HANNAH ARENDT AND MARTIN HEIDEGGER

HANNAH ARENDT AND MARTIN HEIDEGGER

History of a Love

Antonia Grunenberg

Translated by Peg Birmingham, Kristina Lebedeva, and Elizabeth von Witzke Birmingham

Indiana University Press

Bloomington and Indianapolis

This book is a publication of

Indiana University Press
Office of Scholarly Publishing
Herman B Wells Library 350
1320 East 10th Street
Bloomington, Indiana 47405 USA

iupress.indiana.edu

Published in German as *Hannah Arendt und Martin Heidegger: Geschichte einer Liebe.*
© 2006 by Piper Verlag GmbH, München.

English translation © 2017 by Indiana University Press

Manufactured in the United States of America

Cataloging information is available from the Library of Congress.

ISBN 978-0-253-02523-4 (cloth)
ISBN 978-0-253-02537-1 (paperback)
ISBN 978-0-253-02718-4 (ebook)

1 2 3 4 5   22 21 20 19 18 17

Contents

illustrations begin on page 145

Foreword

Arendt and Heidegger: Erotic Reversals, Conflict, and Fissures

Peg Birmingham

OVER THE PAST several decades the question has often been raised: How could Hannah Arendt have reconciled with Martin Heidegger, whom she knew had joined and actively participated in the Nazi Party when taking over the rectorship of Freiburg University? The same question, asked differently: How could Arendt, a Jewish-German refugee who had fled Germany in 1931, have resumed her relationship with Heidegger, her former teacher, on her first trip back to Germany in 1948, a trip undertaken on behalf of the Commission on European Jewish Cultural Reconstruction to recover stolen Jewish cultural artifacts? Grunenberg's biography is remarkable in showing that this way of asking the question is too stark and does not capture the ways in which the history of these two major thinkers of the twentieth century is not simply one of a broken intimacy followed by reconciliation; instead, it is a history marked as much by estrangement, breaks, and distance as it is of proximity, reunion, and resumed friendship. The biography reveals that the history of the love between Arendt and Heidegger is best captured in the English idiom "they have a history," indicating an erotic relationship that is complicated and fraught.

Perhaps the most striking example of the estrangement, distance, and reversals that continued to mark the history between Arendt and Heidegger is the long silence between them that ensued only a few years after the reconciliation in 1948, a silence due not to political or philosophical disagreements—on the contrary, it was personal. The personal silence finds momentary philosophical voice in a note that Arendt sent to Heidegger via her publisher on the occasion of the 1960 publication of *Vita Activa*, the German edition of *The Human Condition*: "You will see that the book does not contain a dedication. Had things worked out properly between us—and I mean *between*, that is, neither you nor me—I would have asked you if I might dedicate it to you; it came directly out of the first Freiburg days and hence owes practically everything to you in every respect."[1] Arendt's note on an absent dedication should put to rest the pervasive assumption by many of Arendt's readers that *The Human Condition* announced a break with Heidegger's thinking; it should also cast doubt on the often-repeated claim that Heidegger's lack of response was due to a philosophical rejection of Arendt's account of the *vita activa*.[2] As the note indicates, this lack of dedication and of response is due to the absence of a personal "between" that renders impossible any philosophical engagement between them. More than a decade later in 1971 there is yet another reversal as Arendt dedicates *Life of the Mind: Thinking* to Heidegger, a dedication that cites several lines from his *Discourse on Thinking*. By this time, another "between" has been established.

As Grunenberg notes, the history between Arendt and Heidegger, a history spanning fifty-one years, takes place against the background of the twentieth century with its violence, catastrophes, wars, and mass migrations. Here, too, Grunenberg adds significantly to Elizabeth Young-Bruehl's biography. She captures—as perhaps only someone who was born during the Dresden firebombing in 1945, who spent her early childhood in East Germany, who then escaped with her family to West Germany, and who as a Berliner participated in the 1989 reunification—the ways in which Arendt lived in two worlds, the European and the American, unwilling and unable to decide between the two. In fact, Grunenberg's biography emphasizes the ways in which Arendt continued to be an exile even after receiving her citizenship papers in 1948. Better, she captures the ways in which Arendt lived a transnational existence after 1941 and how this transnational existence influenced her thinking. Arendt's "fragmented history," her critique of history as process, her critique of the nation-state and a certain conception of human rights and citizenship emerge first from her status as a refugee and then as a nationalized US citizen who never cut ties to Europe generally and to Germany specifically. This experience of exile appears to mark the greatest distance between Arendt and Heidegger, the latter living his entire life in Germany and for much of that life in one city: Freiburg.

Yet here, too, caution must be exercised as Grunenberg's biography shows how Heidegger's world, both personally and professionally, collapsed after the Second World War. Her history of the relationship between these two thinkers raises the difficult question of the difference between a collapsed world and a world of exile and how this difference led Heidegger and Arendt to different understandings of a new beginning, a central concern that runs through each of their work.

Grunenberg's biography of these two thinkers stands between Elzbieta Ettinger's pinched biography of Arendt and Heidegger, in which Arendt is reduced to nothing more than a disciple of Heidegger, and Elizabeth Young-Bruehl's biography of Arendt, in which her relation to Heidegger is briefly discussed. Grunenberg does not reduce Arendt to Heidegger's disciple nor is she interested in adding to Young-Bruehl's account by claiming that Heidegger is more central to Arendt's life than Young-Breuhl admits. Instead, Grunenberg's notable achievement is to show how Arendt and Heidegger's shared history, from their initial meeting in Heidegger's 1924 seminar on Plato's *Sophist*, is the history of a double, inseparable eros: the philosophical and the personal. (At the same time she documents the ways in which this double eros of the philosophical and the personal infuses each thinker's relation with others.) This is not to reduce the work of each thinker to his or her biography or even to a shared biography. Grunenberg is not arguing that Arendt's thinking can be read solely through the lens of Heidegger's thought. It cannot. As she writes in her preface to the English translation, there are significant differences between Arendt's and Heidegger's thought. Nor is she arguing that Heidegger was influenced by Arendt's insistence on the philosophical importance of the *vita activa*. There is no evidence for this. Instead, at the center of Grunenberg's biography is how each thinker engaged with the *vita activa*, how each became aware of its dangers, how one thinker, Heidegger, withdrew from this life, while the other, Arendt, spent her life thinking through its dangers as well as its possibilities for inaugurating the new.

Heidegger's early years, including his involvement with National Socialism, can be read as a cautionary tale of an overzealous commitment to the *vita activa* or, more precisely, of thinking that the activity of thinking can be directly transposed into political action. As Grunenberg describes in detail, and here she makes a significant contribution to the present debate and discussion surrounding the publication of Heidegger's *Black Notebooks*, Heidegger was not alone in thinking this. Her biography, especially chapter 3, goes beyond Heidegger to give a detailed history of the time in Germany between the two world wars. More specifically, she describes the history of the academic community in the 1920s and 1930s, showing that Heidegger was not alone in his commitment to a radical transformation of the public space, particularly the space of the university. Major intellectuals of his day—Paul Tillich, Max Weber, Georg Lukács, and his then "comrade-in-arms," Karl Jaspers, a description both embraced to describe the relationship between them in the years between the two wars—shared this commitment. They all wrote essays on the subject; through newspaper articles and public forums they publicly debated the ways that this *radical* transformation should be achieved. Why Heidegger, nearly alone among this cast of intellectuals and certainly without his comrade-in-arms, went further in thinking that National Socialism offered possibilities for this project is one of the questions Grunenberg explores in this biography.

At the same time Grunenberg's biography corrects the overly determined reading of Arendt as a theorist who celebrates the *vita activa*. While this reading in not entirely incorrect, Arendt, like Heidegger, is engaged in much larger project: to rethink thinking, that is, the legacy of the Western tradition of thought. Certainly her rethinking of thinking includes a rethinking of the *vita activa*: "to think what we are doing," as Arendt puts it in *The Human Condition*. While in the *Life of the Mind: Thinking*, Arendt claims that thinking is a solitary activity that withdraws from the world, Grunenberg's biography shows how Arendt's activities as a thinker belie this claim or at least show that it is only partially correct. For Arendt thinking's *condition* is the same as that of action: publicity and plurality. Certainly, for Arendt, the public space of thinking cannot be conflated with the public space of action; nevertheless, it is a space of talking and debating in concert with others, a concert as rancorous and discordant as it is harmonious.

To put it somewhat differently, for Arendt, friendship is the condition for thinking. For example, Waldemar Gurian, who obtained his position at Notre Dame through Arendt's help, first suggests to her that she write something on National Socialism. Initially Arendt objected, replying that she could not write on this subject. Grunenberg cites Arendt's response to Gurian's suggestion: "I, as a Jew, cannot write on National Socialism at all. It does not behoove me. I have no legitimacy for this. But what I can and would like to do is to write a chapter for *your* book, the one on racial anti-Semitism. This I can and may do and I could do this openly as a Jew: *mea res agitur*. And now write me quickly what you think about this."[3] Gurian refuses to accept this answer. As Grunenberg documents, Arendt had already been working on the history of anti-Semitism since her time as a refugee in Paris. Thus, Gurian was not requesting that she begin an entirely new project. Ultimately, Gurian convinced her to resume this project, and the rest is well-known: *The Origins of Totalitarianism* was published in 1952.

At the same time, the public space of thinking is for Arendt inseparable from journals, newspapers, magazines, and academic institutions: *The Partisan Review*, *Review of Politics*, *Dissent*, *Aufbau*, the *New Yorker*, New School for Social Research, the University of California–Berkeley, and the University of Chicago, to name only a few of the public venues in which Arendt published and taught. Just as she argues that a political space requires public institutions, so, too, she claims that thinking also requires public institutions as the condition for its activity. Her insistence of a public space of thinking reveals Arendt's considerable debt to Kant. It also marks her greatest distance from Heidegger.

Arendt's parable "The Fox" is a thinly disguised description of what she considers to be the condition for Heidegger's disgrace, which she attributes to his understanding of thinking as a leave-thinking from the world. Like a fox who builds a burrow in order to protect itself from the world, Heidegger's builds a burrow in order to protect thinking from the clamor and inauthenticity of the public space. The problem for Arendt is that the protective burrow ends up imprisoning the thinker. The imprisoned thinker ultimately gets burned when the fire comes to its door as it did in Germany in the 1930s.

But, again, as with so many aspects of the relation between Heidegger and Arendt, their respective understandings of thinking cannot be distinguished so sharply. It cannot be so easily concluded that Arendt provides a public notion of thinking while Heidegger does not. While Arendt critiques Heidegger for building an unworldly burrow for thinking, this is not her last word on the subject. First, she does not disagree entirely with him that thinking is *also* a solitary activity that must not be conflated with judging or acting. And, second, she changes her mind—another reversal—on how Heidegger understands the thinking activity. Indeed, Arendt's last *finished* piece of writing before her death is a reading of Heidegger's reading "The Anaximander Fragment." This piece occurs in *Life of the Mind: Willing*, in a penultimate section titled, "Heidegger's Will-Not-to-Will."[4]

Just prior to taking up Heidegger's interpretation of this fragment, Arendt describes his understanding of the thinker as one who "remains the '*solus ipse*' in 'existential solipsism,' except now the fate of the world, the History of Being, has come to depend on him."[5] Yet she immediately qualifies, even rejects, this interpretation by turning to his reading of the fragment: "it is of a different character: it presents an altogether new and unexpected outlook on the whole posing of the problem of Being . . . with its haunting hints at another possibility of ontological speculation."[6] In her reading of the fragment, Arendt argues that Heidegger gives a different view of thinking's response to being, one not caught in an existential solipsism or leave-taking from the world; instead, while certainly solitary, Heidegger understands thinking as a step back from the world, rather than a leave-taking. Indeed Arendt's description of Heidegger's understanding of thinking is one very similar to her own, both as she describes it in *Life of the Mind* and in *The Human Condition*, specifically in her discussion of the work of art. On Arendt's reading, Heidegger's understands thinking as world disclosing, belonging to the realm of history, a realm that Heidegger calls "errancy." Arendt claims that "this realm of error is the sphere of common human history."[7] Closely following Heidegger and agreeing with him, Arendt argues that because every being "lingers awhile in a presence between two absences," it is able to transcend "its own presence . . . and belong to the non-present."[8] The task of thinking for Heidegger is to think the historical epochs of appearance, specifically the moment of transition between one epoch and another.

Strikingly, this moment or gap between one epoch and another is where Arendt also locates the thinker. For example, in her preface to *Between Past and Future*, reading Kafka's "He," she describes the thinker as one who stands between the forces of the past and the future in a "deflected present" in which the thinker has withdrawn but has not taken leave from the realm of appearance. Significantly, in her final finished piece of writing, Arendt's conflicted relationship with Heidegger continues to haunt her work: at once, within the space of two paragraphs, she claims that Heidegger's thinker is a kind of sovereign *solus ipsum* *and* she claims that for Heidegger thinking is not solipsistic, but instead engaged in the activity of a historical world disclosing. This last is in close proximity to her understanding of the thinking activity. To the end, theirs is a fissured eros that marks a personal and philosophical history of proximity and distance, conflict and reconciliation.

Antonia Grunenberg's personal and philosophical history makes her uniquely qualified to undertake this biography of Arendt and Heidegger. In his reflections on writing his biography of Samuel Taylor Coleridge, Richard Holmes argues that the first principle of a biographer is the "physical pursuit" of the subject, what he calls "the footsteps principle": "I had come to believe that the serious biographer must *physically* pursue his subject through the past. Mere archives were not enough. He must go to all the places where the subject had ever lived or worked, or traveled or dreamed. Not just the birthplace, or the blue-plaque place, but the temporary places, the passing places, the lost places, the dream places."[9] Grunenberg's biography is animated by Holmes's footstep principle. In fact, it is marked by a kind of "double footprint" insofar as Grunenberg has physically pursued the places her biographical subjects lived and worked, and these are the same places where Grunenberg has also lived and worked. As mentioned above, she brings a unique European sensibility to writing this biography. Grunenberg has breathed the air of Berlin; she lived through the division and reconciliation of Germany; she studied with Lukács, actively engaging during this time in the student coffeehouse rancorous debates on the direction of leftist politics, debates that give her an intimate, almost sensual sense of the same debates and divisions that occurred in New York intellectual circles, which included Arendt. Grunenberg completed her dissertation with Jacob Taubes, the renowned scholar of Jewish thought, at the Free University of Berlin. For many years she was the director of the Hannah Arendt Archives at the University of Oldenburg (the birthplace and childhood home of Karl Jaspers). Significantly, Grunenberg obtained the archives by spending an entire summer at the Library of Congress, photocopying the entirety of Arendt's papers that comprise hundreds of boxes; she paid homeless people she met on the streets of Washington, DC, to help her. Without romanticizing this situation of homelessness, we can speculate that Arendt would have found something apt in those without a home helping to copy her papers that would then be taken to Germany and archived in the hometown of her mentor and friend.

Grunenberg's biography ends abruptly with the deaths of the main protagonists. At first this may seem jarring, but it is helpful to recall Adriana Cavarero's claim, "Death plays the central role in biography, just as natality plays the central role in action."[10] While recognizing that a biography certainly includes the event of natality, Cavarero sees its primary task, and here she cites Arendt, as rescuing through the "saving power of narrative"[11] singular and unique appearances from the destruction of time. Adding an additional task to Cavarero's, Holmes notes that biography is an act of friendship insofar as it "extends a hand between cultures, genders, times, and ways of life."[12] Grunenberg's biography accomplishes both of these tasks. Her biography extends a handshake between two prominent thinkers of the twentieth century, thinkers divided by war, geographical distance, and political commitments, yet also bound together by a complicated philosophical and personal eros. At the same time, the narrative power of her biography offers a handshake across the divide of appearance and disappearance, thereby saving these lives from the destructive oblivion of time.

Notes

1. Ursula Ludz, ed., *Letters 1925–1975, Hannah Arendt and Martin Heidegger*, trans. Andrew Shields (New York: Harcourt, 2004), 124 (translation modified). Letter dated October 28, 1960, cited in this volume (see chapter 5).

2. See, for example, Jacques Tamineaux, *The Thracian Maid and the Professional Philosopher: Arendt and Heidegger*, trans. Michael Gendre (Albany: SUNY Press, 1997).

3. Arendt to Gurian, letter dated March 21, 1942, Cont.10.7, Archiv des HAZ.

4. This text was published posthumously in Hannah Arendt, *Life of Mind: Thinking and Willing*, ed. Mary McCarthy (London: HB&J, 1971).

5. Ibid., 187.

6. Ibid., 188–89.

7. Martin Heidegger, "The Anaximander Fragment," translated by David Farrell Krell, *Arion*, New Series, vol. 1, no. 4 (1975): 580–81. Cited by Hannah Arendt, *Life of the Mind: Willing*, (New York: Harcourt Brace Jovanovich, 1978), 191.

8. Ibid., 193.

9. Richard Holmes, "A Quest for the Real Coleridge," *New York Review of Books*, December 18, 2014.

10. Adriana Cavarero, "Narrative against Destruction," *New Literary History* 46, no. 1 (2015): 3.

11. Ibid., 5.

12. Richard Holmes, "A Quest for the Real Coleridge," *New York Review of Books*, December 18, 2014.

Acknowledgments

THIS BOOK EMERGED from a world of discussions, readings, and dinners. I thank everyone I met in the course of the work on this book, all those who listened and extended suggestions of all kinds.

Jerome Kohn and Lotte Köhler have given me strength from a distance for many years. Lotte Köhler made original sources available to me, read the book as it progressed, offered critical comments, and very much encouraged me. With his wonderful electronic letters and commentary, Jerome Kohn proved that the age of the culture of letter exchange is not yet past. Edith Kurzweil provided the opportunity of an afternoon's discussion regarding the intellectual atmosphere at the *Partisan Review*.

Hermann Heidegger received me kindly and with curiosity; I thank Elisabeth Büchin for her willingness to give me a tour of Heidegger's hometown.

My dramaturgical reader, Ingrid Karsunke, gave me clear and encouraging comments on our walks. Claudia Schmölders allowed me access to her library and was generous with news and references. Silvia Bovenschen listened and shared with me her saying, "The memory is a machine for lies." Karin Reschke listened to my stories endlessly over her sumptuously prepared dinners. I thank Claus Koch for his willingness to read the text and Peter Merseburger for an inspiring conversation.

A very special thank-you goes to Zoltan Szanky and Gustav von Campe, who continued both directly and indirectly to probe my understanding of the relationship between Arendt and Heidegger.

I thank Erica Stegmann for the successful and friendly work together; she made this book ready for publication. Her husband, Erhard Klöss, supported us with great dinners and the hope of being able to read a gripping book.

This book would not have been possible without the daily, friendly assistance of the professionals of the many different archives consulted. I was warmly welcomed by the New York Public Library staff from the doorman to library information; in their halls I could imagine how thankful the hounded German academics must have been to have such a lovely place in which to study. The same gratitude is extended to the staff of the University Archives in Marburg, Heidelberg, and Freiburg, The Secret State Archives of the Preußischer Kulturbesitz in Berlin, as well as the Marburg Literature Archives and the Archives of the Berlin-Brandenburg Academy of Science.

The staff of the Hannah Arendt Center at the Carl von Ossietzky University Oldenburg fulfilled the most complex requests as well as helped with organizing the references; these include Waltraud Meints-Stender, Sarah Hemmen, Oliver Bruns, Daniel Schubbe, Melanie Rücker, and Heiko Reinwald. Christine Harckensee-Roth read the entire manuscript critically and brought the large quantity of sources and literature into order.

Last but not least, I would like thank two authors whose research into Heidegger or Heidegger and Arendt helped substantially along the way. These are Jacques Taminiaux, author of *La fille de Thrace et le penseur professionel. Arendt et Heidegger* (1992) and *Le theatre des philosophes* (1996), and Dana R. Villa, author of *Arendt and Heidegger. The Fate of the Political* (1996).

As a good reader, Katrin Pollems-Braunfels and I together kneaded the text like dough. I thank her especially for her good humor in the face of all the work and for the strength and imagination she lent to my project.

I thank Marcus Dockhorn and Klaus Stadler of Piper Publishing for their patience, encouragement, and realism. For the English translation, I have to give my special thanks to Peg Birmingham, Kristina Lebedeva, and Elizabeth Birmingham. Finally, it all worked out.

Antonia Grunenberg

Introduction to the English Translation

Antonia Grunenberg

To Save Heidegger from Himself?

Eight years after the initial publication of my book, Martin Heidegger's notebooks from the 1930s and 1940s came out. In the so-called *Black Notebooks* (*Schwarz Hefte*) that Heidegger wrote since the beginning of the 1930s, the philosopher spoke most appallingly about the Jewish people, about the "German essence," about education, and about the task of philosophy. Fundamental questions arise: How are we to understand Heidegger's closeness to National Socialism? Can anti-Semitism be part of a philosophical way of thinking? Can this way of thinking be then called philosophy?

The newly sparked critique of Heidegger as well as the conclusion drawn by some, that is, that Heidegger's entire body of thinking is contaminated by anti-Semitism and thus rendered worthless, forces Heidegger scholarship and all those who are convinced that this philosopher had something new to say into a discussion that has been around for a long time. Since it has reopened, we should seize the opportunity to break free from the old dualism of pros and cons, thereby making a great step methodologically.

It would then be possible to examine the intellectual radicalism that permeated European societies since the turn of the nineteenth century, a radicalism whose hubris, barely traceable today, confronts us in the form of Martin Heidegger and philosophers such as Georg Lukács and writers such as Ferdinand Céline or Filippo Marinetti.

Peter Tawney, the publisher of the *Black Notebooks*, points out that Heidegger's anti-Semitism has two dimensions: "(1) The dimension of the history of Being where the Jews appear as representatives of rationalism, technology, and modernity; (2) The dimension of the history of time wherein Heidegger personally and biographically appears as a philosopher influenced by anti-Semitic ideology."[1]

To understand why the most astonishing philosopher of the twentieth century saw an anti-Semitic attitude as politically, culturally, and philosophically necessary, a person who had great hopes for National Socialism, one has to explore the sociohistorical "origins " of his thinking and those of his contemporaries.

The difficulties begin with the concept of anti-Semitism. This much is clear: modern anti-Semitism is an ideologically fueled hostility toward Jews that ultimately aims at their destruction—then and today. To transpose this definition onto Heidegger's thinking misses the mark. His notes show a personal projection of "Jewishness," as well as a "political" and philosophical critique. Methodologically, Heidegger equates "being Jewish" with an "inauthentic" existence. The fact that his critiques are simultaneously judgments used by the National Socialists should not hinder us from illuminating the different dimensions of his anti-Semitism.

Heidegger rejected tabloid journalism, as well as political journalism and public opinion ("the they, *das Man*"), as he dismissed all the brilliant (Jewish) art critics of the 1920s, from Alfred Kerr to Kurt Tucholsky, from Siegfried Kracauer to Karl Kraus. What does it mean that Heidegger fundamentally rejected journalism and the public sphere because he believed that they abused "the essential"?

Heidegger was—like Hannah Arendt, Walter Benjamin, and many others—an open critic of psychoanalysis: Sigmund Freud was a Jew, like many other of his colleagues and students. Heidegger identified this discipline with Jewishness. He considered their interventions in philosophical problems (what is a human being?) exceptionally dangerous. But is it enough to dismiss his critique of psychoanalysis because of anti-Semitic prejudices?

It clearly has to do with a whole cultural constellation that Heidegger identified, or, better, projected, as "Jewish." This fact does not make his anti-Semitism less reprehensible, but it helps us decipher its underlying structure.

Furthermore, Heidegger's position can be better illuminated by placing it in the philosophical-political controversies of the period between the two world wars. Heidegger formulated a unique philosophical questioning that went beyond the debates of the time (neo-Kantianism, transcendental philosophy, mysticism, life philosophy), but at the same time attempted to answer them.

The influence of the National Socialist "worldview" on the humanities and their representatives of the time must also be illuminated. Heidegger was a college professor who despised the academic university "business," but he also had very strict ideas about the "proper" "German" university. A reform of the university was a necessary consequence of his philosophy of Dasein. One could further ask how an important philosopher could make the enormous mistake of wanting to put a perspective of the history of being in a politico-ideological party name.

Exploring these aspects goes beyond the scope of this introduction; in what follows, I outline only the areas that need to be investigated further.

The Background

Alongside material factors, one of the preconditions for the emergence of modern anti-Semitism in the European and German thinking of the nineteenth century was the unstable social and political standing of Jews—the ideology of the eternal "battle of races." Around the end of the nineteenth century, the biological theory of the time, buttressed by the flourishing of the natural sciences and technology, created a biologically oriented understanding of evolution, wherein the differences between nations were ultimately traced back to racial criteria.[2] Political thinking and acting, as well as the sciences, were mixed with biologism.[3] "Race" was seen as the fundamental principle not only of biology and anthropology but also of modern social development and state formation. The colonial, or rather imperial, powers cultivated a kind of superior thinking based on the higher/elevated position of the "white" (German, English, French, Spanish, etc.) race over and above the other nations of the world.

After the French Revolution, in German states, this constellation appeared as the increasingly stronger reflection on the "German essence." The German essence took hold in the language, and the Germans were declared to be guardians of the human ideal of Greek antiquity. Thus Hölderlin and his cult, and later Stefan George and his circle, stood alongside Goethe, Schiller, and Herder. All human sciences, including pedagogy, were influenced by it. Another trend, represented by Fichte, wanted to awaken the Germanness that was fueled by great national feelings. Their goal was the education of all German people regarding emotional unity, even if national unity was out of reach.[4]

Both camps overlapped in some areas and in time. Some of Hölderlin's epigones twisted the poet's legacy into mawkish national poetry. The main figures of nationalism and imperialism legitimized themselves by appealing to the superiority of the German culture.

This orientation formed the basis of "German attitude" in almost the entire society. Its proponents saw in it the higher meaning of the First World War. The "German essence" was supposed to be acknowledged by the European powers as the highest stage of development among European nations. The utility of this interpretation becomes clear against the backdrop of competition in which the European imperial powers of the time found themselves and in which the German Reich saw itself as the disadvantaged party whose ruling class was suffering from insufficient recognition.

The collapse of the Reich and the European order in 1918 damaged this "worldview" but did not make it disappear. In national and racial circles—and the latter were abundant in academia—the legend of Germany's mission lived on, for instance, in the conviction that the war had not been won decisively but arbitrarily—through the dictate of the winning powers. It awaited, so to speak, its completion.

Martin Heidegger grew up in this political-cultural combination. The home environment and regional peculiarities (peasant view of life, Christian belief, the fostering of folklore, rejection of modernity and technology in his childhood home and the homeland) left an imprint on him insofar as he was thinking racially and nationally to the extent in which the society where he grew up was thinking racially and nationally.

In his youth a heated, long-lasting debate arose as to whether and in what way the Jews belonged to the "German nation." Could they form an entirely different nation within the German nation, thereby entitling them to demand their own state, far away and yet influential?[5] This "Zionism" debate divided the German and European Jews. German-national and liberally inclined Jews rejected Zionist endeavors almost entirely. "The Jews" were collectively branded as "the betrayers of the homeland" by non-Jewish nationalist propagandists. This collective reproach turned into a murderous argument after the end of the First World War. The "stab-in-the-back" myth turned Jews into enemies "in one's own house."

The end of war was seen as a world-shattering event both by Jewish and non-Jewish thinkers. On the basis of the peace treaty not only was the political order in Europe destroyed; not only were the communities of states dissolved; not only did it cost millions of people the loss of their belonging to the state and social life. A whole "world" with its cultural and spiritual orientations collapsed.

The academic spheres were affected by these tectonic jolts. Notable philosophers described the war in 1914 as Germany's cultural mission. After the defeat, German intellectuals reflected philosophically on Germany's way out of the catastrophe. The best of the Weimar intellectuals participated in this: Max Weber, even though he died in 1920, Karl Jaspers, Ernst Troeltsch, Walther Rathenau, Martin Buber, Walter Benjamin, Martin Heidegger, and so on. The problem was the renewal of foundations in the face of the collapse of the traditional world and the philosophical "system."

At that time Heidegger was investigating ontological foundations against both traditional transcendental philosophy as well as Kantianism. At the same time his teacher Edmund Husserl was advocating the phenomenological "return to things" and with it the rejection of traditional metaphysics. Religious, or rather mystical, concepts like "salvation" and "guilt" resurfaced in the political field. Polemical exchanges were forged around the question of whether Jewish "German" or Christian "German" ethics was superior.[6] The differences encompassed fundamental philosophical concepts such as freedom, experience, belief, and knowledge. Like others, Heidegger was convinced that philosophical thinking needed to undergo a catharsis in order to free itself from the impasse of empty discourse regarding the validity of categories and their hierarchy. He took up the Promethean task of renewing the foundation in and against philosophy not only philosophically, but also decidedly personally. He saw it as his own task.

This imperative, however, led him to an insoluble dilemma. He was working on basic philosophical problems: How does human existence stand vis-à-vis being? How can human existence be grounded anew from out of being? These perspectives were possible only when the surrounding world was at an utmost distance. He imagined himself, so to speak, in the position of a "seer" who stands over and above the world and yet claims to know it better than his contemporaries. From the perspective of this abstract height, Descartes, the founder of modern thinking, the bourgeoisie, the university, technology, the National Socialists and the Jews, the socialists, the conservatives, racial thinking all appeared as part of one and the same great problem: the self-alienation of Western culture. Heidegger found himself amid the "decline of the effluent age."[7]

Heidegger saw his task as helping the human being (Dasein) gain self-awareness, and not from out of thinking but from out of being. It had to do with nothing less than an "empowerment of Being."[8] He wrote that we must go back to the great beginning.[9] But "the great beginning" implied a fundamental social transformation. It is no accident that in this context he saw the settlement movement, beloved in the conservative circles—and one he referred to as "military units" of youth "labor camps"—as sites of education from which a new Germany and an authentic thinking were to emerge.[10]

Hubris

However, from his perspective, in order to bring about the new beginning, the old shell of thinking, that is, traditional philosophy, academic pursuit, education, civil society, and civic morality, had to be destroyed.

Given this view, Heidegger greeted the National Socialists as a movement of true "existentialists" who came to the fore despite the "scientific" philistines and pursued a total renewal of Germany.[11]

He considered the National Socialists to be a raw but pliable avant-garde of an all-encompassing future proceeding from the "German essence." He "saw" in their initial anticapitalist and antiliberal ideologies sufficient room for his conviction that a new beginning had to be effected. He noted that he strengthened the least harmful elements in National Socialism.[12] He wanted to educate them, since he saw their ideology as providing a proposal that was meant to help the real Dasein reach a breakthrough.[13] At this time Heidegger's internal emotional state is in utter tension. The basic tone of his communications is "now or never." His entries from the beginning to the mid-1930s reinforce the impression that he saw himself as a part, even as "spiritual leader" of a new movement. It sounds quite unimaginable to us today in the knowledge of the mass murder of European Jews: the "seer" lost his place and rushed into the venture to turn the National Socialist revolution into a philosophy of Dasein.

This hubris merits a critical evaluation.

From out of Germany's sweeping defeat in the First World War hybrid philosophies arose in the German spiritual landscape. They promised religious, political, esoteric, life-reforming, or other types of "salvation."

Everyone who saw the First World War as the break of an era to which one could respond only with an epochal new beginning participated in this emergence. There was a tendency to radical, all-encompassing solutions in the debate culture both of the Right and Left. In the beginning of the 1920s, Lukács demanded that the starting point of every philosophical-political analysis be "the intention vis-à-vis totality" in which anyone able to "think" had to pursue a comprehensive social solution through revolution.[14] Walter Benjamin had been working on a new foundation of the political from out of the in-between world between Messianism and Marxism since the beginning of the 1920s. Martin Buber, Carl Schmitt—all wanted to join the epochal rupture with a new beginning. They wanted to counteract the abyss that had opened up in modernity with an authentic new foundation.

What reads like a philosophical comedy (the philosopher breathing the air of "Be-ing" and thus falling among the barbarians) is that many at the time were caught up in this constellation. Just as the political Right completed the project of filling the role of the leader in Europe, the Left saw the new German beginning as part of the international revolution under the aegis of the Soviet Communist Party.

Their common enemy was liberal modernity, rationalism, pragmatism, positivism, parliamentarism, and so on.

Heidegger acted within this historical constellation. He shared the totalitarian illusion with his admirers and enemies, the illusion according to which it was possible to find a final solution to the fundamental problems of the time.

He found himself, at this time, philosophically and personally in the middle of many contradictions. He attracted a large number of Jewish students and scholars. Some of them did their doctorates under his guidance. He fell in love with a brilliant Jewish student—Hannah Arendt, who, like him, chose philosophy as her life's work.

He intensively engaged with Jewish philosophy, that is, with transcendental-philosophical or rather the mystical traditions in philosophical and political discourse. There is an entry in Heidegger's notebook at the end of 1932 and the beginning of 1933: "Metaphysics as meta-politics."[15] A new politics was to emerge from a renewal of metaphysics. The Jewish philosopher Erich Unger wrote about this in an expressionistic essay in 1921, in which he argued for a metaphysical, if not "mystical," foundation of the political.[16] Other contemporaries took this up, from Martin Buber and Walter Benjamin to Franz Rosenzweig. They all took part in what Heidegger described as a "reflective leap into the whole of being as unconditional, the attempt to think unconditionally within metaphysics."[17]

However, Heidegger wanted to open an ontologically and not mystically (he saw the latter as "Jewish") grounded "German access" to the problem of human existence (Dasein). He saw the German essence preserved in the form of openness to being in German idealism, in Hegel and Schelling. It was not a matter of bringing the German into the national, but rather of grasping the German in idealism.[18]

If one examines Heidegger's position at the time of the emergence of the National Socialist regime, one must remember three elements of his "political philosophy": his transformation of Platonic thinking into the resurgence of the German, his taking up of classical German philosophy as the source of the German essence, and his vision of the National Socialist "revolution" as the medium for the catharsis of human existence.

Whoever reflects on this roughly outlined constellation must ask if and how Heidegger's philosophy is "contaminated" and to what extent it is not only the product of its time—although, as ontology, it presumably stands outside of time—but how it meant to radically overturn this very time. If one fails to consider these factors, one arrives at the conclusion that Heidegger was an anti-Semite who also did philosophy.

The End

After his resignation from the rectorship in 1934, Heidegger spent years trying to understand why he could not reach his goal. Since the middle of the 1930s, he made entries in his notebook where he distanced himself from the violent actions of National Socialism. At the same time, he still criticized the intellectualism of the German intelligentsia, the argument that he used previously primarily against Jewish intellectuals.[19] He parted ways with power and violence, but he still believed that the time to make a decision had come.[20]

His mission ended on a banal and disappointing note. It was not only that the National Socialists did not meet his expectations. He also blamed them for intellectualism, that is, the "misunderstanding of the essence of knowledge."[21] In this context, he claimed that the National Socialist revolution was a part of the self-alienation of the West that he had diagnosed.

The National Socialists separated themselves from him; he was not useful enough, since he was not a pure propagandist of their ideology, even when he approved of it. It was the irony of history that toward the end of the 1930s the official "National Socialist critics" said that Heidegger's thinking was "corrosive" and intellectualist. In other words, Heidegger pursued "Jewish thinking" (see chapter 3, p. 129).

It took Heidegger many years to admit that he fell prey to a double illusion. He made the biggest mistake a philosopher can make: he misconstrued the realm of politics as the space to apply philosophical insights. And he "saw" a potential for renewal in the National Socialist delusion of destruction.

The price he paid for this could not have been higher. His thinking became trivialized, to the point of bordering on the laughable, and he had knowingly affiliated himself with a criminal regime.

Arendt and Heidegger

In 1932 at the latest, Hannah Arendt knew that Heidegger considered National Socialist anti-Semitism as a necessary phenomenon; she also knew that he wrote good recommendations for the Jewish students in jeopardy so that they could study abroad.[22] The break in their relationship between 1933 and 1945 seemed set in stone.

After 1945 their personal friendship aside, the fundamental differences between them are not minor. To the contrary, they stand at the center of Arendt's thinking. This affects not only the question of personal ethics but first and foremost the foundational questions of thinking itself.

Arendt elaborated a different position through the critical reading of his texts and through the critique of his interpretation of Plato. It begins by positioning philosophy vis-à-vis the world. Heidegger withdrew from the political realm after his shameful involvement with the National Socialists. Even though she found Heidegger's voluntary turn toward action bizarre, she considered his personal and philosophical retreat from the world as fundamentally wrong. Indeed, she blamed the distance from the world, with which she diagnosed the whole enterprise of philosophy, for the fact that philosophers or rather intellectuals were so susceptible to totalitarian power.

To name just a few differences between them: Heidegger rejected the public realm, "the they, *das Man*" both in the 1920s and after the war. Arendt believed that the world shows itself only in the public realm, in the plurality of many people, and not in the isolated Dasein.

Arendt was convinced that truth emerged only through diverse perspectives of opinions, it appears among people, it does not reveal itself from out of being, and it is not, as in Heidegger, ontologically grounded.

Heidegger's perhaps greatest innovation in the twentieth-century history of philosophy lay in the fact that he created a subjectless philosophy (the foundation of Dasein from out of being). Arendt desubstantialized the concept of the subject, locating the subjective capacity in acting and in judging. For her, acting and judging in the plurality of many people constituted the uniquely human capacity to be free.

The question remains: What did Arendt value in Heidegger so much that she sought contact with him after the war? Her letters show how conflicted she herself was about it. Nevertheless, even in the face of all criticism of Heidegger, she stayed true to her love.[23]

The story of Hannah Arendt and Martin Heidegger is a parable without a happy end, even if Arendt resumed the connection with her former teacher after 1945. In their last years there was an intimacy that came with a mellow old age, intimacy that resembled their earlier closeness.

Whoever reads Heidegger today has a multifaceted task: Heidegger's personal aberration must be exposed in all its ramifications and contradictions. On the other hand, Heidegger's questions need to be deprivatized so as to be saved from an ideological reduction. One also has to de-ideologize them so as to be able to take his thought further.

Only when Heidegger's "fall" is recognized as part of a historical way of thinking, shared, in its own way, by many important intellectuals and writers in all of Europe, is it possible to analyze his involvement. If one's attention is limited to Heidegger, one loses sight of the intellectual radicalism that lies at the basis of those fatal mistakes that we find in Heidegger or Céline or Lukács.

Notes

1. See Peter Trawny, *Heidegger und der Mythos der jüdischen Weltverschworung* (Hamburg: Klostermann, 2014), 31ff.

2. For example, Darwin's *On the Origin of the Species* (London: John Murray, 1859) and *The Descent of Man and Selection in Relation to Sex* (New York: W. W. Norton, 2005).

3. Houston Steward Chamberlain, *Die Grundlagen des 19 Jahrhunderts* (Munich: Bruckmann, 1899).

4. For example, the war of independence against Napoleon (1812–15).

5. See Heinrich von Treitschke, "Ein Wort über unser Jüdenthus," in Preussische Jahrhücher (1879–1880), 44 und 45; see also, Moriz Goldstein, "Deutsch-jüdischer Parnass," *Der Kunstward* (1912).

6. See Hermann Cohen, "Ausfuhrungen anlasslich des ersten Antisemitismus-Prozesses," in *Astrid Deuber-Philosophie, vergangliche Erfahrung* (Berlin), 132ff.

7. See Martin Heidegger, *Gesamtausgabe Bd. 94, Schwarze Hefte: 1931–1938* (Frankfurt: Vittorio Klostermann, 2014), 109.

8. Ibid., 68.

9. Ibid., 53.

10. Ibid., 59 and 61.

11. Ibid., 22, 132ff.

12. Ibid., 186.

13. Ibid., 190.

14. See Georg Lukács, *Geschichte und Kassenbewusstesin* (Berlin: Malik, 1923), 21ff. and 39ff.

15. See Heidegger, *Gesamtausgabe,* 116.

16. See Erich Unger, "Politik und Metaphysik," *Theorie. Versuche zurphilosophischen Politik* 1 (1921).

17. See Martin Heidegger, *Uberlegungen XII–XV, Schwarze Hefte 193901941, GA, IV. Abt., Band 96* (Frankfurt: Vittorio Klosterman, 2014), 8.

18. Ibid., 8–9.

19. Ibid., 12–13.

20. Ibid., 14.

21. Ibid., 13.

22. From this year there is a letter from Arendt to Heidegger and his response, in which he denies that he is anti-Semitic; see Heidegger to Arendt, letter without date (probably winter 1932–33) in Ursula Ludz, ed., *The Letters of Arendt and Heidegger,* trans. Andrew Shields (London: Harcourt, 1998), 68–69. See also chapter 3 of this volume.

23. See chapter 6 of this volume.

HANNAH ARENDT AND MARTIN HEIDEGGER

Introduction

At the end of her book *The Origins of Totalitarianism*, Hannah Arendt writes about the internal devastation wrought by the power of totalitarianism, "the iron band of terror" that succeeds in creating an atmosphere of desolation around and within each person. One might have the impression, she writes, "as though a means had been found in which the desert had set itself in motion, setting loose a sandstorm that blew over all the inhabited areas of the earth."[1]

My book is about this sandstorm, and its effect on people who, with élan and self-awareness, wished to renew the world.

In the fall of 1924, Hannah Arendt, a young woman from Königsberg, came to Marburg on the Lahn with a group of like-minded friends. She was following a rumor that one could learn to think with a young philosopher at the university there. She was a student hungry for knowledge; he was a rebel among philosophers. She was eighteen years old and a free spirit; he was thirty-five and married. What connected them was the passion of love and the fascination for philosophical thought.

Both entered into a precarious love that was at the same time the beginning of an adventurous path of thought that would push them apart and bring them together time and again. With the publication of *Being and Time* in 1927 Heidegger rose to world fame. He owed this flight of thinking in part to her love. At the same time Arendt turned to Zionism, wanting to fight against murderous anti-Semitism. The seizing of power by the National Socialists ripped both from their paths. She and her friends were forced to flee. He awaited a national awakening and a leading role as educator for himself in National Socialism. Heidegger's "mission" destroyed their love as well as the friendship of many of his teachers, colleagues, and students.

The lovers became enemies. Still, meeting seventeen years later, the old feelings of connectedness surfaced. A friendship of twenty years began, a friendship broken time and again by crises.

Those who came after have had their problems with this history. Not a few contemporaries considered it a scandal. Hannah Arendt and Martin Heidegger! How could a Jewish woman find herself with a Nazi *in spe*? With the abyss that lay between them, how could she seek this connection again after the war, as was clearly the case?

Those who remain as voyeurs cannot understand that in this relationship two themes intersect constantly: love and thought. Along all the meanderings of the story and its characters, the theme that appears is love in all its shadings: eros and agape, faithfulness and betrayal, passion and banality, reconciliation, forgetting, remembering. *Amor Mundi*, "Love of the World," also appears, clearly not a sentimental issue. From Arendt comes the question of how a new beginning may be made after the self-destruction of Europe through war and genocide. With this, however, the question of thinking itself becomes a theme. At the beginning of their relationship stood the following questions: What is the purpose of philosophical thought? Can a well-understood existential philosophy be transferred to the world of human action?

Heidegger failed in his aspiration to be the educator of the nation. When this failure became clear to him, he withdrew deep into philosophy.

Hannah Arendt, violently pushed by her enemies in 1933 into the same question, had a radically different response: thinking must reach into the world and engage human beings and their experiences, ruptures, and catastrophes more profoundly.

Above all, Arendt and Heidegger were painfully aware that they were witnesses to a break with tradition that could not be healed. In their different ways, they were both on the path to a new beginning, a "thinking without banisters," without support in the tradition. One of the richest philosophical discourses of the twentieth century emerged from this political antagonism, a discourse between a thinking of the political world (Arendt) and a philosophical discourse on *Gelassenheit* or letting-be (Heidegger). It is a confrontation that defined the last century and continues today in its endless variations.

The double relationship between Hannah Arendt and Martin Heidegger, as lovers and thinkers, will be told against the backdrop of the last century, its fissures, catastrophes, and personal dramas. The more entwined the history of the century becomes with Arendt and Heidegger, the more characters enter the stage. Karl Jaspers and Martin Heidegger: a young doctor and psychiatrist from the northern German provinces and a young philosopher from the southern Bavarian province link up to radically remake philosophy and with it their universities. Their friendship began as they both followed the same thought: philosophy was no longer adequate to the existential questions of the present. They rebelled against the inherited structures of university philosophy. They would be the emissaries of a new way of thinking, existential philosophy. Their friendship collapsed in 1933 as Jaspers condemned the new leaders and antisemitism. He was driven from the university by these events. Toward the end of the war, he was afraid for his life and that of his wife's. After the war he emerged as a harsh critic of Heidegger—at the same time he appealed to their old connection. Friendship, however, was not possible.

For Hannah Arendt, her doctoral supervisor, Karl Jaspers, was the trusted person she could turn to after 1945 as she encountered a Germany she barely recognized. Jaspers was ever present as the third party to her new relationship to Heidegger. Heidegger suffered under the loss of friendship with Jaspers. Arendt was never able to effect a reconciliation between the two.

Heinrich Blücher, Arendt's second husband, appears; his encouragement of her work was invaluable. Jasper's wife, Gertrud, also emerges. This is the woman who Jaspers thanks for his "humanity" and whose contribution to their discussions in the Jaspers' house can only be surmised. Finally, Elfride Heidegger enters, a woman who embarked on her marriage full of hope as an emancipated woman; she was fascinated with National Socialism early and never escaped from this legacy. Throughout her life she fought against Heidegger's connection to his Jewish students; his insistence on a life with eros made her bitter.

The students appear: Karl Löwith, the talented early critic of his teacher Heidegger; Elisabeth Blochmann, the excellent student with a calling in pedagogy; Hans Jonas, who as Zionist and Jewish scholar studied with Heidegger; Herbert Marcuse, who was fascinated by Heidegger before turning to another fascination, Marxism; the highly intelligent Günther Anders, Arendt's first husband.

What seems to those who come after to have been a clearly delineated world (the teacher as perpetrator, colleagues and students as victims) was at the time a shared world in which the traditions of communists and messianics, Jews and Christians, Zionists, nationalists and racists all interacted with, clashed against, and influenced one another simultaneously. Between the lines we also find the discussion of just how violent the separation of "German" from "Jewish" thinking in the intellectual history of Germany was.

And as though that were not enough for our protagonists, they also lived on two different continents for forty years. Hannah Arendt found a new circle of thinking in the United States, and, with her friends, she made a new home for herself there. She involved herself in the debates surrounding the founding of the state of Israel and worked on establishing a new foundation for political thought. Her friends Mary McCarthy, Alfred Kazin, Waldemar Gurian, Hermann Bloch, Dwight MacDonald, and many others, brought the American world closer to her and debated with her the future of Europe.

Martin Heidegger saw in America the embodiment of the age of doomed technology. Hannah Arendt, on the other hand, wanted to bring the "American perspective" into European thought. Her lifelong disputes also stemmed from this, namely, how the political will of a people could find expression in a form other than that of the European nation-state. In this respect one can rightly speak of a "transatlantic relationship."

Where do the protagonists stand at the end? Unmasked, damaged, rehabilitated? If the book has been successful at counteracting these *images*, then it has accomplished its goal.

Note

1. Hannah Arendt, *The Origins of Totalitarianism* (New York: Harvest/HBJ, 1951), 478.

1 World Out of Joint, or How the Revolution in Philosophy Began

THE TWENTIETH CENTURY began with a stealthy revolution in politics and culture, art and literature, industry, technology, and science. Everyone spoke of great changes:

> Thus it was a world full of antitheses, this *"fin de siècle,"* where everything was chaotically swirling and surging through each other, at once carnival and Ash Wednesday, powerfully emerging Renaissance and pessimistically tired decadence; imperialistic desire for power and craving for peace at any cost; a time of "restlessness and need for stimulation," but also of the need for rest, overly satiated with excitement; of losing oneself in the dispersion of the outside world and of longing to regain the inner and the unitary. And the people of this time were moved, on the one hand, plagued from early youth onwards by a complete overestimation of the intellect, and therefore agitated by unspoken and unspeakable moods, and on the other hand, driven practically, functionally, by will and energy toward the external and internal worlds; pessimistic and indifferent, tired and feeble on the one hand, and, on the other, animated by the will to live, energetically and ambitiously striving forward with vitality and love of life; free from prejudices, unbelieving and critical, cold through and through, and at the same time seized by all kinds of mysticism or at least superficially playing with it, full of curiosity and interest for everything enigmatic and secret, for everything profound and otherworldly, and putting science itself in the service of superstition or pretentiously masking it with a form of occult science.[1]

Theobald Ziegler's painting of fin-de-siècle mores, created with powerful strokes, has its source in the contradictions of such a rich age. *The Intellectual and Social Currents of the 19th Century* was first published in 1899. Ziegler was a sensitive observer of change. He recognized that a contradictory world had emerged wherein unequal forces clashed with one another (natural sciences versus humanities; Marxism versus racism; the Industrial Revolution versus traditionalism; modernity versus antimodern myth), a world where new hierarchies were not yet recognizable.

In 1920 the collection of poetry *Menschheitsdämmerung—Symphonie jüngster Dichtung* appeared. Containing poetry from 1910 to 1919, the collection served as an "anti-anthology" sustained by passionate feelings directed against the predominance of the natural sciences and mathematical rationality over humanities and culture. Its editor Kurt Pinthus wrote in the foreword:

> The humanities of the expiring nineteenth century—irresponsibly carrying over the laws of natural sciences into spiritual occurrences—contented themselves, in the realm of art, with observing, in accordance with the principles of historical development and influences, the successive and sequential; they saw causally, vertically. This book endeavors to become a collection in a different way: it listens to the poetry of our time . . . it listens across, it looks all around . . . not vertically, not successively, but horizontally; it does not separate into pieces what follows in succession, but rather listens to it together, at the same time, simultaneously. . . . Man as such, not his private affairs and feelings, but rather mankind, is a truly endless theme. These poets felt early on how man sank into twilight . . . sank into the night of the downfall . . . in order to reemerge in the clear dawn of a new day. . . . The poets of this book know this just as I do: it saves our youth; joyfully beginning, initially overflowing, disseminating life.[2]

Pinthus's foreword, and this is true of the entire collection, is a manifesto against tradition and a call for a new beginning. It is a skillfully staged call of the young against the old, of life against death and boredom, of the future against the past, of self-confidence against subservience, of anarchic zest against constraining convention.

The eruptions in art, literature, industry, science, and the everyday world took place on public stages, in public discourse, in scientific thought, and in artistic imaginings. The revolutionary moods superimposed themselves upon one another; they provoked one another even as they collided. Each was part of a larger story concocted behind the backs of the actors; it captured and bore them away with the storm of their passions, their desire for disintegration, their creativity, hopes, anxieties, and hubris. And at the center was the longing for a large shocking event that not only Georg Heym yearned for: "Würzburg May 30 [1907] Also I can say: if only there were a war, I would be healthy. One day is like another. No big joys, no big pains. . . . It all is so boring."[3]

Detours to Philosophy: Karl Jaspers

Here we speak of a revolution in philosophy. It announced itself in the proclamations of barely mature young men. It swept across people's homes, the spacious classrooms of sedate educational institutions, the dormitories of secular boarding schools and Catholic convents, to flow into the universities and public life. Scholarly living rooms, hiking trails, auditoriums, journals, book manuscripts, and letters were its arenas. Friendships were made and unraveled in its name.

The philosophical revolution spread like an avalanche. It swept up ever more people—friends, enemies, and the next generation, whose brightest lights (also women!) had craved something like this since grammar-school days.

In the scholarly world, two friends set this avalanche in motion: Martin Heidegger and Karl Jaspers. The two could not have been more different. One was small from birth, sporty, sensitive, awkward, high-strung, and shy to the point of seeming humble. The other was tall, of a noble stature, self-conscious, self-critical, and sickly. Both wanted to found a new way of thinking, a thinking that expressed the Dasein of mankind in this new time. But only one of them would attain world fame. To him alone did posterity bestow the honor of discovering something truly new: that thought comes not from thinking, but from being.

The young men came from opposite poles of the social world. Martin Heidegger was born in 1889, his father a sexton in Meßkirch. His parents' home was Catholic, conservative, and not well off.

Karl Jaspers was born in 1883. His father was a banker; he would later become the director of the Spar- und Leihkasse bank in Oldenburg. He became a member of the federal state parliament and chair of the city council in the county and town of Oldenburg. Jasper's father was a national-liberal and of a tolerant mind.[4] Before the start of his studies, the young Jaspers was diagnosed with a secondary cardiac disorder and severe bronchiectasis. This constrained him throughout his life. Yet, advised by his doctor, Albert Fraenkel, and through a great deal of self-discipline, he succeeded in finding a modus vivendi that allowed him to study.[5] His intellect was sharp, and his interests were so widespread that at first he was not sure of his direction. All authority was foreign to him, and he openly hated the academy. He chose law, but he found the teachers too mediocre.

An early photo of him as a student shows him on a break in Sils-Maria in August 1902 with the physiologist Fano from Florence and the art historian Carl Cornelius from Freiburg. Jaspers is in the middle, sovereign and physically towering over the other two, holding a big book, shyly smiling for the viewers. The professors Fano and Cornelius are kneeling to each side, laying their right hands on the book from opposite sides; the photo is subtitled "Pledge to the Spirit of Science." Both scholars apparently had fun kneeling before the student and passing on to him the role of the keeper of knowledge. At that time, he still did not know where his interests were taking him. In long conversations, the older colleagues advised him to change to medicine or at least to the natural sciences. At home he was uneasy about explaining what was provoking him to switch. In August 1902 he composed a note wherein he explained to his parents the path he wished to pursue: "It has been clear to me for a month that I want to give up law and study medicine. . . . If I had an eminently gifted mind, I would first study the natural sciences and philosophy in order to take up an academic career directly. I would pursue a doctorate in philosophy, and of course also exhaustively study medicine as one of the basic principles upon which physiology and philosophy can be built. . . . Since, however, the requirements have not been met, I will study medicine."[6] He did not send the note, but in a conversation with his father in Oldenburg he was able to convince him of the need for a change. He then studied medicine in Berlin, Göttingen, and Heidelberg. He was, however, interested in all the other natural sciences and also read philosophy in his free time. In 1908 he passed his state examination in Heidelberg with a grade of "good." Having received his doctorate for his work on "homesickness and crime" (summa cum laude), he received his physician's license in Heidelberg in 1909, married and specialized in psychiatry. He wanted to understand both the patient and the illness and to this end he needed psychology and psychiatry. For years, both realms had been recognized as university disciplines. The revolution of the natural sciences in the 1860s and 1870s had paved the way for this. In 1894 Sigmund Freud had first used the concepts "hypnotic" and "clinical-psychological analysis."[7] At first, psychoanalysis influenced this development only marginally, but as the years passed, it proved to be groundbreaking. However, for many in the natural sciences as well as in the humanities, it was psychology and not psychoanalysis that became the guiding science.

For six years Karl Jaspers worked as an assistant in psychiatry in Heidelberg. He was drawn ever more deeply into the field through his experiences with patients, his study of disease patterns and histories and their relationship to the personality of the patient, as well as through reading the professional literature. Much to the dismay of his colleagues who saw medicine as a pure natural science, he engaged in academic debates:

> with ever stranger postulates: One must systematically review the psychiatric literature of the previous decades and centuries in order to avoid the permanent relapse into forgetting; one must draw the conclusion that mental illnesses are indeed psychic illnesses and illnesses of personality; one must orient himself towards the humanities, towards psychology and anthropology; one must find a language that allows for a clear and recognizable description of symptoms; above all, one must know what a theory, what science, what a method, what "understanding" means. To this end one needs philosophy. He who pursues psychopathology must first learn how to think.[8]

His colleagues could not begin to understand his search for a general principle for understanding the social sciences and the humanities. They considered it a waste of time and saw in Jaspers a mischief maker. He, however, had long been caught up in a philosophical train of thought from which he could not detach himself. Also decisive for his turn to psychology was the fact that for some time he had been feeling unfit for the physically demanding work in psychiatry. The frustration resulting from this did not, however, last long: "In looking back it all seems remarkable. What at that time was enforced by my illness and done reluctantly was in fact leading me to the road for which I was destined. From early youth on I had been philosophizing. Actually I had taken up medicine and psychopathology from philosophical motives. Only shyness in view of the greatness of the task kept me from making philosophy my life's career."[9] *Yet* not quite, one could say. What also contributed to his ultimate decision was the fact that since he was not paid, he was under no obligation to the clinic. His father still provided for him financially. He thus did not need to consider the judgment of his colleagues and could follow his own path. However, he approached philosophy differently than the majority of his contemporaries who took philosophy to be the world of transcendent certitudes into which one only needs to become integrated. Is philosophy then not self-evident? For his contemporaries, it was only a matter of reading the doctrines of the great philosophers and interpreting them in accordance with the needs of the age. Jaspers, on the other hand, plunged into philosophy with his entire existence and he expected answers from it. His biographer Hans Saner surmises: "This view of philosophy stemmed from the solitude of his student days and from the awareness of the constant threat of illness. What meaning could there be in an existence that was necessarily detached from that of other people? What meaning did the effort of activity have if there were no objective results to be expected because of the probability of an early death? No science could answer this."[10]

Only Karl Jaspers himself could find the answer: "there remains only one path: philosophy must show the truth, the meaning and the purpose of our lives."[11] Jaspers searched for an existential—in the truest sense of the word—entry into philosophy. The illness might have contributed to this, but it was certainly not the only cause. Coming up against the limits in his study of pathological histories also contributed—as did the restless mood among young people who were at that time searching. Many had been seized by a feeling of discontent with academic philosophy. They felt that something had outlived itself and must give way to the new. But what should the new be? For the time being, Jaspers knew only that thinking emerged from experience and felt existence, a view that was at odds with standard academic philosophy.

Jaspers was an interloper. He had not gone through the traditional discipline of academic philosophy, and yet he had read the classics at an early age: Spinoza, Lucretius, Schopenhauer, Nietzsche, later also Kierkegaard and Hegel. It was solitary reading that led him to tormenting questions: How does one think being? How does it appear?

He had never enjoyed a systematic education in thought. As a doctor who dabbled in philosophy, he now wanted to change gears. This was held against him, above all by the most famous philosopher of his time: Heinrich Rickert. In 1916 the latter took over the key teaching position in philosophy at Heidelberg University. He came from Freiburg where he had supervised Martin Heidegger until his *Habilitation*.

At that time, Heidelberg was one of the strongholds of philosophy. Emil Lask, Moritz Geiger, Max Scheler, and Georg Simmel lived and studied there. Here, the friends Ernst Bloch and Georg Lukács engaged in debates. And here, above everyone, hovered the spirit of Max Weber. Weber, the great cultural sociologist, national economist, a historian of economics, political thinker and failed politician, who sought answers to the questions of his time and who had become the inspiration for an entire generation of thinkers. He was esteemed, if not feared, by everyone. His influence continued to grow well after his death in 1920.

Weber exerted a huge influence on Jaspers in those years: "He became for me the incarnation of philosophy in our time."[12] The puzzling alignment—Weber as a philosopher—is typical for the young Jaspers. For him, anyone he witnessed thinking or whose intellectual testimonies fascinated him was a philosopher. A philosopher was someone who thought through the centuries, who did not take heed of disciplinary borders, and who considered philosophy eternally young, always renewing itself as science. Jaspers admired Weber as a personality, as a responsible politician, historian, national economist, and sociologist. But beyond his interdisciplinary research, the young man esteemed in the older something more. This authentic thinker, with an insightful understanding that spanned centuries, was someone who, going beyond mere description, tried to understand historical and social connections and the ways in which they change. He was someone who could say something about the spirit and the character of the ages, someone who answered the question of meaning without normative assertions. In hindsight, Jaspers justified his admiration as follows: "It was only after his death that it became increasingly clear to me what he [Weber] meant: he is often present in my philosophical writings. . . . Even in those years he had already influenced the draft of my *Psychopathology* and even more that of my *Psychologie der Weltanshauungen*, in the introduction to which I emphasized the meaning which his constructions of ideal types in the sociology of religion had had for my work."[13] Weber recognized in Jaspers a special talent and made it possible for him—along with his employer, Franz Nissel (psychopathology [and head of the psychiatric hospital in Heidelberg, trans. note]) and the Munich philosopher Oswald Kuelpe—to do his *Habilitation* in the philosophy (not medical!) department in 1913.

Weber was thus more than an academic model; he was, in his entire person, someone to whom Jaspers was greatly indebted. Weber showed him the path of independent thinking.[14] This is why Jaspers described him as a "philosopher"—a term that neither his contemporaries nor posterity would apply to him.

In a 1916 conversation with Marianne Weber, who later told her husband in Berlin about it, this special reverence becomes evident:

> Two evenings ago K. Jaspers came to see me, and as so often we spoke a lot about you. He has such a high view of you—a new type who, so he says, is

strong enough to control and rise above enormous inner tensions and conflicts of exterior life . . . who can even afford to be ill or possibly make a fool
of himself. Now, I am impressed by the fact that Jaspers, who regards striving
for knowledge and truth as the highest value in life, said: "It is a pity every day
that this Max Weber wastes on political things instead of on his own scholarly
research."[15]

Could ill health have been a connection between the two of them? Weber, in
whom genius and depression stood in close proximity, and Jaspers, who wrested
his thinking from illness? Both alone and therefore connected? Both learned
through their illnesses how to distinguish the important from the unimportant,
mindless work from serious research, vanity from the ethos of thinking.

After his *Habilitation*, Jaspers taught social and cultural psychology, ethics
and moral psychology, religious psychology and psychology of worldviews.[16] He
still understood psychology as the leading science par excellence; thus, for him
there was also a psychology of scientific knowledge and knowing.

Yet despite his assistant professorship and despite his book *Psychology of
World-Views* (1919), the career in psychology failed. Jaspers was too philosophical for psychologists—and even more so for doctors. He himself was aware of it.
Thus, there was a certain constancy in now trying to establish himself in philosophy. He sought contact with the philosophers in Heidelberg, most directly
with Heinrich Rickert, the leading figure since 1916. Rickert knew that the psychiatrist wished to switch to philosophy and stood in the way of it. He deemed
it improper and considered Jaspers a lightweight who needed to be put in his
place. When Weber died in 1920 at the age of fifty-six, Jaspers had to do without
his role model, who was nineteen years his senior. His colleagues made his life
as difficult as possible. Rickert especially, whom Weber had considered to be his
student, saw it as a pure misreading that Jaspers elevated Weber to the status of a
philosopher: how could Jaspers, thirty-seven at that time and on the brink of an
academic career, dare to declare the esteemed national economist and sociologist
a philosopher? For Rickert this was further proof that the younger man had not
mastered his material.

Looking back over the decades, Jaspers recalled the argument with Rickert:
"'What do you want now,' he [Rickert] said, at our very first meeting, 'since you
are neither in one place nor another, having given up psychiatry and are not yet
a philosopher?' To which I replied: 'I am going to get an academic chair in philosophy; what I shall do after that will be my business according to the academic
freedom of a lecturer, in view of the vague structure of what, in a university, is
called philosophy.' Rickert laughed loudly at this impertinence."[17] Yet what did
Jaspers want? He wanted to propose, against academic philosophy, a philosophical thinking that was closer to life and questions of being than any scientific system. Throughout the years, he argued heatedly with Rickert on this topic:

This became a constantly recurring topic of discussion between Rickert and me: I attacked his philosophy relative to the claim of being a science. . . . In saying this, I developed an idea of philosophy as something altogether different from science. It would do justice to a claim to truth of a sort which science does not know, resting on a responsibility that is quite alien to science. It would perform something unobtainable by any science. On this basis, I declared my opposition to his type of thinking, saying that in reality he himself was no philosopher at all, but was doing philosophy like a physicist. The difference was merely that he was producing cunning logical analyses which on the whole were actually soap bubbles, whereas the physicist was gaining factual knowledge whenever he empirically proved his speculations.[18]

However, his older colleague did not give in. As a "neo-Kantian," he did everything to be in step with his time, in which he wanted to oppose the industrial age's break with certainty with a more secure system of values and norms. Once again, a bastion was to be erected against the violent destructive force of modernity. The "old" were also aware that they were living in a historical turning point.

What made the older colleague angry was the very public calling into question of his authority by the younger colleague. In his well-received *Psychology of Worldviews*, Jaspers presented his transition to philosophy and his critique of it as a *worldview*. Rickert wrote a scathing critique that concluded with a patronizing invitation: "We gladly greet this (philosopher) in his embryonic state."[19] For him, the younger Jaspers was still trapped in his cocoon that held and hindered him. One must wait patiently and see whether he would be able to free himself from this condition.

Rickert conspired against Jaspers in 1922, when the latter was announced as a candidate for the second philosophical academic position in Heidelberg. However, at this point Jaspers had already received two invitations to philosophical positions—one from the University of Kiel and the other from the University of Greifswald. He, however, wanted to stay in Heidelberg. Against the local authorities of philosophy, Jaspers was finally hired by the department and the Ministry. A defeat for traditional philosophy, a rebuke for Rickert, a sign of success for a new direction—and a political mark of Weimar's new culture of democratic practices. However, until the end of his life Rickert would not stop criticizing and speaking ironically about Jaspers's questioning of philosophy.

When he assumed his academic position, Jaspers in no way saw himself as an established philosopher. He wrote, in retrospect: "When on April 1, 1922, I took over the tenured academic position in philosophy in Heidelberg, I was in fact by my own standards not ready for it. I then began to undertake the study of philosophy in a new and more thorough way. . . . It seemed to me that academic philosophy was not a proper [*eigentliche*] philosophy, but had the pretense to be a science; always arguing about things that are not essential for the basic questions of our existence."[20] This is not the triumphant speech of someone who had finally proved something to the old man, but rather the tone of one who is grateful and who has a feeling of personal obligation. Jaspers was a unique individual when in 1922 at the age of thirty-nine he took over the second philosophy professorship at the venerable *Alma Mater Heidelbergienis*. His sense of himself was self-confident and unpretentious, an outsider possessing the courage to attack, having both the experience of illness and the will to live.

Dawn of a New Philosophy: Martin Heidegger

Martin Heidegger's father was a sexton and barrel maker in the service of the archiepiscopal vineyard in the Freiburg diocese. Until the middle of the 1890s, his father's workshop was located in the west section of the so-called Church in Need. Freiburg church leadership had set it up in the 1870s for its Meßkirch flock in its struggle for prestige against the old Catholics. After the purchase of the sexton house, his father moved his workshop to the basement there.[21] Prior to this, the authorities in Baden, in the course of the cultural struggle, granted the joint use of the St. Martin's Catholic Church to the Old Catholics (*Altkatholiken*). [The Old Catholics emerged in 1870 following the First Vatican Council; they did not recognize all the doctrines and practices of the First Vatican Council, and separated from the Roman Catholic Church primarily over the issue of papal authority. Trans. Note.] After this, the Roman Catholics left the church. It was in the Church in Need, whose paintings were done by the monks from the Beuron convent, where Martin Heidegger was baptized in 1889. He visited the church almost daily as a child, often going with his father, who as sexton had the duty to assist at the altar.[22] Later, when the young man wanted to tell his fiancée about himself, he described his childhood:

> But perhaps you have already beheld me in the intuition of your soul—a simple boy, living with modest, pious people in the country, a boy who could still see the glass globe by the light of which his grandfather sat on a three-legged stool and hammered nails into shoes, who helped his father with the cooperage & forced the hoops into place around the barrels, the hammer-blows resounding through the small, winding alleys; who savored all the wonderful poetry open to a sexton's son, who laid for hours up in the church tower & gazed after the swifts & dreamt his way over the dark pine forests; who rummaged about in the dusty old books in the church loft & felt like a king among the piles of books which he did not understand but every one of which he knew & reverentially loved.
>
> And when that boy, who would get the key to the tower from his father, & could choose which of the other boys was allowed up with him & so had a certain prestige & power & was always the leader in all the raids and games of soldiers, he was the only one allowed to carry the *iron* saber.[23]

The famous preacher and writer Abraham a Santa Clara was a distant ancestor of Heidegger's family. Thus there was already a gift for eloquence in the family as well as a sense of mission and a militantly disciplined vein. Abraham a Santa Clara, whose lay name was Johann Ulrich Megerie, was a monk.[24] In 1677 he was appointed imperial court preacher in the service of Kaiser Leopold I in Vienna. Like any critic of civilization of his time, he advocated national unity, esteemed the Germans, and hated the Jews and foreigners. He interpreted the 1679 outbreak of the plague as God's punishment for abandoning the mores of the court, the increasing lack of morality, and godlessness. As the Turks were standing at the gates of Vienna in 1683, he was giving national sermons. Today one would consider Abraham a Santa Clara an exceptionally gifted populist.

Abraham a Santa Clara was born in 1644 in Kreenheinstetten, near Meßkirch. In 1910 a monument was dedicated to him in the same village. Part of the money came at the instigation of Karl Lueger, who was Vienna's mayor at that time and who felt particularly close to the monk. As a student, Heidegger wrote an article about it in the magazine *Allgemeine Rundschau*.[25]

What is important about twenty-one-year-old Heidegger's participation in the 1910 dedication and his subsequent article about the unveiling of the monument for the *Allgemeine Rundschau* is only this: young Heidegger praised his ancestor for his bond with his homeland. Incidentally, the magazine was Catholic to the core, its editorial office being inclined toward anti-Semitism but not toward National Socialism, as will be seen later.

Evidently Heidegger saw no problem that Father Abraham worked in Austria. He took for granted the southern German–Austrian bond, which went very far back and was still connected to the twentieth century. The supporting pillar of this bond was the love of homeland and nature, with its beloved mountains and forests that remained undisturbed by the national boundary markers that were scattered around.

The so-called simple people of this area lived and thought in accordance with faith, accepting fate and the cycle of the seasons. For them, death was the inevitable end of a finite life. For these people, Abraham a Santa Clara was not a distant ancestor but rather a devout man who responded to an important query—that of life coexisting with the presence of death—in a timeless way. In his story about the Vienna plague, Father Abraham described the shifting boundaries between life and death with wordplay:

> It is no accident that one reads the word "life" [*Leben*] back into "fog" [*Nebel*]: No sooner is this vagabond son born on this swampy earth than the sunlight threatens to do him in. Thus it has a perfect similarity to our life: *vix orimur morimur*. Our first breath of life is already a sigh of death and the first moment

of human life falls under the dominion of the grim reaper; the first sip from the wet nurse brings the immature child to a dire worldly storm and the rocking cradle immediately reveals the precariousness of life.[26]

Could one already see here the root of the later existential philosophy? The insistence on "being toward death" would not then be the mere result of a trendy critique of civilization and hostility toward technology but would refer to the constant lingering presence of death that no progress or technology can mitigate. Admittedly, it was Heidegger's brother Fritz whom contemporaries saw as the true successor of Abraham a Santa Clara. The style of his Shrove Tuesday sermons was so similar to his predecessor's that he achieved great fame in Meßkirch.[27]

The people in Meßkirch and surrounding neighborhoods were extremely wary of the new times with their revolutionary changes. They rejected new technology and despised city life. Their anti-Semitism was informed by conservatism and antiliberalism.

Martin Heidegger was also a child of the region and saw Father Abraham as part of his world. He thus could write: "One must know the area of Kreenheinstetten, penetrate its depths, think and live with the people of Heuberg in order to understand fully the singular attraction emanating from Father Abraham."[28] The Augustinian monk, who fulminated against the neglect of mores, was posthumously elevated by the young student to bear witness to the nascent beginning of the self-healing of German culture: "People like Abraham a Santa Clara must continue to quietly nourish the nation's soul. May his writings once again become acceptable currency, may his spirit be a powerful force in the preservation of health and, where need cries out, in the renewed healing of the nation's spirit."[29] One's ears perk up: "the healing of the nation's spirit," "health"? How does the young Heidegger know that the nation is ill? People discuss it, the pastor preaches about it in his sermons, the archbishop says so, it is written about in the newspapers.

In this article, Heidegger appears as a young scholar inserting himself into the public space. He knew perfectly well the attitude he had to adopt. When he had to write an article about an event, he first described it and those involved in a neutral, polite, and correct way; then he wrote openly about what he thought of it, how the event was integrated into his world of experience and thought, and how it was to be interpreted. In this case, he was convinced that the times had become even worse since Father Abraham, threatening homeland, mountains, and the people. Early on, this unique, eloquent young man, certain of his judgment and speech, drew the attention of the circle surrounding him in his community. The local press discussed him.[30]

As to the other predecessor, the composer, conductor, and pianist Conradin Kreutzer, born at Thalmüle in Meßkirch, it is reported that one of his way stations was imperial Vienna, where he was, among other things, Kapellmeister at the Josefstaedter Theater. Leo N. Tolstoy memorialized him in his story "Kreutzer Sonata." We do not know whether Heidegger read the story, but he was quite familiar with Kreutzer's music.

Heidegger's parents and others hoped that he would become a priest. There was an entirely worldly reason for pursuing this profession: the Heideggers did not have enough money to allow their sons to study. Thus they could hope only for a clerical stipend to make school and university possible for their sons. In addition, there was certainly another reason, namely, a higher social status. In this regard, the parents could have been thinking about themselves as well as their son.

Camillo Brandhuber, the Meßkirch parish priest, took in young Martin.[31] In 1903 he enabled Martin's transition to the eighth grade of the classical secondary school in Konstanz, where he became a student at the archiepiscopal Konradinhaus. The costs of school and housing were paid by the Weiss foundation.[32]

The school residence was Catholic, the school itself public; thus the teachers were also Protestant as well as secular humanists. Once again, Heidegger writing about his school days to his fiancée Elfride Petri:

> The little brooder had to "study" & was allowed to go to school on Lake Constance & in the fifth form when he brought home nothing less than a "Schiller" as first prize, he was even in the local paper & from then on, as people still say today, he was never again seen in the holidays without a book. And he delved & sought & became quieter and quieter & already he had a vague ideal—the scholar—in his mind—though his pious, simple mother hoped for a "priest"— it was a struggle for him to win the right to live purely on knowledge, to make his mother believe that the philosopher too can achieve great things for men & their eternal happiness—how often did she ask her son, "what is philosophy, do tell me," & he couldn't give an answer himself.[33]

Clerical, or rather theological, mentors watched over young Heidegger. Pastor Brandhuber looked after him in Meßkirch. Conrad, the director of the Catholic boarding school in Konstanz until 1905 and an extremely distant relative of the family, promoted him and arranged for another stipend for Heidegger to transfer to the Freiburg Berthold Gymnasium, which was necessary after his completion of elementary school in the fall of 1906.[34] Here Heidegger lived in a Catholic dormitory.[35] In the summer of 1909, he passed the high school examination with excellence and decided to enter the Jesuit order in Tisis near Feldkirch (Vorarlberg). In September 1909 he became a novice, but on October 13 of the same year he left the institution.[36] This was prompted by health concerns as the monastic rules of the Jesuits required healthy candidates.[37]

Were there other reasons for his withdrawal? Was this precipitated by something else—suspension rather than withdrawal—covered over, in accordance
with the diplomatic custom, with the irrefutable facticity of a health issue? Or
did a suspicion of the monastic authorities and his own confession that he would
not be able to fulfill his duty with his full strength converge?

There was something in him that was moving in a different direction. And
he was well aware that becoming a priest was not the only, and perhaps also not
the true, calling for anyone who wanted to turn thinking into a profession. Of
course, his withdrawal was disappointing for his parents and supporters. He
might have even had feelings of guilt—had he failed as their hope for the future?

However, he had not yet abandoned theology or his theological sponsors. In
the winter semester of 1909, Heidegger began studying theology at the University
of Freiburg and became a member of the local theological seminary, "Collegium
Borromaeum."[38] His classes and seminars covered the history of the Church and
religious theory, biblical exegesis, and philosophy. Here, too, a teacher was particularly supportive of him: Carl Braig, a philosopher in the theology department. Heidegger was impressed "by the incisiveness of his thoughts."[39] Braig,
with whom Heidegger took an introduction to Catholic dogma in that winter
semester, also introduced him to "the tension between ontology and speculative
theology" and pointed him toward Aristotle and the etymology of fundamental
ontological concepts.[40]

At that time Heidegger began to read the work of Edmund Husserl, but he
was having a hard time, feeling himself a failure. It was also becoming ever clearer
to him that his path led away from theology. Husserlian thinking remained a
challenge for many years, a challenge he took up time and again. It was the relationship to Heinrich Rickert, especially to his text *Der Gegenstand der Erkenntnis: Einführung in die Transzendentalphilosophie*—an investigation that began
in 1890–91 as a habilitation—that helped him bridge the distance to Husserlian
thought. *Die Logik der Philosophie und die Kategorienlehre* (1911) and *Die Lehre
vom Urteil* (1912), both written by Rickert's student Emil Lask, also introduced
him to the mysteries of contemporary philosophy.

Heidegger found it fascinating that Husserl corrected psychology's omni-
present claim to validity. Toward the end of the nineteenth century, its proponents had temporarily succeeded in completely monopolizing philosophy. All
newcomers to philosophy had to pay tribute to them. Husserl titled his habilitation *Über den Begriff der Zahl* (1887) with the subtitle *Psychologische Analysen*.
Paul Natorp, who took up the question, published "General Psychology: Towards
a Critical Method" in 1912. Heidegger wrote his dissertation *Die Lehre vom Urteil
im Psychologismus* in 1913. In 1919 Jaspers published his *Psychology of Worldviews*.
The science of the workings of the psyche called into question the philosophical theory of knowledge, contesting its claim of being the only guiding science.

Concealed behind this was a substantial conflict between the natural and human sciences concerning the validity of facts, or, from the other side, the supremacy of consciousness. The natural and human scientists encountered one another on the ground of psychology, which was understood as the science of knowing (*Erkennen*), the essence of psychic activity, in order to argue about the methods of attaining scientific knowledge. All philosophers considered experts in the field had to work and publish on the influence of psychology on the theory of scientific knowledge.

Husserl emphatically rejected psychology's claim to validity as the guiding science. He provided evidence "that the doctrine of thinking and knowing could not be grounded in psychology."[41] Heidegger was fighting for an entry into phenomenology. Husserl's programmatic essay "Ideas: General Introduction to Pure Phenomenology," first published in 1913, was the breakthrough for him.[42]

Why was it so important to understand the new phenomenological direction in philosophy? Because Heidegger wanted to contribute something to this new thinking. He did not yet know what his own part in it would be. He had to first try to understand the thoughts of others. Husserl was a preeminent authority in his field at the University of Göttingen when Heidegger was struggling to read his work. Young Heidegger was impressed that Husserl was not merely a great interpreter of the history of philosophy but that he philosophized with his entire existence. He understood that Husserl's thinking was a break from idealism and also took its distance vis-à-vis neo-Kantianism. What remained in its place was only thinking itself, and its categories.

At that time the proponents of post-Kantian transcendental philosophy occupied a striking majority of the philosophical academic positions. In Baden they even formed an entire school and, of course, controlled the hiring policy. Their goal was to stave off the attack of the natural sciences, positivism, and psychology, and to develop transcendental philosophy. Natorp's lectures set Heidegger on the path of the tension among thinking, knowing, and being, what was then also called "life." For Natorp, what was decisive was that thought must expose itself to this tension toward being or "life."

During this time Heidegger was still a ward of the theologians. And, at least in hindsight, he was aware of his origins: "Without this theological background I should never have come upon the path of thinking. But origin always comes to meet us from the future," he judged in retrospect.[43] He began to publish poetry. The magazine *Der Akademiker* offered opportunities for publication.[44] Now Heidegger was in good company. He met Romano Guardini and the Jesuit Oswald von Nell-Breuning.[45] In 1923 the high school student Hannah Arendt would listen to seminars by the young professor Romano Guardini at the University of Berlin.

Heidegger did not only have a background in theology; he was also a devout Catholic. However, his studies were leading him away from theology and faith. Some of the theologians with whom he had a connection contributed to this, introducing the young Heidegger, who was increasingly interested in speculative theology, to philosophy (Carl Braig, for example): "On a few walks, when I was allowed to accompany him, I first heard of Schelling's and Hegel's significance for speculative theology as distinguished from the dogmatic system of Scholasticism. Thus the tension between ontology and speculative theology as structure of metaphysics entered into the field of my search."[46] At the time, Heidegger did not experience this with the distance and finality with which he later presented it. A new crisis was on its way. The collision between philosophy and theology, perhaps also the son's duty vis-à-vis his family, plunged him into physical malaise. His physical symptoms returned. He interrupted his studies and returned to his hometown, Meßkirch, for the summer semester of 1911. Ostensibly this was because of the healthy air of the country, but in fact it was also because he did not want to become a burden to the person giving him his stipend. In the summer the crisis came to a head: he wished to give up the study of theology. His parents were speechless when they found out about his renewed change of heart. His brother, Fritz, reported their disappointment: "They had placed high hopes on their son, Martin. They thought he could perhaps one day become, if not an archbishop, then auxiliary bishop and thus a famous man. Giving up the study of theology robbed them of this prospect."[47] Now the inevitable question about the opportunities that were generally open to him arose. Was he still to proceed with theology with a view to a rectorate, where he could pursue his philosophical studies, so as to "mature" there, as his friend Laslowski was advising? This path also seemed, for the time being, financially secure. Or should he change to philosophy? Who would pay for his studies? For the winter semester 1911–12 he finally enrolled in the department of the natural sciences and mathematics. At this point he had four semesters of theology behind him. Now he immersed himself, with the same zeal, in the study of mathematics and physics, but also attended important philosophical lectures.[48]

In summer semester 1912, he received a stipend of 400 marks from the University of Freiburg.[49] Laslowski later organized for him a further loan, which ensured his survival.[50] During this time a difficult situation was at hand. Although he had turned away from theology, Heidegger still had to foster his connections to his theological teachers and colleagues: to the historicist and Privy Council member Heinrich Finke, professor of art history and Christian archeology; to the associate professor of dogmatics in the department of theology, Engelbert Krebs; to the Catholic philosopher in the philosophy department, Arthur Schneider, with whom he would later write a doctorate; to Carl Braig, his mentor; to Conrad

Gröber, rector of Konradihaus in Konstanz and latter archbishop of the archdiocese of Freiburg; and to Josef Geyser, a theologian at the University of Münster. The tension grew. He felt that he was standing on his own feet but still had no corresponding position and thus depended on his supporters and mentors. It was common at the time that anyone aspiring to a university career would make his way under the personal care of an older colleague and would be informed by the latter regarding financing and other career opportunities. Heidegger's financial arrangement, which was endangered time and again, barely ensured his survival. At the same time, in his own way, he was convinced that he had been *called* (*berufen*), without actually having received the call from any particular vocation. He felt in himself an unconditional imperative that he perceived as elevating him well above the average person. He was, however, surrounded by average people; he depended on them. This split must have caused an existential tension from which he could barely recover.

This conflict also manifested itself in relation to his mentors. A letter from May 17, 1912, to his supporter Josef Sauer, a Freiburg theologian and the publisher of the *Literarische Rundschau für das Katholische Deutschland*, is a telling example of this:[51]

> Esteemed Honorable Professor!
> Let me, much respected Professor, congratulate you from the bottom of my heart on your upcoming birthday. May God give you strength and grace to pursue your scholarly studies for many more years to come, that you may continue to work wholeheartedly towards the one true goal of promoting the religious and cultural development of the Church.[52]

These preliminaries were followed by the presentation of a research program on the concept of space and time seen from the standpoint of mathematics and the natural sciences whose tone was not at all that of a dependent student and petitioner. This was an exposition of a study that he would later use for his lecture required for his habilitation: "The Concept of Time in the Historical Sciences" (*Die Zeitbegriff in der Geschichtswissenschaft*).

This letter was written when he had been working for some time on his dissertation; he had, however, not yet detached himself from theology and was not yet free from his dependency on his theological patrons. He thus kowtowed, wished his patron only the best, and a paragraph later made it clear that he was long his peer.

When writing to the famous Heinrich Rickert, he also chose the polite, humble tone that at the time all students and assistants were expected to use until their appointment. It was winter 1912. Heidegger was, in the meantime, Rickert's assistant and still ill. "I suffer so much from complete insomnia that the doctor has forbidden me any extended intellectual exertion."[53] For this reason, he, unfortunately, was not able to deliver his presentation. "May I ask, Esteemed Professor, to be excused from all assignments until my recovery."[54] He had pushed himself to the breaking point. He studied at home and began to recover his strength.

In his dissertation, his first independent work, he confronted the new science of psychology from a philosophical perspective. He submitted his dissertation, titled *Die Lehre vom Urteil im Psychologismus*, to Arthur Schneider, professor of Catholic philosophy; Rickert was the second reviewer. Heidegger passed his oral defense summa cum laude, the highest possible mark for doctoral work.

Two years later, he looks back to the conferral of his doctorate in a letter to his fiancée:

> And his father, whose brooding taciturnity he inherited, was proud & is so to this day, however strange and incomprehensible all his son's work might be to him & when he got his doctorate *summa cum laude*, it was in the local paper & for the small town this was cause for celebration, it had never happened in living memory & his old godmother said, "why, I always knew it, his great-grandfather was just the same, always busy with books; in the Danube Valley where his estate lay among the towering castles of the von Zimmern, he would sit on Sundays with the books he had picked up at the market in Ulm"—You ask how they came to the Danube Valley and the von Zimbern (Zimmern)? The trail leads to South Tyrol, where my ancestors in Switzerland came from—which included a theologian famous at the time [Joh. Henricus Heideggerus] whose many books are catalogued even today in the Freiburg University Library & right below them is his descendant's clumsy dissertation.[55]

He thought himself capable of obtaining a professorship and was now looking for a position. In the same letter, he tells how it happened:

> How it came about that he might write it & rose further & gained access to the university, without having all the wealth & abundance of a refined intellectual education, without the so powerful & much-used expedient of patronage, how it came about—it is a wonder to himself & a reason for deep gratitude & childlike humility; perhaps it is for this very reason that he experiences this priesthood in all its depth, because it long lay dormant within him as a distant ideal to which no path seemed to lead, because to him it is much, much more than an office, a position within society, a career—because to him it is a priesthood, something to which only the 'ordained' may gain entry & this ordination proceeds only from a struggle—from complete submission to its ideal, tortured & full of privation—and whosoever has been ordained in this way—can never be proud, but relates all things in his life back only to his innermost mission—everything apart from this is but a cipher to him.[56]

The awareness of his mission—his "priesthood"—and the will to fulfill it did not free him from earthly cares and tensions. For example, in 1913 he unexpectedly found himself in competition with his friend Engelbert Krebs when he put himself forward as a candidate for the vacant chair for Christian philosophy.[57] Krebs, eight years older, had already finished his habilitation. Heidegger had just completed a doctorate. Krebs obtained the chair.

Now Heidegger had to orient himself anew. He kept attending lectures, this time mainly in philosophy, with Heinrich Finke and Rickert. However, vis-à-vis Rickert, he presented himself ever more openly as an independent thinker.

> Esteemed Professor!
> Unfortunately, it is only today that I can express to you my sincerest gratitude for the strong philosophical motivation and instruction that I took away from your lectures and especially from your seminar. While my basic philosophical intuitions are different, I should like to be the last one to take up the miserable method of seeing contemporary philosophy as a string of "errors," as the spawn of "godlessness" and such. Rather, I am convinced that somehow a common domain must be found and this is to happen by abandoning old-established dogmatic intuitions.[58]

The gratitude concerned Rickert's lecture and his seminar *Übungen zur Subjektslehre*. He then became more resolute and referred to the "Esteemed Professor" by a shared "we": "Above all, before throwing ourselves into a critique too quickly, we must endeavor on our part to address the *formulation* of an understanding so profound that it is often extremely difficult, demanding almost an entire lifetime."[59] He thereby overstepped the boundaries of the teacher-mentor relationship, acknowledging his own voice. Yes, he was grateful to Rickert, but he also showed that he disagreed with him, challenging his professor. After all, he had passed his oral defense summa cum laude in the summer, and Rickert had approved this grade as a second reader.

His "exam," as he wrote disparagingly, was really only the beginning of his studies, and he was asking for a "corner" (*ein Plätzchen*) in Rickert's seminar. At this point he had already inquired—unsuccessfully—as to whether the Münster theologian Josef Geyser had a "corner" available.

He expressed his praise of Rickert in the language and tone of an equal. He read the second edition of Rickert's book *Die Grenzen der naturwissenschaftlichen Begriffsbildung* and admired its content: "the sharpness and the striking force with which the *logical* emerges in the first edition."[60] There is a hint of something patronizing here. We thus should not be deceived by the forms of politeness and humility of the time. Heidegger demanded recognition and respect for himself. He was then only twenty-four years old, and Rickert was fifty.

Nevertheless, Rickert took his time. Both skeptical and encouraging, he protected his position as academic teacher against a young doctor whose sights were high. In 1915 Heidegger submitted his habilitation "Die Kategorien- und

Bedeutungslehre des Duns Scotus" to Rickert. Rickert's review was critical; he found the historical foundation of the investigation weak, but he gave his approval and therewith also the conferral of the authorization to teach.[61] In the same year, Heidegger was allowed for the first time to conduct his own independent lectures and seminars.

At that time it was common in academic circles for professors to have an open house and organize evening discussions to which their colleagues, spouses, and students were invited. Students, too, paid their respects to professors at their houses and announced their visits in advance by letter. Heidegger also respected these customs. His overly polite—by today's standards, obsequious—style has led some biographers to impute opportunism to young Heidegger. That is indeed likely, but it says little about the forces that motivated him. It is first of all necessary to understand his tone as indicating an inner conflict, and this is accomplished only when we take into account the manners and social constructs of the time. Heidegger came from a hierarchically structured social milieu. Hierarchies demand subordination, particularly from those who wish to rise above the level proscribed by their social origins. Heidegger's letters speak to this.

In 1914 Heidegger's tone in his letters to Rickert became more straightforward. He had informed him about his research on Duns Scotus and sent him a copy of his habilitation. He wanted to make sure that the critique of Rickert that he had mounted there would be taken as a philosophical critique and not personal. Heidegger's self-confidence was now reinforced by the fact that he was, in the meantime, in military service. He was conscripted early in 1914, at the beginning of war. Excused from direct combat duty because of "neurasthenia and heart disease," he was first stationed at a postal checkpoint (as a censor) and then at meteorological posts in different places, ending in Freiburg itself. He served there until the demobilization in November 1918.

The revolutionaries of spirit went happily to this war. From it, they expected the necessary momentum for a spiritual renewal of Germany and Europe for which they so passionately yearned. In 1915 Max Scheler published his *Der Genius des Krieges und der Deutsche Krieg*. In the same year Paul Natorp presented his "Der Tag der Deutschen" and in 1918 delivered a two-volume work entitled *Deutscher Weltberuf. Geschichtsphilosophische Richtlinien* (volume 1: *Die Weltalter des Geistes*; volume 2: *Die Seele der Deutschen*). Heidegger, too, as most others, saw the war as a revelatory event. Even if he was excused from active military service, he participated, lest it be said afterward that he was a weakling.

Like many artists, poets, and thinkers of this time, he believed that the war would lead to a profound transformation of human and social existence. Philosophy, too, was to be affected. He wrote to his teacher Rickert, "As useless as philosophy seemed when the war broke out, all the more meaningful it will become in the future, especially a philosophy of culture and the system of value."[62] Fortunately relocated to Freiburg, he could continue with his philosophical studies. In the winter semester of 1915–16, he resumed his lectures and seminars.

On the one hand, it is remarkable just how sharply the aforementioned people, Heidegger included, separated real life from the world of thinking by being openly disinterested in the political realm. On the other hand, however, it is no less interesting to note how they were driven, for the very same reasons, to submit real life and the political realm to the world of thought. The war became, thus, an abstract event, perhaps something given through divine provenance. In order to make it an object of their philosophy, these intellectual creators praised it as the source of the German spirit's convalescence. Still, the material reality of the gruesome slaughter caught up with them: one lost a son; another was said to have welcomed his death; still another complained that he now had only women in his lectures (not the real addressees!) and that, generally speaking, the lecture halls were empty. Where would this lead?

It is almost impossible for a reader born after the Second World War to understand this philosophically embellished, ideologized understanding of war. We must be aware that many philosophers, when encountering nationalist propaganda, were mentally disarmed. They had not developed a capacity to judge independently. What was only an echo, they took as a calling, and thought with all seriousness that the war was an instrument of education and they the educators. They therefore obscured lived reality with their philosophical constructions mapped within large coordinates. The "Great War" was thus turned into an emanation of the movement of the highest consciousness—one would like to declare it rather "a schizophrenic consciousness," except that it was a matter of the normal attitude of almost two generations of scholars whose professional understanding distorted their view of the reality of the world.

Although Heidegger experienced the war from a safe position, it could not stop the reality of the war from disillusioning him. On October 17, 1918, just a month before his discharge, twenty-nine year-old Martin wrote to his young wife from the "field":

> Only the young will save us now—& creatively allow a New Spirit to be made flesh in the world—Come what may, we must keep our belief in the spirit so surely & trustingly alive within us that we are capable of building up—building perhaps in outward poverty and privation—with many a hindrance—but only times such as these have ever awakened the hour of the birth of spirit—we are bogged down in a horribly deformed culture with a spurious appearance of life—in most people all root connections with the fundamental sources of true life have withered away—superficial existence prevails

everywhere, but is all the more brazen, insistent, demanding—we lack the great enthusiasm of the soul & spirit for the true life & experience of valuable worlds—which is why the people from the front today lack any truly rousing sense of purpose—given the sufferings of 4 years, great maturity of spirit & a radical awakening are required to rouse people to sacrifice for true values. Instead, people have been systematically nauseated by pan-German pipe dreams, & as the instruments of power for realizing them are now failing, they're faced with a hollow-eyed aimlessness—they labor under a sense not of national belonging based on true love & helpfulness—but of being deceived & abused for the selfish purposes of spiritually misguided or indeed completely unspiritual, backward power groups. In recent decades or even during the whole of the last century we've not taken enough care—if any at all—of the inner human being in ourselves & *in others*. Values such as soul & spirit have been lacking, their meaning could no longer be experienced—or at most as a perfect object of destruction for exact scientific (both natural sci. & "history") analyses—This whole aimlessness & hollowness & alienation from values has dominated political life & the concept of the state in general. The only thing that can help here is the appearance of new human beings who harbor an elemental affinity with spirit & its demands, & I myself recognize ever more urgently the necessity for leaders—only the individual is creative (even in leadership), the masses—never.[63]

Here sits a no-longer-young man in a barracks behind the front in the meteo-rological service. He is bored; he knows that the war will soon come to an end. He sees through the slogans; perhaps he feels a vague sense of anxiety and is reflecting on the beginning after the end. He wants to impress his young wife. All the intellectual markers of a young scholar of the time are to be found in this let-ter: cultural critique, worldview, bias, personal experience, awareness of mission, political judgment. Heidegger thought nationally, but he does not come across as nationalistically narrow-minded. The analogous metaphors of language and thought flowed as a matter of course from his pen: foundational origins and the young, the birth of a new spirit, deformed culture and a spurious appearance of life, superficiality, enthusiasm of the soul and spirit, radical awakening, hollow-eyed aimlessness, national belonging, the inner human being, alienation from values, the necessity for leaders, the herdlike nature of the masses. The ingredi-ents for a conservative revolutionary critique of modernity are gathered here. In this creative mind, the values of the youth movement, the critique of the avant-garde culture and society, the nationalistic consciousness, and the ideal of the "leader" resulted in a mixture that was typical of the time. In the rear echelons, on the front, in scholarly studies and in letters between friends, the idea of the leader took on the hint of a metaphysical meaning, which would then be carried over to National Socialism and its Führer Hitler in 1933. In fact, the war effected a caesura in the lives of the young soldiers, even if one different than expected.

The war made it impossible for them to return to their point of departure. That was also the case for philosophy. Hans-Georg Gadamer, a student and later a friend of Heidegger's, recalls almost sixty years later the mood of this generation: "In the realm of philosophy, too, it was no longer possible for us, the younger ones, to simply continue with whatever the older generation had created. Neo-Kantianism, which had previously enjoyed a genuine, if controversial international value, collapsed in the material massacres of trench warfare as did the proud cultural consciousness of the liberal age and its scientifically grounded belief in progress."[64]

Karl Jaspers was excused from active combat participation as a result of his lung disease. In his philosophical autobiography, he describes, from the distance of almost forty years, how the outbreak of the First World War changed him. Until then his life had been carefree. Belonging to the intellectual elite, he, like most others, naturally mocked real politics and was instead dedicated to his own tasks:

> However, in 1914, with the outbreak of the war (I was 31 years old) things became different. The historical earth trembled. With one stroke, everything that seemed long secure became threatened. We felt that we had gotten into an irresistible, opaque process. Since that time our generation has known itself primarily as having been thrown into the vortex of catastrophic events. Since 1914 it has not stopped. It keeps going in a frantic tempo. This is our human fate that I sought from then on to comprehend, not as the knowable necessity of a dark supernatural process of history, but as a situation whose results—on the basis of what is properly knowable, which is always something specific—are decisively determined by our human freedom. What I have thought since the outbreak of the war in 1914 has stood under the influence of Max Weber. Through him my political attitude underwent a change. Until then the national idea had been foreign to me. Through Max Weber I learned to think in national terms and took that type of thinking to heart.[65]

Take note: Jaspers began to think nationally, not nationalistically. Unlike Heidegger, Jaspers was interested in politics via Weber. He went so far as to picture himself in Weber's place, Weber who saw the future of Germany as the mediation between the Eastern and Western worlds: "It is our task and opportunity to salvage between those two a third: The spirit of liberalism, the freedom and manifoldness of personal life, the magnitude of the Occidental tradition. This was Max Weber's attitude which I now shared."[66]

Jaspers thus stood on the national side. Heidegger, too, was thinking nationally. The war reaffirmed for both their discomfort and increasing distance from transcendental philosophy. The question concerning the meaning of life arose from the war and demanded new answers. While their experience of the detachment of philosophical discourse from the existential problems of human beings had already developed before the war, the importance of this insight was powerfully reaffirmed by the conflict. In what followed, both Jaspers and Heidegger, in their respective realms, led a war within a war: the battle of life or existential philosophy against neo-Kantianism and transcendental philosophy. Finally, both turned against conventional metaphysics, to which theology also belonged.

In 1915 Heidegger met the student of economics Elfride Petri. Elfride came from an evangelical Lutheran family of officers. Her father had been in the Saxon military service. She was an intelligent and independent woman who spoke French and traveled alone in England, learning the language along the way. In 1914 she passed her teacher's education exam. During the war she worked at the National Women's Service (Nationaler Frauendienst) and was a follower of Gertrude Bäumer. She received her high school diploma in Kassel and went to Freiburg University in the winter of 1915–16 to study economics. Elfride loved the outdoors and was an enthusiastic skier, things that bound the two of them together.[67]

When she married Martin Heidegger, she gave up her study of economics, but she was by no means an old-fashioned spouse: she made up her own mind and maintained a connection to a male childhood friend. It becomes clear time and again that Heidegger appreciated women with intellect and femininity. He now entrusted his "mission" to Elfride:

> And this lofty, solemn, timeless mission has now been placed in the angelic hands of a "saint," the whole torrent of deepest experience engulfs the hard struggle—my Dearest Soul scatters the roses on the steep mountain path up to the towering peaks of pure knowledge & most blissful experience in these two creatures whom God was leading along their paths, his inscrutable path, until suddenly, filled with the pangs of holy craving, they found one another; the two of them will build themselves a happiness in which spirit, purity, goodness rush together and, overflowing, pour forth into the languishing souls of those who thirst—Dearest Soul, clasp your pure hands together & place them in mine—take my soul, it is yours—you saint—and let the flames and glowing heat come together and as they flare up consume one another in the longing for "the divine itself in its unchangeable beauty."[68]

His problematic relation to the Catholic Church once again became difficult because of his marriage to Elfride. He could not hurt his parents by foregoing a Catholic wedding. It was already painful for them that that their son had chosen a Protestant. Thus they had a Catholic wedding in the chapel at Freiburg University, officiated by Heidegger's friend Engelbert Krebs. Five days later they had an Evangelical ceremony in Wiesbaden, where her parents lived.[69]

The tensions with the Catholic Church became deeper after Heidegger's application for a vacant teaching position in the philosophy department was declined in 1916. In the process of application, it became discouragingly clear to

Heidegger just how far apart his own view of himself was from the older colleagues' view of him. His mentor Rickert did not lift a finger for him, and the newly appointed Edmund Husserl made no attempt to speak in his favor. During the process, he was deemed fit for a teaching position as associate professor in theology only if the sole nominee, the theologian Geyser from Münster, declined.[70] He was, however, given to understand that he did not have the stature for a proper professorship. In this way, the denial came close to being a reprimand, perhaps provoking a gnawing anger in the ambitious young scholar.

At the beginning of 1919, Heidegger confirmed his departure from Catholic theology in a letter to Engelbert Krebs, friend and priest, in which he outlined his thinking. First he described what he had worked through in the past two years and then stated his position: "Epistemological insights applied to the theory of historical knowledge have rendered the *system* of Catholicism problematic & unacceptable for me—but not Christianity *per se* or metaphysics, the latter albeit in a new sense."[71] Admittedly, he assured his friend, "in modifying my fundamental position, I have not allowed myself to sacrifice objectivity of judgment, or the high regard in which I hold the Catholic tradition, to the peevish and intemperate diatribes of an apostate."[72] His rejection was directed against "the *system* of Catholicism," by which he apparently meant the Catholic networks that were reaching far into academic and private lives, this combination of dogmatic doctrine, professional connections, and control that had destroyed the wishes and dreams of so many.

Heidegger had often made clear just how problematic he found Scholastic philosophy. Why was he now counting on a profession in this very field? Apparently he thought he was ready to occupy a teaching position even as an enemy of the "Catholic system." We do not have to see this attitude necessarily as hubris. We can also understand it as the expression of an extreme objectivity. He had pursued philosophical thinking so thoroughly that he thereby spotted the fault lines in the logic of Catholic philosophy. In so doing, he did not reject Scholasticism wholesale. In his view, the politics of professorial appointments must emerge from real philosophical merits, not from dubious claims to validity and certainly not from the opinion of the majority or those in power. Admittedly, he will later act in a similar manner, that is, more or less decisively intervening in the hiring politics of his university.

The lack of Rickert's support must have been for Heidegger at least as discouraging as the rebuke from the Catholic network. This mentor welcomed all signs of respect but gave little back.

However, the tone of Heidegger's letters to Rickert did not change. He continued to express gratitude, to show his respect for the philosophical achievements of the older colleague, and to act like an earnest philosophical partner. His grudge against Rickert was, however, growing steadily and indeed turned into cold, negative passion, as will be seen a few years later in the correspondence with Jaspers. Rickert suspected none of it; he had, in the meantime, gotten used to Heidegger's esteem, and had even begun to take him seriously as a philosophical opponent. Rickert's engagement with the philosophy of life (*Lebensphilosophie*) can be seen as a sign of this esteem. The book that he wrote on this would lead to Heidegger's (and Jaspers's) internal break with Rickert. The correspondence itself did not end until 1933.

In the meantime, Heidegger's relationship with Husserl took a positive turn. After Husserl ensured that the teaching position was not filled by any serious competitor, he turned to the aspiring talent of Heidegger, who had stayed on as his assistant through his predecessor Rickert. In 1917 Heidegger's name came up again, this time as a professor of the history of medieval philosophy in Marburg. Paul Natorp, the leading scholar in the Marburg philosophy department and an associate professor after his habilitation, asked for Husserl's advice: whether Heidegger was a capable teacher and particularly—what irony of history!— "whether with him one was really safe from confessional oppression."[73]

Husserl answered that Heidegger was indeed bound by the confessional, but that he had married a Protestant who did not convert. Heidegger had relatively little teaching experience, and the feedback on his teaching activity was divided. As a former student of Rickert, Heidegger was now trying to come to terms with phenomenology.[74] As a result, Heidegger was placed third on the Marburg list. Barely two and a half years later the position became available again, and this time Husserl hurried to put in a good word for Heidegger to whom, in the meantime, he had become attached. Earlier he had spoken a bit ambivalently as he did not know Heidegger that well. But now he could affirm that Heidegger was not in any way to be considered a Catholic philosopher:

> In the past two years, he has been my valuable philosophical co-worker; I, as an academic teacher and a philosophical thinker, have the best impressions of him and have high hopes in him. His seminars are just as well attended as mine & he knows how to attract both beginners and advanced students. His very famous lectures, both perfectly complete and profound, are very avidly attended (about 100 students). He familiarized himself very energetically with phenomenology and is generally striving after the most secure foundation for his philosophical thinking. His erudition is extensive. A genuine person.[75]

All the reproaches and ambivalences of 1917 were now rescinded. A better recommendation was unthinkable. Husserl's about-turn was now complete, one even detected admiration. Heidegger, even though recommended with greater force than in 1917, was again put in the third place on the list. Nicolai Hartmann was put in first place.

In 1922 the constellation repeated itself when Natorp was looking for a phenomenologist to take up his position in Marburg, a position that became available as a result of his retirement. All the old reproaches to Heidegger resounded. Natorp particularly feared that Heidegger was still more an epigone than an independent philosopher, that he was more engaged with "listening attentively and with understanding and then continuing along the same lines with whatever material he had received . . . rather than creating something out of any original productivity of his own,"[76] a judgment that is a bit surprising considering Husserl's praise of 1919. Still, it is telling that Heidegger also could not be ignored. The reason for this was banal and revealed much about the condition of universities in the Weimar Republic: Natorp would have gladly presented his list with Nicolai Hartmann, Moritz Geiger, and Richard Kroner on it: "However, the faculty would be opposed to *three* Jews on the list; and anyone adhering to the strictest impartiality cannot help thinking that he, by the—ever so false—*illusion* of being biased toward the other side—only strengthens the resistance even against the most capable Jews & that he hurts the case that he wanted to help."[77] Because he wanted to appear to be making every attempt to look for good non-Jews, Heidegger's name came up again.

Husserl energetically rejected Natorp's suspicion that Heidegger was an epigone. No, he was an independent, "original individual," both as a teacher and as a philosophical thinker. It was important for Heidegger's development that he come to Marburg; in the same way, "his appointment to M[arburg] would mean a lot *for M[arburg] itself!*"[78] If Hartmann became his successor, Heidegger could take his assistant professorship. And he added that Heidegger's potential departure would be "an irreplaceable loss for him."[79] And so it proceeded as follows: Nicolai Hartmann received the chair. His vacated position of assistant professor was given to Heidegger. After this, Heidegger rushed to produce a manuscript, the so-called Aristotle manuscript, from his lecture notes and sent it to Marburg. Hartmann was particularly enthralled by the "extraordinary originality, depth, & rigor which was so much better relative to the others who were second rate, at best."[80] Heidegger "found the warmest reception" in Marburg.[81]

Heidegger and Jaspers: The Encounter

Karl Jaspers and Martin Heidegger first met on April 8, 1920, at Edmund Husserl's sixty-first birthday. Jaspers recalls on that day he felt "as if we two younger men were in solidarity against the authority of abstract rules and regulations."[82] Their correspondence began immediately after their meeting. Jaspers visited his colleague in his "cabin," the newly built wooden house at Todtnauberg in the Schwarzwald, given to him as a gift by his wife, Elfride, so that he could work in peace during the school breaks. It was a modest house: a study, kitchen, bedroom, and no separate room for the children. Heidegger's first visit to Jaspers's house in Heidelberg must have taken place soon thereafter.

At that time Jaspers was already well known. His *Psychology of Worldviews* came out in 1919. In retrospect, the title suggested a false proximity to the literature of worldviews of those years, for example, Oswald Spengler's main work *The Decline of the West* that came out in 1918. But for Jaspers it was not a question of a political doctrine of worldviews, but rather of world*views* (*Welt-Anschauungen*) in the literal sense. It had to do with thinking the conditions, possibilities, and various ways of comprehending the world in its "totality," as Hegelians were saying. Content-wise, Jaspers's book marked his transition from psychology to philosophy; more precisely, it marked his search for a middle ground between psychology and philosophy. He called his approach to the worldview "comprehensive psychology." The latter struck him as "a vast and substantial area, rich in content."[83] He separated it from psychology that purported to be a substitute for philosophy. Jaspers included in it what we today understand as psychoanalytic theory: Sigmund Freud, Alfred Adler, Carl Gustav Jung, and others.

What was at stake for him in his *Psychology of Worldviews* was "not select worldviews, but rather their pointing towards the ungraspable whole of mankind's true-being."[84] Jaspers was attempting here a kind of systematization of mental attitudes, views of the world, and spiritual epochs. Seen from today's viewpoint, what stands out about the book is how experimentally Jaspers developed categories in the area between psychology and philosophy. Admittedly, this did not win him any friends among the systematic thinkers who demanded clear answers. In retrospect, Jasper's book marks, in its own way, the beginning of existential philosophy, just as *Being and Time* would do eight years later. However, the two authors were thinking from opposite poles: one was coming from an attempt to philosophize the psychology of the time; the other from the thoroughgoing questioning of fundamental philosophical categories. Also their style of argumentation was fundamentally different: Jaspers was daring, moving back and forth, almost dancing in his arguments. Heidegger was a woodchopper strenuously clearing his way through the forest. One wonders today why these two men were so drawn to each other. Was it the pressure from outside, the lack of recognition and massive criticism to which both were exposed? They felt close to each other in that one was waiting impatiently for his first professorship and the other was struggling for recognition in the philosophical guild. Both were working on a new relationship between thought and being.

They later developed an almost symbiotic relationship to which Jaspers was especially attached. Both passionately rejected German academic philosophy and its protagonists (especially Heinrich Rickert and the declining Marburg School of neo-Kantianism). Both were driven by the thought of renewing the university.

On June 27, 1922, thirty-two-year-old Heidegger wrote to his colleague Jaspers, who was six years older: "Your work has made it clearer to me that in the critique of the psychology of worldviews, your investigations are set in the correct positive direction towards the problem, and that strengthens in me the consciousness of a rare and independent comradeship in arms that I otherwise—not even today—do not find anywhere."[85] Jaspers was moved: "I especially thank you for your friendly sentiments and for your consciousness of a *comradeship-in-arms* in all of your careful attacks and jabs, which gives me pleasure."[86]

The men felt like kindred spirits in their passion for the renewal of philosophical thinking in Germany. They agreed that German universities had to be reformed from the ground up. In their letters they mocked the old guard still chewing on the same neo-Kantianism, in their eyes a misguided religion of reason. The old guard were sloppy thinkers and hindered the advancement of the young to boot. "Even the Negroes do not have such representations of *Dasein* as those that circulate in today's scientific philosophy," Heidegger called out—in playful despair—to Jaspers on June 27, 1922. He claimed in the same letter that philosophy must be radical, that "the true philosopher must confront himself and his work in a principled struggle which takes him to the knife's edge." Those who did not do this remained outside of philosophy. One had to "give hell" to the old guard.[87] He declared this after he had finally been appointed to Marburg. He brought sixteen students with him from Freiburg to Marburg (among them Karl Löwith and his friend Walter Marseille, as well as Walter Bröcker) whom he wanted to use as "shock troops" for a new thinking.[88] When he departed from Freiburg at the end of the summer, his student Hans-Georg Gadamer reported that he had a celebration on the Stübenwasen near his cabin. They piled up logs, lit up a fire: "And Heidegger gave an impressive speech that began with the words: 'Be awake to the fire of the night.' His next words were: 'the Greeks. . . . ' Certainly, the romanticism of the youth movement was in the air. But there was more. It was the decisiveness of a thinker who beheld as one our time and old times, the future and Greek philosophy."[89] Gadamer formulated what Heidegger himself saw as his mission or rather what was for him the taking on of a mandate that remained unfulfilled since the time of Plato. He saw himself as charged with philosophically refounding thought. This he wanted to accomplish within the framework of radical university reform that would have at its center the education of young students.[90] A half a century later, Hannah Arendt characterized her friend Karl Jaspers as a true educator following in the tradition of Goethe, whereas Heidegger was a teacher.[91]

At times the letters between the friends reached the point of being militant. Strong feelings of passion and rejection, resolve and boasting came from both sides. Heidegger was the more active party. While his use of rousing rhetoric reminds us today of the National Socialist use of language, it was then on the lips of all the poets, from Stefan George to the futurists. Jaspers joined this readiness for battle as a rather passive party.

Their mutual convictions at times appeared downright dramatic. Heidegger to Jaspers on April 17, 1924: "Since that September 23, I have continued to live, with you, under the assumption that you are my friend. That is the all-sustaining faith in love."[92] This was no longer a conversational tone, but rather an expression of a strong feeling of connection whose origin could also be glimpsed in the youth movement. Heidegger's remark to one of his students, as reported by Paul Hühnerfeld, presumably arose out of this feeling: "Jaspers has his own unique path of beauty."[93]

Jaspers reciprocated these feelings. He showed them openly when he visited Heidegger, which gave rise to the intimacy of thinking together that was dear to both of them. The conversations at Jaspers's house in Heidelberg became world famous. What made these conversations unique was that all conventions and clichés were to be avoided. Anyone not conforming to this structure was reprimanded rather clearly.

Two Couples

What was also unique about the conversations is that Gertrud Jaspers participated in them as an equal, just as she did in the correspondence by adding her own postscripts to the letters. In June 1923 it was she who wanted to lend Heidegger a million Reichsmark; he had complained that he needed travel money in order to proceed with negotiations in Berlin regarding his appointment to Marburg. This million, at the peak of increasing inflation, would have barely covered the travel and lodging expenses in Berlin. Great openness and trust must have reigned between Karl Jaspers, Gertrud Jaspers, and Martin Heidegger. Elfride Heidegger, on the other hand, always remained in the position of the spouse and mother in the correspondence, although at first she also made friendly postscripts to her husband's letters. However Heidegger never tried to integrate her as a partner in conversation.

Gertrud Jaspers, née Mayer, was from the outset more of a partner than a "devoted" wife who remained in the background. Jaspers came to know his Gertrud as the sister of his school friend Ernst Mayer. She and Ernst came from an Orthodox Jewish family. They were self-confident, educated, and open-minded people. At the time Gertrud was preparing for her high school examination. She was well read and knew Greek and Latin. She had already experienced deep suffering at a very young age: she had lost one of her sisters and a close friend had committed suicide. Ernst was a doctor, like Jaspers. An intense connection formed between the two men: "The community of philosophizing goes so far that my main work (*Philosophie*[94]) is unthinkable for me without Ernst Mayer. He has collaborated. Some ideas came from him. We have him to thank for making the work better formulated, better written, more precise and more literary. In this book . . . we were as one identity, an unforgettable experience for me."[95] Jaspers looked for symbiotic connections and maintained them not just with Heidegger. Here symbiotic means to be united while working on a common project. This also included, of course, argument and contradiction. The relationship with Gertrud must have been built similarly. With remarkable openness, Jaspers depicts the transformation that Gertrud had worked on him: "Up until now I was—despite dissatisfaction and longing—a cold man who wanted to know, who strove after truth. Now I am a human being who is daily reminded that he is a human being. Not by words, but rather by the reality of my life partner who demands silently: you cannot mean that you have already done enough with your intellectual achievements!"[96] Perhaps the secret of this harmony lay in the fact that it was the expression of a friendship between two kindred spirits rather than a usual bourgeois marriage, as Jaspers's biographer Hans Saner discreetly implies.[97] Gertrud Jaspers was thus much more than a professor's wife who "covered her spouse's back." She was an acknowledged partner and cothinker. A 1911 picture of the couple shows him sitting down and her standing with her hands crossed behind her back—a pose of natural authority. What is astonishing is Gertrud's facial resemblance to the woman whom Jaspers was to esteem tenderly in his later years: Hannah Arendt.

Thus Jaspers and Heidegger were talking about "comradeship in arms," about "kinship spirits," and about the goal of effecting an "overthrow" of the German university. A rebirth of Plato's Academy was to emerge from this overthrow. There was to be an "aristocratic university," a real "imperial university," where only the best could study. The correspondence provides eloquent information about the two thinkers who were searching for their place and found it in opposition and a vision of an entirely different philosophy and an entirely different university than that in which they found themselves. In a thank-you note after Heidegger's first visit to Heidelberg in 1922, Jaspers characterized their situation as paradoxical: "And neither of us know what we want; that is, we are both borne up by a knowing that is not yet explicit."[98] Here Jaspers transferred his feelings of dissatisfaction and the need to still learn to his friend. Heidegger shared this modesty personally, but not factually, not in philosophy, where he conducted himself much more self-confidently than did Jaspers. Still, Jaspers knew that he and Heidegger had both been called to this vocation.

A curious pair of friends, blown together by a contrary wind. Decades later, Arnold von Buggenhagen, one of Heidegger's students, described the appearance of Heidegger and Jaspers in the university landscape of the early twenties, where existential philosophy was struggling for recognition: "To be sure, it [existential philosophy—author's note] was presented as an academic subject. But Jaspers and Heidegger were *homines novi* (= newcomers, new professors of philosophy)."[99] The public image of the two philosophers must have been striking:

> Anyone who had the eyes to see and ears to hear was bound to discover that the two people took charge not because of their acquired positions, but due to their humanity; not on the basis of some entitlement of reason, but because they *were*. But who, in the twenties, had the eyes to see and the ears to hear that in philosophy, the scepter and the crown were wrested from reason and that the command over thoughts was given to the authority of an irrational ground, that from now on the subject of philosophy was rooted in violence and its normative power! Hardly anyone thought that the friendly and ill, inevitably bed-bound Jaspers was the gentle, corn-munching lamb, not by a long shot, but rather that he belonged to the species of hawks. Those who saw Heidegger as a stunning, soaring eagle surely missed the degree and extent of the violent energies of these angry men. The lawful ground of existential philosophy? It was the *fait accompli* right of conquest.[100]

Arnold von Buggenhagen's critical remarks were composed five decades later. In them the experience of the catastrophe is superimposed on the earlier fascination, inserting what was known later into the flow of story. Still, it is clear that with regard to their intellectual projects, Karl Jaspers and Martin Heidegger had the rigor that their peers sought.

Having obtained the position of assistant professor in Marburg, Heidegger first rented a room there. The apartment exchange with Freiburg he had hoped for fell through. He let his friend know that he no longer believed in an academic vocation. It was the language of someone who wanted to intimate that he was no longer concerned with the rancor associated with hiring. A letter from July 17, 1923, outlines just how profound his discouragement was:

> The fundamental reconstruction of philosophizing in the universities (i.e., in and with the sciences) will never be achieved by merely writing books. Whoever still doesn't notice this and leads his pseudo existence in the humdrum of today's busyness does not know where he stands, and the more organically, concretely and inconspicuously the downfall occurs, the more persistent and certain he becomes. To that end, we need an invisible *community*—that term is actually already too much and looks like *coalition, circle*, and *alignment*. Much preaching must be wiped out (i.e., the medicine men of today's philosophy must have their dreadful and pitiful handiwork exposed) in their own lifetime, so that they don't believe that the Kingdom of God has appeared with them today.[101]

The commitment to his own vocation always resonates between the lines. "I am thankful," he writes to Jaspers on December 16, 1925, "that fate protected me from corrupting Kant and Hegel by looking at them through any of the eyeglasses currently on sale. I believe that the spirit of the world can be perceived close to these two."[102]

Martin Heidegger and Karl Jaspers wanted to compel all existing philosophies to declare bankruptcy and then begin a new structuring of philosophy through their way of thinking, which did not speak of things, but rather wanted to bring Dasein itself into philosophy. They saw it as a truly national task.

In doing so, Jaspers did not use the militant language of war and national tradition in which Heidegger sometimes expressed himself, but he, too, saw himself in an uncompromising battle against what was superficial, untrue, and dishonest in German intellectual and cultural life. He admired his friend for pursuing this critique to the extreme.

A letter to his student Karl Löwith reveals Heidegger's condition at the beginning of the twenties. Even as a student, Löwith was an independent person. He used the skill of thinking that he learned from Heidegger to critique the master himself. Heidegger must have been provoked by Löwith's critical remarks when he gave a kind of self-disclosure in his response on August 19, 1921:

> I must now direct this talk at myself. The discussion hinges first of all on the fundamental mistake that you and Becker make in measuring me (hypothetically or not) against standards such as Nietzsche, Kierkegaard, Scheler, and various other creative and deep philosophers.[103] You are free to do so—but in consequence it will have to be said that I am not a philosopher. I do not picture myself as an object of comparison; this is simply not my intention.
>
> I do only what I must and what I consider to be necessary, and I do so as I am able; I do not slant my philosophical work toward cultural tasks for the sake of a "universal present." I also do not have Kierkegaard's inclination.
>
> I work in a concretely factical manner, from out of my "I am"—from out of my spiritual, indeed factical origins—milieu—life contexts, from out of that which thereby becomes accessible to me as the living experience in which I live. As existential, this facticity is no mere "blind Dasein"; Dasein is proper to existence, though this means that I live it—the "I must," about which one does not speak. With this *facticity of Being-thus*, i.e., with the historiological, existence rages; but this means that I live the inner obligations of my facticity just as radically as I understand them to be. Proper to this facticity of mine is—to state it briefly—my being a "Christian theologian": therein lies a definite radical concern for self, a definite radical scientific character—*in* this *facticity* there lies a rigorous objectivity; in it there lies "intellectual historical" historiological consciousness—and this is what I am in the everyday life of the *university.* "Philosophizing" is connected with the university only in a factically existential manner, i.e., I do not maintain that there could be philosophy only

there but rather that philosophizing has its own executed facticity [*Vollzugs-faktizität*], and hence its boundaries and limitations, precisely on account of its fundamental existential meaning in the university.

This does not exclude the possibility of a "great philosopher," a creative one, emerging from the universities; and it does not exclude the possibility that philosophizing in the university will be nothing but *pseudo-science*, i.e., neither philosophy nor science. What university philosophy is in such a case, one can demonstrate only in the course of his life.[104]

Heidegger took up his first professorship with this consciousness of being other, of feeling the necessity of existentially binding the person and the vocation, of living the task of thinking. With regard to those who interacted with him, encountered him, befriended him, distanced themselves, or even aggressively confronted him, this meant that Heidegger forced them into the tension between social conventions and his existential life project as well as into his dissent with philosophy.

Decades later, one still feels the *furor teutonicus* driving Heidegger forward. In the meantime, he was writing the first part of *Being and Time*, which was already widely talked about before it appeared in 1927.

In April 1924 the rage receded once again; it was replaced with loneliness:

My talk about *comradeship-in-arms* was written from my loneliness. Along with this, I was thinking about coming to terms with the present; however, since those days, I have become more and more unpolemical—not in the sense of not disputing anything, but from a growing understanding that what is decisive is correctly directed, positive work—and you have awakened this in me.[105]

It is telling that in this conversation Jaspers speaks of overcoming loneliness, while Heidegger places himself in his loneliness; a motif that will return in their correspondence after 1945.

An unending source of anger was the constant animosity of and toward Heinrich Rickert. Rickert's book *Die Philosophie des Lebens* came out in 1920. In it he presented himself as a polemical critic of the new philosophy of existence. He harshly attacked its representatives. He made fun of it, called the new direction that was in the meantime officially certified in Berlin a "fad," and predicted its upcoming demise.[106] In the preface to the second edition, he added that he himself wanted to found a philosophy of life, a meaningful rather than a nihilistic one—and fight against those who glorified or negated life itself: "I consider bare life to be senseless."[107] The death of philosophy as science was to be feared if "the misogynist modern philosophy of life" gained the upper hand.[108]

With broad strokes he painted those currents of life philosophy that, in his view, veered into the irrational: the young Goethe and Schelling as its forerunners, Friedrich Nietzsche as its herald, Henri Bergson as its popularizer, William James, the founder of pragmatism, as its American relative, Georg Simmel, Wilhelm Dilthey, Max Scheler, almost the entire new philosophy of the 1920s. Edmund Husserl, too, was presented as related to life philosophy. And of course Oswald Spengler, bent on decline, was among them.[109]

Rickert attacked the book of his younger competitor, *Psychology of Worldviews*, as unsystematic and accused Jaspers of biologism.[110] Jaspers himself reports that Rickert had once called him "the seducer of the young."[111] Rickert also sarcastically called into question Heidegger's understanding of being as temporal and his fundamental rejection of traditional metaphysics.[112]

Rickert had a good eye for the weak points of what appeared in the new life philosophy. He saw the crossing over to political irrationalism; he noticed what was anti-Enlightenment and atavistic in it. But could Jaspers and Heidegger really be aligned with Gertrud Bäumer, who was so well versed in nationalizing language and was speaking as a representative of life against philosophy, as Rickert implied?[113]

Heidegger's reaction to Rickert's attack oscillated between noble contempt and cold rage.[114] Regardless, Heidegger continued assuring Rickert of his appreciation, but it was becoming ever clearer that he was doing it from the standpoint of an enemy.[115] For instance, he thanked Rickert for enabling him to depart from Scholastic philosophy—what double-edged praise!

In the postscript to a 1931 letter to Jaspers, he openly spoke against Rickert: "With his shameless 'Heidelberg tradition'[116] (which is pathetic), Rickert will probably want to publicly commit himself for the coming political battle over appointments."[117] But at that point Heidegger himself had risen so far that Rickert asked him to visit, somewhat upset after the Davos debate of 1929 where Heidegger had also attacked him.[118]

The frictions and debates that Heidegger and Jaspers suffered drove them together time and again. Yet the first trial of the friendship showed that the symbiosis—which Jaspers longed for—was fragile. Jaspers hoped that his friend would recognize his struggle for a new philosophizing and positively review his book *Psychology of Worldviews*. After all, he had already expressed his agreement.[119] In June 1921 Heidegger sent his review, followed in August by Jasper's disappointed comment. He acknowledged that Heidegger was the most insightful among all other reviewers: "however, what I missed is . . . the positive approach."[120] He had had high expectations, "which were disappointed and found myself *so* far from where we had come."[121] Some of the critique he found to be unjust. He consoled himself with the thought of the next conversation, which, however, did not happen immediately.

In any case, it was painful for Heidegger that his friend did not accept his critique.[122] And yet he was certain about his judgment of Jaspers. The year before, he had summarized his objections to Jaspers's approach in a letter to Rickert: his conceptualizing, his methodical instruments were much too vague: And perhaps every philosophical judgment will not do justice to Jaspers' book, for it does not generally fit in this dimension."[123]

He was also far beyond Jaspers's distinction between thought and worldview. One can read this letter as an expression of the betrayal of friendship; after all, both Jaspers and Heidegger saw a common enemy in Rickert. But one can also read it as an expression of an unbridled devotion to philosophizing that broke through the borders of interpersonal consideration.[124] Or was it only part of the usual academic bickering?

Heidegger repeatedly tried to lessen Jaspers's shock,[125] but the disappointment—one of many—was deep. In October or November 1922, the much-awaited conversation that lasted several days took place in Heidelberg. Heidegger was moved by it: "The eight days spent with you are continually with me. The suddenness of these days, which were externally uneventful, the sureness of *style* in which each day unaffectedly grew into the next, the unsentimental, rough step with which friendship came upon us, the growing certainty from both *sides* of a mutually secure comradeship-in-arms—all of that is uncanny for me in the same sense as the world and life are uncanny for the philosopher. I thank you again warmly for these days."[126] Heidegger did not publish the review.

The roles had settled in their relationship. Jaspers was the solicitor who wanted to have his friend close to him and who was subsequently disappointed time and again. He wanted a more substantial clarification and was increasingly put off by Heidegger's responses. A letter that Jaspers wrote on January 4, 1928, after Heidegger's visit in October 1927, describes the mood of the end of the 1920s:

> I have gladly thought about the days when we were together; the complete loneliness to which one is condemned in philosophical thinking is then lifted for a moment. That another finds this intellectual exertion important—or even more important than me—is not only a satisfaction, but the fact as such is a strong impulse. It covers over the soft pain that remains, because I have the feeling that, in a sense, the answer is sometimes not forthcoming from you— without my knowing what kind of answer I mean and would like.[127]

The resigned undertone came from the feeling that his friend was not wholeheartedly open, that he kept something to himself. And Heidegger himself could not really claim that he was open toward his friend in all matters.

On the Way to Philosophy: Hannah Arendt

Then something happened that completely bowled him over. The event was called love. Her name was Hannah Arendt. She was born on October 14, 1906, the only child of the engineer Paul Arendt and his wife, Martha, née Cohn, in Hannover, Lindener Markt 2. In 1909 the family moved to Königsberg in East Prussia because the father fell ill with syphilis. Prior to the discovery of penicillin, syphilis often forced families into economic hardships and downgraded them to the status of social outsiders. Martha Arendt retreated with her family to the circle of relatives from both sides of the family. In Königsberg she found support and security for herself and her daughter. Arendt's father soon had to go to a nursing home. Her mother sought to protect her, but the child surely saw her father's physical decline.

Her paternal grandparents were well off. Max Arendt was a tea trader, chair of the Königsberg city assembly, member of the progressive party, and liberally minded. From 1910 until his death, he was the director of the assembly of representatives of the Jewish community and chair of the local Armenkommission (Commission to Aid the Poor).[128] He initiated the child into the art of storytelling, which was to play such a significant role in her life and work. For young Hannah Arendt, whose childhood was marked by the disease and death of her father and grandfather—both died in 1913—friends would later substitute for family. She built a network of personal relationships, people who supported one another through life and who ensured survival in hard times. In Königsberg, primary among these relationships were Anne Mendelssohn, Ernst Grumach, Victor Grajev, Heinz Lichtenstein, Jens Litten, and the children of the Fürst and Jacoby families.

Arendt's schooling in Königsberg lasted from 1913 until 1924—much too long in her own view. Biographers point out early independence, the love of Greek literature and philosophy, intellectual curiosity, and boredom in school. The young girl read Latin and Greek fluently and was interested in ancient poetry and philosophy. She participated in a reading group for Greek literature. A few years earlier, the collection of ancient art at Königsberg Museum had been expanded with a few significant pieces. Already at the age of fourteen, she was reading the works of the Königsberg philosopher Immanuel Kant, whose work would play a significant role in her thinking. She was also impressed with Søren Kierkegaard, the companion of so many adolescents from all levels of education.[129]

For seven years she attended a general school (*Realschule*), the former Szittnick'sche Lyceum. From 1919 to 1922 she attended "the secondary school section of the Studienanstalt of the State Königin-Luisen-School" in order to complete her high school education preparing her for university studies.[130]

The gifted student was clearly bored and stubbornly rebelled against the meaninglessness of school drills. A reprimand from school would then arrive promptly, accompanied by the message "he who breaches discipline has no business being in school." At the end of the lower secondary, Hannah Arendt left the Lusienschule. In her curriculum vitae it says simply: "I was then educated privately and passed the first set of exams at the public Hufengymnasium in Königsberg on April 30, 1923." In one stroke, she succeeded in transforming the discouraging school reprimand into freedom. With the help of relatives and friends she finally went to Berlin and in the winter semester of 1923–24 audited philosophical seminars and lectures at Berlin Friedrich Wilhelms University, from, among others, the young philosopher of religion Romano Guardini. In spring 1924, back in Königsberg, she had private lessons, preparing for the *Matura*, the exams that would enable her to matriculate at university. As an independent student, a *Matura* in fact meant taking the examinations under more demanding conditions. But, like a good swimmer, she pulled past it all. In September 1924 she passed the final examination at the city *Wilhelmgymnasium*. She was awarded a gold medal for outstanding achievement.

Daily life in Hannah Arendt's childhood and youth was marked by the everyday kind of hatred of Jews that was glossed over in "normal times," but that could transform into open hysteria in crises and revolutions. Citizens expressed their aversion to the Jews usually off the record, as a kind of social convention that they nevertheless denied officially. The tensions between Jews and non-Jews led to both hidden and open hostilities. This strengthened the feeling of belonging within Jewish families and circles of friends. One could gauge the real hostility of this society from the behavior of the children. In one of her few autobiographical disclosures, Arendt brings up the anti-Semitism among the children that led to the experiences of loneliness and peculiarity.[131]

> My mother was always convinced that you mustn't let it get to you. You have to defend yourself! When [some of] my teachers made anti-Semitic remarks . . . I was instructed to stand up immediately, leave the classroom, come home, and report everything exactly. Then my mother wrote one of her many registered letters; and for me the matter was completely settled. I had a day off from school, and that was marvelous! But when it came from children, I was not permitted to tell about it home. That didn't count. You defended yourself against what came from children. Thus these matters never were a problem for me. There existed rules of conduct, by which I retained my dignity, so to speak, and I was protected, absolutely protected, at home.[132]

Many years later, Arendt wrote to Jaspers about her mother: "I owe her a lot, most of all an upbringing without prejudices and with all possibilities open to me."[133] The maternal protection lessened the ever recurring experiences of foreignness, but could not abolish them.

For, against all expectations, anti-Semitism was not declining in proportion to the successful integration of the Jewish middle class. The political culture of the city was fragile. At the same time, since the eighteenth century, Königsberg had had a prosperous citizenry in which the Jews were strongly represented.

To name just three: Johann Jacoby, Eduard von Simson, and Fanny Lewald. Both men were Democrats with a Republican bent and were fearless fighters for the freedom of the city and its citizens. Simson was one of the "fathers" of the 1848 constitution and the voice of the citizenry against nobles and the king. Johann Jacoby was a member of the first German National Assembly and later a member of the Prussian Parliament. He switched to the Social Democrats when the liberals, with whom he associated himself, became more and more involved in imperialistic power frenzy. Fanny Lewald, who admittedly relocated her influence to Berlin, was a fearless observer of the times and on the side of the Democrats.[134]

The Shattering of the Assimilatory Culture

At the beginning of the twentieth century, Königsberg Jews were the supporting pillars of the city as members of the mercantile community and banking industry, as well as, to a smaller extent, middle-class intellectuals. They were represented in all branches of industry, but overproportionally in independent occupations, since the road to civil employment was for the most part denied them.

A large part of commerce with Russia ran through the Königsberg Jews. Königsberg was the largest European hub for the tea business in which Arendt's grandfather made his fortune. In the summer months there were streams of visitors from Russia, including merchants, academics, and parents who brought their sons who were students to Königsberg or were visiting them there. There were also job seekers of all kinds; many of whom were Jews fleeing from pogroms in Russia and Ukraine.[135]

The Jewish community possessed the right to collect taxes from its members, which made them independent of state subsidies and random donations. The Königsberg Jews were to a large extent liberal and loyal to the state in the republican sense. In these liberal Jewish families religion was considered a private affair, just as it was—at least officially—with Catholics and Protestants. Children were sent to religious classes and went to the synagogue for celebrations. There were five synagogues in Königsberg. Only a minority chose to be baptized during the wave of conversion in the nineteenth century. Still, the Orthodox Jews, who were more numerous among those who came from the East than among the already assimilated "Western" Jews, disagreed with the secularization of Jewish life and bemoaned the loss of Jewish identity. Hence, the Jewish community was religiously partitioned in several ways.

In political life, the Königsberg Jews were represented on every level. They were deputies in the Reichstag (Hugo Haase) as well as members of the city council assembly. Max Arendt was chair of the city council for many years.[136]

Social democracy was firmly anchored among the workers and intellectuals of the city, including those who were Jewish. In the electoral district of

Königsberg, "a Social Democrat was almost always" elected in the Reichstag already before the First World War.[137]

Yet, beneath the surface of a common German-Jewish culture lurked, as almost everywhere in Europe, deep-seated frictions between the Jewish and the Christian factions of the German population—better said, between the Jewish and the Christian middle and lower middle classes. On the one hand, city society benefited from the wealth of Jewish business enterprises and the culture of Jewish families. On the other hand, the Christian educated middle class looked down on the Jews, just as, conversely, the educated Jews looked with contempt on the German plebeians. In many places one read that the Jews stood out too much. This referred to, among other things, their high percentage in the intelligentsia, their self-confidence, and their critique of the ongoing unequal treatment of non-Jews and Jews. And of course it also referred to the critical publications of the time in which Jews were well represented.

Most Jewish families hoped that these frictions would go away as ever more Jewish artists and scientists, pedagogues and politicians contributed to the development of German society and the German state. Furthermore, in Königsberg, one was confident that the stable political culture of the city could keep those political passions that were repeatedly jolting the capital of Berlin in check. There a racist anti-Semitism had emerged that questioned the degree to which Jews contributed to the development of the city and society and stigmatized them as foreigners, as intruders. Still, little by little, the ideology of race came to Königsberg. It was an anti-Semitism that degraded Jews as a social group and turned them into the object of dissatisfaction and eventually hatred. It was fueled by the massive flight of Jewish from the East. Königsberg was the port of hope for these refugees. This influx brought huge social and cultural problems to both the city and the Jews community. Poverty and disease in the city increased; xenophobia was on the rise. Deportations began. In fall 1900 the local press reported the deportations of Russian Jews as "burdensome foreigners."[138]

When the war broke out in 1914, one of the first measures that the Königsberg authorities enacted was to declare a large part of non-naturalized Eastern Jewish citizens hostile foreigners and detain them.[139] During the Revolution of 1918–19, the nationalist circle again demanded the deportation of Jews as foreigners.[140] Since the passing of the equality laws, such an emotionally charged public space had been rare, but it now became the undercurrent of society.

Since the 1890s the cultural assimilation, celebrated by many as a "Golden Era," had also been attacked from within Jewish community. This Jewish reform movement that manifested itself everywhere at the time had many faces: it was the mystical Messianic renewal movement; it was the youth movement in the style of

German reform pedagogy (Gustav Wyneken); it was the youth revolt against the conformism of the parents; it was a political or reformist revolution. Many of its political protagonists advocated a Jewish state in Palestine.

In all their multiplicity and diversity, the disgruntled and the frustrated shared the conviction that German-Jewish assimilation was an illusion that poorly concealed the old injustices and humiliations. As to what should take its place, many answers were proffered.[141]

After the outbreak of the First World War, the tsarist army temporarily occupied parts of East Prussia. In Königsberg, the fear of a siege was growing, and Arendt's mother fled with her daughter to relatives in Berlin. They returned after several weeks. The victory of the German army in the "Battle of Tannenberg" in the end of August 1914 brought the advance of the Russians to a standstill.

The end of the war brought no relief to the situation. In the winter of 1918–19, a peculiar mood prevailed in the city. The anxiety and expectations vis-à-vis revolutionary Russia—the Bolsheviks seized power in October 1917—created a wild confusion of news and rumors.

After the collapse of the German Empire in the winter of 1918, the German East was an ideal area for dissatisfied and dismissed officers, Kaiser loyalists and militarists, radicalized workers, adventurers of all kind, and soldiers who were putting out different fires against many different enemies. They fought against civilians or soldiers, against civil servants, against gangs and paramilitary groups, against democrats or Spartacists, against Poles, Lithuanians, or Russians, against Jews.

In Königsberg, which then had a quarter million residents,[142] also had all the different groups of the political tableau that existed elsewhere: groups of revolutionary and reactionary soldiers and officers, disgruntled, embittered workers, frightened citizens, courageous democrats, cowardly informers, and bureaucratic counterrevolutionaries. The public life of the city was defined by spontaneous crowds of people, organized party assemblies, and secret meetings. The war split the civil and political landscape into various camps.

Workers' and soldiers' councils were created in Königsberg and East Prussia soon after the cease-fire.[143] The situation was in no way relieved after the National Assembly elections of January 19, 1919, which showed that East Prussia, adjacent to the district of Frankfurt/Oder, was the strongest Social Democratic Party (SDP) bastion, which together with independent Social Democrats, brought in more than 51.1 percent of the votes.[144] An assembly of East Prussian workers and soldiers councils took place in Königsberg on February 7–8, 1919. It is possible that Martha Arendt and her daughter went to this meeting, which included a large number of the populace who were interested in politics. In any case, Arendt mentions a public event that she attended with her mother around that time. At this assembly it was decided that the councils should form an interim government until the newly elected National Assembly took over. The workers' and soldiers' councils presumed themselves to be under the authority of the East Prussian Provincial Council,[145] clearly not wanting a confrontation with the new government, but rather wanting to secure the seat.

Yet the actual events lent themselves to other interpretations. The whole situation—with regard to economic exigencies and the separateness of East Prussia and Königsberg from the empire—seemed to become more radical. This was certainly no surprise. After the cease-fire, Königsberg was in a most problematic position. In March and April 1919, the city, as well as all East Prussia, was still cut off from the empire owing to the provisions of the Versailles peace treaty. Ships were not sailing, nor were the railroads functioning through the newly set up Polish corridor. This was fertile ground for a hectic public space governed by rumors, news, slander, wishful thinking, and propaganda.

Seen in retrospect, one has the impression that during the winter months of 1918–19, in Königsberg as well as elsewhere, various political and military camps—including the East command, the Prussian government, the imperial government, workers' and soldiers' councils, parties, and spontaneous mass gatherings—were all vying for power simultaneously, although certainly in different directions.

In Königsberg the first experimental ground for an alliance that would later so successfully bring National Socialism to power emerged: the alliance between the mob and elite. Thirty years later Hannah Arendt described this in her book *The Origins of Totalitarianism.*

In March 1920 the continuing unrest in Germany culminated in the so-called Kapp-Lüttwitz Putsch. Wolfgang Kapp, the East Prussian *Generallandschaftsdirektor* in Königsberg, supported by the disgruntled army command, his party and parts of the armed forces, again tried to wrest the power from the majority Social Democrats and the newly formed government centered in Berlin and install a military dictatorship. The imperial government took the putsch so seriously that it temporarily moved to Weimar. Many institutions in Königsberg were implicated in this coup, including the postal service and the judiciary. The putsch collapsed a few days later lacking sufficient support. In the same year, the imperial government passed a law on exemption from punishment, granting amnesty to the participants. The investigations against the institutions petered out. Admittedly, August Winnig, the Social Democrat Oberpräsident of East Prussia who was involved in the putsch, was dismissed and later expelled from the SPD.

The adolescent Johanna, Arendt's registered name, was influenced by this political disorder, whose center up until now had been in distant Berlin. Above all, the assembly of people at the meetings of the spontaneously formed workers' and soldiers' councils must have made a clear impression. She would also have understood a few things relating to the situation indirectly from her mother. She would later take up the idea of councils again and again.

Notes

1. Theobald Ziegler, *Die geistigen und sozialen Stroemungen in Deutschland in neunzehnten Jahrhundrert* (Berlin: Georg Boni, 1911). 457.

2. Kurt Pinthus, Foreword to *Menschheitsdämmerung* (Berlin: Reinbek Rowohlt, 1959), 22 and 25.

3. Georg Heym, "Taegebueche Traeume und Briefe," *Dichtungen und Schriften* 3 (1979): 89.

4. Cf. Saner, *Karl Jaspers. In Selbstzeugnissen und Bilddokumenten* (Berlin: Reinbek Rowohlt, 1970), 10.

5. Cf. Wolfgang Häubner, "Albert Fraenkel," in *Den Unvergessenen*, ed. Maas/Radbruch, (Heidelberg: C. F. Müller Juristischer Verlag, 1952), 49 ff; and "Jaspers to Fraenkel," letter from June 1, 1934, in Saner, *Jaspers*, 57ff.

6. Saner, *Jaspers*, 20.

7. In Sigmund Freud, "The Neuro-Psychoses of Defense," in *The Standard Edition of the Complete Psychological Works of Sigmund Freud* (New York: Basic Books Early Psycho-Analytic Publications, 1893–1899), 3:41–61.

8. Saner, *Jaspers*, 29–30.

9. Karl Jaspers, "Philosophical Biography," in *The Philosophy of Karl Jaspers*, ed. Paul Arthur Schlipp (La Salle, IL: Open Court, 1981), 23–24.

10. Saner, *Jaspers*, 31.

11. Karl Jaspers, "Mein Weg zur Philosophie," in *Rechenschaft und Ausblick* (Munich: Piper, 1958), 383.

12. Ibid., 389.

13. Karl Jaspers, *Philosophical Autobiography*, in *The Philosophy of Karl Jaspers, Karl Jaspers and Paul Aruthus Schilpp* (New York: Tudor Publishing, 1957), 29.

14. See Dieter Henrich, "Karl Jaspers: Denken im Blick auf Max Weber," in *Max Weber*, ed. Wolfgang Mommsen and Wolfgan Schwentker (Göttingen: Vandenhoeck and Puprecht, 1988), 726ff.

15. Marianne Weber, *Max Weber*, trans. Harry Zohn (New York: Wiley-Interscience Publication, 1975), 570–71 (translation modified).

16. See Saner, *Jaspers*, 35.

17. Jaspers, *Philosophical Biography*, 30 (translation modified).

18. Ibid., 31 (translation modified).

19. Cited in Jaspers, *Philosophical Autobiography*, 30.

20. Ibid. (translation modified).

21. See Heinrich Heidegger, letter to author, January 1, 2007, 1.

22. Also, when in 1895, the Martinskirche was taken over again by the Catholics, Martin Heidegger remained the altar boy. It was he who gave over the key at the ceremony that returned the church to the Catholics as the old Catholic sexton found the entire situation so embarrassing that he preferred to have this done by an altar boy as opposed to a priest; see Hugo Ott, *Martin Heidegger: A Political Life* (New York: Basics Books), 44.

23. Heidegger to Elfride Petri, letter dated December 15, 1915, in Martin Heidegger, *Letters to His Wife* (Cambridge: Polity Press, 2008), 5.

24. Abraham a Santa Clara (1622–1709) belonged to the reformed Augustinian-Barbusse order.

25. My description is also supported by Victor Farias, *Heidegger and Nazism*, ed. Joseph Margolis and Tom Rockmore, 24–37 (Philadelphia: Temple University Press, 1989). The French sections were translated by Paul Burrell, and the German sections translated by Gabriel Ricci. Farias takes this event and Heidegger's involvement with it as an occasion to draw a line of continuity from the seventeenth century to Heidegger's later involvement with National Socialism. For him, Abraham a Santa Clara is *cum grano salis* an ancestor of National Socialism. The agent who connects into the new era is Karl Lueger, an admirer of the monk, sworn anti-Semite and conservative, antimonarchist politician of the turn of the nineteenth into the twentieth century. As proof for Abraham a Santa Clara's entanglement via Lueger, Farias cites Adolf Hitler, who was present at Lueger's 1910 burial in Vienna. Hitler records the event in *Mein Kampf*, wherein Lueger is belittled as a weakling in state matters (Farias, *Heidegger and Nazism*, 68ff).

26. Abraham a Santa Clara, *Wien* (1895), 18.

27. Hans Dieter Zimmerman, *Martin Heidegger und Fritz Heidegger: Philosophie und Fastnacht*, (Munich: Beck, 2005), 27ff., 34ff, 43ff.

28. Martin Heidegger's article on Abraham a Santa Clara, cited by Farias, *Heidegger and Nazism*, 31.

29. Cited by ibid., 32.

30. See ibid., 33ff.

31. Ott, *Martin Heidegger*, 47.

32. Farias, *Heidegger and Nazism*, 14.

33. Heidegger to Elfride Petri, letter dated December 15, 1915, in Heidegger, *Letters to His Wife*, 5.

34. See Ott, *Martin Heidegger*, 49.

35. Ibid., 53–54.

36. See ibid., 56.

37. Johannes Baptist Lotz, "Im Gespräch," in *Erinnerung*, ed. Neske (1977), 155; Lotz rightly noted that the news that Heidegger had left the monastery because of health reasons "sounded somewhat strange." Admittedly, this strangeness is only so if we leave aside the psychosomatic side of illness.

38. Hugo Ott, *Martin Heidegger, A Political Life*, trans. Allen Blunden (New York: Basic Books, 1993), 57.

39. Ibid.

40. Ibid.

41. See Martin Heidegger, *My Way into Phenomenology*, cited by Walter Biemel, *Martin Heidegger: An Illustrated Study*, trans. J. L. Mehta (New York: HBJ, 1976), 11.

42. Ibid., 12.

43. Martin Heidegger, "Aus einem Gespräche zur Sprache. Zwischen einem Japaner und einem Fragenden," in *Unterwegs zur Sprache* (Frankfurt: Vittorio Klostermann, 1985), 91. English translation: Martin Heidegger, "A Dialogue on Language: Between a Japanese and an Inquirer," in *On the Way to Language*, trans. Peter D. Hertz (San Francisco: Harper and Row, 1971), 10.

44. Cf. Ott, *Martin Heidegger*, 59–60.

45. Romano Guardini (1885–1968) was a Catholic priest and a philosopher of religion and theory who in 1923 accepted the chair for Philosophy of Religion and Christian Studies at

Berlin University. Oswald von Nell-Breuning (1890–1991) was a Jesuit and in 1928 became a professor of moral theology, church law, and social science, at the St. George Philosophical-Theological High School in Frankfurt am Main.

46. Biemel, *Martin Heidegger*, 10.

47. Lotz, "Im Gespräch," 155.

48. The information regarding Heidegger's lectures and seminars as a student was obtained from the list Alfred Denker has set up of all seminars and lectures given by Heidegger. He completed this task on the basis of the documents in the archive of Freiberg University (UAF). Heidegger's correspondence and his college books are cited at www/freewebs.com/m3smg2/ Heidegger Student.html; see also the collected attachments from the thinker on the published book: Alfred Denker, ed., *Heidegger-Rickert: Briefwechsel* (Frankfurt: Vittorio Klosterman, 2002), esp. 77; see also Heidegger's curriculum vitae for his application seeking promotion (1913), translated by Thomas Sheehan, http://religiousstudies.stanford.edu/wp-content/ uploads/CURRICULUM-VITAE-1913.pdf.

49. Ott, *Martin Heidegger*, 72.

50. Ibid.

51. Ibid., 69–70.

52. Ibid., 70 (translation modified).

53. Heidegger to Rickert, letter dated December 13, 1912, in Denker, *Heidegger-Rickert*, 11.

54. Ibid.

55. Heidegger to Elfride Petri, letter dated December 15, 1915, in Heidegger, *Letters to His Wife*, 5–6.

56. Ibid., 6.

57. Ott, *Martin Heidegger*, 75.

58. Heidegger to Rickert, letter dated October 12, 1913, in Denker, *Heidegger-Rickert*, 11ff.

59. Ibid., 12.

60. Ibid., 13.

61. Cf. Rickert's assessment of Heidegger's Habilitationsschrift dated July 19, 1915, UAF, B 3, Nr. 522.

62. Heidegger to Rickert, letter dated November 5, 1914, in Denker, *Heidegger-Rickert*, 20.

63. Heidegger to Elfride Petri, letter dated December 15, 1915, in Heidegger, *Letters to His Wife*, 55.

64. Hans-Georg Gadamer: *Selbstdarstellung*, in: ders: Werke Bd. 2 (1986), S. 479f.

65. Jaspers, *Philosophical Autobiography*, 55 (translation modified).

66. Ibid., 55–56.

67. Cf. Gertrud Heidegger's accompanying textual commentary in Heidegger's letter dated December 13, 1915, and letter dated December 16, 1915, in Heidegger, *Letters to His Wife*, 6–7.

68. Ibid., 7.

69. Cf. ibid.

70. Cf. Ott, *Martin Heidegger*, 92.

71. Ibid., 106.

72. Ibid., 107.

73. Natorp to Husserl, letter dated October 7, 1917, in Kurt Schumann, ed., *Husserl: Brief-wechsel, Bd. V* (New York: Springer, 1994], 130.

74. See Husserl to Natorp, letter dated October 8, 1917, in ibid., 131ff.

75. Husserl to Natorp, letter dated February 11, 1920, in ibid., 140.

76. Natorp to Husserl, letter dated January 29, 1922, in ibid., 145.

77. Natorp to Husserl, letter dated January 29, 1922, in ibid.

78. Husserl to Natorp, letter dated February 1, 1922, in ibid., 150.

79. Husserl to Natorp, letter dated February 1, 1922, in ibid., 151.

80. Natorp to Husserl letter dated October 30, 1922, in ibid., 161.

81. Husserl to Natopr, Letter from 1.2.1922, in ibid., 151.

82. Cf. Jaspers, *Philosophical Autobiography*, 75.

83. Cf. Karl Jaspers, *Weltanschauungen* (Berlin: Springer, 1990), 11.

84. Ibid., 12.

85. Heidegger to Jaspers, letter dated June 27, 1922, in Walter Biemel and Hans Saner, eds., *Heidegger-Jaspers Correspondence*, trans. Gary E. Aylesworth (New York: Humanity Books, 2003), 36.

86. Jaspers to Heidegger, letter dated July 2, 1922, in ibid., 37.

87. Heidegger to Jaspers, letter dated June 27, 1922, in ibid., 36 (translation modified).

88. Cf. Hans-Georg Gadamer, *Philosophical Apprenticeships*, trans. Robert R. Sullivan (Cambridge, MA: MIT Press, 1985), 38.Cf. Heidegger to Jaspers, letter dated July 14, 1923, in Biemel and Saner, *Heidegger-Jaspers Correspondence*, 46.

89. Gadamer, *Philosophical Apprenticeships*, 48.

90. It is astonishing just how much Heidegger continues to follow Plato, especially his understanding of the relation between philosophy and political thinking, and his view of the meaning of the university and of the aims of education. Cf. also Ersnt-Wolfgang Böckenförde, *Rechts-und Staats-philosophie* (Stuttgart: Atelier Reichert, 2002), 70ff.

91. "Heidegger is a teacher" in Hannah Arendt, *Denktagebuch* (Munich: Piper, 2002), 13.

92. Heidegger to Jaspers, letter dated April 17, 1914, in Biemel and Saner, *Heidegger-Jaspers Correspondence*, 50.

93. Cited by Hühnerfeld, *In Sachen Heidegger* (Hamburg: Hoffman and Campe, 1959), 57.

94. Karl Jaspers, *Philosophie*, 3 vols. (Berlin: Spring Verlag, 1932).

95. Karl Jaspers, "Self-Portrait," in *Schicksal and Wille,* edited by Hans Saner (Munich: Piper, 1967), 31.

96. Ibid., 32.

97. Saner, *Jaspers*, 26.

98. Jaspers to Heidegger, letter dated November 24, 1922, in Biemel and Saner, *Heidegger-Jaspers Correspondence*, 41.

99. Buggenhagen, *Philosophische Autobiographie*, 102.

100. Ibid., 108.

101. Heidegger to Jaspers, letter dated July 14, 1923, in Biemel and Saner, *Heidegger-Jaspers Correspondence*, 47.

102. Heidegger to Jaspers, letter dated December 16, 1925, in ibid., 62 (translation modified).

103. Oskar Becker (1889–1964) was an assistant professor with Heidegger in Freiburg from 1928 to 1931; he received an appointment in Bonn in 1931.

104. Heidegger to Löwith, letter dated August 19, 1921, in Karl Löwith, *Martin Heidegger and European Nihilism*, ed. Richard Wolin, trans. Gary Steiner (New York: Columbia University Press, 1998), 236.

105. Heidegger to Jaspers, letter dated April 17, 1924, in Biemel and Saner, *Heidegger-Jaspers Correspondence*, 51.

106. Heinrich Rickert, *Philosophie* (Toronto: University of Toronto, 1922), 8.

107. Ibid., 11.

108. Cf. ibid., 14.

109. Ibid., 19ff.

110. Cf. ibid., 155.

111. Jaspers, *Philosophical Autobiography*, 36.

112. Cf. Rickert, *Philosophie*, 143.

113. Ibid., 184.

114. Cf. Heidegger to Jaspers, letter dated December 26, 1926, in *Heidegger-Jaspers Correspondence*, 72–73.

115. Cf. Heidegger to Rickert, letter dated February 15, 1928, in *Heidegger-Rickert*, 58ff.

116. Meant here is Heinrich Rickert, *Die Heidelberger Tradition in der deutschen Philosophie* (Tubingen: Mohr Siebeck, 1931).

117. Heidegger to Jaspers, letter dated July 24, 1931, in Biemel and Saner, *Heidegger-Jaspers Correspondence*, 136.

118. Ibid., 157ff.

119. Heidegger to Jaspers, letter dated January 22, 1921, in ibid., 27n8; and Jaspers to Heidegger, letter dated January 24, 1921, in ibid., 28n1.

120. Jaspers to Heidegger, letter dated August 1, 1921, in ibid., 31.

121. Jaspers to Heidegger, letter dated August 1, 1921, in ibid.

122. "That I have done you many injustices, Husserl also says. For me, that is only proof that I have at least *tried* to throw myself into it. The point is made if you get some kind of stimulus out of it, perhaps one that I didn't even intend. Judged by the standards I hold for my work, it's a laughable, pitiful, beginner's attempt, and I don't imagine myself to have gone further than you, especially since I have it in my head to make a few detours. Whether I can also find my way into the clear, or whether I go only so far and stop, or even *go* at all, I don't know" (Heidegger to Jaspers, letter dated August 5, 1921, in Biemel and Saner, *Heidegger-Jaspers Correspondence*, 32).

123. Heidegger to Rickert, letter dated August 27, 1920, in *Heidegger-Rickert: Briefwechsel*, (2002), 51.

124. Rickert had already used the argument that Jaspers did not understand the tools of philosophy for years. Heidegger knew this. And in order to make the confusion complete, Rickert may well have read Heidegger's remark, that some phenomenologists manipulated evidence too "generously" and thought that he was also implied in this remark; see ibid., 52.

125. Cf. also Heidegger to Jaspers, letter dated June 27, 1922, in Biemel and Saner, *Heidegger-Jaspers Correspondence*, 33.

126. Heidegger to Jaspers, letter dated November 19, 1922, in ibid., 40 (translation modified).

127. Jaspers to Heidegger, letter dated January 4, 1928, in ibid., 84.

128. Cf. Günther Jacoby, *Königsberg 1881–1969 Greifsweld*, ed. Hans-Christoph and Frank Harwise (Lubeck: Schmidt-Romhild, 2004), 32.

129. Elizabeth Young-Bruehl, *Hannah Arendt: For Love of the World* (New Haven, CT: Yale University Press, 1982), 36.

130. Hannah Arendt, curriculum vitae included with the dissertation file, Box marked "UAH, H-IV-757/24."

131. "The word 'Jew' never came up when I was a small child. I first met up with it through anti-Semitic remarks—they are not worth repeating—from children on the street. After that I was, so to speak 'enlightened.' . . . I thought to myself, that is how it is. . . . I knew that I looked Jewish. I looked different from other children. I was very conscious of that. But not in the way that made me feel inferior, that was just how it was"; see Hannah Arendt, "Interview with Günter Gaus," in *Essays in Understanding*, ed. Jerry Kohn (New York: HBJ, 1994), 6–7.

132. Ibid., 8.

133. Arendt to Jaspers, letter dated March 23 and 25, 1947, in Lotte Kohler and Hans Saner, eds., *Arendt-Jaspers Correspondence*, trans. Robert Kimber and Rita Kimber (New York: Harcourt Brace, 1992), 80.

134. See Manthey, *Königsberg: Geschichte einer Weltbürgerrepublik* (Munich: Carl Hanser, 2005), 442ff., 486ff., 493ff.
135. Cf. Jacoby, *Königsberg*, 9.
136. Cf. ibid., 13.
137. Ibid., 8.
138. Cf. ibid., 55.
139. Cf. ibid., 65.
140. Ibid., 65ff.
141. Anson Rabinbach explicates four different dimensions to Jewish messianism at the time: (1) the idea of restoration, that is, the return of a utopian past of Judaism; (2) the redemptive utopian aspect that wears the double garment of religion and politics such as *Georg Lukács in History and Class Consciousness*; (3) the apocalyptic idea as the sudden eruption of a messianic age; (4) messianism as separated from the profane and an ambivalence toward practical everyday life which only the Messiah will bridge; see Anson Rabinbach, *In the Shadow of the Catastrophe* (Berkeley: University of California Press, 1977), 31ff.
142. On December 1, 1919, according to a population census, the state of Königsberg had 245,994 inhabitants; see Prussian Privy State Archives (GSTAPK) Berlin, File: HA XX, Rep 2 II, Nr. 2983.
143. Already on January 8, there was a gathering of all East Prussian workers and soldiers in the state of Insterburg; cf. Protokoll der "Verhandlungen der vereinigten Arbeiter-und Soldatenräte Ostpreussens in Insterburg am 8. Januar 1919," GSTAPK Berlin, HA XX, Rep 2 II, Nr. 2983.
144. See Winkler, *Revolution* (Hannover: Sammlung Vandenn, 1984), 139.
145. Cf. GSTAPK Berlin HA XX, Rep 2 II, Nr. 2983.

2 Life's Transformation, or the Sudden Eruption of Love in Life

An everyday love story. Life has written this story many times, yet something is different here. When the eighteen-year-old student Hannah Arendt from Königsberg met the thirty-five-year-old professor Martin Heidegger from Meßkirch in the winter of 1924, something happened.

Martin Heidegger was a reclusive scholar, at five three rather short and slender, with an athletic build. Hannah Arendt was a young student eager to learn, slim, with a beautifully proportioned face, shining eyes, and lightning-quick intelligence.

Heidegger harbored contradictions within himself. He was ascetic but could also break suddenly into joie de vivre. He was a thinker par excellence. He followed the style of a country worker both in dress and in demeanor. He was full of high-strung intensity but also displayed a perplexing shyness. Platonic gesture and lyrical rigor were mixed in his language. He spoke in a soft, almost thin, high voice. Thus it was no wonder how different, even contradictory, the depictions of his appearance and influence were. Karl Löwith, the aspiring young philosopher, who early on measured himself against, as well as argued with, Heidegger, wrote from the distance of decades: "We nicknamed H[eidegger] 'the little magician from Meßkirch' . . . He was a small dark man who knew how to perform magic tricks, making what he had just presented to his listeners disappear."[1] His student Paul Hühnerfeld noted:

> Heidegger [was] stocky and dressed in a peculiar kind of clothing. When he came to Marburg, he had a suit made which evoked the efforts of the artist Otto Ubbelohde who had passed away the year before. This post-Romantic Biedermeier artist became famous not only because of his paintings and children's illustrations, but also because he was concerned with the reform of German men's clothing. It was to resemble once again traditional wear. Thus Heidegger wore tight breeches and a long overcoat: the Marburg students quickly dubbed this "the existential suit."[2]

Eighteen-year-old Hannah Arendt was also a person of contradictions. She was a well-behaved young woman who was shy and self-confident, modest and sometimes arrogant, judgmental and eager to learn, capable of criticism and receptive to critique from others. She could be passionate and was always ready to argue. When she was fascinated with something, her face lit up.

Arendt consulted her friends as to the best place to study and which academic teachers were interesting. These prospective students, who flowed into Marburg from the entire country, were ambitious. Endowed with clarity of thought and well versed in ancient philosophy, these young people could tell the difference between the epigone and the authentic thinker. Their attention was awakened whenever there was the promise of a return to the original sources (*ad fontes*). Arendt's friend Ernst Grumach had already attended Heidegger's lectures in 1923 and was impressed with the young philosophy professor in Marburg with whom one could learn how to think independently, not simply how to reconstruct the existing philosophy. In retrospect, Arendt wrote about that stormy time:

> In the German universities at the time, after the First World War, there was no rebellion but widespread discontent with the academic enterprise of teaching and learning in those faculties that were more than mere professional schools, a disquiet that prevailed among students for whom study meant more than preparing for making a living. Philosophy was no breadwinner's study, but rather a study of resolute starvelings who were, for that very reason, all the harder to please. They were in no way disposed toward wisdom of life or of the world, and for anyone concerned with the solution of all riddles there was a rich selection of world views and their partisans available: it wasn't necessary to study philosophy in order to choose among them. But what they wanted they didn't know. The university commonly offered them either the schools—the neo-Kantians, the neo-Hegelians, the neo-Platonists, etc.—or the old academic discipline, in which philosophy, neatly divided into its special fields—epistemology, aesthetics, ethics, logic, and the like—were not so much communicated as drowned in an ocean of boredom.[3]

Hans-Georg Gadamer later recalled a "distinctly frantic search for direction confronting the young people at that time."[4]

On the one hand, the universities seemed undisturbed by the revolutionary and reformist zeitgeist. Universities like Marburg, Freiburg, or Heidelberg were academic hothouses, rooted in the cultures of small towns while enlivening them. On the other hand, one could feel a peculiar unarticulated restlessness among the students which was marginally also related to political events.

However, those who viewed themselves as intellectuals did not lower themselves to the level of politics. Many smart young scholars were clearly not interested in current events. They found the hostile camps narrow-minded and abhorrent in their violence; they refused to get involved with the weak Weimar Republic just as they ignored nationalist currents. Their intellectual contempt for politics manifested itself in the complete abstinence from participation in political life. This attitude was also typical for the educated middle class of the nineteenth century with whom the young people of the 1920s most certainly wanted nothing to do. True, Thomas Mann's openly celebrated "transition" from the nationalist to the republican camp in 1922 caused some commotion on the intellectual scene, but it had no real effect. Revolution and antirevolution, radical change and tentative reform influenced the universities both indirectly and directly, but the fermentation remained in a peculiar in-between realm. For instance, Gadamer tells about a revolutionary discussion club where political and philosophical ideas were scrutinized for their potential for salvation. Stefan George competed against Rabindranath Tagore, Max Weber's sociology against Otto von Gierke's cooperative rights and Edmund Husserl's phenomenology.[5] Political revolution and philosophical unrest were brought together in academic discussions, which, however, wanted nothing to do with the political present.

Academic Life

Marburg was a small town brought to life by its university. The Berlin spirit occasionally influenced the university, most notably with hiring decisions. But in the end it only mattered if one counted for something in the social and academic hierarchy of university life. This included, for example, invitations to the social evenings of Mrs. Councilor Hitzig, on Rotenberg 1a, provided that one was already established socially. It was said that Frau von Hitzig, a great-grandchild of Leopold von Ranke, was related to ninety-one German Ordinarien professors, a title that at the time was considered to be one of the highest social distinctions, just below the conferral of knighthood or aristocratic status.[6]

The entry of Heidegger onto the stage of this academic environment struck these restless young people. For many, an encounter with him was a dramatic, life-changing experience. For instance, Gadamer notes in his memoir that "my first meeting with Martin Heidegger came as a complete shock to my premature self-confidence."[7] A somewhat peculiar, but never hitherto experienced charisma lay behind it: "A basic event, not only for me but for all of Marburg of those days. He demonstrated a well-integrated intellectual energy laced with such a plain power of verbal expression and such a radical simplicity of questions that the habitual and more or less mastered games of wit with logical categories or modalities quickly left me."[8] His behavior in the classroom was at the very least idiosyncratic:

> He entered the lecture hall, barely glanced at the crowd, went to the window, and began to speak in a low voice. His first words were often not understood and perhaps were not meant to be because Heidegger wanted to impose utter concentration. As he continued to speak, his voice became louder, often ice cold, derisive . . . The audience was captivated. The thirty-four year-old

man emanated a brittle charm, a dark fascination. It was not only the appeal of a truly creative philosopher; it was also the fascination for one of the great people of the 1920s.[9]

His student Heinrich Schlier said: "Heidegger's way of teaching was fascinating. He taught us how to think and keep on thinking. Not that we understood much of anything. At first it was too enigmatic for us."[10] His student Hans Jonas spoke of an enigma behind the influence of Heidegger's teaching: "One came under his spell rather than understanding him."[11]

The word certainly traveled about the appearance of someone with such an extraordinary charisma. It did not take long before interested young students flowed in from around the country. At sixty, more than forty years later, Hannah Arendt attempted to describe the force that had gripped her eighteen-year-old self as well as her friends: "The rumor about Heidegger put it quite simply: Thinking has come to life again; the cultural treasures of the past, believed to be dead, are being made to speak, in the course of which it turns out that they propose things altogether different from the familiar, worn-out trivialities they had been presumed to say. There is a teacher; one can perhaps learn to think."[12] To this still-young professor, it seemed possible that one could address in an original way the questions posed time and again by the history of Western thought. Phenomenology for him was the proper orientation for encountering the world, thereby shattering the idealistic or positivist foundation of the modern understanding of being. He wanted to turn the past into the present and to read the ancient Greeks in such a way that they appeared as contemporaries. He thereby became "the hidden king [who] reigned therefore in the realm of thinking, which, although it is completely of this world, is so concealed in it that one can never be quite sure whether it exists at all; and still its inhabitants must be more numerous than is commonly believed. For how, otherwise, could the unprecedented, often underground, influence of Heidegger's thinking and thoughtful reading be explained, extending as it does beyond the circle of students and disciples and beyond what is commonly understood by philosophy?"[13] The names of those who heard Heidegger's lectures and his colleagues reads like a who's who of the twentieth-century schools of thought: Hans-Georg Gadamer, Max Horkheimer, Fritz Kaufmann, Herbert Marcuse, Hans Jonas, Karl Löwith, Leo Strauss, Benno von Wiese, Ernst Grumach, Günther Stern (who later called himself Günther Anders), Hannah Arendt, Walter Bröcker, Walther Marseille—not to mention many others whose intellectual development was influenced by Heidegger but who did not later make an academic career. Most were simply drawn into his orbit, having an experience of awakening. Hans Jonas, a young Jewish philosopher committed to Zionism and well versed in the art of textual interpretation, first came to Freiburg for the summer semester of 1921 to attend lectures by Husserl and his not-yet-established assistant, Heidegger:

From the beginning Heidegger was—this was my first impression—much, much more difficult than Husserl . . . One had [with Heidegger—author's note], without even understanding anything, the immediate impression: Here is something new, here new vistas are opened up and new linguistic paths are elaborated. I know that I became fully convinced in this semester, without understanding very much, that here a significant and essential philosophizing was at work. Here was a man thinking in front of his students, who was not reporting on thought, as it was with Husserl, but rather enacting the act of thinking itself in the presence of his students. And it was shattering. To use an example, a purely external detail: it often happened that he was not facing the audience at all, but was rather looking out of the window or in fact looking into himself and thinking aloud. One had the feeling that one was witnessing here the inaugural activity of an entirely original, distinct new thinking, discovering, and opening up. And at the same time he was an excellent pedagogue. I remember even today that it had to do with Aristotle's *De Anima*, with the Aristotelian treatise on the soul. I do not think that we moved past the first three or four chapters of the whole book. But, as he interpreted sentence after sentence—of course, the text was read in Greek, as was natural at the time—he would not let go until the innermost chambers of the Aristotelian thinking and seeing were penetrated. And it was also always the case—which, incidentally, has become for me something from Heidegger that I have kept my entire life—that someone would say something and use professional language. He would then say: "too scholarly, much too scholarly, please express yourself in a way that is not so scholarly." He wanted to get rid of fixed, already coined terminology in the professional language of philosophy in order to arrive at the originary phenomena. He wanted one to see things simply, which is not to say lightly, because for him simple insights lay in the depth and not on the surface.[14]

The intellectual and human shattering did not necessarily come in lofty garb. This professor stirred his students—including female students—in a special way. Löwith describes how many students had to struggle with the influence of this charismatic teacher and how ambivalent Heidegger's appearance could be. His characterization of Heidegger dates back to 1926; he reproduced it, with minor changes, in his autobiography written in the 1940s:

Heidegger's face can be described only with difficulty, because he was never able to look at us directly or openly for long. The natural expression of his countenance can be described as an animated forehead, a veiled face and downcast eyes, which only from time to time checked on the situation by looking up a second. If he was forced to look directly at someone during a conversation, his expression would become reserved and unsteady as if relations with others were difficult. Conversely, he expressed the cautious and prudent distrust of a peasant. He read his manuscript with an air of concentration, avoiding gestures or empty phrases. His sole rhetorical device was a very studied soberness and rigorous construction of a thesis that was designed to create a suspense. With the effort of such concentration, his face would become very expressive with plain but interesting asymmetries. His forehead, marked by a prominent vein, was the sole animation. We could see it working of its own accord without consideration for the audience who was aroused rather than addressed.[15]

Of course, Heidegger participated in many social events, as was common in the academic life of the day. He visited student and professorial circles and he pursued sports, participated in volleyball games and boccie contests on the Dammelsberg. He put on his skis as soon as the first snow fell. Skiing connected him with his origin, the beloved Schwarzwald. Here once again it becomes clear that the fascination Heidegger exercised on young students stemmed from a peculiar confluence of action and contemplation, doing (*Tat*) and reflection, thinking and existence in his lectures and in his demeanor. It must have appeared to his young students as well as some young professors as a radical act of questioning. Hans-Georg Gadamer reports that it was only in his encounter with Heidegger that for the first time he learned how to do philosophical work properly.[16] One learned how to think by first working through the old texts themselves—against the standard interpretations. Heidegger did not make it easy for his students; he lectured early, in the summer already around seven in the morning, thereby unsettling their routine.[17]

It is striking today that so many Jewish students flocked to Heidegger. In retrospect, Hans Jonas writes about the mood of these young Jewish students who went to Marburg for Heidegger:

> I was active in the Zionist movement and to this extent I was thoroughly politically oriented, yet I took no part in German politics, except for following it with some attention. But Hannah Arendt and I shared this with a whole lot of these passionate Heideggerian students who came together in Marburg. We had a certain beautiful noble disdain or rejection of the world of politics. There was the German, or at least widespread in Germany, prejudice that the higher life of the mind was not compatible with common everyday affairs and one did not engage with them or at least it had to be limited to the minimum of attention and interest. This is the life devoted to theory, the contemplative life; the *bios theoretikos*, the *vita contemplativa*, which is to say the highest form of life. It became detached from the Aristotelian context where man is a political being. Somehow this foundation was ignored. Hannah Arendt had a childhood where she had completely isolated herself from the reality of the world around her via a small chosen, and mutually choosing, circle of young fellow students, who, I believe, were all Jewish. I do know that Hannah Arendt appeared in Marburg with a small group of friends from Königsberg . . . I believe they were all filled with the same disdain for political engagement as Hannah. It was . . . a typical group phenomenon.[18]

In his bitter memoir, *My Life in Germany before and after 1933*, Löwith recalls his position vis-à-vis the Weimar Republic in a very similar manner: "The struggle of the political parties did not interest me, for both the left and the right were arguing about things that did not concern me personally and only irritated me in my development. Thomas Mann's 1918 text, *Reflections of an Unpolitical Man*, gave me a kind of justification for this."[19] The irony of history is that even this book, from which its author distanced himself in the beginning of the 1920s, fed into the national agitation and arrogance among the young creative minds of the time. The mixture of open political disinterest and an awareness of how the First World War destroyed the old world and its ideals, educational values, and ways of thinking, brought many young intellectuals either to the national right or radical left camps. And it led particularly gifted students to a teacher like Heidegger.

First Encounter

In winter 1921 Hans Jonas began his studies at the Higher Institute for Jewish Studies (Hochschule für die Wissenschaft des Judentum), a rabbinical seminary in Berlin. He then came to Marburg for Heidegger in the Winter Semester 1924–25 at the same time that Hannah Arendt began to study there. They first met during this semester. Arendt was attending Heidegger's lectures on Plato's *Sophist* and *Philebus*. She was a pretty young woman who caught the attention of both younger and older men. Gadamer calls her in his memoir "the striking girl who always wears a green dress."[20] She was a dark-haired, graceful person with a clearly defined oval face, high forehead, and shining eyes, whose quick mind and power of judgment were present. It was natural that she would study philosophy and Greek philology because she had already excelled in these subjects in high school. But why did she choose evangelical theology? Apparently she wanted to study theology as part of her philosophical studies; she also took the biblical texts to be part of thinking about the world and human beings. Furthermore, the famous Rudolf Bultmann was teaching evangelical theology in Marburg.

Arendt was as fascinated with the young professor Heidegger, as were, presumably, her fellow students. In November 1924 she went to see him during his office hours.[21] Prior to that, there must have been a look between them during one of the lectures, a look through which those in love make themselves known. In any case, in 1950 Heidegger returns to the look that he saw during a lecture.[22]

One can easily imagine what fascinated Heidegger about the young student: the rare mixture of beauty, cleverness, foreignness, shyness, and self-confidence. But what fascinated Arendt about Heidegger? One can certainly see how a young, highly intelligent woman falls in love with a charismatic teacher twice her age. Löwith introduced a metaphor that expresses the enigmatic aspect of this relationship: the magician. Heidegger, "the little magician from Meßkirch,"[23] met the young student Hannah Arendt, who had, as attested to by Hans Jonas, "an intensity, an inner direction, an instinct for quality, a search for essence, a depth which gave her a magic."[24]

So, two magicians? Or was it an entirely mundane story?

Toward the end of the semester she received this letter:

X.II. 25

Dear Miss Arendt!

    I must come see you this evening and speak to your heart.

    Everything should be simple and clear and pure between us. Only then will we be worthy of having been allowed to meet. You are my pupil and I am your teacher, but that is only the occasion for what has happened to us.

    I will never be able to call you mine, but from now on you will belong in my life, and it shall grow with you.

    We never know what we can become for others through our Being. But surely some reflection can make clear how destructive or inhibiting the effect we have might be.

    The path your young life will take is hidden. We must be reconciled to that. And my loyalty to you shall only help you remain true to yourself.[25]

In the meantime, an intimacy—even though still using the formal "you" (*Sie*)—developed between the two that allowed them to become bolder. In all likelihood, they saw each other often during office hours or on other academic occasions. But the first letter reveals someone who is struggling for composure.[26] The letter was a kind of probing, a questioning self-reflection on what the eruption of love had brought about. It unsettled the teacher-student relation. The protective social boundaries were about to become undone. Heidegger was trying to understand the relationship within the coordinates of his thinking. Yet something happened that exceeded the limits of his power of understanding: he knew that this young woman did not belong to him. He was oscillating between paternal, caring feelings and an inexpressible passion, between proximity and distance: "We have been allowed to meet: we must hold this as a gift in our innermost being and avoid deforming it through self-deception about the purity of living. We must not think of ourselves as soul mates, something no one ever experiences."[27] The last sentence could—perhaps unwittingly—be read as a commentary on his relationship with Jaspers. For the latter was still professing intimate friendship, although such a thing was very difficult for Heidegger; he took it to be dishonest because detachment, distance, and remoteness, which for him were always present even in the relationship between friends, was suppressed.

To this young woman, on the other hand, he spoke of the sphere of the "between" that showed itself in experiencing their difference. However, he did not understand this difference as static; it was changing, transforming itself. Symbiosis and diversity, proximity and remoteness did not stand in an antithetical relation to each other. They conditioned each other, not in a dialectical way, but rather as a relation of being.

They must have gone on a walk between the first encounter during office hours and this letter, since he apologized for his strong feelings on their walk. Perhaps he had spontaneously pulled her to himself. He concluded the letter by integrating this experience into his work: "But just once I would like to be able to thank you and, with a kiss on your pure brow, take the honor of your being into my work."[28]

The structure that contained him had not yet completely burst, it still held. The existential shattering still lay ahead. For the time being he was trying to interpret what had happened by philosophizing existentially. His words were long-winded, stilted. But he spoke like that to his wife, as well. It is unclear if he spoke this way to his sons.

As love overtook him, Friedrich Schiller's poem flashed in his mind:

The Strange Maiden
A vale there was, whose simple folk
Perceived with each returning year,
Just as the earliest larks awoke,
A strange and lovely maid appear.

Her birth the valley could not boast,
Where she had come from none could tell;
And every trace of her was lost
The moment she had bid farewell.

Her presence caused an honest mirth
All hearts and spirits to invade,
And yet her dignity and worth
Familiarity forbade.

Enchanting blooms and fruits she bore
With gay profusion in her hand,
Grown on some more prolific shore,
The products of a sunnier land.

To everyone she gave a share—
To this some fruit, to that a bloom;
And whether young or bowed with care,
All turned their footsteps richer home.

Welcome were all, but if by chance,
Hand clasped in hand, some lovers passed,

For them was her most favored glance,
And they received her very best.[29]

His letters suggest that in February 1925 their relationship turned passionate. He now uses the informal "you" (*Du*), and he no longer speaks in the double role of the teacher-lover, but instead as the lover who is also a teacher. The topic of "proximity and distance in love" surfaces in the letters time and again:

Dear Hannah!
Why is love rich beyond all other possible human experiences and a sweet burden to those seized in its grasp? Because we become what we love and yet remain ourselves. Then we want to thank the beloved, but find nothing that suffices.

We can only thank with our selves. Love transforms gratitude into loyalty to ourselves and unconditional faith in the other. That is how love intensifies its innermost secret.

Here, being close is a matter of being at the greatest distance from the other—distance that lets nothing blur—but instead puts the "thou" into the mere presence—transparent but incomprehensible—of a revelation. The other's presence suddenly breaks into our life—no soul can come to terms with that. A human fate gives itself over to another human fate, and the duty of pure love is to keep this giving as alive as it was on the first day.[30]

Thus begins a passionate relationship, which, as both of them understand, ought not to be, but also cannot not be. They must hide their feelings from all others; he from his colleagues and few friends (like Jaspers). Above all, his wife—he was, after all, the father of two children—had to know nothing about this love. Elfride had a hard time with his openness toward young women. Moreover, she had tolerated Heidegger's exchanging letters with their friend Elisabeth Blochmann—a smart young woman, but not of the extraordinary brilliance as this Hannah. The latter upended him, made him insecure. He was moved and agitated. His passion elevated him to unknown heights of feeling. Hannah, on the other hand, had to consider her circle of friends and other fellow students only in a limited way. She could wholly devote herself to this love.

They were now seeing each other during discussion nights. He hosted evening events in honor of Edmund Husserl when the latter visited Marburg: "What was unpleasant about the Husserl evenings was the striving to top each other. So I was all the more pleased that you sat quietly in the corner."[31] Supposedly, she said nothing at all. Perhaps she was so fascinated by the intense academic *logos* gathered there that she did not feel the need to say anything.

Love shattered him.

27.II.25
Dear Hannah!

The demonic struck me. The silent prayer of your beloved hands and your shining brow enveloped it in womanly transfiguration.
Nothing like it has ever happened to me.[32]

It was the end of semester, students were going home. Hannah's departure home was imminent. In the meantime, her mother had married the widower Martin Beerwald, father of two daughters, Eva and Clara. They now lived on Busolstraße 6 in Beerwald's house.

Heidegger sent her a "small book," as a "symbol" of his gratitude. He asked her to send him a small token before her departure, a greeting, a couple of lines. At the end of the letter he wrote: "I am looking forward to seeing your mother." Was her mother planning to visit her daughter at her university, perhaps in the beginning of the new semester? In the meantime, Hannah's stepsister Clara Beerwald had moved to Marburg. He was interested in Hannah's origin, her family background. Perhaps she showed him a picture of her mother, perhaps she told him that Martha Arendt was an educated and intellectually involved woman. Did she also tell him that her mother was a leftist social democrat who esteemed Rosa Luxemburg? In all likelihood, he knew she was Jewish. But were not all his smartest students Jewish?

Then both left; she for her mother and relatives in Königsberg and he for his "cabin" in Todtnauberg. He wrote to her from there on March 21, 1925: "When a storm rages outside the cabin, I remember 'our storm'—or I walk on the quiet path along the Lahn—or during a break I daydream about the young girl who, in a raincoat, her hat low over her quiet, large eyes, entered my office for the first time, and shortly and shyly gave a brief answer to each question—and then I transpose the image to the last day of the semester—and only then do I know that life is history."[33] Heidegger felt confused and clear-sighted, overpowered and strengthened, distracted and focused. This young woman threw his life into disarray but also helped him regain clarity. He had never encountered such a relationship. In the meantime, he pulled himself together; the work came to the fore again. Passionate feelings were the driving motor for his work: "I live in the frenzy of work and of joy at your impending arrival."[34]

In the middle of April, Hannah went with her childhood friend, Paul Jacoby, to Kassel where Heidegger was giving several lectures. He wrote to her about the topics he was going to cover in his lectures. He was concerned with his disagreement with Jaspers: "Right now, it is important for me to distinguish clearly between how worldviews are formed and how scientific-philosophical research works, in particular by addressing the concrete issue of the essence and meaning of history. Of course, this clarification is itself possible along scientific-conceptual paths. And so my studies always end up with the lectures becoming an absurdity before a 'general' public. But I have made a commitment and now

I have to muddle through as best I can."[35] He appreciated her for being a silent brilliant listener; he also spoke to her, let her in on his concerns. One of these concerns was that he hopelessly overestimated his public, even in his lectures to an educated middle-class audience. But he could not help it, philosophy was difficult; it could not be translated for a public that liked what was easy to digest. On the other hand, people were curious about this new philosopher; they came even if they did not understand him.

The secret meetings after the lectures were meticulously planned: "At any rate, *after* the lecture I will—as I now do every day—take leave of my acquaintances and hosts and get on the No. 1 tram to Wilhelmshöhe, the last stop—perhaps you can—discreetly—take the next tram. After that, I'll take you home."[36] Earlier, in March or the beginning of April, she had sent him a text called "Shadows," saying that she had dedicated it to him. The title refers to Plato's cave allegory as well as to Heidegger's lectures on *The Sophist* and *Philebus* in the winter semester 1924–25. The text is a kind of self-analysis undertaken by the young student on the basis of Heidegger's exercises for thought, written after a semester of his lectures. It is a heartfelt text that goes back and forth between the immediacy of feelings and intense theoretical abstractions. Her difficulty with her own feelings becomes clear in the transformation of the narrative "I" into a "she." A powerful anxiety is at its center: "an animal anxiety to be sheltered, because she could not and would not protect herself, combined with an almost calculated expectation of callousness, made the simplest, most natural things in life increasingly impossible for her." Anxiety resurfaces in this text in many formulations: "anxiety of reality," "she had fallen prey to anxiety," "anxiety of existence," being anxiety's "prey." The opposite of anxiety is "fixation on a single thing,"[37] searching and passion. In this text Arendt depicts her inner conflict: "a Here and Now and Then and There."[38] She speaks of "a true passion for anything unusual" and marvels at everyday banalities. "Shadows" is an autobiographical text. Its author attempts to interpret her oscillating state of mind in terms of Heideggerian thinking. The image that emerges is that of a young woman who had become estranged to herself in the face of her first passion, suffering from the fears of separation, torn out of the path of the everyday. The outsider's position of the author as a woman and a Jew is mentioned only implicitly, in the awareness of her peculiarity, in the insight that she did not belong "to anything, anywhere, ever," in the fear of vulnerability, in the feeling of the uncanny. It is an open text, without boundaries. The young woman sees herself as walking a thin line and communicated this to him. She wanted him to perceive this precariousness and to accept that his beloved was frightened. The outcome of this walking on the edge was left open; perhaps she would fall, perhaps she would find a new self: "Perhaps her youth will struggle free of the spell, perhaps her soul will realize what it is to speak out and to be released under a different sky, and thus overcome sickness and confusion and learn patience and the simplicity and freedom of organic growth. But more likely she will continue to pursue her life in idle experiments and a curiosity without rights or foundation, until finally the long and eagerly awaited end takes her unawares, putting an arbitrary stop to her useless activity."[39] She was not doing well; she had thoughts about death. He was touched and consoled her like an older father. In the meantime, on April 24, she was once again in Marburg. He spoke to her:

> "Shadows" were cast by your surroundings, by the age, by the forced maturity of a young life. I would not love you if I were not convinced that those shadows are not *you* but distortions and illusions produced by an endless self-erosion that penetrated from without. Your startling admission will not undermine my belief in the genuine, rich impulses of your existence. On the contrary, for me it is proof that you moved into the open—although the way out of such existential contortions, which are not really yours, will be long.[40]

In her first semester, she had entered into his realm and the intensive contact with new philosophical thinking and her love for him clearly unsettled her. In Königsberg, she was still the daughter and a friend of carefree young people. The contrast between everyday life, things that had become insignificant and yet now important again, and the memory of the philosophical world at Marburg must have tormented her. He, however, spoke of her strength. He believed that "an unbroken certainty and security resides in your life."[41]

Meanwhile he was sitting in his cabin, writing her about the glorious winter, and that he wished to have her near him but could not bring her there. He even began to reconcile himself with Marburg, this narrow academic town: "Since this past winter, Marburg has seemed more appealing to me, and for the first time I am looking forward to returning. The mountains, forests, and old gardens will be beautifully adorned by the time you come back. And perhaps the atmosphere I've always found so numbing about the place will finally be driven off."[42] But this did not last long. Marburg became bearable only for a short time. Three years later he would write to Jaspers: "I cannot tell you anything that speaks for Marburg. I haven't felt at ease here for a single hour."[43] Hannah had by that time left him and no longer enlivened his existence there.

In the meantime, the letters were going back and forth every few days. Since only his letters remain, several things can be said about his state and only a little about hers.

When she returned from Königsberg to Marburg for the summer semester, he observed that she was glowing. In the meantime, a profound intimacy, an almost painful directness, developed between them. He gave her a manuscript and was happy about her joy over his proof of trust. It was during this time that she gave him "Shadows," presumably her first independent text, which was dedicated to him; he was touched.[44] He accidentally met her at a concert and could not bear seeing her without approaching her.[45]

In the meantime, he advised her not to take notes but rather to listen and follow the line of thought in his four-hour lecture "History of the Concept of Time: Prolegomena to a Phenomenology of History and Nature" (*Geschichte des Zeitbegriffs. Prolegomena zur Phänomenologie von Geschichte und Natur*).[46] They exchanged poems. He asked her to bring with her the George poems of which she had spoken.[47] Heidegger loved Stefan George's poems, even if he was not a fan of the public persona of the master. His thinking was diametrically opposed to George's emphasis on sympathy.

He was so stirred by one of the meetings with her that he cried. He read Augustine's *De Gratia et Libero Arbitrio* to calm himself down.[48] She would later write her doctoral work on the concept of love in Augustine. The church father was more than a spiritual consoler; he was chosen to be the bridge between antiquity and modernity and the witness to their love.

Love aside, Arendt led a normal life. She wandered around the neighborhood with her friends, participated in academic circles and student debates. During this time, he thought longingly about her.[49] The secret meetings continued to require much organizational skill and were affected by his duties as a university teacher.[50] The relationship settled down and was no longer so eruptive. In the meantime, she recovered her self-confidence and he could see it. "You have a different expression now—I saw it at the lecture—and I was completely stunned."[51] She had been with friends for Pentecost, and her anxiety had dissipated.

They were concerned with love as a phenomenon at least as much as it was a bodily encounter; he often wrote to her about "love."[52] He knew of course that the secret of love lay in the encounter in which each overstepped the boundary of being strangers and was defined anew. But it also bothered him when he ran into her by herself or accompanied by her friends; he had to communicate these sentiments to her. They had all the little signs by which lovers recognize each other. Thus a delightful summer semester for both, for which he thanked her at the end. Then he left once again to the "cabin" in Todtnauberg and she to Königsberg.

He did well in the fresh air of meadows and forests, with the hills of the Schwarzwald surrounding him. He recovered from the semester and took solitary walks. It was the atmosphere in which he could work. "Roaming amid the firs is wonderful meditation. . . . I know every firebreak or little spring, or deer run—or grouse site. In such an environment, the work has a different texture than when one is surrounded by squabbling, conniving professors."[53] He gave her reading suggestions for her next Bultmann seminar. Rudolf Bultmann's lectures would be on the apostle Paul. Hölderlin's *Hyperion*, on his desk in the cabin, was for him a sign that "you and your love are a part of work and existence for me."[54] Her mother was supposed to send her ski equipment for the winter. He wanted to go with her on ski trips around Marburg and envisioned Clara Beerwald, Hannah's stepsister and an aspiring pianist, playing something for him. In the fall he came down from the cabin to Freiburg, where he spent two days with Husserl. In addition, he visited his elderly parents in Meßkirch. He then went to Jaspers in Heidelberg. He exhorted his Hannah one more time to prepare for Bultmann's seminar. They met again secretly around the beginning of the semester. Heidegger's next letter is dated January 10, 1926. At least two letters from Arendt must have preceded it wherein she told him of her decision to leave Marburg, perhaps because she was under the impression that he had forgotten her. In Heidegger's letter a disconcerting personality trait appears, namely, his ability to withdraw completely from all human relationships when he was working. What sounds like a confession is nonetheless only the description of the condition that for him meant ecstatic happiness, but which could cause suffering for his fellow human beings:

> I forgot you—not from indifference, not because external circumstances intruded between us, but because I had to forget and will forget you whenever I withdraw into the final stages of my work. That is not a matter of hours or days, but a process that develops over weeks and months and then subsides.
>
> And this "withdrawal" from everything human and breaking off all connections is, with regard to creative work, the most magnificent human experience I know—with regard to concrete situations, it is the most repugnant thing one can encounter. One's heart is ripped from one's body. And the hardest thing is—such isolation cannot be defended by appeal to what it achieves, because there are no measures for that and because one cannot just make allowance for abandoning human relationships. But all of that has to be borne—and while talking about it as little as possible, even with those one is closest to.[55]

This passage could be read as an expression of harshness toward his beloved. It could also be read as a thinker completely immersed in thought, an understandable attitude given his profession. During this time he was engaged in focused work on *Being and Time*, which we now know he had been working on throughout 1926. This was possible only at the price of complete withdrawal from all human relationships.[56]

But one can also recognize a trap of his own making. He was caught up in a situation where he retreated to thinking and where he forcefully detached himself from everyone and everything. He suffered from this and at the same time built up an immense strength. Yet, after the subsiding of thought's intoxication, he had to turn once again to togetherness, to proximity, until the next moment of deep concentration. When he writes in the same letter about his "times of violence" he himself suggests that there was something traumatic about this process.[57] The oscillation between rupture and rejoining, attraction and rejection, warmth and cold, symbiosis and cold separation not only exposed his beloved time and again to an emotional roller coaster; it damaged something in him, as well.

In this letter, Heidegger tried to avoid the breakup of the relationship and to interpret her departure as a transition. He refused to see their good-bye as painful, envisioning it rather as a new phase between them. She was much better off going away. The alternative was to remain stuck, risking boredom. By this, of course, he did not mean himself; rather, her decision helped them "clear the air. If it has a good effect, it can only be because it calls for sacrifice from both of us."[58] His sacrifice was to let her move; his gain was that he was free to work unencumbered. Her sacrifice was to tear herself away; her gain was "a new world," new experiences, new people, new challenges in thought.

She packed her things toward the end of winter semester 1925–26. A time of uncertainty began. Judging by the letters, she was silent, apparently wanting to show him the same distance that he had shown toward her. Half a year later she sent him greetings—presumably through her friend Hans Jonas. He answered happy and relieved, admitting that he had longed for her. He wanted to see her. This meeting did not take place. Yet, he kept track of her and during a visit to Heidelberg in October 1927 he tried to meet her without success. He asked Jaspers about her, without revealing anything of their relationship, and Jaspers told him that Hannah Arendt was engaged. He transformed this shock immediately into a gift of renunciation: "Dear Hannah, for me it was as if I had been favored to give away something ultimate and great, so as to receive it, the gift and the giving, as a new possession. I still haven't come to grips with it, much less comprehended the unsuspected things I saw in our existence in those hours. I searched for you constantly to be happy with you—until I was overcome by joy and departed."[59] He took a step back, asking almost humbly if he could have another photograph of her—perhaps from her vacation on the Baltic Sea?[60] But she was by no means engaged to Benno von Wiese, the gifted son of the famous Leopold von Wiese, as Jaspers assumed. However, she wanted to free herself from the overpowering presence of Heidegger and for this reason was with von Wiese at the time. Jaspers apparently had to formalize this liaison in order to be able to accept it.

The year 1927 was eventful. *Being and Time* was published, and Heidegger was appointed to a full-time chair as Nicolai Hartmann's successor, a position for which he had already been recommended in 1925—a belated satisfaction. The Prussian Ministry of Science insisted that the holder of the teaching position should have published something of importance. For this reason Nicolai Hartmann and others urged him to speed up the publication of *Being and Time*, which he did. The manuscript, which he had sat on for years, was hurriedly prepared for publication. It would make him world famous.

Being and Time

Being and Time was planned in two volumes. In the first part, Heidegger wanted to discuss the temporal dimension of his fundamental ontology. The second part was to work through the tension between ontology and temporality in individual thinkers (Descartes, Aristotle, and Kant). Only the first part, and not even in its entirety, was completed. The last section of the first part and the entire second part were never written. However, there is a book on Kant—*Kant and the Problem of Metaphysics*—stemming from the plan of the second part. This was published in 1929 after the famous *Davos Debate* between Heidegger and Ernst Cassirer.

Being and Time became a sensation. Many colleagues perceived it as a call to arms; others felt that this book caused a radical rupture in the history of philosophy. "The title is a manifesto. Traditionally, *Sein* is timeless. In metaphysics after Plato, the investigation of being, of the essence within or behind appearance, is precisely a quest for that which is constant, which stands eternal in the flux of time and change. Heidegger's title proclaims otherwise: *Sein und Zeit. Being is itself temporal.*"[61] In this work Heidegger viewed neo-Kantianism not so much as a school, but rather as a last gasp Idealism. He "grounded" both knowing and the rational subject in a way that subverted the strict dualism of neo-Kantianism.

Being and Time was both a radicalization as well as a break from phenomenology. Here Heidegger presented a so-called *phenomenological method* that went far beyond Husserl. Decisive in both the radicalization and the break was that Heidegger's subject is situated completely differently than was possible in the various transcendental doctrines of the subject. In the classical sense, it was no longer the autonomous subject; it was being-there (Dasein). No longer the master of the situation, the subject was now understood as being-exposed. Heidegger was able to make this theoretical leap because he approached the question of truth completely differently, namely, not normatively. Heidegger's Copernican turn was to understand the human being from being rather than from ideas. He worked his way like a lumberjack through the history of philosophy, stripping away all the encrustations and the twists and turns in the history of philosophy, in order to pose *the* question of the relation between human being and being as the central and basic question of philosophy since antiquity. But this did not go far enough: he did not simply juxtapose his thinking against modern philosophy; rather, he set free the temporality of being, that is, the historicity of philosophical thinking concerning the question of being, thereby putting into question all classical truth claims. Thus, in one stroke he overturned the metaphysical grounding and the meaning of being. Transcendental subjects and transcendental values—whether they be reason or a priori ideas—were thus mere temptations that led one astray. Truth and standards for action would have to be attained in a different way. Many of his contemporaries supposed, out of astonishment and terror over the radicalness of this claim, that a revolutionary was at work here. After 1945 there were those who wanted to detect the seeds of inhuman thought in *Being and Time*.

The surprising step in *Being and Time* was that Heidegger opened up a completely new approach to the question of the subject, now understood as thrown and exposed to being. This subject could come to itself only by understanding itself as being-there (Dasein) and in questioning itself in its relation to being.[62] Thus, the subject was now understood as an everyday "anyone" (*Jedermann*).

It is clear already here that Heidegger described in a fundamentally different way the relation between the subject and the world. This happened not through transformation or neglect of traditional theses, but through the almost brutal uncovering of the fact that the subject is always already in the world that surrounds it without the safety net of traditional sources of meaning.

Therefore, the main theses in the first part of *Being and Time* were that the being of the human being is Dasein (being-there); the core of Dasein is everydayness.[63] Dasein determines itself from the human being's existence as anxiety toward death, not by ideas or other transcendental sources of meanings; Dasein exists as possibility. An authentic Dasein is a being-in-the-world; it is care and solicitude. The human being must question after being in order to awaken the possibility of Dasein; authentic Dasein is possible only through this questioning.[64]

In a letter to his student and early critic Karl Löwith, written from Todt-nauberg on August 20, 1927, Heidegger tried to present a summary of *Being and Time* as a response to Löwith's critique of his fundamental ontology. Löwith had expressed this critique in his Habilitation—a courageous, provocative recognition of this demanding undertaking: "The 'nature' of human being is therefore not something for itself and adhering to 'spirit.' The question is: is it possible to obtain the foundation and a guiding thread for the *conceptual* interpretation of Dasein from *nature* or from 'spirit'—or from neither of these, but rather originally from the '*wholeness*' of the understanding of being."[65] The old duality between spirit and nature, upon which theology and metaphysics had grounded its thinking, must be "overcome."

If there is no dualism of nature and intellect, mind and body, essence and existence, then there is also no dualism between knowing as a purely intellectual activity and Being as neutral facticity. Knowing then must be a way of being of Dasein and, as such, part of being as being-in-the-world. "That which is to be known is a concrete form of being-in-the-world."[66] Heidegger thus overturned the Cartesian vision of the world. What mattered was not "I think, therefore I am" but rather, "I am Dasein, therefore I think."

A second, confusing element of Heidegger's philosophical advance was that he rethought the classical subject as a peculiar hybrid being. On the one hand, the subject as singular was thrown into the world and was in no way the master of things; on the other hand, Dasein was always already being-with. Being-with as being-in-the-world was "to be with others."

From this arose two possibilities. First, the danger of losing oneself is bound up with this being-with. It is embodied in the "anyone" (*Man*) and in the worldly being-with of the many "they" (*Mans*). There was something threatening about the "they":

> The *they* is everywhere, but in such a way that it has always already stolen away when Dasein presses for a decision. However, because the they presents every judgment and decision as its own, it takes the responsibility of Dasein away from it. The they can, as it were, manage to have "them" constantly invoking it. It can most easily be responsible for everything because no one has to vouch for anything. The they always "did it," and yet it can be said that "no one" did it. In the everydayness of Dasein, most things happen in such a way that we must say "no one did it."[67]

Inauthentic existence is always already given in being-with alongside others, which is to say, it is unavoidable. One notes here the outline of a critique of urban culture and the way of life, of mass society and the public space. Also noted is a critique of democracy and a principle of equality articulated since antiquity. George Steiner sees here a pitiless critique of the "they" in totalitarian society.[68] One can, however, also connect this critique to democratic mass society. The temptation to reduce Heidegger's theoretical figure of the "they" to such real historical phenomenon is great. Heidegger himself rejected this.[69]

The "fallenness" of the "they" in being-with is also not unambiguous. It is given with Dasein itself, but Heidegger also qualifies it as a "positive possibility." It is positive in the sense of being the "struggle" for authentic Dasein. The intermediary concept in Dasein's struggle for its authentic way of existence is the anxiety of perishing in fallenness and the possibility of care.[70] "Under the stress of the uncanny, *Dasein* comes to realize that beyond being *Dasein*-with and *Dasein*-in—which are the ineluctable modes of the everyday—it must become *Dasein*-for. Care is the means of this transcendence."[71] A kind of "ethics of care" develops from this. Steiner uses this to rework Descartes's maxim anew. It is not "I think, therefore I am" and also not "I am, therefore I think" but "I care, therefore I am."[72] Care is thus the constitutive possibility of Dasein's solicitous comportment in the world.

The second part of *Being and Time* concerns Dasein's insertion into the temporality of being. For Heidegger this means that only a Dasein who dares to experience its finitude does not distort its access to being. Heidegger's concept of time, which is paradoxical in our eyes, comes to us as a question: the past and future can "be" only as long as Dasein is.

The relation to time is marked by "thrownness" in the world and toward death. Behind this do we perhaps see again the return of a theme whose nihilistic consequences theology seeks to overcome in new ways?

In any case, the theme of death was a pervasive theme at that time. In expressionism, life and death collided directly with each other. In the First World War, the explosive force of life and the destructiveness of death pervade each other.

In this year a new approach to the human being's relation to death appeared with Sigmund Freud. Freud comes up against the conflict between life and death. To be sure, Heidegger (and Jaspers) rejected Freud because they equated him with psychologism, but whence came the simultaneity of the motif of death in Heidegger and Freud? In any event, Heidegger brought together the facticity of death and the meaning of life.

Heidegger's introduction of death into Dasein and thereby also in thought had its roots in Romanticism, especially in Romantic poetry, whose sensibility was close to Heidegger's. But it also came out of the Catholic tradition. How close did Heidegger feel to the thematic of death already mentioned in Abraham a Santa Clara? "No sooner had the vagabond son been born onto the muddy earth than the sun's rays threaten him with horror. Thus there is a perfect similarity to our life: *vix orimur morimur.* The first breath of our life is already a sigh of death and the first glance of human life falls on the dominion of the grim reaper; the first suck from the wet nurse brings the small child to an arid worldly storm, the rocking cradle readily shows the inconstancy of life."[73] The ancestor concluded that only the God-fearing, ascetic life and grace that God alone can grant can alleviate the fear of this inevitability in life. However, his descendant pursued the opposite direction: death must be accepted, not as blind fate, but rather as the certainty that allows for the possibility of meaning. In contrast to Abraham a Santa Clara, the fact of death did not lead to the meaninglessness of life without God; rather, the resolute facing of Dasein's death is the condition for the constitution of meaning: "A true being-towards-the-end is one which labors consciously toward fulfillment and refuses inertia; it is one which seeks an ontological grasp of its own finitude rather than taking refuge in the banal conventionality of general biological extinction."[74] Let us ask once again: what was revolutionary? What invited astonishment or horror in this incomplete work that had the effect of an explosion? It lies in the return to categories like being, Dasein, death, and time, that together form the axis of a new realm of thinking that is not simply intellectual; it lies in the radically a-theological this-worldliness of meaning that opens up a sphere of thinking that had been inaccessible to theology, and—last but not least—it lies in the critique of inauthentic life, from which one can draw connections to the Marxist critique of alienated (reified) life, but also to the national-conservative critique of technology and urban life. To be sure, the difference is that Marxism begins with the material determinations of existence, and the nationalist critique begins with a sacred past, while Heidegger identifies the origin in the temptation of inauthenticity rooted in the distractions of everyday life. From this, the category of possibility in Dasein is introduced. Following from this, life does not unfold in accordance with a plan or destination; rather, it must be projected and fulfilled as possibility. With the rejection of the concept of objective time and the introduction of time as finitude, the homogeneous present of the physicalist-biological understanding of being is subverted by the past and the future. In affirming its facticity, death becomes the possible source of meaning instead of destroying it. Meaning no longer comes from the promise of the salvation of faith—or from other transcendental sources.

The First Reactions of Readers

Many testified to the "shattering" experienced by the first readers of *Being and Time*, "when it almost incidentally appeared in Husserl's *Jahrbuch für Phänomenologische Forschung* (spring 1927)."[75] In any event, the work and its author had a tremendous impact: "Within half a year of publication, Heidegger's reputation in philosophic and theological circles was assured. By 1930, the secondary literature was extensive. Heidegger's repeated that the manuscript had been more or less taken away from him (for motives of academic promotion) and that the work, as it stood, was a fragment, added to the general sense of strangeness and revelation."[76] Even in retrospect, his student, the Marxist social theorist Herbert Marcuse, still expressed himself reverently: "Heidegger's work seemed to me and my friends like a new beginning: we experienced his book (and his lectures, from which we had notes) as, at long last, a *concrete* philosophy: it had to do with existence, our existence, with anxiety, care, boredom, etc."[77] The historian Hermann Heimpel recalled that "*Being and Time* hit like a rock causing ripples of waves or like a magnet gathering particles."[78] Reading it seemed like an existential experience to the philosopher Otto Friedrich Bollnow: "After the transition from physics to philosophy and pedagogy, at the time of my first probing inquiries, the appearance of *Being and Time*, was for me a truly subversive event. Everything that I had attempted before then seemed provisional and noncommittal, for here I felt a genuine, passionate philosophizing that was surging from the depth, like an elemental natural event, a thunderstorm for example; a philosophizing that called into question what I had up until now understood by philosophy."[79] However, Edmund Husserl must have been disappointed. He had thought that Heidegger would continue his work, but his former assistant went in an entirely different direction. Of course, Heidegger was aware of that. *Being and Time* was dedicated to his teacher and supporter for his sixty-fifth birthday, as if to soothe his fatherly friend.

Dedicated to
Edmund Husserl

in friendship and admiration
Todtnauberg in Baden, Black Forest
8 April 1926

As the text appeared as volume 8 of *Jahrbuch für Philosophie und phänomenologische Forschung* in spring 1927, this dedication was not surprising. Yet, the symbolic content was meaningful, a significant birthday gift. Heidegger placed his work on his mother's deathbed, but he dedicated it to Husserl. A sign of recognition, bound up with a request to be recognized. The first footnote in the section entitled "The Phenomenological Method of Investigation" makes this clear: "If the following investigation takes any steps forward in disclosing "the things themselves" the author must above all thank E. Husserl, who by providing his own incisive personal guidance and by very generously turning over his unpublished investigations, familiarized the author during his student years in Freiburg with the most diverse areas of phenomenological research."[80] Here appears the Heidegger who needed friendship and support, but demanded these on the basis of equal standing. In this mutuality, he expected something that not all people could offer: the acknowledgment of someone who had surpassed them. Husserl reacted ambivalently to the gift of his former assistant. However, the joint work, especially the work on Husserl's texts, continued for the time being.

Hannah Arendt was also a witness to the genesis of this book. He told her many times how much her love inspired him in his work on this massive text. At the same time, he also showed her that whoever dared to go so far into the world of thinking distanced himself from the world of the living, although he always emphasized that being-with was always part of him. But the student Arendt resisted the role he intended for her. Even if her beloved suggested this, she had no intention of being content with a passive role. She went away, left him, and yet took him with her. She strove to transform her wounds into intellectual exercises— doctoral work! He made her way easier by seeing that her connection to him extended to his work. Thus, for him the fact that she read *Being and Time* was an expression of her love. More precisely, it was the expression of the fact she could combine her love for him with her new happiness.[81] Her desire for this work of transference becomes very clear in a letter she wrote to Heidegger upon a reunion at the end of April 1928, more than two years after her departure from Marburg.[82] "What I want to tell you now is nothing but, at heart, a very frank assessment of the situation. I love you as I did on the first day—you know that, and I have always known it, even before this reunion. The path you showed is longer and more difficult than I thought. It requires an entire long life."[83] In the same letter, she again picks up the motif of anxiety from "Shadows." She feared isolation preserving the connection with Heidegger in the face of this abandonment. But she also saw this isolation as a "task" that the connection with Heidegger assigned to her.

> I would lose my right to live if I lost my love for you, but I would lose this love
> and its *reality* if I shirked the responsibility it forces on me.
> "And, if God choose,
> I shall but love thee better after death."[84]

There again was the magic pertaining not to the persons, but to the relationship
itself, something that she was to retain through all the distance and the rupture
of the physical love affair. Absolute abandonment seemed near. She felt the need
to protect the relationship in the face of it. Thus, her reference to death. Why did
the motif of death resurface not in the philosophical sense that Heidegger introduced in *Being and Time*, but rather in the immediate sense of a possibility that
she had already envisioned in "Shadows"? Arendt must have been filled with a
tension that threatened to overwhelm her.

Shortly thereafter she entered into a relationship with Günther Stern, a cousin of
Walter Benjamin, with whom Arendt was also friends. She met Stern at events organized by Heidegger and ran into him at a masquerade ball in Berlin.[85] In 1924,
at twenty-one, Stern had done his dissertation "Die Rolle der Situationskategorie
bei den logischen Sätzen" with Edmund Husserl. His doctoral director found the
work stimulating, but too loosely formulated; thus, Stern obtained his title only
on the condition of revision.[86]

This was Günther Stern of all people, the very person Heidegger had ridiculed
in an earlier letter! On October 18, 1925, he had written to her from the cabin:

> Shortly before coming down[87] I received a letter from Dr. Stern, in which he re-
> lated the embarrassing situation he finds himself in. Namely, this summer he
> wrote an essay (on environment—situation—resistance), and while preparing
> it, he could not distinguish which "ideas" were *mine* and which were his own.
> Well, Jonas read my summer lecture to him, from which he could see that he
> agrees with me completely. He asked me, however, to read his work before its
> publication so he can be sure he is not interpreting me incorrectly.
> Mr. Stern is the only person who can get away with something like that.
> For years he has been getting hold of everything I say in courses and seminars.
> I answered him briefly that "in a case where I cannot decide which ideas are
> my own and which are someone else's, I don't consider publication. Sincerely
> yours."—
> Well, perhaps Mr. Stern is just one of the worst—but such experiences
> do make one wonder sometimes whether it is worth putting so much energy
> into teaching and whether it would not be much better to concentrate entirely
> on research. But in the end, the potentially positive effect of teaching remains
> hidden, and that is good.[88]

Günther Stern's lack of modesty must have greatly annoyed Heidegger. At
the same time, he was well acquainted with Stern's parents, who were child

psychologists. And now his beloved was together with this Stern. She used the words *homeland* and *belonging* to describe this relationship, not the word *love*.

When she encountered Heidegger in September 1930, a scene took place that shook her to the core. She described it for her beloved without the protective cloak of philosophical language and concepts:

> I had already stood before you for a few seconds, you had actually already seen me—you had briefly looked up. And you did not recognize me. When I was a small child, that was the way my mother once stupidly and playfully frightened me. I had read the fairy tale about Dwarfnose, whose nose gets so long nobody recognizes him anymore. My mother pretended that had happened to me. I still vividly recall the blind terror with which I kept crying: but I am your child, I am your Hannah.—That is what it was like today.

This scene repeated itself in their departure at the same train station: "And then when the train was about to leave. And it was just as I had imagined moments before, and so, it seems, had wanted: you two up there and me alone, completely powerless. As always, nothing was left for me but to let it happen, and wait, wait, wait."[89] Her trauma, which she had told him about over and over again since "Shadows," suddenly repeated itself twice. Do these two scenes illustrate Heidegger's thoughtlessness? Or did he get so accustomed to the inward turn of thinking that it precluded the outward look of daily life? Did he even want to punish her? The response of the beloved to this letter is not preserved.

After the Separation

In summer semester 1926, after their separation, Hannah first went to Heidegger's friend Karl Jaspers in Heidelberg and not, as Heidegger advised her, to Husserl in Freiburg. She studied philosophy with Jaspers, classical philology with Otto Regenbogen, and theology with Martin Dibelius. With Freidrich Gundolf, she listened to lectures on Klopstock and German literature of the seventeenth and eighteenth centuries. She took a sociology class from Karl Mannheim, the rising star in the academic world. She requested permission to choose the history of early Christianity as her area of concentration required for the conferral of a doctorate. In winter semester 1926–27, she transferred to study with Edmund Husserl in Freiburg, but after one semester she was back in Heidelberg. She received permission from Jaspers to do her doctoral work. The subject was ambitious and complex: "The concept of Love in Saint Augustine: An Attempt at a Philosophical Interpretation." In winter semester 1927–28, she asked for time off in order to work on her dissertation in Königsberg. In summer semester 1928, she submitted her work. In her curriculum vita, which was part of her doctoral documentation, she concluded with: "Now I would like to express my gratitude to my teachers,

Herr Prof. Jaspers and Herr Prof. Heidegger."[90] At this point Hannah Arendt was just twenty-two years old.

The oral exam took place on November 26, 1928. She received a "satisfactory" grade in all three subjects. But since for Jaspers, her major professor, the written work merited between a "very good" and "good," the final grade ended up being "good"—a very honorable mark.

Her dissertation appeared in 1929 in issue 9 of the *Philosophical Investigations* series, edited by Jaspers and published by Springer Verlag in Berlin.

Arendt's academic subject was intertwined with a subject in her own life. Saint Augustine's writings had already played a significant role in Heidegger's philosophical formation. It was a remarkable confluence that she took up a central theme of her personal life and treated it in philosophical form. Thus one could see this work also as an attempt to grapple philosophically with a painful and earthly love. Incidentally, one notes that not only Arendt but Hans Jonas, as well, worked on Saint Augustine. In 1930 he published an investigation titled "St. Augustine and the Pauline Principle of Freedom."

In her introduction, she describes how she wanted to work through the multiple facets of Saint Augustine's thought. Above all, she intended to demonstrate—via the example of the concept of love—Augustine's rootedness in Greek thought and in the culture of his time. These roots had been relegated to secondary importance in the face of Augustine's purportedly timeless contribution to Christian dogma. The Augustine that appeared in her text was thus a double figure: a thinker of post-antiquity and an early church father, whose absorption in ancient philosophy made it possible for him to formulate a foundation of love that was both transcendent to the world and yet present in it. At the beginning of the thesis, Arendt described her own trajectory of thought in the dissertation to follow:

> This essay offers three analyses. The first begins with love understood as craving (*appetitus*), which is the only definition Augustine gives [A:033248] of love. In the presentation of "well-ordered love" at the end of this analysis, we see the incongruities to which this definition of love leads Augustine. Thus we are led to a very different conceptual context, which is incomprehensible from the first analysis and yet in an oddly peripheral sense suggests the attempt of deducing neighborly love from love as craving (*appetitus*).The second analysis permits us merely to understand in what sense our neighbor is loved in adhering to the commandment of neighborly love. Not until the third analysis is any light thrown on the incongruity of the second. This incongruity is pointed out in the question of how the person in God's presence, isolated from all things mundane, can be at all interested in his neighbor. This is illuminated by proving the neighbor's relevance in a wholly different context.[91]

In the end, she sought to demonstrate that Augustine's concept of love was entirely worldly. In retrospect, some of the key points of her later thought already appear in this first published text, such as the occasional polemical confrontation with Christianity, whose dogmatists she charged with resisting the worldly orientation of love. In this early work, it is also clear just how differently Arendt interpreted the categories of "with-world" and "being-with" from Heidegger.

The reviewers' reception of the book was divided. Her doctoral director, Karl Jaspers, had some criticisms about it. At the same time, he saw it as a serious attempt to apply the Heideggerian approach to Augustine's philosophy. Not suspecting anything about the reality of the love between Arendt and Heidegger, Jaspers asked his friend for a positive review of the research proposal that Arendt wanted to present: "The work, on the whole, did not turn out as brilliantly as we had expected after the first part, but it is still good philosophically. . . . As an actual matter of what she methodically learned from you, the work is superb, and there is no doubt about the genuineness of her interest in the problems."[92] Jaspers saw a gift ripening in Arendt, a gift that he deemed worthy of his further support. He had given his recommendation for a dissertation scholarship from *Notgemeinschaft der Deutschen Wissenschaft* and recommended a follow-up scholarship for her next proposed project on the cultural history of German youth in the nineteenth century, using the example of Rahel Varnhagen's life. Heidegger, too, supported the new project with his positive recommendation.

Heidegger and Cassirer at Davos

Their paths parted: Arendt was on her way to new horizons, while Heidegger was celebrating a triumph. The breakthrough had finally arrived with *Being and Time*. He was no longer lacking recognition. The University Weeks at Davos (*Hochschulwochen Davos*), founded the year before, took place at the Swiss resort of Davos—given eternal fame by Thomas Mann in *The Magic Mountain*. In 1929 the meetings took place from March 17 to April 6. Professors and students came together to work with one another, exchange ideas, and relax in a collegial atmosphere. The meetings were initiated in 1928 by the Swiss dentist Dr. Müller, who wanted to awaken the "spirit of Locarno" within Europe. In 1925, in Locarno, the European powers had settled the German questions left open in the Treaty of Versailles in an amicable atmosphere. From that moment on, Locarno became the metaphor for the new spirit of peace in Europe.

The events at Davos were thought of as a forum for young European intellectuals from France, Germany, Switzerland, Italy, the Netherlands, and other European countries. German and French scholars and students came together here.[93] In peace and seclusion, the younger generation was to listen to lectures from important scholars, educate themselves and debate one another, thereby going beyond individual national borders. The time between seminars, lectures, and events was filled with informal discussions and sports. All of this was organized by the Frankfurt sociologist Gottfried Salomon.[94]

The second University Weeks of 1929 was eagerly anticipated because the two opposing camps, considered to be the two main intellectual currents of the time, were to come together there: the camp of neo-Kantian transcendental philosophy, represented by Ernst Cassirer from Hamburg, and the camp of fundamental ontology, also known as existential philosophy, represented by Martin Heidegger from Freiburg. The event took place under the general topic "Man and Generation."

Ernst Cassirer was one of the founders of Davos. Such an undertaking was close to his political convictions and social gregariousness. In contrast, such involvements in the political culture of the time were foreign to Heidegger. His professional self-understanding, his "calling" placed strict boundaries on his life. He did not enter the social realm, much less the political. It was not in his nature. He did not enjoy it, but he also did not have time for it. He held strictly to his motto: no concessions in thinking. He was so convinced of the correctness of his critique that he wanted to radically deconstruct this philosophical current. His magnum opus, *Being and Time*, published in 1927, not only had made him known to the philosophical world; he was now considered to be an insurgent against the tradition, an innovator. In February 1928 he finally received the long-desired chair of philosophy in Freiburg. Freiburg had always been Heidegger's preferred university. The detour through Marburg allowed him the—triumphant—return to Freiburg. He had defeated his enemies; even Rickert, who was so skeptical toward him, had seen no alternative to his appointment. His mentor Edmund Husserl, who suggested Heidegger as his successor and accomplished it with Rickert's help, was pleased about the appointment: "because of his philosophical originality," he wrote to Heinrich Rickert: "Because of his entirely unique teaching ability, he [Heidegger] is the right choice. There is no one in Germany who captivates the hearts of the youth like this. And with it a pure, completely selfless personality, so fully devoted to the great matters of thinking. I am curious to see how he will develop further; however, I hope that he will continue on the upward trajectory that I foresee for him."[95] Husserl, the great phenomenologist, had not seen the hidden side of Heidegger, a side that was much more difficult, the side that Heidegger showed in his relations with his colleagues and students, friends or enemies.

In the meantime, Heidegger was well known throughout Germany. At that time, Ernst Cassirer also enjoyed a less controversial fame. He was considered to be a thinker who had advanced the legacy of transcendental philosophy. In 1923 and 1925, he published the first two volumes of *Philosophy of Symbolic Forms*. The third volume appeared in the same year as the famous Davos debate. In

1928 Heidegger reviewed the second volume of Cassirer's *Philosophy of Symbolic Forms* (1925). Cassirer would review Heidegger's *Being and Time* in 1931.[96] The two thinkers had already met in Hamburg where Heidegger gave a lecture in 1923.

The University Weeks thus promised a great, eagerly anticipated event. Three months prior to the debate, Heidegger had nonchalantly announced to Jaspers: "I will accept, if nothing else for the mountain skiing. . . . Please come, too."[97]

The fascination that resulted from the debate between Cassirer and Heidegger is clear in the reports of their contemporaries. The personal dimension of this intellectual confrontation was more visible here than in the universities where each worked:

> On the one hand, this small dark-brown man, this accomplished skier and athlete, with his energetic, but impassive features, this sharp and dismissive, sometimes almost rough man . . . who, in impressive detachment, is totally committed to setting and solving problems with the deepest moral seriousness; and, on the other hand, this man with his white hair, Olympian, not only in appearance but also in spirit, with his open mind and wide-ranging way of looking at problems, with his cheerful countenance, indulgent amiability, his vitality and adaptability, and, last but not least, his aristocratic nobility.[98]

This was written retrospectively by one of the students who was present at the debate.

Ernst Cassirer was aristocratic: tall, slender, with a high forehead, an expressive direct glance, full lips, and thick, white, curly hair. He dressed with elegance, was sociable, although resolute in action. Heidegger, on the other hand, was of a small, wiry stature; he almost disappeared behind his students—for instance, Löwith or Gadamer. Some perceived his penetrating gaze as stinging, others as concentrated. His body language was dismissive when he spoke. His appearance came off as rather awkward; he seemed to some brusque, to others, exceedingly modest. This was underscored by his clothing: the aforementioned "traditional German" suit, pointing to his antiacademic streak. Certainly, he knew what was "appropriate" socially, he also wore normal suits at Davos, but he did not place much value on social customs in academic circles. He wore his rejection of the "they," of the mores and conventions of society, on his sleeve. In an argument, he set aside all social niceties. His speech took on an intensity that was sometimes wounding. We have already encountered this quality in his love affair with Hannah Arendt.

There was skiing in the free time between lectures. A math student from Leipzig commented on it in the style of the academic language of the day: "We were particularly glad that professors also went skiing, and it seemed to us symbolically significant for Heidegger that he cited Nietzsche's saying that a philosopher must be a good mountain-climber."[99] The appearance of Heidegger and Cassirer took place within the context of a larger program of lectures. Among others the speakers were the Jesuit Erich Przywara (Munich), the philosopher Karl Jöel (Basel), the philosopher Kurt Riezler (Frankfurt am Main), the famous doctor Ferdinand Sauerbruch, and the art historian Wilhelm Pinder.[100] The list of participating students was impressive. The most famous among the French were Emmanuel Levinas, Leon Brunschvicg, and Jean Cavaillès; on the German side, several of Heidegger's students traveled from Marburg and Freiburg, Otto Friedrich Bollnow, Joachim Ritter, but also Alfred Sohn-Rethel, Eugen Fink, Herbert Marcuse, and Leo Strauss among them.[101] The students met independently and organized their own courses. They also discussed political topics such as Marxism and nationalism.[102]

Prior to the debate, Cassirer and Heidegger gave their own lectures. Cassirer gave three lectures concerning the fundamental problems of philosophical anthropology and a single lecture on "Spirit and Life in Scheler's Philosophy." He lectured in the mornings. In the afternoon of the same days, Heidegger lectured on "Kant's *Critique of Pure Reason* and the Task of Laying the Foundation for Metaphysics." There he attacked the widespread understanding of Kant that reduced him, on the one hand, to a theory of knowledge and critique and, on the other, to an idealism of practical reason.

Heidegger began with a critical assessment of the triumphant procession of the natural and human sciences in the nineteenth century that "claimed the totality of the knowable." As a consequence of this development, philosophy was reduced to a knowledge of science, not of being (*Seienden*).[103] Out of this background, Kant had been construed as a critic of what came before him, while Heidegger wanted to present him anew (especially in *The Critique of Pure Reason*) as the founder of a transformed metaphysics, a metaphysics that finds its source not in transcendence, but rather in its finite formulation. It corresponded to the argument that he presented in *Being and Time*. Contrary to this, Cassirer took up Kant's "practical reason" with its references to "spirituality" and wanted to further develop the Kantian power of imagination into a cultural anthropology in his *Philosophy of Symbolic Forms*. The lectures formed the foundation for the greatly anticipated debate between the two men.

The debate took up the entire Tuesday morning. The philosopher H. J. Pos from Amsterdam moderated it. The students writing the protocols were Otto Friedrich Bollnow (for Heidegger) and Joachim Ritter (for Cassirer).[104]

Two kinds of Kantian interpretation stood at the center. Cassirer argued for the autonomous and creative character of the Kantian concept of reason. He assigned it to the symbolic-cultural space, arguing that the constitution of meaning should occur in this space. He thereby drew a first line of separation between himself and Heidegger, since for the latter the rejection of the duality between the normative dimension of spirit and anthropological cultural theory was central to his reading of Kant.

A further difference between the two emerged from the problematic of death. Cassirer interpreted death in relation to transcendence, as a chance to overcome the fear of finitude in the transition to infinity. "Man is the finite being, who *knows* his finitude—and who in this knowing overcomes his finitude and becomes certain of his infinity."[105] Heidegger, on the other hand, insisted on the unavoidable finitude of Dasein, on the pure facticity of death. The possibility of Dasein grasping itself must first arise out of finitude.

Cassirer faulted Heidegger for a disguised theological understanding of the world and bemoaned the absence of any symbolic transcendence. Heidegger mocked the weakness of Cassirer's category of symbolic transcendence. It becomes clear that behind the polemic both had a concept of transcendence, but these concepts were fundamentally different. With Heidegger, transcendence unfolds in the historicity of Dasein. This going-outside-oneself is shown in the human being projecting its own possibilities, but it is always related to the human being; it proceeds from it and returns to it, and opens no separate symbolic sphere.

Of course, Cassirer and Heidegger had fundamentally different conceptions of the subject. Heidegger viewed Dasein as facticity that was not itself creatively constituting. Against the neo-Kantian view of reason as the creator of being (*Seienden*), he argued that the human being could never be unlimited and absolute. Ontology is the doctrine of this-worldliness and finitude. Cassirer saw the subject as simultaneously imperfect and capable of perfection. He insisted that philosophy harbored a task greater than merely commenting on Dasein in its existential anxiety; its first goal should be human freedom.[106] This also meant freedom from anxiety. Heidegger considered this to be impossible. His concept of freedom was based on the thesis of "becoming free for the finitude of Dasein."[107]

In the eyes of one faction of those interpreting this debate, the clash of these two dissimilar philosophies manifests itself in the confrontation between the weak post-Idealist philosophy represented by Cassirer and the strong philosophy of life embodied by Heidegger.[108] Accordingly, Heidegger emerges as the glowing victor and Cassirer as the defeated warrior.

Heidegger himself did not by any means see it like this. In his descriptions to his confidant Elisabeth Blochmann, a more clear-sighted view prevails:

> Objectively, I did not gain anything philosophically, but I did profit personally from the exchange with Riezler, the curator of Frankfurt University, and with Karl Reinhardt and Cassirer. The fact that he concentrated his lectures on my book and that others were interested in it pushed me into the spotlight more than I would have liked. Fortunately, I had chosen Kant as my own subject and could therefore, through historicity, steer the conversation away

from me and toward the central, fundamental problem . . . In the discussion, Cassirer was extremely noble and almost too obliging. I thus found too little resistance, which made it difficult for me to formulate the problems with necessary precision. In essence, the questions were much too difficult for a public discussion.[109]

He was also critical of the debates in a letter to Bultmann, but at the same time he said he had learned a few things from the discussions of his book *Kant and the Problem of Metaphysics.*[110]

Students and critics, contemporaries and those who came later, created legends around the "Davos debate." Some participants saw the public debate of the philosophers as the "meeting of the representatives of two epochs."[111] Levinas, Husserl's student at the time, formulated it as follows: "as a young student, one had the impression that one had witnessed the creation and the destruction of the world."[112] Otto Friedrich Bollnow, psychologist, pedagogue, and philosopher, who studied under Heidegger, experienced the debate as a major earthquake in the philosophical world: "And in spite or perhaps because of the uneven opposition, the participants had the exhilarating feeling of being present at a historical hour, very similar to Goethe as described in 'Campaign in France': 'from this place and from this day forth commences a new era in the world's history'—in this case philosophical history—'and you can all say that you were present at its birth.'"[113] In retrospect, some even wanted to give a political dimension to this meeting. The debate thus represented certain camps at the end of the Weimar Republic, which already stood on the edge of the abyss. Indeed, Cassirer, who on several occasions voiced approval for Weimar's republican constitution, notably in 1928 at the celebration of the tenth anniversary of the Republic at Hamburg University, emerged as a republican.[114] Heidegger did not join any camp.

It is of course tempting to impose a pseudo-political category on Heidegger retrospectively. Did Heidegger not "win" later, awarded the NSDAP badge of honor, as well as give his valuable philosophical insights to National Socialism? And did Cassirer not have to give up and leave the country? This kind of speculative classification, however, leads to a dead end.

Cassirer was a convinced republican, rather unusual for an intellectual at that time. Perhaps he was even a typical republican. Heidegger, however, was not a typical nationalist. He was apolitical by conviction, oriented toward an antistate point of view, and showed great sympathies for the national populist movement. Yet his support for these groups did not lead to nostalgia for the "Mythos." It is an open question as to where each of these thinkers stood beyond the philosophical currents with which they are more or less associated.

Cassirer and Heidegger's debate and their lectures touched on something disturbingly contemporary, namely, the empty space of meaning and the role of philosophical thinking in relation to it.[115] Cassirer clearly filled the emptiness with a symbolic space, where reason stands at the center. The constitution of meaning unfolds in the renewal of this symbolic space and in the adhering of the subject to this space. Heidegger wanted to end this discussion once and for all with his fundamental ontology. From his perspective, the constitution of meaning emerges from existence, not from the side of value giving. This results not in a turn toward abstraction but, rather, toward what is concrete. There could be no victor in this controversy because it could not be resolved. The discussion continues up to the present.

The famous debate made such an impression on the students that not long afterward they dramatically staged it. The young Levinas assumed the role of Cassirer. He powdered his hair white to make himself look like the philosopher. Bollnow took the role of his teacher Heidegger. Levinas prepared the dialogue, in which he put together paradoxical sentences such as "interpretation means turning a thing on its head."[116]

Heidegger's fame grew even more after this event. He was now considered a public person and as the champion of his own coherent philosophical direction. Within three weeks, he turned his Davos lectures into a book, *Kant and the Problem of Metaphysics*. It appeared in 1929. He thus published two books within two years.

Yet Cassirer's followers also saw him emerging from the conflict as victorious. The news of the duel of the giants spread from Davos to Berlin. Newspapers reported on it. Those who were present spread the news further. How would Hannah Arendt have discussed the event in conversation with Günther Stern?

Heidegger's student Löwith related a puzzling insight after the war. Shortly before his death, Franz Rosenzweig, whose main work, *Star of Redemption*, came out in 1921, had written a kind of short review of Hermann Cohen's *Religion of Reason: Out of the Sources of Judaism*. Hermann Cohen was and is considered to be the founder of the southern German school of neo-Kantianism.

Rosenzweig wrote a short text conveying his impressions of the report he received on the Davos debate. He claimed therein that in Davos Heidegger had defended the true Hermann Cohen against his student Cassirer. He argued that both Cohen and Heidegger understand the human being in terms of finitude and, moreover, the human being's value did not begin with "the intellectual transport to the eternity of culture."[117]

This is true despite the fact that Cohen wanted to embed the human being in his "religious idealism" (Löwith) and supply "the vanity of the earthly with the glory of the eternal," "whereas Heidegger does not want to have anything to do with eternity and understands Being from out of time."[118] From this perspective, Rosenzweig argues that Heidegger was the true successor of Hermann Cohen in Freiburg; a claim that provoked outrage as well as the opposition of some neo-Kantians.

Löwith thus points to the connection between the Jewish thinkers Hermann Cohen and Franz Rosenzweig, on the one hand, and Heidegger, on the other—a line that nearly disappears in the critical assessment of Heidegger after the Second World War.

Hannah Arendt and Günther Stern

On September 26, 1929, Hannah Arendt married her friend Günther Stern in Nowawes, today a part of Babelsberg, on the outskirts of Berlin. They were wed in an almost village-like city hall, a red neo-Gothic brick construction of the turn of the nineteenth century, presumably in the small room available for weddings. Stern and Arendt were then living in Babelsberg, on Merkurstraße 3, in a modest one-family house just outside town. One cannot help but wonder what drove them into the solitude of an isolated settlement on the edge of the city.

With the marriage, many pressures abated for Hannah. Her mother wanted to know that she was in a secure relationship and a marriage to a highly gifted school colleague from a good family promised a secure future.[119] Furthermore, in the golden 1920s marriage was a prerequisite for a young woman who wanted a professional career as well as to participate in public life. The strict moral codes of Wilhelminian society with regard to gender relations and the position of a woman in the public space were not yet past. Perhaps Stern's parents also hoped that their occasionally unfocused son would settle down in the care of a highly intelligent and ambitious young woman.

After she submitted her dissertation for publication, Arendt dedicated herself to her new project: researching Rahel Varnhagen's biography. She managed to have the project supported with a stipend. Her income ensured the survival of the young couple, since they otherwise had no steady income. Stern wanted to do his habilitation in Frankfurt am Main. Both moved to Frankfurt, Oederweg 128, in April 1930. They wanted to be on-site in order to press for Stern's acceptance to do his habilitation at the university there. Arendt would then be able to work on her Rahel project independently. With her research project, she was not bound to a place. The matter, however, turned out differently. After several conversations with Paul Tillich, the person who needed to strongly support Stern's habilitation project—above all, against Theodor W. Adorno—"the situation was completely untenable, that is, for all parties degrading," she wrote to Jaspers on November 2,

1931, already in Berlin. "We preferred to leave Frankfurt and for the time being try to make a living outside the academy."[120]

She decided to be done with the university and its "business." In some ways, this judgment was fitting for two former Heidegger students. Certainly, they had learned much at the university, but they also despised its "business," the empty talk, the bureaucracy, and the competition.

Thus, there was nothing else for the two of them to do other than to freelance in the marketplace. The new existence was nonetheless not easy to endure, even less so as Heidegger's students. It is said that Bertolt Brecht gave full rein to his prejudice against Stern, "the Heideggerian."[121] Yet, it was on his recommendation that Stern finally managed to find employment in the newspaper field. He worked as a boy Friday for Herbert Ihering's *Berliner Börsen Courier.*[122] He began to sign his articles as "Günther Anders." His income was not enough to live on. It was therefore fortunate that Arendt received a steady income for two years.

Heidegger and Jaspers: The Silence Begins

The friendship between Heidegger and Jaspers seemed to come to life again at the end of the 1920s. Jaspers's overall view of philosophy, on which he labored for more than ten years, was progressing very slowly. He was all the more yearning for conversation. In general, he was much more dependent on communication than Heidegger. The latter was forcing his way unflinchingly through the "forest" of the history of philosophy. In December 1929 Heidegger came to visit once again. He visited his old friend and longtime comrade-in-arms on the occasion of a conference for German student organizations in Heidelberg. A small card that Jaspers gave him documents his gratitude:

> Dear Heidegger!
> I cannot think of a time when I listened to anyone as I did to you today. I felt as if I were free in the pure air of this incessant transcending. I heard in your words, at times strange to me, but as identical, what is so completely self-understood between us. There is still philosophizing!
> Good night!
> Most sincerely
> Your, Karl Jaspers[123]

Then Heidegger visited Heidelberg again in April 1930. He had received an offer for a philosophy position in Berlin and wanted to discuss it with his friend. After an initial hesitation, he declined the offer and remained in the province. Now Jaspers wanted to bring his friend to Heidelberg, but he complained about his silence: "When I think upon the possibility of your coming here, I experience a vitality that strengthens a wish—but then I think about your silence in our conversations, and I long most of all for the mutual and radical discussion that took place earlier but now rests for so long. For a year, to be sure, the blame rests essentially with me."[124] He was still busy with his *Philosophy*.

In December 1931 Jaspers's three-volume *Philosophy* was delivered to Heidegger. The correspondence around the new work picked up where it had ended in the twenties on Jaspers's *Psychology of Worldviews*. Heidegger said how impressed he was. However, the *way* in which Heidegger praised Jaspers unsettled him. Heidegger called him "victor": "It remains essential that, with your work, there is finally in philosophy today something *indispensable* and *whole*. You speak from the clear and decisive comportment of the victor and from the richness of one who has been existentially tested."[125] But this is not how Jaspers sees himself: "I don't feel like a *victor*, as your friendly but dangerously distancing formula puts it, but as if I stand *before* the door, as if what is extraordinary would still have to be revealed, as if I can't do enough to grasp it in thought . . . as if, nevertheless, a common power were capable of capturing what is anticipated and showing a direction for the future."[126] Here again Jaspers was referring to the common project, to the common intellectual sculpture on which both of them were working. He reminded Heidegger of their mutual undertaking, although he was aware that he could not impose collaboration. For both were on their own paths. Still, he called for the renewal of the impulse that had attracted them earlier. They had wanted to revolutionize philosophy, not become the authors of books in which they praised each other in turn. He knew that he was not up to the task physically; he could never be anything more than a bookworm. Thus Heidegger had to accomplish the actual revolution. But Heidegger was no longer listening. Did Jaspers still get through to him? Or was he caught up in his inner dialogue? In these years, critical commentaries on Heidegger piled up in Jaspers's notes. On dozens, even hundreds of pieces of paper, Jaspers jotted down his thoughts while working through Heidegger's texts:

> Lack of freedom through lack of irony.[127]
> Ambiguity.[128]
> Heidegger's philosophy godless and worldless up until now.[129]
> Without love. For this reason not worthy of love also in style.[130]

The differences were becoming greater, the unresolved questions, the feelings of estrangement were growing. Still, neither of them said a word to clarify the situation. Heidegger did not want to end the friendship and Jaspers did not want to demand the explanations that Heidegger could not give. The comradeship in arms—a great misunderstanding?

Heidegger's letter from December 1932 talks about peaceful serenity, about the retreat to the Greeks in the face of the rejection of his way of thinking by his colleagues. Finally, he wrote, the hype around *Being and Time* was behind him and he could work again. "Will it succeed in providing philosophy with ground and space for decades to come? Will there be men who carry within themselves a distant readiness?"[131]

The idea of the revolution of spirit withdrew into the distance but was not forgotten. It was to return within several months.

Notes

1. Karl Löwith, *My Life in Germany before and after 1933* translated by Elizabeth King (London: Athlone, 1994), 44–45.

2. Paul Hühnerfeld, *In Sachen Heidegger: Versuch über ein deutsches Genie* (Hamburg: Hoffmann und Campe, 1959), 54ff.

3. Hannah Arendt, "Martin Heidegger at Eighty," in *Heidegger and Modern Philosophy*, ed. Michael Murray (New Haven, CT: Yale University Press, 1978), 294.

4. Hans-Georg Gadamer, *Philosophical Apprenticeships* (Boston: MIT Press, 1985), 7 (translation modified).

5. Cf. ibid., 15.

6. Cf. ibid., 17.

7. Ibid., 14.

8. Ibid., 19.

9. Hühnerfeld, *Heidegger*, 56 and 57.

10. Heinrich Schlier, "Denken im Nachdenken," in *Erinnerung in Erinnerungen an Martin Heidegger*, ed. Günther Neske (1977), 218.

11. Hans Jonas, *Wissenschaft* (Göttingen: Vandenhoeck & Ruprecht, 1987), 14.

12. Hannah Arendt, "Martin Heidegger at Eighty," in *Heidegger and the Modern World*, ed. Michael Murray (New Haven, CT: Yale University Press, 1978), 295.

13. Ibid., 295–96.

14. Hans Jonas, *Erkenntnis* (Göttingen: Lamuv, 1991), 41–42.

15. Löwith, *My Life*, 45–46 (translation modified).

16. Hans-Georg Gadamer, *Philosophical Apprenticeships* (Cambridge, MA: MIT Press, 1985), 14.

17. Cf. ibid., 49.

18. Jonas, *Erkenntnis*, 46–47.

19. Löwith, *My Life*, 18 (translation modified).

20. Hans-Georg Gadamer, "Einzug in Marburg," in *Erinnerung*, 111.

21. This decision is alluded to in a poem by Heidegger from March 1950, entitled "November, 1924." In this poem he refers to the beginning, ending, and renewal of love.

22. See Heidegger to Arendt, letter dated May 4, 1950, in *Hannah Arendt and Martin Heidegger, Letters, 1925–1975*, edited by Ursula Ludz, translated by Andrew Shields (New York: Harcourt, 2004), 78–79. (Hereafter referred to *Arendt-Heidegger Correspondence*.).

23. Cf. Löwith, *My Life*, 44–45.

24. Hans Jonas, in his obituary for Hannah Arendt, for the journal *Social Research* (Winter 1976), cited by Young-Bruehl, *Hannah Arendt*, 1982), 468.

25. Heidegger to Arendt, letter dated February 10, 1925, in *Arendt-Heidegger Correspondence*, 3.

26. There is only one letter remaining from this exchange of letters. There are rumors about the so-called letter of response (destroyed, still held back) but no concrete knowledge.

27. Heidegger to Arendt, letter dated February 10, 1925, in *Arendt-Heidegger Correspondence*, 4.

28. Heidegger to Arendt, letter dated February 10, 1925, in ibid., 3.

29. Friedrich Schiller, *Collected Works* (New York: P. F. Collier, 1875), 271–72.

30. Heidegger to Arendt, letter dated February 21, 1925, in *Arendt-Heidegger Correspondence*, 4–5.

31. Heidegger to Arendt, letter dated March 21, 1925, in ibid., 8.

32. Heidegger to Arendt, letter dated February 27, 1925, in ibid., 6.

33. Heidegger to Arendt, letter dated March 21, 1925, in ibid., 9.

34. Heidegger to Arendt, letter dated April 12, 1925, in ibid., 10.

35. Heidegger to Arendt, letter dated March 21, 1925, in ibid., 9.

36. Heidegger to Arendt, letter dated April 4, 1925, in ibid., 11.

37. Hannah Arendt, "The Shadows," in, *Arendt- Heidegger Correspondence*, 14 (translation modified).

38. Ibid., 12.

39. Ibid., 16.

40. Heidegger to Arendt, letter dated April 24, 1925, in *Arendt-Heidegger Correspondence*, 17.

41. Heidegger to Arendt, letter dated May 1, 1925, in ibid., 18.

42. Heidegger to Arendt, letter dated March 21, 1925, in ibid., 8.

43. Heidegger to Jaspers, letter dated May 13, 1928, in *Heidegger-Jaspers Letters*, 95.

44. Heidegger to Arendt, letter dated April 24, 1925, in *Arendt-Heidegger Correspondence*, 16.

45. Heidegger to Arendt, letter dated May 8, 1925, in ibid., 19.

46. Ibid., 20.

47. Ibid.

48. Heidegger to Arendt, letter dated May 13, 1925, in ibid., 21.

49. Heidegger to Arendt, letter dated May 20, 1925, in ibid., 22.

50. Cf. ibid., 23, 24, 26, 27.

51. Heidegger to Arendt, letter dated June 14, 1925, in ibid., 24 (translation modified).

52. Cf. Heidegger to Arendt, letter dated June 22, 1925, in ibid., 25.

53. Heidegger to Arendt, letter dated August 23, [1925], in ibid., 32.

54. Ibid., 33.

55. Heidegger to Arendt, letter dated January 10, 1926, in ibid., 40.

56. Cf. Hans Ulrich Gumbrecht: "Stichwort: Tod im Kontext: Heideggers Umgang mit einer Faszination der 1920 Jahre," in *Heidegger Handbuch*, ed. Dieter Thomas (Stuttgart: J. B. Metzler, 2005), 98.

57. Heidegger to Arendt, letter dated January 10, 1926, in *Arendt-Heidegger Letters*, 42 (translation modified).

58. Ibid.

59. Heidegger to Arendt, letter dated December 7, 1927, in ibid., 45.

60. Heidegger to Arendt, letter dated February 8, 1928, in ibid., 46.

61. George Steiner, *Martin Heidegger* (New York: Viking Press, 1979), 78 (emphasis in original, translation modified).

62. See Walter Biemel, *Heidegger: An Illustrated Study* (London: Routledge and Kegan Paul, 1973), 44ff.

63. Cf. Steiner, *Martin Heidegger*, 82.

64. Cf. ibid., 81.

65. Three letters of Martin Heidegger to Karl Löwith, in Dietrich Papenfuss Otto Pöggeler, ed., *Zur philosophischen Aktualität Heideggers* (Frankfurt: Vittorio Klotserman, 1990), 36.

66. Steiner, *Martin Heidegger*, 83.

67. Martin Heidegger, *Being and Time*, trans. Joan Stambaugh, rev. and ed. Dennis Schmidt (Albany: SUNY Press, 2010), 124.

68. Steiner, *Martin Heidegger*, 93.

69. "The peculiar *neutrality* of the term 'Dasein' is essential, because the interpretation of this being must be carried out prior to every factual concretion . . . Neutrality is not the voidness of an abstraction, but the potency of the *origin*, which bears in itself the intrinsic possibility of every concrete factual humanity"; Martin Heidegger, *The Metaphysical Foundations of Logic*, trans. Michael Heim (Bloomington: Indiana University Press, 1984), 136–37; also cited by Johannes Weiss, *Die Jeminigkeit des Mitsein* (Constance: Uvk Verlgs GmbH, 2001), 24n16.

70. See Heidegger, *Being and Time*, part 1, chap. 6.

71. Steiner, *Martin Heidegger*, 100.

72. Ibid., 101.

73. Abraham a Santa Clara, *Wien* (1895), 28.

74. Steiner, *Martin Heidegger*, 105.

75. Ibid., 76.

76. Ibid.

77. Herbert Marcuse, "Enttäuschung," in *Erinnerung*, 162.

78. Hermann Heimpel, "Der gute Zuhörer," in *Erinnerung*, 115.

79. Otto Friedrich Bollnow, "Gespräche in Davos," in *Erinnerung*, 25.

80. Heidegger, *Being and Time*, footnote 5 in section C of part 7, 36.

81. Cf. Heidegger to Arendt, letter dated December 12, 1927, in *Arendt-Heidegger Correspondence*, 44.

82. This is the first preserved letter from Arendt other than the "The Shadows."

83 Arendt to Heidegger, letter dated April 22, 1928, in ibid., 50 (translation modified).

84. Ibid. This letter contains a quotation from a poem by Elizabeth Barrett Browning (1806–1861), translated by Rainer Maria Rilke, which Arendt must have highly esteemed. See Elizabeth Barrett Browning, *How Do I Love Thee? 43 Sonnets from the Portuguese*, trans. Rainer Maria Rilke (Leipzig: Homeyer, 1991), 90–91.

85. Cf. Young-Bruehl, *Hannah Arendt*, 77.

86. Cf. Husserl's report on Stern's dissertation, "Die Rolle der Situationskategorie bei den logischen Sätzen," July 12, 1924, in Edmund Husserl, *Briefwechsel, Bd. III* (Berlin: Springer, 1994), 501–2.

87. Referred to here is Heidegger's moving down from the cabin in Todtnauberg at the end of summer 1925, on the way to Husserl in Freiburg.

88. Heidegger to Arendt, letter dated October 18, 1925, in *Arendt-Heidegger Letters*, 37.

89. Arendt to Heidegger, letter dated September 1930, in ibid., 51–52.

90. Hannah Arendt, curriculum vitae, in UAH H-IV-757/24.

91. Hannah Arendt, *The Concept of Love in St. Augustine*, ed. Joanna Vecchiarelli Scott and Judith Chelius Stark (Chicago: University of Chicago Press, 1996), 7.

92. Jaspers to Heidegger, letter dated June 20, 1929, in Walter Biemal and Hans Saner, eds., *The Heidegger-Jaspers Correspondence*, trans. Gary Aylesworth (New York: Humanity, 2003), 118.

93. See Heinz Paetzold, *Cassirer* (Darmstadt: Wissenschaftliche Buchgesellschaft, 1995), 86.

94. Ibid.

95. Husserl to Rickert, in *Husserl: Briefwechsel Bd. V.* (Berlin: Springer, 1994), 187. From the report of the search committee for philosophy, from January 28, 1928, signed by Dean Honecker: "The commission charged with filling the chair left vacant by Edmund Husserl unanimously recommends Martin Heidegger of Marburg." The commission argued further that "the high standard of this position which has made Freiburg one of the main centers for the study of philosophy, must continue to be preserved."

96. Cf. Michael Friedman, *A Parting of the Ways: Carnap, Cassirer, Heidegger* (Chicago: Open Court, 2000), 6–7n9.

97. Heidegger to Jaspers, letter dated December 21, 1928, in *Heidegger-Jaspers Correspondence*, 115.

98. Englert, "Davoser Hochschulkurse," cited by Schneéberger, *Nachlese*, 4–5.

99. Ibid., 4.

100. Paetzold, *Cassirer*, 87.

101. Cf. ibid.

102. Cf. ibid.

103. Cf. "Die Davoser Disputation zwischen Ernst Cassirer und Martin Heidegger," in Heidegger, GA 1, ABT., Bd 3 (1991), Anhang 274.

104. Cf. Dieter Thomä, "Die Davoser Disputation zwischen Ernst Cassirer und Martin Heidegger, Kontroverse Transzendenz," in *Heidegger Handbuch*, ed. Dieter Thomas (Stuttgart: J. B. Metzler, 2005), 111.

105. Cited by Paetzold, *Cassirer*, 90–91, who has taken the citation from Cassirer's literary estate at Yale University.

106. See Gordon, *Rosenzweig* (Berkeley: University of California Press, 2003), 286.

107. See "Die Davoser Disputation zwischen Ernst Cassirer und Martin Heidegger," in Heidegger, GA 1, ABT., Bd 3 (1991), Anhang 275.

108. See Jürgen Habermas, "The German Idealism of the Jewish Philosophers," in *Philosophical-Political Profiles*, trans. Frederick G. Lawrence (Cambridge, MA: MIT Press, 1983), 32ff. Cf. Karlfried Gründer, "Cassirer und Heidegger in Davos 1929," in *Cassirers Philosophie der Ssmbolischen Formen*, ed. Braun, Holzhey, and Orth (Frankfurt: Suhrkamp, 1988), 297ff.

109. Heidegger to Blochmann, letter dated April 12, 1929, in *Heidegger-Blochmann: Briefwechsel* (Marcbach: Deutsches Literaturarchiv, 1990), 29–30.

110. Cf. the unpublished letter of Heidegger to Bultmann dated May 9, 1929, cited by Dominic Kaegi, "Davos und davor—Zur Auseinandersetzung Zwischen Heidegger und Cassirer," in *Cassirer-Heidegger*, ed. D. Kaegi and E. Rudolph (Hamburg: Felix Meiner Verlag, 2002), 67.

111. Cf. Gordon, *Rosenzweig*, 277.

112. François Poirie, *Emmanuel Levinas: Qui êtes-vous?* (Lyon: La Manufacture, 1987), cited by Gordon, *Rosenzweig*, 279.

113. Otto Friedrich Bollnow, "Gespräche in Davos," in *Erinnerung*, 28.

114. Cf. Friedman, *Parting of the Ways*, 4.

115. Cf. Martin Heidegger, "Zur Geschichte des philosophischen Lehrstuhles seit 1860," in Heidegger, GA, 1, Abt., Bd. 3, Anhand (1991), 306–7.

116. Cf. Gordon, *Rosenzweig*, 278.

117. Cf. Karl Löwith, "M. Heidegger und F. Rosenzweig. Ein Nachtrag zu *Sein und Zeit*," in *Heidegger—Denker in dürftiger Zeit*, in Löwith: Samtliche Schriften Bd 8, 1984, 73–74.

118. Ibid., 74.

119. The parents, Lewis William Stern and his wife, Clara, were pioneers in the field of child psychology. Together they wrote *Psychologie der frühen Kindheit* (The Psychology of Early

Childhood), a book that is still considered pathbreaking today. The book was based to a degree on their diaries about the growth of their three children—Günther among them. L. W. Stern achieved international renown through his research on IQ, especially in children. From 1915 on, he was a professor for philosophy and psychology at the Hamburger Allgemeine Vorlesungswesen und Kolonialinstitut, a forerunner to the Universität Hamburg, which Stern helped found in 1919. He was forced from the university by the National Socialists in 1933 and he and his wife emigrated to the United States in 1935. There Stern taught at Duke University and took part in the army's program of research into intelligence. Stern died in 1938, his wife, Clara, in 1945.

120. Arendt to Jaspers, letter dated November 2, 1931, in *Arendt-Jaspers Correspondence*, 50.

121. Elizabeth Young-Bruehl, *Hannah Arendt: For Love of the World* (New Haven, CT: Yale University Press, 1982), 83.

122. Ibid.

123. Jaspers to Heidegger, letter dated December 5, 1929, in *Heidegger-Jaspers Correspondence*, 125.

124. Jaspers to Heidegger, letter dated May 24, 1930, in ibid., 131–32.

125. Heidegger to Jaspers, letter dated December 20, 1931, in ibid., 139.

126. Jaspers to Heidegger, letter dated December 24, 1931, in ibid., 141 (translation modified).

127. Jaspers, *Notizen zu Martin Heidegger* (Munich: Piper), 31.

128. Ibid.

129. Ibid., 33.

130. Ibid., 34.

131. Heidegger to Jaspers, letter dated December 8, 1932, in *Heidegger-Jaspers Correspondence*, 143.

3 The Failure of the German-Jewish Symbiosis, or Friends Becoming Enemies

THE EVENING BEFORE Hitler's nomination as Reich Chancellor, Hannah Arendt and Martin Heidegger found themselves on opposite sides of German society. As a Jew, she was pushed to its margins, while he was elevated to the status of one of the greatest German philosophers.

With *Being and Time*, Heidegger led the philosophical community to entirely new dimensions of thinking. Prior to this he had been a well-known and respected figure in professional circles, one who was occasionally feared because of his uncompromising character. Overnight the book made him famous even for those who rejected it or, indeed, those who had never read it at all. His 1929 critique of neo-Kantian philosophy, *Kant and the Problem of Metaphysics*, was closely related to *Being and Time* and was declared by Heidegger himself to be a kind of introduction. This deepened the impression that here was a highly significant thinker who had opened a path to a completely new way of thinking.

In 1928 he finally received the long-desired offer of a position at the University of Freiburg. He was *uni loco*, that is, the only candidate put forward on the list of possible candidates and was recommended to the Ministry as the successor of the famous Edmund Husserl. Heidegger hastily left the University of Marburg, where he felt he was not valued highly enough and, in addition, where he had never liked the landscape.

The offer meant greater financial benefits which only increased when in 1930, he received an offer from the University in Berlin; he declined after some thought,[1] but not before negotiating with the University of Freiburg for more benefits as part of the conditions for him to remain in Freiburg. As a result, a typist paid 240 Reichsmarks was made available to him and the *aversum* (a kind of research budget) for the philosophical seminar, was doubled from 500 to 1,000 Reichsmarks. This was a lot in those days and added to his reputation. It also increased the number of those who were jealous of him.

With Martin Heidegger's return to Freiburg, it seemed as though the domination of the neo-Kantians was irrevocably broken. Heidegger advanced to the leading position in the university, although he always irritably denied this aspiration. However, he had great ambitions and felt the need to transcribe everything he thought and wrote. He also wanted to search practically for access to the "authentic life (*eigentliches Leben*)." In a congratulatory letter to Jaspers on December 20, 1931, on the occasion of the publication of his three-volume *Philosophy*, Heidegger addresses Jaspers in a way that could characterize himself, as well: "May the joyfully animated relaxation after the completion of *this* step make you ready for the *second* decisive step of the knowing leader and guardian of the *authentic (echte)* public domain." In the same letter, Heidegger described himself as "an overseer in a gallery, who, among other things, must see to it that the curtains in the windows are correctly opened and closed so that the few great works of the tradition are more or less properly illuminated for the randomly gathering spectators."[2] "Knowing leader and guardian"—allusions to Greek antiquity—both thinkers choose these metaphors to describe themselves in their correspondence regarding the project of academic renewal in the early twenties. The secret of their common project lay in the space that opened up between a "leader" and a "guardian." Leaders and guardians outlined the tasks they saw before them. And the *authentic public realm*? It is not the public realm of the "they" (*das Man*) that Heidegger saw as a cacophonic confusion of liberal democracy, but rather one of *aletheia*, the unconcealment of being. This domain had nothing to do with plurality and debate, but rather with the shining emergence of the spiritual "leader" vis-à-vis those who were meant to follow him. Those who followed would then find themselves within this domain. This type of thinking was common in many circles of that time.

Heidegger envisioned a twofold educational project: first, he wanted to counteract the tendency in German university politics of making academic study widely available to everyone, a tendency toward education for the masses. Second, the university itself was to be radically cleaned up.

In 1931–32, the newspaper *Frankfurter Zeitung* published a series of articles on the reform of universities and professional schools.[3] There were many controversial points of view. Among the contributors were the social scientist Emil Lederer, pedagogue and philosopher Eduard Spranger, religious philosopher Paul Tillich, philosopher Karl Jaspers, Jesuit priest and philosopher Erich Przywara, and cultural sociologist Siegfried Kracauer.[4] These articles were written by scholars in the humanities who defended the ideal of humanism, but they were also written by specialists in the respective fields of teacher's training and elementary school education. The relationship of education with the economy was discussed and students also contributed to the debate. One nationally minded student criticized the institution of the university using the same stereotypes of the popularized philosophy of life (rigid institutions, dead knowledge, useless thinking) that would later resurface in anti-Semitic propaganda. Other students in the series pleaded for a more demanding academic curriculum.

Paul Tillich began with a plea for separating professional training from the university. His first sentence was "the university has become a fiction."[5] By this he meant that the university, which over decades had gradually fused with modern mass society, had lost its unique character. He demanded a clear separation between the training necessary for a profession, for example, teaching or the applied sciences, and the training necessary for what he called the fundamental human sciences that are meant to educate future generations of scholars.

The majority of the authors did not embrace this radical model and pleaded for reforms of specific educational levels. Jaspers, too, no longer advocated this radical break between professional and scholarly training. Instead he and others recommended moderate reforms, arguing against the tendency of the university to entrust higher education to underpaid and underqualified staff rather than to professors.

However, Tillich's suggestion was very similar to what Heidegger had repeatedly advocated since the 1920s, a suggestion Jaspers never opposed. Tillich called for the separation between elite education and training for the masses. Jaspers and Heidegger put forward the idea that the university needed to be cleaned up, nonprofessorial staff expunged, and the number of professors and thus also the number of students drastically reduced.

The discussion continued after the emergence of National Socialism. Heidegger, who had not contributed to the series of articles in the *Frankfurter Zeitung*, offered his opinion *ex post et cathedra*. In his speech accepting the rectorship at the University of Freiburg in May 1933, he announced a program for a new university: elite education, integrating physical and intellectual studies, separating academic education from professional training.

One of his first actions as rector in 1933 was to work with other professors in the university on a project that sought to remove the leaders of university associations. The latter exemplified for him and for other conservative revolutionaries the irrevocable movement toward making the university a place for the masses. But more on this later.

Heidegger now wanted to practically implement what he and Jaspers had been discussing, namely, the transformation of the university into an institution that produces intellectual leadership. Plato's idea of the academy resonated in the background. Hannah Arendt would take up this idea in her plan for a book on politics. Of course, such an elite concept required the right students. They should be highly intelligent, but not studying out of purely theoretical interest. Heidegger and others accused the Jewish intelligentsia of just this, being too one-sided, living only in their heads, neglecting the other side of life: embodiment, work. Against this, the new students were to be exhorted to lead an authentic life, to engage in physical as well as intellectual exercise. Heidegger had already diagnosed the alienation between the two poles of human existence as a sign of self-alienation in the age of the masses. Already in the 1920s, there were reports of the campfire romanticism at the Todtnauberg cabin where visitors told ancient myths, sang songs, and played sports.

Academic teaching was to be completely transformed. Many complaints about the faculty in the 1920s—especially in letters between friends—often culminated in the derisive cry that the majority of colleagues did not belong in a university deserving of its name. Competitive thoughts and feelings of social inferiority may well have been at play here, but so was the conviction that too many compromises had been made in academic teaching. True thinking, however, as Heidegger had learned under difficult and trying circumstances, did not admit compromises. Those born after the Second World War were the first to understand that while lack of compromise can be fruitful and inclusive, under different circumstances, it can also be devastating and destructive. However, in the time after the First World War, another idea held sway, namely, that the renunciation of radicalness leads to mediocrity. It remains a mystery as to why so many people of that time consciously accepted the view that uncompromising thinking, in circumstances where it seeks to make an impact, may become violent, indeed, must become violent. Was it the First World War that made the dimension of violence in thinking so acceptable? An entire generation in different camps (socialism, communism, messianism, Zionism, national ideology) enthusiastically welcomed radical thinking. They believed that only those who pushed thought to its most extreme consequences could accomplish something in this world of decay. The danger of this uncompromising thinking escaped Heidegger, as well. He was certainly not alone in this.

But what astonishes us even more, from today's point of view, is that the philosopher Heidegger must have really believed that he could leap from thinking to action, without first crossing over the transitional space where the two seemed to directly oppose each other.

In *Being and Time*, Heidegger foreclosed the possibility of thinking this transitional space; there he thoroughly demonstrated that authentic Dasein exists in the rejection of everything having to do with the "they," of everything having to do with the evental-historical with-world (*Mit-Welt*), with the public domain, culture, and technology. From the background of this exclusion of the everyday world, a world defined as distracting, emerges this naïveté—a naïveté that seems so monstrous to us today—out of which Heidegger saw the euphoria of National Socialism materialize as a convincing concept. Hannah Arendt would later write a parable about this: Heidegger, the fox, fell into the trap that he himself set.

Heidegger hoped that the new way of thinking that he was working on would lead to a new kind of academy, a new form of thinking, teaching, and educating at the University of Freiburg. He believed that the opportunity to accomplish his project would present itself in one way or another. Did he hope that the National Socialists would come into power? He certainly did not wish for the banal orgies of violence that began after 1933. However, early on he saw in the "movement," and apparently also in its militarization, the auspicious alternative to the everydayness of the 1920s, to the boring monotony of democratic procedures and practices. He saw a possibility, a forum, for the renewal of the nation's spiritual potential. He must have believed that there was a task left unaccomplished by the ancients, a task that was now possible to fulfill with National Socialism. Not that he thought the task would be fulfilled by the National Socialist movement itself. In his view, the latter needed to be educated. The task was up to him; he had taken it upon himself long ago. He wanted only to be called.[6]

Heidegger shared the epochal illusion of the emergence of National Socialism with many others, from Gottfried Benn to Carl Schmitt to Arnolt Bronnen, and others. National Socialism became the bearer of hope; many people saw in it an alternative to the chaos of the mass age, to being at the mercy of technology, to the self-forgetting loss of German culture, and the decline of the national state. The return to the "German essence" was the promise that hid the violence and terror, the modern means of technological domination and the formation of the totalitarian system.

The utopia of Russian socialism was bound up with the vision of a *new human being*. Socialism represented the modernist image of the human being in a much more unambiguous way than National Socialism. Lenin's mathematical equation, "Communism = Soviet power plus the electrification of the entire country" (1920) presented socialism as the greatest project of modernization in Russian history. The new person had to be *produced* by technology and, if necessary, by force. Many projects of the twenties—individualistic and collectivist, artistic and political—resurfaced here, from the reform of education and dance to Zionist Nationalism.

Both utopias were founded on the idea of self-purification and renewal. The choice between these alternatives divided the German and European intellectual scene into several camps.

The French historian François Furet has shown that the attraction to both utopias, aiming at totality, went back to the growing hatred of European intellectuals of their own class, the bourgeoisie.[7] From a different perspective, one could also say that the totalitarian utopias were a response of the self-loathing of European intellectuals. They gave support and direction to the angry, sentimental aestheticizing, ideologized, but always radical rejection of the bourgeois society. They offered answers both for ordinary people and for the Bohemians.

It often depended on chance and the personalities of individuals whether those confronted with the temptation resisted it. Karl Jaspers, for instance, who had been fascinated by Heidegger's world of thinking for a long time, became aware at an early stage of the deadliness of anti-Semitism. His wife was Jewish; her nephews were exposed early on to the fear of persecution in Berlin. That, however, was an exception. The rule was rather the young intellectuals who, through one of these two utopias and strategies of power, wanted the opportunity to live out their own possibility of heroic transcendence, a sense of power, and the phantasy of the absolute.

Assimilation and Career at an End: Hannah Arendt

In this constellation, the fundamental conflict of the intellectual became the life-long theme for Hannah Arendt. Her path ran counter to that of her former lover and was doubly disrupted in 1933 when her academic career ended abruptly and her life in Germany became impossible. Apart from professional concerns, Arendt and her husband encountered something that they could not avoid: they were increasingly confronted with being Jewish.

In the meantime, anti-Jewish propaganda was no longer the exception but rather the rule; it was socially acceptable. German public opinion slid into a swirl of envy, hatred, and scorn regarding the Jews. Since the end of the nineteenth century, anti-Semitic hate propaganda had already been common practice among the students and the faculty at most German universities. What was new after the end of the First World War was that professors dropped their facade of academic reserve. They came forward with judgments, prejudices, and feelings of envy regarding the Jews. University annals of that time detail disciplinary proceedings against Jewish student groups opposed to nationalistically minded student associations. These Jewish youth groups in large part rejected the German-National alliance culture in which an anti-Jewish mood was cultivated and where violence was clearly manifest. The defeat of the First World War was attributed to the Jews. The most brutal expressions of growing anti-Semitism were the assassinations of Jewish politicians (Kurt Eisner, Hugo Haase, Walter Rathenau, and others), the rioting marches of nationalist student organizations, and later the pogroms and street killings carried out by the violent SA.

Zionism and Existential Philosophy

The world of escalating violence, on the one hand, and, on the other hand, Zionism that emerged in their fathers' generation at the end of the nineteenth century resulted in a current that swept up many Jewish youth. Unlike their fathers, they were moved by *political* self-consciousness.

Hannah Arendt belonged to the generation of those who grew up within the erosion of the German-Jewish "symbiosis." As an adolescent, she and her friends participated in a movement that already had a history. Important Jewish student fraternities as well as new hiking organizations and debate clubs had been founded at the beginning of the new century and were now being taken over by the next generation. The Königsberg "Zionist Organization" and the "United Jewish Students" were founded in 1901 and 1904, respectively. Their members came primarily from Jewish families from the East.[8] The goal of these and other Zionist organizations, such as the hiking clubs founded later, was to educate the upcoming generation of youth in Jewish culture and consciousness. To this end, they clearly followed conventional social forms. The student organizations were formed utilizing the model of the existing nationalist alliances. Zionist hiking clubs, seen from the outside, were difficult to distinguish from their nationally oriented competitors.

The adolescent Hannah directly experienced the pedagogical reform movement emerging in her childhood with protagonists like Gustav Wyneken, Siegfried Bernfeld, and the young Walter Benjamin. In Königsberg, too, there were school groups. As the records of the Königsberg Jewish community show, Arendt belonged to a circle of the young people "who, without denying their Judaism, did not belong to any of these [Zionist—author's note] organizations."[9] Among these non-Jewish groups was the circle of high school students, gathered around Ernst Grumach,[10] who excelled in ancient philology and who was Arendt's first love. The students who gathered in this circle read Plato in the original, knew Immanuel Kant's texts by heart, and discussed new literary publications. Thus emerged that "peer group," with which Arendt remained connected her whole life.

Max Fürst, another childhood friend of Arendt's, reports on the tumultuous time of their youth in Königsberg, when he joined a youth group called "Black Mob": "It was a witches' caldron which we cooked, where we were concerned with everything that our time subjected us to. Beginning with Wyneken . . . lyricism, songs, hiking, solstice celebrations, we came to. . . . Expressionist poetry, the confrontation with nationalism of every kind . . . with the generation of parents and their gods, with Judaism and other religions, and always with Marx and the effort to clarify our position on current events."[11] At first, the Jewish youth movement was rejected by both conservative and liberal-minded Jews. Kurt Blumenfeld, the influential Zionist who was a welcome guest at the house of Arendt's parents, reported that Arendt's beloved grandfather Max Arendt reacted to the impertinence of Zionism with the words: "He who contests my Germanness, I consider a murderer."[12] However, he later supported the Zionist youth groups in Königsberg. Königsberg Rabbi Hermann Vogelstein was also an enemy of Zionism at the time: "Judaism is a religion, not a nation" were his words.[13] For this reason, the Jewish community at first closed itself off from the youth activities, although as time went on the representatives of the older generation always appeared at the celebrations of the "Jewish Student Clubs."[14]

For Hannah, Zionism was primarily an intellectual counterculture. Although clearly separate from the main discourse, Theodor Herzl's and Max Nordaus's writings, Max Goldenstein's articles, Martin Buber's or Leo Baeck's books were part of the general framework of German, even European, political and cultural currents of the time. These thinkers participated in scientific and intellectual discussions of the day and they immersed themselves in the key precepts of the socialist movement. They shared the maxims of the race doctrine because they considered them to be scientifically supported. The young Zionists in Königsberg and elsewhere in the Reich held aesthetic ideas similar to the German avant-garde, even if they did not belong to it. The separation between the "Jewish" and "German" discourse, a fundamental distinction in Zionism, was more symbolic than real. The majority of Zionists were modernists of the first order. Modernism, messianism, nationalism, traditionalism, youth movements, race doctrine, and socialism entered into a unique configuration. Still, these young Zionists represented something entirely different.

Heinrich Graetz, the great Jewish historian who had discovered the writing of Judaism's history, summarized the history of the Jews with the thesis that only Jews had a sense of history, not Germans—and this despite the fact that German-national history proudly presented itself as a high science.

Buber, Baeck, and others were speaking of the convalescence of the people, of the selection of only those who were strong as pioneers in the building of Palestine, excluding the weak. Strong young men, blond and blue-eyed, served as models for the pioneers in Palestine. The youth group "Blue White" represented the elite consciousness of the movement. The Leader Principle (*das Führerprinzip*) was inscribed in its charter.[15]

The Zionism of this time was socialism infused with nationalism. The "new man," so talked about in Soviet Bolshevism, in expressionist-messianic poetry, and in parts of racial-nationalist ideology, also made an appearance in Palestine. His prototype was the free, physically productive worker at whose hands modern industry was to be born. Political Zionism emerged, therefore, as the ideology of this projection of modernity. It is this which differentiates it from the populism of National Socialism of the 1920s.

Zionism in eastern Germany also profited from the exchange with the movements, groups, and people who came from pre-revolution Russia. Königsberg was the German town closest to them.[16] In Königsberg, Zionism could successfully merge with Social Democratic culture and thinking. Hannah's parents belonged to the circle around the *Socialist Monthly* (*Sozialistische Monatshefte*). Its publisher, Josef Bloch, was close to the revisionist Bernstein wing of the Social Democratic Party and had corresponded with Friedrich Engels. Because he was so cultured—he spoke and read Yiddish and Hebrew—he played the role of intermediary between the socialists and the Zionists.[17] Not just in Berlin but elsewhere in Germany, the magazine became a forum for passionate, self-conscious Zionism, and if not actually organizing a direction for Jewish socialism, it separated itself from the liberal, assimilated Jewish milieu.

In the meantime, Hannah's mother, who was highly sympathetic with Rosa Luxemburg, hosted a discussion circle in her apartment that was attended by Königsberg leftist intellectuals. Not only reform socialists but also radical independent Social Democrats were among the guests.[18] Her daughter would later write an important essay on this Jewish, Polish-German revolutionary, Rosa Luxemburg.

Against the backdrop of a public discourse that was becoming increasingly forceful and threatening, it was no accident that at the end of the 1920s, Arendt, after revising her dissertation as Jaspers had asked her to do, turned her attention to the recent history of the Jews. She pursued her studies of German-Jewish assimilation with a feeling of uncertainty and a need for reassurance. She sensed her world tottering, a feeling perhaps stronger when she was outside Königsberg. Hans Jonas reports that the young student had always dealt with anti-Semitism rather self-confidently. In Marburg, prior to attending Rudolf Bultmann's theological seminars, she had gone to his office hours seeking assurance of his support should she be confronted with anti-Semitic hostilities.[19] Bultmann reassured her.

In Heidelberg, the same nationalist-racist unrest was felt. The student organizations and their members from the faculty were already fighting against "the system" in the 1920s. Zionist students attempted to defend themselves against discrimination.

The extent to which anti-Semitism had wormed its way into the political culture became clear in two affairs, both of which had far-reaching effects on the country's politics. In Heidelberg, the case of the pacifist untenured assistant university lecturer Emil Julius Gumbel had stirred feelings for many years. After many attempts by his detractors to unseat him, Gumbel, an economist, mathematician, statistician, unionist, and militant USPD-follower, was ultimately stripped of his right to teach in 1932. He was soon removed from the university. Gumbel had established the connection between the political murders of the 1920s and the people in the secret societies who were behind them. In books and pamphlets, he exposed the antidemocratic stance within the legal system. One of these investigations brought him to trial on charges of treason, but the charges were dropped because the facts that Gumbel gathered were indisputable.[20] What finally tipped the scale toward an internal academic investigation was a public antiwar announcement on July 26, 1924, in Heidelberg. Referring to the many who had been murdered, he said, "I will not say they died on the field of dishonor, but rather they died in an awful fashion."[21] Since then, "the Gumbel case," which was the name of the disciplinary proceeding, continued to percolate in the dean's office and the university Senate. As a member of the Gumbel committee, Jaspers tried to de-ideologize the proceeding. He writes almost forty years later: "From the very first moment it was clear to me: what is at stake is academic freedom. The latter is destroyed at its very roots if the faculty member's opinions are used as a litmus test."[22] Evidently, the social-democratic minister of the interior, culture, and education Adam Remmele and part of the state government supported Gumbel for a while. The facts on which his claims rested were indisputable, making the nationalists just that much angrier. During this time, Gumbel was receiving a *Privatdozent* stipend from the university. In 1932 Gumbel's enemies managed to convince the department to take away his right to teach. Jaspers did not give his agreement to this unparalleled action, but he could do nothing about it.

The second case concerned the national-populist *Privatdozent* Arnold Ruge. Ruge wrote nasty anti-Semitic flyers in which he presented himself as a victim of "Jewish terror."[23] His shattered academic career lay behind it. In 1920 there was a professorial protest against his actions in Heidelberg, in which Professors Ludwig Curtius and Eberhard Gothein, among others, participated. The philosophy department finally justified taking away his right to teach by saying that Ruge was dismissed not because of his anti-Semitism, but rather because of his offense to the ideals of the university.[24] Such a downplaying of conflict was not atypical at the time. Ruge went to Marburg and continued his anti-Semitic badgering as an assistant in philosophy seminars. This episode had repercussions. In December 1933 Heidegger declined the request of the Reich Governor Robert Wagner, who was looking for a professorship for the party member Ruge, with the following justification: "As long as there is a merit system for the election of leaders and responsible directors of positions in National Socialism, Herr Ruge, in the final analysis, does not come into consideration for a philosophical professorship."[25]

It is against the backdrop of cases like this, among other things, that the Minister Adam Remmele encouraged the University of Heidelberg in 1931, "before hiring anyone, consider the candidates who support the state." Indignantly, the department refused this attack on academic freedom. It considered itself obligated to "refuse to comply with directives like this." At the same time, the university Senate was asked "to endorse this point of view in the interest of the University and bring it to the attention of the Ministry."[26]

In 1933 the new Ministry of Culture and Education pointedly provoked the university by giving a NSDAP-friendly professor a top position. The untenured assistant professor and Privy Councilor, Dr. Paul Schmitthenner, received the professorship for history specializing in "the science of war and defense" without following appointment protocol. The philosophy department announced their agreement "with joy and gratitude," and welcomed "the enrichment of their curriculum with such a significant subject." They did add that they wished to point out, however, that appointments were really a university matter.[27]

From these incidents, one can understand how the university was in a persistent struggle that had simultaneously a protective and a self-destructive effect. The university committees generally proceeded in the following way: one deferred legal disputes, for instance, the National Socialist slander of a Jewish university teacher, by subjecting them to lengthy democratic proceedings. That took some time. But, little by little, the barriers collapsed. The universities increasingly tolerated undemocratic activities so as not to disturb the peace of the university as a whole. They were surprised when this practice was seen as agreement with hostility against the German Republic, which then led to more unrest. Thus, in the university as a whole, the understanding of academic freedom oscillated between nationalist and antipolitical sentiments. Many people thought that the most important thing was to keep politics outside the university.

The matters were similar in Heidelberg, as well. Young Hannah Arendt would certainly have followed these "cases" and critically commented on them.

Yet, apart from this, everything seemed to be as before: appointments were negotiated, careers were planned, careers failed, academic talk made the rounds, books and essays sought readers. Gradually, however, the polarizing mood on the streets penetrated the university; the alma mater, too, became the battlefield of political interests.

In Berlin, Hannah could feel the looming disaster with her own skin; she could smell, hear, see, and sense it. In the city she was lacking the protection she had enjoyed at the universities. In Marburg, there were Heidegger and Bultmann, in Heidelberg, Jaspers and several Jewish professors were protective of her, and there were, of course, her friends from Königsberg and elsewhere. Some, such as Hans Jonas, came from the Zionist camp, others, like Benno von Wiese, were apolitical.

In Berlin, spring 1930, Hannah gave a lecture on her new research topic: "Rahel Varnhagen and Jewish Existence in Modernity."[28] She sent the text to Jaspers, who immediately felt her strong inner turmoil, a turmoil that could not have been caused by academic problems. The lecture disturbed him. He wanted to talk to her about it, "to ask my questions and get a clearer idea in the give and take of our conversation of what you mean. For merely to write you a few dicta seems to me an inadequate response when I can see that, despite the deliberate objectivity of your presentation, something else is going on here."[29]

And then he did write a couple of "dicta" to her:

> You objectify "Jewish existence" existentially—and in doing so perhaps cut existential thinking off at the roots. The concept of being-thrown-back-on-oneself

can no longer be taken altogether seriously if it is *grounded* in terms of the fate of the Jews instead of being rooted in itself. Philosophically, the contrast between floating free and being rooted strikes me as very shaky indeed.

The passages from the letters, which you have chosen so well, suggest something quite different to me: "Jewishness" is a *façon de parler*, a manifestation of a selfhood originally negative in its outlook and not comprehensible from the historical situation. It is a fate that did not experience liberation from the enchanted castle.[30]

Of course these were not objections. Arendt's reply shows that she was struggling with the subject but was, at the same time, still confident. She knew how to defend herself against Jaspers's reservations:

I was not trying to "ground" Rahel's existence in terms of Jewishness—or at least I was not conscious of doing so. This lecture is only a *preliminary* work meant to show that on the foundation of being Jewish a certain possibility of existence *can* arise that I have tentatively and for the time being called fatefulness. This fatefulness arises from the very fact of "foundationlessness" and can occur *only* in a separation from Judaism. I did not at all intend to provide an actual interpretation of this having-a-fate. And for such an interpretation the fact of Judaism would be of no importance anyhow.

An objectification is in fact there in a certain sense, but not an objectification of Jewish existence (as a gestalt, for example) but of the historical conditions of a life which can, I think, mean something (though not an objective idea or anything like that). It seems as if certain people are so exposed in their own lives (and only in their lives, not as persons!) that they become, as it were, junction points and concrete objectifications of "life." Underlying my objectification of Rahel is a self-objectification that is not a reflective or retrospective one but, rather, from the very outset a mode of "experiencing," of learning, appropriate to her. What this all really adds up to—fate, being exposed, what life means—I can't really say in the abstract (and I realize that in trying to write about it here). Perhaps all I can try to do is illustrate it with examples. And that is precisely why I want to write a biography. In this case, interpretation has to take the path of repetition.[31]

Decades later she would vehemently deny having written a biography and insist on having retold a history—just as Rahel herself would have done.[32] But that would be later. What is interesting here is that behind the project of the individual Rahel Varnhagen was something more than the desire to simply provide an interpretation of an historical figure. Arendt also wanted to narrate a typical phenomenon from the history of modern Judaism. This figure became for her emblematic of a rupture in Judaism itself: the rupture between the yearning for belonging and knowing that no identity could emerge from the parvenu-existence of an assimilated people. However, something surfaced in her as she reflected upon this break. She was not sure what it was, but she felt that it had to do with something so fundamental that could it not be discounted. Later, in her

Parisian exile, she was to find the figure of the *pariah*, the ostracized one who can maintain his or her dignity only by remaining outside.

It was natural for a young existential philosopher influenced by Heidegger's thought to undertake this project. *Dasein* existed as possibility, but it had to be lived. Lived how? By facing up to givenness. For Heidegger, this included death, anxiety, the "they," idle talk, but also the care of Dasein. Heidegger did not formulate these reflections in terms of the "Jewish question," but this did not bother Arendt. Why should the self-reflection of Judaism in the figure of Rahel Varnhagen not be part of the realization of an already existing possibility? Why should that which Heidegger—convincingly, in her view—presented as the dualism between the Dasein that loses itself and the Dasein that finds itself, not apply to the self-reflection of Judaism?

Certainly, Heidegger was not the only source of inspiration. The young, inquisitive woman was also reading contemporary Zionist literature. At lectures and discussions she picked up the ideas of great Zionists such as Martin Buber, Leo Baeck, Theodor Herzl, and her friend Kurt Blumenfeld. Their conversations and texts had to do with a sense of destiny and awakening to authentic existence. At the same time, these authors spoke of failed existence and true vocation. Today one would say they talked about the true sense of identity and what is truly at stake.

Arendt met Kurt Blumenfeld at one of his lectures in summer 1926, during her first semester in Heidelberg.[33] Like Arendt, Blumenfeld came from East Prussia, but, born in 1884, he was a generation older than she. He had studied in Berlin, Freiburg, and Königsberg. It was at Königsberg that he embraced Zionism. From 1909 onward, he worked tirelessly in the Jewish communities, especially with student alliances and associations in Germany, so as to transform Zionism into an important political movement. In 1911 he became the general secretary of the World Association of Zionists (*Zionistischer Weltverband*). With this appointment, he became the first permanent Zionist politician in Germany. In 1924 he was elected as the president of the Zionist Union of Germany (*Zionistische Vereinigung für Deutschland* [ZVfD]). In the Berlin phonebook of 1933, he is listed as a merchant.

His charismatic way of speaking must have particularly appealed to young Jewish men and women who were looking for an authentic life and action beyond assimilation. Moreover, Blumenfeld was a brilliant organizer; he knew how to obtain donations with great style and how to impress the celebrities of the time. Over the years, he worked closely with Albert Einstein, who played an important role in winning over important and wealthy persons, even non-Jewish, to the cause of Zionism. Until his flight to Palestine in 1933, Blumenfeld fought tirelessly for the cause of Zionism in Germany.

As a rule, young Hannah Arendt was rather shy with people, but with Blumenfeld something in their first encounter must have broken through. In any event, the day ended quite joyfully. Hans Jonas had invited Blumenfeld to participate in a dinner at the Jewish students association in Heidelberg. He invited Arendt, as well. It is reported that after dinner, during a stroll through the city, she held hands with Blumenfeld, and they sang songs loudly. Her shy admirer, the student Hans Jonas, tagged behind.[34] A friendship that was to last a lifetime, albeit with major crises, connected her with Blumenfeld. The young, fatherless student "adopted" him as her father.

From the distance of years, Arendt herself defined her relationship with Zionism before 1933, in the following way: "I was close friends with some of the leading people, above all with the then president, Kurt Blumenfeld. But I was not a Zionist. Nor did the Zionists try to convert me. Yet in a certain sense I was influenced by them: especially by the criticism, the self-criticism that the Zionists developed among the Jewish people. I was therefore influenced and impressed by it, but politically I had nothing to do with it."[35] In 1972 she responded to Hans Morgenthau's question about her political "belongingness": "I belong to no group. The only group to which I belonged, was, as you know, the Zionists. But, of course, it was only against Hitler. And it lasted from 1933 to 1943. Then I broke away from them. The Zionists offered the only possibility of defending oneself as a Jew and not as a human being—I took the latter to be a great mistake because if one is attacked as a Jew, one must defend oneself also as a Jew."[36] It was a kind of intellectual self-reflection of Judaism that she took part in—and of course the practical relief work that she accomplished. Certainly, she did not agree with the Palestine political project and the tactical strategies which Jewish organizations were using at the time to realize the goal of a Jewish Palestine.[37]

Exposed simultaneously to Heideggerian thinking, Jaspers's existential philosophy and Zionism, Arendt found herself in a peculiar dilemma, as did her friends who had also studied with Heidegger and Jaspers and opened themselves up to Zionism. She was working from conflicting sources that seem contradictory from today's point of view. At that time, however, one could take what one had learned from Heidegger and think as a Zionist. One could think with Jaspers in a Jewish-national way. Zionism could also be understood as a kind of Jewish existential philosophy. Zionism was not only that. It had many, sometimes contradictory, aspects; it is an extremely complex topic, and we cannot discuss it in detail here.

The shock came at the end of 1932, beginning of 1933: Heidegger, Jaspers, and Zionism were no longer facets of a unified cosmos. Some distinguished professors were now literally standing on the other side. That must have shaken Arendt to the core.

Forty years later, Georg Lukács, at that time a young Jewish intellectual like Arendt, diagnosed this shock as an expression of a preceding "disavowal of reality." In his view, this dilemma was the unforeseen result of the conflation of "a leftist ethics oriented towards radical revolution coupled with a traditional-conventional exegesis of reality from the right."[38] He saw it as a generational phenomenon: "A considerable part of the leading German intelligentsia . . . have taken up residence in the 'Grand Hotel Abyss' . . . a beautiful hotel, equipped with every comfort, on the edge of an abyss, of nothingness, of absurdity. And the daily contemplation of the abyss between excellent meals or artistic entertainments, can only heighten the enjoyment of the subtle comforts offered."[39] Lukács's diagnosis referred to the joy of thinking on the edge of the abyss that was widespread at the time. Not only was the danger seen as an intellectual and aesthetic challenge but the actual endangerment was also presented aesthetically. Stories have it that a short-lived attempt to implement a communist Soviet Republic in Hungary was masterminded by Budapest coffee-shop intellectuals (the young Lukács among them) who argued all night long, in the style of Dostoevsky's heroes, about the relationship between good and evil in the times of revolutionary change.[40] There are similar stories from the Bavarian Soviet Republic and from some revolutionary intellectual circles in Russia. In all of these groups the idea of a salvation or redemption that becomes secularized through the revolution circulates.

Some of these intellectuals leaning toward radical thinking were out of touch with reality. They were, therefore, not aware of how dangerous this kind of thinking had become for them. Everything was fine as long as the political barriers and democratic rules respected by all held strong. When these broke down, there was no longer any restraint. The messianic hopes of Ernst Toller, Erich Mühsam, Eugen Leviné, Georg Lukács, Ernst Bloch, and Walter Benjamin were harshly dashed with the onset of the persecutions.

This is *one* possible explanation of this mixture that is for us so unsettling today—that of a groundlessness combined with intellectual radicalism found among many young thinkers of the 1920s and the beginning of the 1930s.

Rahel Varnhagen's Dilemma

Arendt stayed at the "Hotel Abyss" only temporarily. All the evidence shows that she was an unusually practical and sober young woman. Her great self-confidence, her healthy common sense, and her contact with the Zionist activist circles prevented her from succumbing to illusions.

The political situation worsened, factions were formed and solidified. The threatening escalation of violence was reflected even in political discourse. The underlying awareness of something looming and frightening would explain the uneasiness of Hannah Arendt and her friends, the uneasiness that vexed

Jaspers. She was caught between her conviction that in these times one had to affirm oneself as a Jew and her drive to independence. This became clear to her in the historical figure of Rahel Varnhagen, who had not yet taken this step, or not completely, or had done so in a way that was not satisfactory for Arendt.

Why did she choose Rahel Varnhagen to discuss this dilemma? Was her friend Anne Mendelssohn's enthusiasm for Rahel Varnhagen the reason why she chose this woman as the "embodiment" of the German-Jewish dilemma? Later she dedicated this book to Mendelssohn. It is perhaps revealing that in August 1936, Hannah, who had just fallen in love with Heinrich Blücher, writes from Geneva to Paris that Rahel Varnhagen is her "very closest woman friend, unfortunately dead for a hundred years now."[41] Here we see ardor, a good mood, intimacy, which she immediately counteracted with the powerful paraphrase from a letter Rahel Varnhagen sent to Rebecca Friedländer: "The reason it is so horrible to be a Jewess is because one must constantly legitimize oneself."[42]

Whoever reads this becomes aware of the extent to which anti-Semitism was confronting Arendt with existential questions, which, up until now, she had been exposed to primarily as theoretical.

Hannah's dilemma in her love for Martin Heidegger becomes even clearer against this backdrop. This love was authentic, but it put the young woman in a hopeless situation. She was hearing rumors about the increasingly anti-Semitic Heidegger. The letter she wrote to her lover on this subject is not preserved. But he must have received her questions: Are the rumors true? Do you sympathize with National Socialism?

Annoyed, Heidegger reacted:

The rumors that are upsetting you are slanders that are perfect matches for other experiences I have endured over the last few years.

I cannot very well exclude Jews from the seminar invitations; not least because I have not had *a single* seminar invitation in the last four semesters. That I supposedly don't say hello to Jews is such a malicious piece of gossip that in any case I will have to take note of it in the future.

As a clarification of how I behave towards Jews, here are the following facts:

I am on sabbatical this Winter Semester and thus in the summer I announced, well in advance, that I wanted to be left alone and would not be accepting projects and the like.

The man who comes anyway and urgently wants to write a dissertation is a Jew. The man who comes to see me every month to report on a large work in progress (neither a dissertation nor a Habilitation project) is also a Jew. The man who sent me a substantial text for urgent reading a few weeks ago is a Jew.

The two fellows of the *Notgemeinschaft* whom I helped get accepted in the last three semesters are Jews.[43] The man who, with my help, got a stipend to go to Rome is a Jew.

Whoever wants to call that "raging anti-Semitism" is welcome to do so.

Beyond that, I am now just as much an anti-Semite in university issues as I was ten years ago in Marburg, where, because of this anti-Semitism, I even earned Jacobsthal's and Friedländer's support.

To say absolutely nothing about my personal relationships with Jews (e.g., Husserl, Misch, Cassirer, and others).

And above all it cannot touch my relationship to you.

For a long while, I have been quite withdrawn in general, not least because my work has been met by hopeless incomprehension, but also on account of some less-than-pleasant personal experiences that have resulted from my teaching. In any case, I have long since given up expecting any sort of gratitude or even just decency from so-called "disciples."[44]

Heidegger wrote matter-of-factly, almost impatiently, emphasizing how much he supported his Jewish students. He implicitly reminded Hannah that he wrote one of the recommendations for obtaining the grant from *Notgemeinschaft der deutschen Wissenschaft* for her.[45]

Apparently it was not just the spatial distance that contributed to the alienation between them. Hannah had become more politically aware. She lived in Berlin in an atmosphere of intellectual friction and polemical public speech. Through Bertolt Brecht, Kurt Tucholsky, Carl von Ossietzky, and other intellectuals related to the leftist camp, she encountered another dimension of political discourse, without realizing at first just how much it would affect her personally.

In Marburg, she concentrated on her studies. In Heidelberg, her connections with Zionist organizations made her aware of her situation as a Jew. In Berlin, however, she was confronted with the German-Jewish antithesis.

In 1932 she told her astonished friend Anne Mendelssohn that, in her view, as a Jew, one had to emigrate. Clearly, the militant anti-Semitism of the early 1930s in Berlin outstripped everything that she herself, as unflappable as she was, had experienced in Königsberg, Marburg, or Heidelberg.

Radical openness was the foundation of her relationship with Heidegger; in any event, *she* had shown this openness. Her question regarding his stance vis-à-vis the Jews introduced something into the relationship that until then had been painstakingly kept outside, namely, an aggressive external world that had pushed them to opposite sides of the political landscape.

She also had a peculiar experience with her teacher Karl Jaspers. The tension between them had to do not only with the Jews, but also with the "German essence." In 1932 Jaspers published an appraisal of Max Weber and sent it to his former doctoral student. Hannah Arendt responded very soberly:

> The title and the introduction made it difficult for me from the start to comment on the book. It does not bother me that you portray Max Weber as the great German but, rather, that you find the "German essence" in him and identify that essence with "rationality and humanity originating in passion." I have the same difficulty with that as I do with Max Weber's imposing patriotism itself. You will understand that I as a Jew can say neither yes nor no and that my agreement on this would be as inappropriate as an argument against it. I do not have to keep my distance as long as you are talking about the "meaning of the German world power" and its mission for the "culture of the future." I can identify with this German mission, though I do not feel myself unquestioningly identical with it. For me, Germany means my mother tongue, philosophy, and literature. I can and must stand by all that. But I am obliged to keep my distance, I can neither be for nor against when I read Max Weber's grandiose sentence where he says that to put Germany back on her feet he would make an alliance with the devil himself. And it is this sentence which seems to me to reveal the critical point here. I wanted to convey this reservation to you, although it faded as I read further.[46]

Jaspers justified himself in a peculiarly defensive manner: the "German essence," to which she belonged, as well, was not a generic concept, but rather "an indeterminate and emerging historical totality."[47] He wanted to bring nationalist youth back into the general consciousness of what it meant to be German. To this end, he published the text with a nationalistic publisher. He did not, however, compromise as to the content. Still, the fact of her disagreement gave him pause.

But she extended no forgiveness. She did not understand his view of an emerging "historical totality" and found it to be idealist and nationalist in a bad sense.[48] Of course she was still a German, but Jews entered this German history belatedly and partially, and for this reason they did not belong to it.

Jewish destiny—Jewish self-reflection—German essence—historical totality. What was at stake in this dispute?

Karl Jaspers's attempt at reconciling the national with the democratic, the philosophical with the national, was not obvious to everyone. His former student's response made this clear to him. He was only trying to connect the national with the democratic project. In doing this, he was trying to accomplish something similar to what Max Weber in 1919 and Thomas Mann in his first democratic speech in 1922 had also attempted: to speak to the nationalistic youth so as to bring them to the side of democracy. Hannah Arendt, however, was speaking to him, the well-meaning and somewhat naive representative of the German essence, as a politically aware Jew.

Seen from today's perspective, one finds in these letters between Arendt and Jaspers an irremediable and irrevocable separation of the Jewish from the German. As someone from Königsberg, one who had experienced political hatred in the microcosm of her city, she knew what was going on. She was well aware of the new dimension of anti-Semitism. Something irreversible had occurred within her.

At the time of the collapse of the Weimar Republic, the twenty-seven-year-old Arendt was in a transitional phase: her great love frozen under the icy circumstances of the time, her promising academic career interrupted, her bare existence threatened. Her non-Jewish friends, for the most part, came to terms with the new regime. This was a profound shock to her, equal to the separation from Martin Heidegger. Thirty years later she judged the consequences of this failure of intelligence in the face of National Socialism:

> Among intellectuals *Gleichschaltung* was the rule, so to speak. . . . No one ever blamed someone if he "conformed" because he had to take care of his wife or child. The worst thing was that they really believed in Nazism! For a short time, many for a very short time. But that means that they made up ideas about Hitler . . . things far above the ordinary level! I found that grotesque. Today I would say that they fell into the trap of their own thinking.[49]

In this unreal time, when the Weimar Republic stumbled toward its breakdown and no one knew what tomorrow would bring, she housed several fugitive communists and persecuted intellectuals in the apartment on Opitzstraße in Berlin. The apartment she and Stern rented had several makeshift beds for the guests in transit.[50]

The contemplative life of academic intelligentsia was now over. With her remarkable sense for atmospheric shifts, she was one of the first in her circle who felt it. Her worry was not so much about her destroyed career as a philosopher; rather, she was suddenly confronted with the insight that something so decisive had happened that it demanded a definitive break with what had been her life up until this time. The shock that she experienced in 1933 resonates even thirty years later. In 1964 she responded to the journalist Günther Gaus on the question of the decisive event in the transition from the Weimar Republic to National Socialism:

> I would say February 27, 1933, the burning of the Reichstag, and the illegal arrests that followed during the same night. The so-called protective custody. As you know, people were taken to Gestapo cellars or to concentration camps. What happened then was monstrous. . . . This was an immediate shock for me, and from that moment on I felt responsible. That is, I was no longer of the opinion that one can simply be a bystander. I tried to help in many ways. . . .

I intended to emigrate at any rate. I thought immediately that Jews could not stay. I did not intend to run around Germany as a second class citizen, so to speak, in any form.[51]

Daily Arendt heard from friends about arrests, torture, and murders. Almost everything that one had feared was coming true: the black lists were compiled well before 1933 and immediately enacted when on January 30, 1933, Hitler was charged with forming a government. The terror was directed at the enemies of National Socialism, most commonly at intellectuals, communists, Social Democrats, and Jews.[52]

Persecution and Flight

Those who were politically clear-sighted felt that a systematic persecution was about to begin. However, only a few described the situation as clearly as Kurt Blumenfeld: "On February 28 [1933—author's note] all guarantees of civil freedom were eliminated by a so-called emergency decree 'about the protection against Communist violence.' That day was the end of the history of Judaism."[53] Günther Stern fled to Paris in January. Arendt was arrested in March. She had been doing research on behalf of *Zionistische Vereinigung für Deutschland* on everyday anti-Semitism in the trade publications of business and professional organizations read by the German middle class. The Zionists wanted thereby to convince the international public to renounce its tolerant attitude vis-à-vis National Socialist Germany. She was released after a short while. She was lucky in that the criminal police were still not entirely co-opted. The leading criminal officer could not get her to admit anything and promised her that he would release her soon.[54] She trusted this man; she did not get a lawyer and was released a couple of days later. Still, she had to leave Germany under the cover of darkness. Via Prague she landed in Paris, where Günther Stern had already settled. The estrangement that surfaced between them in Berlin could not be undone in the emergency situation of exile. Soon they started to live separately.

The flight in 1933 turned her life upside down. All continuity was undermined. She lost a secure network of friendly academic connections and reacted decisively—even from a distance of more than thirty years—in her own way:

You see, I came out of a purely academic background. In this respect the year 1933 made a very lasting impression on me. First a positive one and then a negative one. Perhaps I had better say first a negative one and then a positive one. People today often think that German Jews were shocked in 1933 because Hitler assumed power. As far as I and people of my generation are concerned, I can say that that is a curious misunderstanding. Naturally Hitler's rise was very bad. But it was political. It wasn't personal. We didn't need

Hitler's assumption of power to know that the Nazis were our enemies! That had been completely evident for at least four years to everyone who wasn't feebleminded. We also knew that a large number of the German people were behind them. That could not shock us or surprise us in 1933. . . . First of all, the generally political became a personal fate when one emigrated. Second . . . friends "conformed" or got in line. The problem, the personal problem, was not what our enemies did but what our friends did. In the wave of *Gleichschaltung* (conformity), which was relatively voluntary—in any case, not yet under the pressure of terror—it was as if an empty space formed around one. I lived in an intellectual milieu, but I also knew other people. And among intellectuals *Gleichschaltung* was the rule, so to speak. But not among the others. And I never forgot that. I left Germany dominated by the idea—of course somewhat exaggerated: Never again! I shall never again get involved in any kind of intellectual business. I want nothing to do with that lot. Also I didn't believe then that Jews and German Jewish intellectuals would have acted any differently had their own circumstances been different. . . . I thought that it had to do with this profession, with being an intellectual.[55]

In the following years, she had important things to do: practical work had top priority; academic discussions, in contrast, became unimportant.

In the Zionist circles, the dangers that emerged with National Socialism had been under discussion for a long time. All one had to do was to read the relevant propaganda and Nazi pamphlets and draw political conclusions from what was being said.[56] To be sure, no one could know that the murderous declarations would soon be implemented, nor could Arendt foresee that some of her friends would become co-opted.

One can still hear her reaction to the monstrosity of this experience thirty years later:

I realized what I then expressed time and again in the sentence: If one is attacked as a Jew, one must defend oneself as a Jew. Not as a German, not as a world citizen, not as an upholder of the Rights of Man, or whatever. Rather: what can I do specifically as a Jew? Second, it was now my clear intention to work with an organization. For the first time. To work with the Zionists. They were the only ones who were ready. It would have been pointless to join those who had assimilated. . . . But now, belonging to Judaism had become my own problem, and my own problem was political. Purely political! I wanted to go into practical work, exclusively and only Jewish work.[57]

Zionism, which previously had been for Arendt more of a network of relationships, a source of an alternative intellectual culture rather than a sphere of organizational affiliation, now offered her the necessary support. Compelled by circumstances, and yet of her own accord—as paradoxical as that sounds—she became a Zionist.

Heidegger: Philosophy of Action

The new era threw Arendt out of her previous life; she had to invent a new one. Spring 1933 also brought a change for Heidegger. In March he once again visited Jaspers in Heidelberg; his visits had by then become infrequent. Jaspers wrote about it in retrospect from the 1950s: "The last time Heidegger paid us a lengthy visit was at the end of March 1933. Although the National Socialists had been victorious during the March elections, we conversed as we always had. We listened to a record of Gregorian church music that he had purchased for me. Heidegger left earlier than originally planned. 'One has to join in,' he remarked regarding the rapid development of the National Socialist reality. I was surprised but did not question."[58] Heidegger's letter reached Jaspers on April 2, 1933: "So much is so dark and questionable that I sense more and more that we are extending into a new reality and that an age has grown old. Everything depends on whether we prepare the right point of engagement for philosophy and help it find the right words."[59] At that time the violent persecution of the oppositionists and intellectuals had already begun. On February 27, the Reichstag stood in flames. This letter to his friend marked Heidegger's transition from the realm of philosophy to that of action. He was still speaking of "we," and it seemed that Jaspers was included in this "we."

On April 21, 1933, Martin Heidegger was elected as rector of the University of Freiburg. On May 3 he joined NSDAP,[60] claiming later that he did so "upon the request of the Freiburg direction (NSDAP)."[61] After the fall of National Socialism, Heidegger generally tended to attribute his activities and duties in National Socialism to the suggestion of others. This must be understood not only as evasion or even conscious opportunism. Indeed, after the war, he freely admitted to Jaspers: "I immediately fell into the machinery of the office: the influences, the power struggles, and the factions. I was lost and fell, if only for a few months, into what my wife describes as an 'intoxication of power.'"[62] A report of the "Purification Committee" established by the University in the fall 1945, states laconically: "power stimulated Herr Heidegger. . . . What attracted him was the prospect of exercising a stronger influence."[63]

It might have been that colleagues pushed him to take up the rectorship. However, after the end of National Socialism, Heidegger himself made clear that there was no pressure from his colleagues.[64] After all, the rectorship was also an honorary post not offered to just anyone, and it was to a large extent connected with recognition. Clearly, Heidegger wanted this specific recognition that went beyond his philosophical work and enabled him to influence others. In any event, the University Senate was not forced to elect Heidegger. On April 21, 1933, Martin Heidegger was elected as rector by the Senate of the University of Freiburg, with two votes against him, not unanimously, as he claimed in his November 4, 1945, report to the academic rectorship.[65] His predecessor, Wilhelm von Möllendorf, who had just assumed the position, was, as an openly non-Nazi, forced to leave the office. After the war, Heidegger wrote in a letter to the rector that the unacceptable request of the Ministry to fire the deans of the Department of Law and the Department of Medicine (Dr. Wolf and Dr. von Möllendorf, who became dean again after his failed rectorship) was a reason for his resignation just a year later.[66]

On May 27 Heidegger gave his inaugural address upon the acceptance of the rectorship. The address can be understood only if it is taken as an "inflammatory text." This speech on the German university was shaped by the discourse of crisis in the Weimar Republic. Here is the philosopher who, on the one hand, had for many years been part of the critical discourse on university education, which, for example, took place in 1931–32 in the *Frankfurter Zeitung*. On the other hand, he is in the role of the rector of the university speaking as a politician.

The speech is carefully crafted. Heidegger begins with the responsibility that goes with this position. It consists in taking up "spiritual leadership." This mission is not solely up to him; it concerns the entire body of faculty and students; indeed, it is related to the entire society. The university elite is required to bring this mission into the greater society: "The will to the essence of the German university is the will to science as the will to the historical spiritual mission of the German Volk as a Volk that knows itself in its state. Science and German fate must come to power *at the same time* in the will to essence."[67] He addressed the university as a unified body and its members—professors and students—as the spiritual leaders of the nation, who at the same time had to be the true representatives of the people. The speech ends with a call for university education to be closely bound together in "service to labor, service to the military, service to knowledge."[68]

In the address, Heidegger fell into a pseudo-Hegelian conflation of the Prussian military state and the history of philosophy. The reader is aware that Heidegger wanted to enforce something: "will to essence . . . will to science . . . will to historical spiritual mission." And for this purpose he needed a transference. He transferred his mission onto the German people and thus lapsed into the thinking he had always despised: he described German reality in terms of the dichotomy between essence and appearance. The text is a document of triumph and failure at the same time.

In the time that followed, Heidegger's announcements and decrees as rector complemented the measures of the Ministry and the actions of the local NSDAP units. As a result, Freiburg University was transformed into an ideological institution. This transformation included the prohibition on Jewish student associations, the total inclusion of autonomous university organizations under the umbrella of the university's administration, the introduction of proof of Aryan ancestry, lifting the prohibition on dueling, the burning of books (following the example in Berlin), obligatory military sports class and ideological education of professors and students, establishment of a student race office, closure of a Jewish fraternity house, introduction of the Hitler greeting, introduction of "scientific camps," the alignment of the university constitution with the Führer's ideas, purging the university of "antistate elements," dismissing professors for racial reasons, withdrawal of the right to teach from Jewish faculty, introduction of the German greeting in lectures and seminars, the introduction of work service, and a loyalty oath to the Führer.[69]

In 1933 Heidegger did not miss any opportunity to speak publicly of his view of university reform. On the occasion of the tenth anniversary of the death of nationalist Freiburg student Albert Leo Schlageter, who had been executed by the French and elevated to the status of a martyr by the National Socialists, he spoke to the university about the idea of the "university in the new Reich."[70] He spoke at the opening of a new student dormitory, at the introduction of public service programs, at the student solstice celebration, even at the Twenty-Second Congress of the National Association of Baden Master Carpenters.

Platonic Academy and National Socialist University Reform

On May 3, 1933, the newly elected rector of Freiburg University sent a telegram to the Rector of Frankfurt University, Ernst Krieck:

> Dear Herr Krieck!
> My warmest congratulations on the acceptance of rectorship.
> I hope for a good camaraderie-in-arms.
> Sieg Heil!
> Your Heidegger[71]

Heidegger now wanted to accomplish his project of university reform with the influential Ernst Krieck, later his arch-enemy, not with Karl Jaspers. The term "camaraderie-in-arms" and "comrade-in-arms" had been for many years reserved for Jaspers. However, Heidegger had long understood that Jaspers and his wife had reacted with profound unease to the street violence and anti-Semitic marches even before 1933, but all the more so after Hitler and the SA assumed power. Jaspers once mentioned such incidents in a letter. However, Jaspers could not be a real comrade-in-arms at any rate, for purely physical reasons. He was able to travel only to a limited extent and was active only in a small radius. His public presence—aside from several lectures—was limited to his courses. In Heidegger's view, however, all these arguments were now superfluous, because Jaspers was married to a Jew. Unspoken words had been accumulating between them since the beginning of the 1930s. Jaspers complained about it, Heidegger remained silent for the most part.

At the end of May 1933, he visited Jaspers for the last time. As Jaspers notes in his biography:

> [He visited] on the occasion of a lecture that he—now rector of the University of Freiburg—gave for students and professors at Heidelberg. Scheel, chairman of the Heidelberg Student Organization, introduced him as "Comrade Heidegger," it was a masterly lecture as to form; as to content it was a program for the National Socialist renewal of the universities. He demanded a total transformation of the intellectual institutions. The majority of the professors still holding office would be unable to meet the new challenge. A new generation of able lecturers would be educated within ten years. We would then turn our duties over to them. Until that time we could be in a transitional phase. Heidegger expressed anger about many facets of university life, even about the high salaries. He was given a tremendous ovation by the students and by a few professors. I was sitting at one end of the first row, with my legs completely stretched out, my hands in my pockets; I did not budge.
>
> After that, for my part, conversations with him were guarded (*unoffen*). I told him that he was expected to stand up for the university and its great tradition. No answer. I referred to the problem of the Jews (Jüdenfragen) and the malicious nonsense about the sages of Zion.[72] He replied: "There really is a dangerous international fraternity of Jews." At the dinner-table he said, in a slightly angered tone, that it was foolish to have so many professors of philosophy; one should keep only two or three in the whole of Germany. "Which ones, then?" I inquired. No answer. "How shall a person as uneducated as Hitler rule Germany?" "Education," he replied, "does not matter. You should just see his wonderful hands![73]

Evidently, Heidegger saw in Hitler an authentic, "genuine" personality. He projected onto him his idea of "true education (*Bildung*)." Germany's most famous philosopher was fascinated by the convulsive speech, the anticapitalist attitude of the early Hitler, his logic that appeared cogent to many people, in which he simplified world history and Germany's destiny to the point of rendering them all but incomprehensible, and by his dichotomist worldview.

To return to May 1933, this is Jaspers's description of their meeting:

> Heidegger himself seemed to have changed. Already from the time of his arrival, a mood separated us. National Socialism had grown rampant among the populations. To extend my welcome, I visited Heidegger in his room upstairs. "It is like 1914 . . ." I began and wanted to continue by saying, "Again we have this treacherous mass-hysteria," but, as Heidegger was beaming in agreement with my first words, the rest of them stuck fast in my throat. This radical rupture [between us] gave me extraordinary concern. I had not experienced

the like with anybody else. It was all the more upsetting because Heidegger seemed completely unaware of it. Yet he revealed himself by never visiting me again after 1933 and by not writing when I was removed from office in 1937. But I heard still in 1935 that during a lecture he had spoken of his "friend Jaspers." I doubt whether he grasps even today the rupture in our relationship.[74]

This, then, was the end of the friendship between kindred spirits that had lasted thirteen years. It was destroyed by the circumstances and at the same time by what had not been spoken between them for many years. After 1933 they exchanged a number of their texts for a while but did not say whether or how they had read them. In 1937 simultaneous with Jaspers's removal from his position, the contact broke off completely.

However, in what followed, Heidegger did not let go of the conflict with Jaspers. He now publicly subjected him to a critique that he had not dared to express in personal interaction. In the Nietzsche lecture course in the winter semester 1936–37, Heidegger writes:

> Jaspers discerns that here we are in the presence of one of Nietzsche's decisive thoughts. In spite of the talk about Being, however, Jaspers does not bring the thought into the realm of the grounding question of Western philosophy and thereby also into actual connection with the doctrine of will to power. The reason for this not immediately obvious attitude is that, for Jaspers, to speak with utmost clarity, philosophy as such is impossible. Philosophy is essentially an "illusion" for the purpose of moral illumination of human personality. Philosophical concepts lack a force of truth, if not *the* force of truth of essential knowledge. Because in the final analysis, Jaspers does not take philosophical knowledge seriously, there is no real questioning any longer. Philosophy becomes a moralizing psychology of human existence. This is an attitude that, despite all efforts, denies him the capacity to penetrate in a questioning and critical way into Nietzsche's philosophy.[75]

An annihilating judgment! Jaspers, for his part, was constantly preoccupied with Heidegger up until the end of the 1930s. His notes sound as if he had been fighting with a demon. He noted in his short text "A Critique of Heidegger," composed in 1938:

> Content-wise, he stands entirely in the unconscious tradition of recent philos. Externally: the quotations in *Being and Time*—.
> The dedications to Rickert, Husserl, Scheler—
> Then the type: starting from scratch, true philos. begins now for the first time.
> 1. The latter was the enthusiastic reality of personality that emerged in the Renaissance philosophy;
> 2. It was style and sense in Descartes;
> 3. It became tragedy in Kant . . . ;

4. It became subsequent satire in Husserl;
5. It is nihilistic hubris in Heidegger.[76]

But is it really nihilistic hubris that Heidegger manifested? Both friends remained a mystery to the other. They would never again meet personally, but one would always be a presence for the other. After her reconciliation with Heidegger in 1950, Hannah Arendt will repeatedly try to bring the two together again—in vain.

In May 1933 the Reich's chancellery invited the board of university directors to a reception with Adolf Hitler. Evidently, new guidelines for university policy were to be announced there. In agreement with the rectors of other universities, the rector of Kiel University sent a telegram to the Reich Chancellor asking to postpone the date. The reason was that the association first needed to be organized. Furthermore, the present association of the board of directors did not yet enjoy the trust of the student body. The old conflict between the university as a place of professional training or intellectual pursuit was behind this.

Apparently Heidegger sent a similar telegram on May 20, 1933, to the Reich Chancellor in support of his colleagues.[77] He wrote about it after the war:

> My opposition to the University Association did not first date back to spring 1933. Because of the famous blue notebooks, I had for years agreed with K. Jaspers, my friends and students, that no inner transformation of the German university in the sense of a *universitas* emerging from a philosophical spirit could be achieved this way. The universities had become ever more influenced by "colleges," that is, the professional and vocational schools had increasingly become the priority. Technical education, technical administration, and questions of pay were top priorities. The "spiritual" was treated occasionally, only "in addition." Furthermore, I saw since the Frankfurt meeting in the spring of 1933 . . . that even the "old party comrades" among the university professors came mainly from technical colleges, medical, and law departments, and that the latter were, entirely consciously, pushing for professional universities, which then had to be politically oriented in accordance with the Party and its worldview.[78]

With his like-minded colleagues (the Kiel rector Wolf, the Göttinger rector Neumann, and the Frankfurt rector Krieck), he wanted to avoid this tendency. With his colleagues, he basically opposed Alfred Rosenberg and Ernst Baeumler.[79] He wanted to pit the position of the Ministry, which was closer to his idea, against that of the party ideologists, but did not succeed.

> When I speak in the telegram of coordination (*Gleichschaltung*), I meant it in the sense in which I also understand the name "National Socialism." It was never my intention to deliver the university over to the party doctrine; on the

contrary, it was to attempt to initiate a spiritual change *within* National Socialism and in relation to it. It is not true to the facts to claim that National Socialism and the Party had no spiritual goals with regard to the university and the concept of science. They only had to *decide* on it and drew on Nietzsche, according to whose doctrine, truth did not in itself have its own foundation and objective content, but was rather only a means of the will to power, that is, a mere "idea," that is, a subjective representation. And the grotesque thing was and is that this "political concept of science" in principle agrees with the doctrine of "ideas and ideology" of Marxism and Communism.[80]

He was thus negotiating not for the sake of a clear separation between the old University Association and the National Socialist Party, but for the sake of the opposition between—in today's terms—the concept of professional colleges, an idea supported by many National Socialist strategists already at that time, and a program of university reform in the sense of *universitas*, a university for the education of the best.[81] However, in the following years, the NS-leadership strengthened colleges rather than universities. Only a few, including Heidegger, saw then that "this recognition of the sciences was guided by the intention to expand and exploit the professional achievement and expertise of science."[82] Since the 1930s, he had been writing against the erosion of the sciences and their reduction to technical understanding. The party ideologists had understood this very well and turned against him. Was the telegram, then, an act of resistance?

Heidegger was not defending a general idea of the university; he simply wanted to implement *his* idea of the university. In retrospect, he was in complete agreement—*post festum*—with his onetime friend Jaspers, whose name is invoked in a quite calculative manner. Heidegger knew that Jaspers was well regarded at the university after 1945, and he played the Jaspers card.

Heidegger's argument in fact strengthens the thesis that for him this was the continuation of an already existing project and not a completely new beginning with National Socialism. He wanted to use the new regime to advocate for a position he had been championing for years. Already in the 1920s, this position implied a *coup de force* against the members of the university who opposed such reforms.[83]

Heidegger and His Colleagues

As for the treatment of Jewish university professors, Heidegger did not oppose the "law to reorganize civil service," and therefore he did not oppose their removal; he shared this stance with most German university faculty. Yet he repeatedly attempted to help his students as well as his esteemed colleagues, such as Eduard Fraenkel and Georg von Hevesy.[84] He supported his assistant Brock, who was fired in April 1933, by writing a recommendation when he sought a position in England.[85] He helped his students Helene Weiß and Elisabeth Blochmann, the latter a friend of his wife who had also been friends with him since the 1920s.[86] He recommended that his student Paul Oskar Kristeller continue his habilitation with his Basel colleague Paul Häberlin.[87]

Under pressure from the publisher during the National Socialist rule, he removed the dedication in *Being and Time* to his fatherly friend and patron Edmund Husserl, but left the footnote dedicated to Husserl in section 7.

A 1945 report of the University Purification Committee on Heidegger's behavior during National Socialism read: "Certain of his actions are to be understood as stemming largely from concern, particularly as regards his behavior towards Jews." He was not a strict anti-Semite, he defended Jewish professors during his rectorship, and, furthermore, he had contact with some Jewish friends. "However, he held his distance with regard to many other Jews, apparently because he feared inconveniences for himself and his position."[88]

In December 1933 Heidegger wrote a recommendation for the young scholar Dr. Eduard Baumgarten, whom he knew well. Apparently, this was a response to a request by the NS Union of University Faculty; he was to judge the scholarly expertise as well as the National Socialist aptitude of the younger colleague. He first described his personal impression of Baumgarten. He characterized him as unsuitable for a university career under National Socialism both academically and in terms of character. For this reason, he had refused to direct his habilitation in 1932 and had broken off contact with him. He then described Baumgarten's background. According to Heidegger, he came from the "liberal Democratic Heidelberg circle around Max Weber." He was surprised that Baumgarten had been able to complete his habilitation work on American pragmatism in Göttingen even though he had rejected him, and offered a reason for this: "After Baumgarten had failed with me, he very actively mixed with the Jew Fränkel, who had previously been active in Göttingen and is now dismissed from there. I suppose that in this way Baumgarten succeeded in being accepted in Göttingen. . . . I currently judge his integration into the SA to be *just as impossible* as his integration into the University faculty." Direct and indirect judgments followed: "In any event, in the realm of philosophy, I consider him a fraud without basic and solid knowledge. . . . Because of his stay in America, during which he became noticeably Americanized in his behavior and way of thinking, he undoubtedly acquired good knowledge of the country and the people." The concluding political evaluation was: "but I have serious reasons to doubt the rectitude of his instincts and his capacity for political judgment." And then almost a retraction: "in the final analysis, it is always possible that Baumgarten would fundamentally change and settle down. But for this purpose is required a more serious. . . ." Here the transcript breaks off, with the supposition of the transcribing secretary that the next word was "probation." The concluding sentence is not in the transcript.[89]

This recommendation was composed in a formal, customary manner: first one described his personal relationship with the person in question, then weighed arguments for and against the candidate, and finally proposed a course of action. Apparently this kind of activity was one of Heidegger's duties in the context of the National Socialist purification of the universities.

One notices that Heidegger lists belonging to Max Weber's circle, to which Jaspers had also belonged, as a point against him.

The formulation of the recommendation was ambivalent, yet it was clearly meant to be negative. The concluding suggestion for a probationary period would not have been taken seriously, since prior to it Heidegger gives the decisive arguments, which—from the National Socialist perspective—spoke against Baumgarten's promotion: severe "deficits" in expertise and character, previous promotion by a Jew, American experience (apparently synonymous with political unreliability), weak sense of National Socialism, questionable capacity for change.

Years later, when the University of Freiburg formed a "Purification Committee" to investigate the National Socialist involvement of its members (from university teachers to concierges), the director of the committee, von Dietze, sent the text of the recommendation for Baumgarten, discovered only belatedly, to his colleague Gerhard Ritter, a man completely sympathetic toward Heidegger. It had a note: "the present text in its entirety became known to me only a few days ago. In January 1946, the Committee had only Jaspers' letter that contained excerpts from Heidegger's letter from January 16, 1933."[90]

Jaspers's letter from January 1945, in which he judged Heidegger's role in National Socialism, was based on another transcript of the Heideggerian recommendation and he cited it with a different conclusion: "the judgment about Baumgarten certainly cannot yet be final. He could still develop himself. But one must wait until the probation is over before he can be integrated into a division of the National Socialist Party."[91] The difference between the two texts led Heidegger, in 1946, to write his own version of the facts and to declare the version cited in Jaspers's letter as false.[92]

The Rectorship

We should not be deceived by the high tone that Heidegger set as rector. His rectorship was not "a happy time." As one of the later evaluative reports of the Purification Committee said, his rectorship brought about an "unusually agitated time" for the University of Freiburg.[93] Heidegger interfered in the life of the university in a brusque manner, making enemies in all departments. Clearly he was serious about changing the entire way of doing things at the university. In the face of resistance from senior professors, he sought new allies among young assistants, faculty, and students. His appeal to the Freiburg student body at the opening of winter semester 1933–34 was charged with the pathos of a revival, as though Heidegger was in a state of extreme intellectual agitation:

German Students

The National Socialist revolution is bringing about the total transformation of our German existence [Dasein].

In these events, it is up to you to remain those who always urge on and who are always ready, those who never yield and who always grow.

Your will to know seeks to experience what is essential, simple, and great.

You crave to be exposed to that which besets you most directly and to that which imposes upon you the most wide-ranging obligations.

Be hard and genuine in your demands.

Remain steadfast and sure in your rejection.

Do not pervert the knowledge you have struggled for into a vain, selfish possession. Preserve it as the necessary primal possession of the leaders in the national professions of the State. . . . You can no longer be those who merely listen to lectures. You are obligated to know and act together in the creation of the future university of the German spirit. Every one of you must first prove and justify each talent and privilege. That will occur through the force of your aggressive involvement in the arena of the struggle of the entire people on its own behalf.

Let your loyalty and your willingness to be led be daily and hourly strengthened. Let your courage ceaselessly grow so that you will be able to make the sacrifices necessary to save the essence and to heighten the inner strength of our people in their State.

Let not propositions and "ideas" be the rules of your Being (*Sein*).

The Führer alone is the present and future German reality and its law. Learn to know ever more deeply: from now on every single thing demands decision, and every action responsibility.

Heil Hitler!

Martin Heidegger, Rector[94]

No one who has doubts about himself or the state of affairs speaks like this. But one questions again the image Heidegger had of National Socialism. Looking at the military, rough demeanor of the SA leaders in public, one wonders about the sophisticated, indeed classicist, tone of Heidegger's written statements. Presumably he was acting in accordance with a positive fiction of National Socialism that he superimposed on the reality of the SA leaders with their boots and uniforms and their markedly proletariat manner. However, this is only partially accurate, insofar as Heidegger was no idealist, as subsequent history shows. He was also fascinated by the antitraditionalist aspect of National Socialism. He had long wanted to declare war on the traditions at the university, traditions against which the NSDP also turned.

Unfortunately, there are few direct reports about Heidegger's rectorship. We are limited to testimonies written in retrospect. We must keep in mind shifts of emphasis affected by temporal distance. In 1945 the president of the Purification Committee, Constantin von Dietze, writes:

> He fought, without allowing for a discussion, against the "reactionary" views opposing his own and sought support from young professors, assistants, and students. Some of his declarations had the effect of direct instigations. The repeated instructions that Herr Heidegger meted out to the professors, for instance about the length of lectures and the conduct in the office, were understandably seen as signs of arrogance. In December 1933, the rector sent a note to the professors in the department of law and political science, with whom the tensions were particularly strong, in which he strongly advised them to adopt a different attitude. He stated that, in the future, the recommendation of colleagues would depend on the personal assessment of Herr Heidegger. Such a declaration—the text is no longer available—must have been understood by the younger professors or doctoral students as a threat to their future.[95]

Dietze argued that Heidegger violated the university statutes, for instance, by co-opting students into the university senate: "His solicitation of the young professors, assistants, and students went so far that it was seen as incitement against the older professors."[96] The Purification Committee also reproached Heidegger for collaborating on changing the university constitution by seeking to assign a larger role for the rector. Worse, he was above all in favor of the Ministry appointing university rectors as well as for the right of the rectors to name "professors without chairs to be faculty members."[97]

From this perspective, the resignation from the rectorship once again appears in a somewhat different light. It was not, as Heidegger later emphasized, only the swift disillusionment as regards the National Socialists and their banal praxis that led him to leave the office. Heidegger must have become aware that entire groups at the university were against him and that he would not be able to persevere for long at any rate.

In 1933 young Professor Karl Löwith visited Heidegger in his office. His report on Rector Heidegger stems from 1940:

> When I called on him in his Rector's office in 1933, he was sitting there forlorn, morose and ill at ease in the large elegant room, and one sensed his discomfort in his commands and movements. He himself further provoked this distance by his unconventional dress. He wore a kind of Black Forest farmer's jacket

with broad lapels and semi-militaristic collar, and knee length breeches, both from dark-brown cloth—an "authentic" style of dress, which was supposed to antagonize the "they" and amused us then, but at that time we did not recognize it as a peculiar temporary compromise between the conventional suit and the SA uniform. The brown color of the cloth went well with his jet-black hair and his dark complexion.[98]

Heidegger had worn this style of clothing since the 1920s. He wanted thereby to set himself apart from others. The change in men's clothing, modeled after traditional dress, was part of the reform of lifestyle in the 1920s. By the 1930s, however, traditional wear was out of fashion, a sign of the swift transitions between the culture of the 1920s and the anticulture of the 1930s. Thus, Löwith's bitter memoir needs to be read with a grain of salt.

Everywhere in Baden—in Freiburg, as well—the restructuring of the universities through their coordination with National Socialism was linked to the destruction of university autonomy. Colleagues not convinced by National Socialism were sickened by the fact that Heidegger generally had no reservations about the coordination. It must have been painful for the entire university, particularly given that a large majority had wanted him as rector. After the defeat of National Socialism, it also explains why they let him endure a six-year process of purification, marked by real difficulties between occupation authorities, the Ministry, and university committees—the conciliatory tone of the correspondence notwithstanding. They neither would nor could spare him the shame of a public trial.

The Withdrawal Begins

According to his own admission, Heidegger decided to step down from the rectorship at the beginning of 1934.[99] In the 1945 report, the reason he gave—aside from the frustration of disappointed expectations—was the fact that he had to fire two deans (including his predecessor von Möllendorf). But, in fact, he left the office in April 1934, shortly before the beginning of the summer semester. According to Heidegger, this was because it took the Ministry so long to find a suitable successor.

During this time he held lectures and seminars. In winter semester 1933–34, he offered a seminar on "The Essence and Concept of Nature, History and the State." In summer semester 1934 he offered "Hegel: On the State."

In the years that followed, he worked on timeless themes: logic; Kant: *Critique of Pure Reason* (summer semester 1934); Hölderlin; Hegel's *Phenomenology of Spirit* (winter semester 1934–35); Introduction to Metaphysics; Hegel on the State (summer semester 1935); Basic Problems of Metaphysics; Leibniz's Concept of the World (winter semester 1935–36); Schelling: *On the Essence of Human Freedom*; Kant: Critique of the Power of Judgment (summer semester 1936); Nietzsche: *Will to Power* (winter semester 1936–37); Schiller's philosophical writings on art (winter semester 1936–37); Nietzsche's foundation in Western thought and Schiller's philosophical writings on art (summer semester 1937).

During the war, the titles of his lectures did not become more ideological; indeed, one gets the impression that he had completely turned away from modernity, devoting himself to antiquity and working on fundamental concepts of philosophy.

In the meantime, the university curriculum had become more regimented, a result of Heidegger's efforts and National Socialist university politics. Courses were now divided into intermediate and higher levels, in addition to the already common divisions of lecture, practicum, and professional or advanced seminars. During their studies students had to attend military sports and work camps, activities that Heidegger had championed as an integral component of university education.

The list of Heidegger's students in these years again reads like a who's who of the next generation of academic and political intelligentsia: Werner Marx, Walter Schulz, Jan Patocka, Ludwig Thoma, Jeanne Hersch, Walter Bröcker, Adolf Kopling, Hans Filbinger, Georg Picht, Ernst Schütte, Karl Rahner, Gerhard Ritter, Karl Ulmer, Friedrich Tenbruck, Hermann Heidegger, Margharita von Brentano, Walter Biemel, Ernst Nolte.[100]

Official academic trips were very unusual during National Socialism; they were not part of the rights of university professors. Decisions were based on who was traveling and for what purpose, and whether some propagandist success could result. When evaluating trips, the appropriate Ministry and party leaders placed the highest value on propaganda. The "foreign world" played an almost magical role in the German Reich that was increasingly cut off from the outside world. Thus, if a German university professor was invited by a foreign institution, he traveled *not* just as a representative of his discipline and his university but as a representative of National Socialist Germany. The trips were charged with symbolism. A professor was required to verify the diplomatic opportunities and needed to follow up with comments about them. Whoever obtained the permission of his university and the green light from the Nazi Party and the Ministry of Foreign Affairs did not have to pay high traveling fees, which increased when traveling abroad.

Heidegger made several trips to lecture, but he also declined some invitations. In April 1936 he traveled to Rome and gave a lecture at the Istituto Italiano di

Studi Germanici entitled, "Hölderlin and the Essence of Poetry." His sojourn in Italy lasted for more than two weeks, during which time he and his family—his wife, Elfriede, and his sons—went on all kinds of excursions and he refreshed his knowledge of ancient Rome. He met with Karl Löwith and his wife. At this meeting Löwith surely hoped that Heidegger had distanced himself from National Socialism. Perhaps Löwith expected some word on what the next step might be, since he (Löwith) was in a precarious situation. Since the 1934 summer semester he had been relieved of his professorship, a professorship he had obtained with Heidegger's help. Löwith fell under the race paragraph, but not under the "law to reorganize public service," since he was not an official (*Beamter*). Initially he had gone to Rome with the support of the Rockefeller Foundation and lived there with his wife in poor conditions, frequently changing apartments. He maintained his connections with his alma mater in Marburg for a time. A legal loophole allowed the dean of his department to support him financially to a very modest degree. It is clear from his correspondence with the dean's office in the philosophy department that until March 1, 1936, with some interruptions, Löwith's stay in Rome was supported in part by financial aid from the University of Marburg and that he could therefore count on the powerful support of Dean Walter Mitzka, against all resistance from the university chancellor and the Ministry.[101] Then the connection abruptly broke off. On February 14, 1936, the Ministry of Culture and Education announced the withdrawal of Löwith's right to teach. Even the dean's mention of the serious war wounds that Löwith received during the First World War no longer helped.[102] Heidegger either knew all this or Löwith had told it to him, for after Löwith's habilitation, Heidegger had emphatically advocated for a paid position for him as an assistant professor.

The meeting with Löwith and his wife in Rome, however, was a catastrophe. Löwith's bitter rejection of Heidegger was confirmed: Heidegger promenaded around Rome with his party badge, maintaining no distance at all from National Socialism.[103]

After this disappointing meeting, Löwith drew a line through his relationship with Heidegger. His biography, *My Life in Germany before and after 1933*, as well as his critical text on Heidegger,[104] attests to the difficulty of this break.

For many intellectuals who had joined the ranks of National Socialism in 1933 with high expectations there was always one particular moment when enthusiasm no longer carried them and disillusionment began, when the truth of reality could no longer be suppressed. This moment occurred when one became aware that terror had assumed an independent existence and friends as well as acquaintances were its victims. Or it was the moment when one suddenly became aware of the banality of National Socialist politics. Some of those affected by this moment reacted by withdrawing from the evil.

Heidegger reacted in two ways: he withdrew and he fell silent. At times he expressed himself cryptically and left his listeners unclear about his actual meaning.

For instance, in his memoir, Heinrich Schlier reports on the following event from the year 1934:

> [Heidegger] was invited to his friend Bultmann. We spent the evening talking of all sorts of things but, of course, especially about the so-called "Third Reich." Heidegger was pressed very hard because of his conduct in 1933. He then turned to me as he was leaving and said cautiously: "Herr S., we have not yet seen the end of the matter." I understood well what he meant. But had he clearly said: "I was mistaken," we would certainly have thrown our arms around him.[105]

Heidegger's hidden dissatisfaction also showed during these years in his correspondence with the dean's office, the rector's office, and the Reich Ministry of Culture and Education.

In 1936 Heidegger received an invitation to Paris for the three hundredth birthday of Descartes that would take place in 1937. It was not just any congress, but rather an extremely important event in National Socialism's struggle for international recognition. Almost all the German academic exiles lived in Paris. These exiles were waiting for the opportunity to publicly criticize representatives of National Socialist Germany. They intended to turn the congress into a stage for the encounter between fascism and democracy. Heidegger foresaw this and wanted to plan the appearance of the delegation from Nazi Germany strategically.

Instead his invitation was left hanging in the parallel bureaucratic channels of the Ministry of Education, the NSDAP, and the Foreign Ministry. In any event, it took a year before Heidegger received any news on the matter. On June 14, 1937, he told his rector that he thought the entire affair was impossible.[106] For this reason he did not tell him of the many repeated invitations to attend the event. Under these circumstances, a mere one and a half months before the congress, he was not willing to join a delegation whose composition and direction were unknown to him. A month later, on July 17, 1937, the minister told the rector that he would very much welcome Heidegger's participation in particular at this congress. He named him as a member of the official delegation and promised him travel financial assistance of 200 Reichsmarks.

Heidegger withdrew from the affair elegantly and yet firmly. On July 24, 1937, he wrote to the minister that he considered it his duty to participate in the congress, since the minister wished it, but, unfortunately, he was not able to do so for health reasons. A medical note was attached. He added that "he was always available for the wishes of Herr Reich Minister."[107]

Karl Jaspers was allowed to publish an essay in *Revue Philosophique* on the occasion of Descartes's birthday, but he was not permitted to participate in the Paris congress. It was the year of his removal from the university. On June 25 of the same year, the minister told him that he was "retired according to §6 of the law of the reorganization of public service from April 7, 1933."[108] Two months later his professor's (*Ordinarius*) salary was suspended. The rector's office and Jaspers himself tried to transform the dismissal into a discharge owing to health reasons. This would have entailed a higher retirement pay and, in addition, would have been a more honorable departure from the university. All in vain. Three years earlier he had refused to sign a loyalty oath to Adolf Hitler. In the same year, 1937, Jaspers went to Geneva to give a lecture. In 1941 he was no longer allowed to travel. The invitation from Basel University to teach there for two years, endorsed by Heidegger's archenemy Ernst Krieck, who was rector in Heidelberg at the time, was rejected by the Ministry. Apparently they did not want Jaspers to leave, expecting that he would emigrate with his Jewish wife.

In 1942 Heidegger declined a second planned trip to Rome. He explained:

> That I, during the upcoming Winter Semester, when the soldiers leaving the front come to study again, could neither interrupt my teaching activity for a long time nor compromise it. . . . With regard to the longer duration of the war, the studies of returning soldiers attain a greater significance over simply teaching. It no longer suffices to attend to these students separately and also alongside others. These students must, for the time being, be recognized as the core of the audience and everything that exceeds mere instruction in teaching must be tailored to their needs.[109]

He thus asked to dedicate himself fully to this work. At some later point he would gladly give lectures, but the latter required *proper* preparation, since the translation of his texts was extremely difficult. Again an act of insubordination, but finely presented. Heidegger was angry that he had difficulties with the publication of his texts. The reference to "returning soldiers" was clear: it pointed to his service for his fatherland. In return, he expected due respect or rather appreciation, which had to be expressed in the form of paper allotted to his publisher.

In 1943 he declined a trip to Spain and Portugal for similar reasons. Apparently, he did not want to accept travel abroad as compensation for the refusal of more paper. At this time he had already fought several battles with National Socialism. We turn now to one of the most decisive battles.

Heidegger also had enemies within the National Socialist Association of Professors. Ernst Krieck was among them. Both shared a genuine aversion toward the other. The eighth 1938 issue of *Meyers Konversations-Lexikon* published an article about Heidegger, an article in which the tone was not far from that of National

Socialist hate propaganda against Jewish thinkers. The author argued that Heidegger's philosophy in *Being and Time* was "an image of what Nietzsche meant by 'nihilism' and 'decadence'; it fascinated the individual before 1933 because he believed to have found in it an intellectual and mystical explanation for his own inner and exterior hopelessness."[110]

Here Heidegger became the object of a critique that he himself used against others. Since the beginning of the thirties, he had introduced similar arguments as a way of distancing himself from his Jewish colleagues or "Jewish thinking."

Heidegger needed years to recover from his downfall. He began dedicating himself to poetic thought and poetic language inspired by his reading of Friedrich Hölderlin. The excitement of the 1920s and early 1930s, the underlying search for the magical passage from thinking into praxis, from contemplative thinking to applied thinking, now shifted to the entry of thinking into the house of language. "Poetically Man Dwells . . . ," Heidegger placed this Hölderlin poem at the center of his turn away from politics and power. Poetic thinking was not action. Since the 1920s, he had worked with a thinking that was also an acting. Now there emerged a concept of "letting be" (*Gelassenheit*) in his thinking, something he had not permitted until this point.

Heidegger took the step toward the poetic in the mid-thirties on the basis of his critique of the potential nihilism in Nietzsche's philosophy. It had to do with what he repeatedly said to his enemies after 1945: he had, in thinking, freed himself from the trap into which he had fallen while seeking the path from thinking to action. Hannah Arendt would later introduce this metaphor when she told the fable about the fox who got caught in its own trap.

The Heidegger of the 1920s saw the break from philosophy into revolutionary action as necessarily prescribed. He shared the view of an entire generation who returned home from the First World War disappointed and frustrated; they regarded the mission for which they had been mobilized as incomplete, not yet achieved. This "front generation," as Hannah Arendt called it in *Origins of Totalitarianism*, felt itself responsible for saving Germany and Europe from the quagmire of obsolete tradition and soulless modernity.

Like Heidegger, those who had lived from childhood with the conviction that Germany and the West were in a profound crisis—and those were not few among the intellectuals—must have seen the weaknesses of the Weimar Republic as a sign of a much greater underlying crisis. Whoever thought as he did that the crisis could be solved was attracted to those who promised to resolve it.

Of course, it was possible to choose communism as the "solution." Many people in his generation made this leap. In the twenties, the Hungarian philosopher Georg Lukács, only four years older than Heidegger and an esteemed student of Rickert's and Weber's in Heidelberg, undertook a renewal of philosophy vis-à-vis the metaphysical foundation of Marxist thought. He had resolved to do this already at the end of World War I.[111] His friend Ernst Bloch approached a philosophy of action starting from the Marxist-messianic point of view.

The fact that Heidegger did not succumb to the attraction of the communist promise of salvation can be explained by the traditional fear of communists of his immediate and remote homeland and by the heritage of Catholicism, to which he was still connected. But he was susceptible to that mixture of radicalness and patriotism, populism and belief in salvation, which the National Socialist leaders offered in the first years. This language spoke to him. However, this, too, does not entirely explain why he became so completely involved. His brother Fritz came from the same tradition of Meßkirch Catholicism, and yet he never succumbed to the promise of National Socialism. The philosophical thinking, which he was well capable of following (he transcribed many of his brother's manuscripts), did not override his healthy common sense.[112]

Thus it was not just the generational pull and the culture of his homeland that led Heidegger to offer himself to the National Socialists and somehow see in their ideology something with which one could work. Moreover, Heidegger did not decide on National Socialism because its Führer promised him concrete opportunities for action. He thought—like many intellectuals of the time—that National Socialists *must* offer him possibilities for influence since he possessed the correct grasp of the situation.

There must have been a fortuitous moment in the leap. It was the moment when Heidegger felt that he *must* leap from thinking into action. There are moments in the history of political action when *virtù* and *fortuna*, the capacity for action and the situation that confronts those who act, come together. When this happens, it is called the historical event. Niccolò Machiavelli, at the end of the fifteenth century, considered these two moments together; he saw the spark of successful political action emerge from their friction. But this moment is not infallible. One could err, and come to see only after the fact that one had misjudged the situation.

Satisfactory explanations for the "Heidegger phenomenon" are not possible without taking the element of contingency into account.

His thinking was marked by a profound unrest and the possibility of the aleatory inherent in it. This unrest leads us to the elements in his thinking that drove Heidegger to this unique moment of the "leap," the moment wherein he could decide correctly, or not.

We must keep in mind this unrest with regard to people in general, to women, to his lover Hannah, and in this context also mention the peculiar *furor teutonicus* in his judgment. With Heidegger, thinking emerged out of intellectual agitation. In his philosophical soliloquies, Heidegger time and again circled the abolition of the separation between nature and intellect, body and mind. The agitation emerged when questioning thought exposed itself to being, when it did not think of *something*, but opened itself up to the flow of thinking. Evidently, Heidegger experienced this movement of thinking physically, as well. Two things thus came out of this agitation: ecstatic thinking and openness toward erotic experiences. When the two converged, trouble was not far off.

Already during the 1920s, he experienced states of agitation. They were kindled—this becomes clear in the correspondence with his friend Karl Jaspers—by the most diverse situations: the miserable state of universities, the handling of his own career path, the reflection over Germany and contemporary philosophy—and by women. This agitation increased in the face of the National Socialist movement that swept everything along with it, the youth and women's movements, students and professors, intellectuals and middle-class citizens, public and private thinking—until it overflowed and reached a climax. The telegram to Hitler is indicative of Heidegger's confrontational engagement with the university during the short time of his rectorship.

Being and Time was therefore not an intellectual preparation for the fall but rather the text of a thinking that put its author under so much pressure in the tension between cultural critique and systematic thinking that he felt compelled to turn to action. Through action, the actual world of experience had to be abolished, to be replaced by a world whose framework he had laid out in its analysis of authentic Dasein.

In retrospect, one could say that Heidegger wanted to prepare an atheological ethics of Dasein in *Being and Time*. Such a gesture harbored the possibility of a transition to an ideology. If this ethics was to become effective, it had to be accomplished against the resistance of the "they," of the with-world and its thoughtlessness. He saw the chance to make a transition from the possibility of authentic Dasein to its actuality. For this transference he needed the medium of applied philosophy, which he would criticize after the war in "The Letter on Humanism." He clearly thought that his fundamental ontology could result in a collective education for true Dasein. *Being and Time* offered neither fascist nor nationalist ideology, but rather a unique mixture of the systematic exposition of the question of Being and the attempt to extend it to the requirements of Dasein's ethics, without touching on the question of actualization. The question of *why* Heidegger made the leap from pure thinking to National Socialism cannot be reduced to a simple cause-effect relation. Explanations such as "since Heidegger wrote *Being and Time* in this way and not in some other way, he had to turn to the Nazis," or "Heidegger's involvement with National Socialism can only be understood after years of philosophical preparation" mean precious little. Heidegger's commitment to National Socialism lay in the realm of the possible, not of the necessary. The longing for a practical revolution was a temptation for an entire generation, demonstrated once again by Georg Lukács, Ernst Bloch, and a generation of intellectuals of bourgeois background who converted to communism, as well as Carl Schmitt, Gottfried Benn, and others, who followed National Socialism for a short period of intoxication.

Certainly, there was a series of "favorable" preconditions: Heidegger's inclination to understand a general cultural critique as a critique of loss from which the West was suffering. They also involved his rejection of modern mass democracy and the republic as inauthentic forms of German existence, the swift linking of traditional culture and national ideology, and, fueled by Teutonic fire, his scorn for all compromises in thinking and of liberalism, as well as his dream of a collective Dasein.

When he became aware of his mistake, it was already too late. He had made himself look ridiculous. How shameful must have been the moment after the end of the intoxication, when the awakening took place. Still, he believed for a while that the higher echelons of the regime were more open to his ideas than those in the lower levels. He did not come to this critical understanding of National Socialism through his own common sense. It took him a long time to understand that power was in the hands of evil. That he saw only later.

However, he never came to a political critique of National Socialism; such a critique was foreign to him. After all, he always thought nationally and accepted it as self-evident that National Socialists were nationalists. He did not see as acutely as he perhaps should have that they were racists. After 1934 Heidegger tried to get out of the impasse into which he had maneuvered himself. His preference now was to work on the themes that fell under the general notion of a "critique of modernity." Some of these include contemporary science and technology, the culture industry, de-mythologization, and nihilism.[113]

Beginning in winter semester 1936–37, Heidegger worked for three years on Nietzsche's philosophy of power and his over-turning of the Western philosophical tradition. Altogether he prepared four lecture courses on Nietzsche between 1936 and 1940.[114] We owe his detailed critique of Nietzsche to these lectures, where we see, among other things, his increasing distance from National Socialism. He now saw National Socialism as the rule of soulless technology, coupled with an irrepressible will to power. He saw the special connection between technology and absolute rule as a particularly modern phenomenon, one that had conquered the human being. And, he saw the coordination, uniformity and bureaucratization, practiced by National Socialism, taken up in the wider context of modern technology.[115] Silvio Vietta argues that in National Socialism, Heidegger "realized for the first time the aggression of modern technology and of modern rational thinking."[116]

Nihilism was for Heidegger "the basic movement of Western history,"[117] embodied in Nietzsche's thought of the Übermensch and power. Now Heidegger also recognized the self-assertion of power in this thinking oriented toward action.[118]

Heidegger's essay "Nietzsche's Word 'God Is Dead'" (1943), which emerged from the 1936–40 Nietzsche lecture courses, culminates in the insight: "Thinking does not begin until we have come to know that reason, glorified for centuries, is the most obstinate adversary of thinking."[119] This insight reflects the critique of modernity made by the critical philosophies of the twentieth century. We can establish ties between Heidegger's insights and Theodor W. Adorno's and Max Horkheimer's thought, as well as Hannah Arendt's critique of modernity. They were all aware that the Enlightenment brought with it not only progress but also the potential for self-destruction.

Therefore, Heidegger's *turn* (*Kehre*) was a philosophical not political turn. In turning away from power, he also abandoned the absolute will to change. This was the utmost point of criticism he could think of.

Hannah Arendt: Propelled into Politics

While Heidegger withdrew from politics, Arendt was violently drawn into it. Later, she used the figure of the pariah to describe the situation into which she had been thrown with the rise of National Socialism. The pariah is the excluded figure who fights for his or her self-understanding and finds it through the commitment to being an outsider. In the figure of Rahel Varnhagen, she describes Jews as torn between the desire for recognition and their experience that they would never belong "to society." She supplemented the book, which she had written primarily in Berlin, with two chapters written in Parisian exile, in which she led her figure to the voluntary decision to be an outsider. This interpretation was a bit far from the historical figure of Rahel Varnhagen, but it revealed the many inner tensions of its author. From the personal context of exile, Arendt's book on Rahel Varnhagen appears in retrospect as a precursor to her own existence as a fugitive, as a pariah, one who draws her new consciousness from being an outsider. This subject occupied Arendt time and again in the 1940s.

In one of the two concluding Parisian chapters, Arendt writes about the tensions between the dimensions of the pariah and the parvenu in Rahel's self-understanding:

> This longing to be grateful [earlier Arendt describes this quality as belonging to the Pariah and suggests that Rahel's self-reproach regarding the most benign gestures of friendliness is indicative of this gratitude—author's note] would only be a fault if it were not accompanied by another trait equally characteristic of the pariah: what Rahel called 'too much consideration for a human

face. I rather can hurt my own heart than hurt someone else's and watch his vulnerability.' This sensitivity is a morbid, exaggerated understanding of the dignity of every human being, a passionate comprehension unknown to the privileged. It is this passionate empathy which constitutes the humaneness of the pariah. In a society based upon privilege, pride of birth and arrogance of title, the pariah instinctively discovers human dignity in general long before Reason has made it the foundation of morality.[120]

In the 1940s, Arendt took up this figure of the pariah as a way of describing the refugee's existence. At the same time, by choosing the extreme point of view of the outcast, she made clear that refugees were not defined by their existence as refugees. They were neither hunted animals nor objects of pity. Insofar as they suffer with others, they retain a dignity inaccessible to the parvenu who is obsessed with appearing as part of the society at any price.

This view from the perspective of the millions of persons who were stateless, persecuted and fleeing was fundamentally different from the approach to the refugee problem taken by political and relief organization of that time.

The insights into political reality that Hannah gained in the last months of 1932, the experiences that she had up until her flight from National Socialist Germany, pushed her into practical work. If it was right that one "had to defend oneself as a Jew," then it was only logical to help with the organizations that provided practical help.

When she arrived in Paris, the French political landscape was shaped by the Left; the country was considered the democratic bastion of Europe. In the Spanish civil war (1936–39), France took the side of the republicans. After the victory of General Franco, France accepted tens of thousands of Spanish refugees. France's reputation as having an open refugee policy made it a destination for refugees not only from Germany, but later also those fleeing from Middle or Eastern Europe. Because of this the French republic found itself in an unstable situation. The precarious situation of these refugees became very clear in 1937 with the collapse of the Popular Front under Léon Blum. Anti-Semitism, which had been rekindled time and again since the 1894 Dreyfus Affair, found increasing support from powerful social and political groups—including the Catholic Church. This change was felt in a particularly drastic form when, in the summer of 1939, the French government declared war on National Socialist Germany and for the first time interned a large number of refugees as "hostile foreigners."

After Arendt's arrival in Paris, she was immediately faced with pressing practical issues: documents (in 1937 she was expatriated from Germany and of course did not obtain French citizenship), money to live on, an apartment, food, clothes, and so on. She was continuously searching for lost or new friends, books, vital contacts, and long-term prospects of residence and work. The psychological and cultural dimension of exile manifested itself in the constant questioning of one's own identity on the basis of a precarious legal status, a foreign language, lack of everyday normalcy, worry about friends and family members, and feelings of anxiety and depression. It took a huge toll mentally and physically. Presumably Arendt did not often show her exhaustion; she was an energetic person who upon arrival in France immediately looked for possibilities to earn money and who also helped others searching for work.

She took Hebrew classes from a new friend, Chanan Klenbort, a Polish Jew and intellectual, who, like Arendt and thousands of other refugees, was constantly looking for a job and money to survive. "I want to know my people," she replied when asked why she wanted to learn the language.[121]

At first Arendt lived in Paris with her husband, Günther Stern, who had fled Germany in January 1933. What remained of this marriage was more a coexistence of necessity than a loving relationship. They had already separated in Berlin, but they managed to transform their relationship into a friendship. Their separation became public for the first time when Stern moved to New York in 1936. They maintained the appearance of marriage up until then, divorcing in 1937.

Arendt obtained her first position in 1934 at the Jewish organization, Agriculture and Artisanship (*Agriculture et Artisanat*), a relief organization for Jews (particularly German) who wanted to emigrate to Palestine. She had to demonstrate her office skills in order to get the position. Her job at Agriculture and Artisans was to organize clothing, education, documents, and medications for Jewish youth who came from Germany and Central European countries. She also prepared them for their emigration to Palestine. There, the young people were to help with the building of settlements, local industry, and the construction of roads.

Youth-Help was part of the Jewish activist movement that was introduced shortly after the 1933 "seizure of power" and after the dismantling of the Jewish bourgeoisie began.[122] The "Youth-Alijah," as the emigration of young people to Palestine was called, was founded in 1934 by Chaim Weizmann: "The idea of Youth-Alijah came from Recha Freier, the wife of a Berlin rabbi, who, already in 1932, had transferred a group of young people from Germany to Palestine for technical education. But in reality the fulfillment of the idea to transplant children and young people from the middle class milieu of Central Europe to Israel and to educate them for agricultural work lay in the hands of Palestine's collective settlements which declared themselves ready to host a two-year stay and the education of young emigrants from Germany."[123] Between 1934 and 1939, 4,635 young boys and girls, mostly from Germany and its neighboring countries, arrived in Palestine under the auspices of this organization that created for Jewish youth a bridge between Europe and Palestine.[124]

In 1935 Hannah Arendt accompanied one of her groups to Palestine; there she met the family of her cousin Ernst Fürst and traveled around the country. Presumably, she also saw again her old university friend Hans Jonas, who was there at the same time regarding Zionist matters.

During these years, Arendt developed a close connection with Salomon Adler-Rüdel. Robert Weltsch, the main editor of *Jüdische Rundschau*, wrote that Adler-Rüdel, who later called himself Scholem Adler-Rüdel, was "one of the most experienced and knowledgeable veterans of Jewish social work in Germany."[125] Adler-Rüdel, like Arendt, first fled to France in 1933 and then to London after England's entry into the war. There he worked as the "chief diplomat" of Jewish refugee relief. He traveled tirelessly to find suitable countries for refugees—above all, Switzerland, England, Denmark, Sweden, and, of course, the United States—and to negotiate refugee quotas. He was also involved in the refugee, as well as emigration, transfers to Palestine. In Paris Arendt regularly discussed with him the situation of the relief organizations in which she was actively involved.

Traveling as a Jewish refugee in the thirties and the beginning of the 1940s in European countries or the United States always meant having to engage with the Jewish political organizations in those countries as well as with their relationship with Palestine.

In the 1930s it was not yet clear whether the Zionist international movement would reach its goal, namely, the founding of a Jewish state in Palestine. In 1933 Arendt joined the World Zionist Organization. She participated in Zionist debates in Paris, Geneva, and other places. It is clear from the notes of her friend Lotte Köhler that in August 1933 she participated as a protocol taker in the Eighteenth Zionist Congress in Prague.[126] However, she soon came into conflict with Jewish politics.

Arendt wanted to accomplish real resistance work against National Socialism, for example, to organize a boycott against German goods. She was also working hard on behalf of international support for David Frankfurter, who had shot a National Socialist functionary in the Swiss town of Davos in 1936 and was now facing trial. She wanted to strengthen the resistance against the cooperation of European states with the National Socialists; however, she quickly confronted insurmountable obstacles.[127] Among other things, there were French Jews who feared anti-Semitism and xenophobia in their own country, causing many Jewish functionaries to reject out of hand any Jewish political engagement. Moreover, the French Jews were convinced that they were more cultivated than many uprooted refugees from Germany and Austria, not to mention the Eastern European countries. Here Arendt encountered firsthand the dilemma that she brought to the fore in her book on Rahel Varnhagen and later in *The Origins of Totalitarianism*: the self-disempowerment of the Jews.

Arendt experienced another kind of existential jolt in spring 1936 in the figure of Heinrich Blücher. The latter, once a Spartacus fighter in the communist circle, not a Jew, was also on the run. At that time Blücher had distanced himself from his communist past and did not belong to the group of exiled communists. As a man of many talents, he wrote cabaret texts in the twenties and was friends with the well-known songwriter Robert Gilbert with whom Arendt would later have a lifelong friendship. Blücher, born in 1899, came from a poor background. He passed the teacher's exam but did not work as a teacher; rather, he eked out a living as a freelance journalist and as an assistant in film and cabaret. Otherwise Blücher led the life of an exiled intellectual: constantly in search of identification documents, money, and intellectual exchange.

Despite her angry vow to never to set foot in academia again, Arendt diligently visited libraries in Paris and met significant European intellectuals of the time. She already knew Alexandre Kojève from Heidelberg; he had done his doctoral work with Jaspers. At that time, Kojève was already a recognized Hegel specialist, whose reading of Hegel she in time endorsed. Beginning in 1936 she regularly met with Walter Benjamin. He was a distant relative of Günther Stern and also exiled in Paris. She also met Alexandre Koyré who studied with Edmund Husserl and who introduced her to Jean Wahl in Paris. She did not want to become friends with Jean-Paul Sartre. She met Bertolt Brecht and Arnold Zweig. Brecht deeply impressed her; she would later devote an essay to him in her book *Men in Dark Times*. In Paris she also met again Anne Mendelssohn, her friend from Königsberg.

Hannah Arendt and Martin Heidegger could have met at the 1937 Descartes Congress in Paris, he as a representative of National Socialist Germany, she as an outspoken Zionist. Arendt surely would not have missed this opportunity. But it did not happen; Heidegger had already fallen out with the Nationalist Socialists.

On September 3, 1939, France declared war on National Socialist Germany. Two days earlier, Heinrich Blücher had already been detained as a "hostile foreigner," but was released in December 1939 when their common friend, Lotte Kleinbort, intervened. In this extremely difficult situation, further complicated by the tensions between Martha, Hannah's mother, and Heinrich Blücher, Hannah and Heinrich married on January 16, 1940.[128]

On May 10, 1940, German troops invaded France. They divided the country and occupied the northern part of France. The French government negotiated a ceasefire. In Vichy, a small town in central France, an emergency administration was established. From there, the French, the l'État Français of Marshell Pétain administered the unoccupied part of France.

From May to July 1, 1940, Blücher was again placed in a detainment camp.[129] In June 1940 Arendt was transported to the women's camp, Gurs, in the south of France. After five weeks, possessing forged documents and shortly before the German security forces arrived, she took part in a mass flight from the camp under the benevolent blind eye of the French authorities.[130] She had arranged with Blücher to meet in Montauban, a small town in the unoccupied part of southern France, in whose vicinity the Kleinborts had rented a house. She ran into Blücher by chance on the street in Montauban, in the middle of the stream of refugees. They rented a small apartment. In January 1941 they crossed over the Pyrenees to the Spanish border on the escape route arranged by Lisa Fittko and her husband. Upon arriving in Spain, they took a train to Lisbon.[131]

Her letters of the time to Adler-Rüdel were marked by the chaos of flight and the disorder that prevailed in the unoccupied zone of France. She told him about the peculiarities of French nationalistic anti-Semitism.[132] Adler-Rüdel, in his turn, shared news from England about the German bombings of London, detainment hysteria, and the pervasive common sense of the English despite everything.[133] Arendt responded by reporting on the situation in the French detainment camps, which became more serious as the activities of German secret police in the unoccupied part of France became officially more tolerated. Then the deportations began. The first famous deportees were the Social Democrats Rudolf Breitscheid and Rudolf Hilferding. Arendt and Adler-Rüdel exchanged news almost up until the final hour of their stay in Europe. He let her know how pessimistically he saw the situation of Jewish refugees. In 1941 he thought that it would come to a German mass murder of Jews in East Europe and that the Western public would know only a fraction of it.[134] In 1943 he was sure of it:

> I have the impression, on the basis of the material I gathered there [on his trip to Sweden—author's note] that our knowledge from the press reports about the events on the continent and what is being done to Jews is more understated than overstated. The feeling that the Jewish problem will find its natural resolution through extermination in Europe has turned into certainty.... Unless in the next few days or weeks a miracle happens and the Germans fail, there will hardly be any more Jews after the war in the world, as at the time of the Dreyfus affair.[135]

In Lisbon, in May 1941, Arendt and Blücher finally obtained an American visa.

During these two years, 1940 and 1941, Arendt accumulated, willingly and unwillingly, the experiences on which she would draw for a lifetime. The collapse of tradition and morals, the destruction of the political space—these fundamental elements of her political thinking stemmed from the perceptions and experience of those years. She would incorporate them in numerous articles and, above all, in the first and second part of her book *The Origins of Totalitarianism*.

Notes

1. Heidegger's letter to the Dean of the Philosophy faculty dated March 29 and June 11, 1930, UAF Akte Heidegger B 3, Nr. 788.

2. Heidegger to Jaspers, letter dated December 20, 1931 in Walter Biemal and Hans Saner, eds., *Heidegger-Jaspers Correspondence*, trans. Gary E. Aylesworth (New York: Humanity Books, 2003), 139–40.

3. See *Frankfurter Zeitung* from October 1931 to January 1932.

4. After he was forced to leave Germany and after his arrival in the United States as an exile, Lederer (1882–1939) belonged to the original founders of the New School for Social Research in New York, also known as the "University in Exile."

5. Paul Tillich, "Gibt es noch eine Universität?," *Frankfurter Zeitung*, November 22, 1931.

6. Heidegger to Jaspers, letter dated April 3, 1933 (shortly before the assumption of the Rectorate) in Biemal and Saner, *Heidegger-Jaspers Correspondence*, 145–46.

7. "Der Haß auf den Bürger, der aus der Demokratie entstand, und in ihr weiter wächst, kommt nur dem Anschein nach von außen. Im Grunde genommen ist es der Haß des Bürgers auf sich selbst" ("The hatred of the bourgeoisie, out of which democracy emerged and out of which it continues to grow, does not come from something outside of itself; rather, the ground of the hatred of the bourgeoisie is from the bourgeoisie itself"); see François Furet, *The Passing of an Illusion* (Chicago: University of Chicago Press, 1999), 28; see also especially 8–9.

8. Jacoby, *Königsberg 1881–1969 Greifsweld*, ed. Hans-Christoph and Frank Harwise (Lubeck: Schmidt-Romhild, 2004), 42.

9. Ibid., 91.

10. Ibid.

11. Fürst, *Fisch Eine Jugend in Konigsburg* (Berlin: Verlag der Nation, 1973), 94.

12. Kurt Blumenfeld, *Jüdenfrage* (Stuttgart: DVA, 1962), 45.

13. Jacoby, *Königsberg*, 49.

14. Schüler-Springorum, *Minderheit* (Göttingen: Vandenhoeck & Ruprecht, 1996), 147ff.

15. Ibid., 276ff.

16. Blumenfeld, *Jüdenfrage*, 46ff.

17. Ibid., 57.

18. Elizabeth Young-Bruehl, *Hannah Arendt: For Love of the World*, (New Haven, CT: Yale University Press), 27.

19. Ibid., 61–62.

20. Renato de Rosa, "Nachwort," in *Jaspers: Erneuerung* (März: Schneider Lambert, 1986), 344.

21. Cf. ibid., 345. Jaspers himself cites Gumbel's own words: "the men who—I would not say fell on the field of dishonor, but—lost their lives in an awful fashion"; Karl Jaspers, *Philosophical Autobiography in the Philosophy of Karl Jaspers*, ed. Paul Arthur Schlipp (Chicago: Open Court, 1957), 50.

22. Jaspers, *Philosophical Autobiography*, 50.

23. See Aken Universität Marburg betreffend Politisches, StA MR, 305 a, ACC 1959/9, Nr. 584, Rector u. Senat, Sect. 1, Lit. T Nr. 7.

24. See Akten Rektor u. Senat, StAMR, 305a, Acc 1959/9, Nr 584, Sect.1, Lit. T Nr. 7.

25. Martin Heidegger, "Report Concerning Herrn Arnold Ruge," dated December 18, 1933, in Heidegger GA, 1, Abt. Bd. 16 (2000), 223.

26. Letter of the Philosophy Faculty, Dean Sölch to the Engeren Senat, dated May 11, 1933, UAH, H-IV-102/153 Akten der Phil. Fak 1930–1931, Bd 1ato Dekan Sölch.

27. See faculty letter to Ministry, dated May 18, 1933, UAH, H-IV-102/157, Files of Philosophy Faculty, Dean Arnold von Sallis Bd. 1.

28. Jaspers mentions this lecture in a letter to Arendt dated March 20, 1930, in Lotte Kohler, ed., *Arendt-Jaspers Correspondence*, trans. Robert and Rita Kember (New York: Harcourt, Brace, 1992), 10.

29. Jaspers to Arendt, letter dated March 20, 1930, in ibid.

30. Ibid.

31. Arendt to Jaspers, letter dated February 24, 1930, in ibid., 11–12.

32. In the correspondence she joked about a suitable subtitle for the book that Piper was to publish: "Rahel Varnhagen. The melody of an offended heart, whistled with variations by Hannah Arendt. That is exactly what I have done" (Arendt, Brief an Hans Rössner, 12. Januar, 1959, Nachlaß Piper Verlag, DLA Marburg).

33. See Young-Bruehl, *Hannah Arendt*, 71.

34. Ibid.

35. Hannah Arendt, interview with Günter Gaus, in "'What Remains? The Language Remains': An Interview with Günter Gaus," in *Essays in Understanding*, ed. Kohn (New York: Harcourt, Brace, 1994), 6.

36. Arendt, *Diskussion mit Freunden und Kollegen in Toronto (November 1972)*, in Arendt, *Ich will verstehen* (Hannover: Piper, 1996), 107.

37. Palestine was put under the British Protectorate in 1920 after the fall of the Ottoman Empire and as part of the postwar treaty.

38. Georg Lukács, *Theory of the Novel*, trans. Anna Bostock (London: Merlin Press, 1971), 21.

39. Ibid., 22. See also Lukács's book *The Destruction of Reason*, trans. Peter Palmer (Atlantic Highlands, NJ: Humanities Press, 1980), 243.

40. Antonia Grunenberg, *Bürger und Revolutionär. Georg Lukacs 1918–1928* (Bücher vom Verlag Europ Vlg -Anst H, 1976), 63ff.

41. Arendt to Blücher, letter dated August 12, 1936, in Lotte Kohler, ed., *Within Four Walls*, trans. Peter Constantine (New York: Harcourt, Brace, 2000), 10.

42. The actual quotation states: "It is so beastly to always have to legitimate oneself. This is why it is so repugnant to be a Jewess." See Arendt-Blücher, letter from August 12, 1936, in Kohler, *Within Four Walls*, 10. See also footnote 28 of Lotte Köhler (editor) to this letter from Geneva.

43. With Heidegger's mediation, Karl Löwith had obtained a stipend in Rome.

44. Heidegger to Arendt, letter without a date (winter 1932–33) in Ursula Ludz, ed., *Arendt-Heidegger Letters*, trans. Andrew Shields (New York: Harcourt, Brace, 2004), 52–53.

45. Heidegger had been asked by Jaspers to write a recommendation for Hannah Arendt's project, a cultural historical work regarding the German-Jewish assimilation in the nineteenth century, using Rahel Varnhagen as an example. See *Heidegger-Jaspers Correspondence*, letters 83 and 84, 118 and 119.

46. Arendt to Jaspers, letter dated January 1, 1933, in *Arendt-Jaspers Correspondence*, 16.

47. Jaspers to Arendt, letter dated January 3, 1933, in ibid., 17.

48. Arendt to Jaspers, letter dated January 6, 1933, in ibid., 18.

49. Kohn, *Essays in Understanding*, 11.

50. Hannah Arendt, Lebenslauf, in Folder Blücher, Hannah Arendt Archive at the University of Oldenburg (HAZ).

51. Kohn, *Essays in Understanding*, 4–5.

52. Axel Eggebrecht has written vividly of this time. See Axel Eggebrecht, *Volk ans Gewehr. Chronik eines Berliner Hauses 1930–1934* (Bonn: J. H. Wl Dietz, 1980).

See also Axel Eggebrecht, *Weg* (Hamburg: Rowohl, 1974).

53. Blumenfeld, *Jüdenfrage*, 205.

54. Kohn, *Essays in Understanding*, 6.

55. Ibid., 11.

56. Blumenfeld, *Jüdenfrage*, 186.

57. Kohn, *Essays in Understanding*, 11–12.

58. Jaspers, *Philosophical Autobiography*, 75–78.

59. Heidegger to Jaspers, letter dated April 3, 1933, in *Heidegger-Jaspers Correspondence*, 146.

60. Membership number 3 125 894. Later explanations from Heidegger followed the enlistment on April 30 or May 1, 1933, respectively. Compare Heidegger's statement in the questionnaire for de-Nazification, UAF B 133/34.

61. See UAF B 133/34.

62. Heidegger to Jaspers, letter dated April 8, 1950, in *Heidegger-Jaspers Correspondence*, 188.

63. Report on the results of the Process for Purification from December 11 and 13, XII.45, Freiburg, 19.12.1945 (Reporter Constantine von Dietze), UAF B 34/31–2, P. 13ff.

64. Compare Hermann Heidegger in his critique of his father's biography by Hugo Ott, in which he writes that his father was pressured by von Möllendorf who lived across the street in Rötebuckweg. Heidegger's wife was against it. Heidegger himself had gone to the Senate in order to turn down the offer but was pressured into it by many colleagues. Hermann Heidegger, "The Economic Historian and the Truth. Necessary Remarks on the Public Remarks of Hugo Ott about Martin Heidegger," *Heidegger Studies* 13 (1997): 181.

65. Heidegger, letter to the rector of Freiburg University, letter from November 4, 1945, in Richard Wolin, ed., *The Heidegger Controversy* (Cambridge, MA: MIT Press, 1993), 61.

66. Ibid., 63.

67. Martin Heidegger, "The Self-Assertion of the German University," lecture given on the assumption of the rectorate, May 27, 1933 (ibid., 30).

68. Ibid., 37.

69. The examples are from Hermann Heidegger's collection of documents taken from this time; see Heidegger: *Reden*, in GA 1, Abt. Bd 16 (Frankfurt: Vittorio Klostermann, 2000) and from Schneeberger's edited volume, *Nachlese* (Suhr: Auflage, 1962).

70. Compare Schlageterfeier der Freiburger Universität, Report of the newspaper *Der Alemanne, Kampfblatt der Nationalsozialisten Oberbadens*, Number 145, May 27, 1933, Cited after Schneeburger, *Nachlese*, 47ff.; See also Paul Hühnerfeld, *Heidegger* (Istanbul: Gundogan Yayinlar, 1959), 102.

71. Martin Heidegger, copy of a telegram to the rector of the University of Frankfurt am Main, Ernst Krieck, UAF B 24 Nr. 1277.

72. The fictitious "Protocol of the Elders of Zion" about a supposed Jewish conspiracy, appeared in France in the 1890s, written up in 1905 for the Russian secret service, appears in Berlin in 1919 in an anti-Semitic paper, exposed as a forgery in 1924, used to spread anti-Semitism.

73. Jaspers, *Philosophical Autobiography*, 75–79.

74. Ibid.

75. Martin Heidegger, *Nietzsche: Der Wille zur Macht als Kunst*, in Heidegger: GS, II, Abt., Bd. 43 (1985), 26. English translation with introduction and notes by David Farrell Krell, *Nietzsche: Will to Power as Art* (New York: Harper and Row, 1979), 1:23.

76. Karl Jaspers, "Zur Kritik Heideggers," in *Notizen*, ed. Hans Saner (Munich: Piper, 1978), 41.

77. Martin Heidegger, telegram to Reichskanzlei Berlin dated May 20, 1933, Abschrift, UAF B 34/31 2.

78. Martin Heidegger, letter to Dietze dated December 15, 1945, 1, UAF B24 Nr. 1277.

79. Ernst Baeumler, one of the earlier philosophers of National Socialism, from 1934 on head of the economic section of the "Amt Rosenberg."

80. Martin Heidegger, letter to Dietze dated December 15, 1945, 1ff, UAF B 24, Nr. 1277.

81. Ibid.

82. Ibid.

83. When Heidegger's work in National Socialism is addressed, it is with the background of the following sources: (1) original sources from the NS time itself; (2) secondary sources from the "Purification Process" of 1945, concerning the case of Heidegger and the procedures advised and the several nonprimary facts of the case as well as eyewitness accounts from colleagues; and (3) other sources, such as the memories of Heinrich Heidegger, Karl Löwith, and other students.

84. Martin Heidegger, Stellungnahme zur Beurlaubung der Kollegen von Hevesy und Fraenkel, in Heidegger, *Reden*, GA 1, Abt. Bd. 16 (2000), 140ff, and Heidegger, Stellungnahme zu Professor Dr. Eduard Fraenkel, in Heidegger, *Reden*, GA, 1, Abt. Bd. 16 (2000), 144ff.

85. Jaspers to Rektor Oehlkers, letter dated December 22, 1945, in Wolin, *Heidegger Controversy*, 148.

86. See Heidegger's correspondence with Elisabeth Blochmann dated April to October 1933, in *Martin Heidegger-Elizabeth Blochmann: Briefwechsel* (Marbuch: Deutsche Schillerges, 1990).

87. Martin Heidegger, Empfehlung für Dr. Kristeller, in Heidegger, *Reden*, in GA, 1, Abt. Bd. 16 (2000), 89.

88. Report on the results of the purification hearings from December 11 and 13, 1945 (Chair von Dietze), UAF B 34/31–2, s. 14.

89. Martin Heidegger, letter from December 16, 1933. Copy of the second transcript included in the purification hearings of 1945 UAF B 43/31–2. See also Hugo Ott, *Martin Heidegger: A Political Life*, trans. Allan Blunden (New York: Harper, 1993), 190.

90. Handwritten addition from Dietze to G. Ritter dated June 21, 1949, on the copy of Heidegger's report dated December 16, 1933, UAF B 34/31–3.

91. Jaspers's letter to Friedrich Oehlkers dated December 22, 1945, in Wolin, *Heidegger Controversy*, 148.

92. As Hans Saner reports, Jaspers had indeed never seen the original of the report. Marianne Weber, a relative of Baumgarten, had let Baumgarten see a copy of the report. In 1945 Baumgarten himself once again asserted, this time for the report, that Jaspers had sent his recollection of the report to the University of Freiburg. It is therefore easy to see how a divergence in the reports emerged (see *Heidegger-Jaspers Correspondence, 1920–1963*). Footnote 6 indicates that letter number 125 was not sent from Jaspers to Heidegger, dated March 1, 1948, 158.

93. Report on the result of the of the Purification hearings from 11 and 13.12.45 (Chair von Dietz), UAF b 34/31–3. s.13.

94. Jaspers's letter to Friedrich Oehlkers dated December 22, 1945, in Wolin, *Heidegger Controversy*, 46–47.

95. Report on the result of the Purification hearings from December 11 and 13, 1945 (Chair von Dietze), UAF b 34/31–3. s.12.

96. Report on the result of the Purification hearings from December 11 and 13, 1945 (Chair von Dietze), UAF b 34/31–3. s.13.

97. See Martin Heidegger: Proposals for further provisions in the Badische University Constitution from December 18, 1933. Heidegger: *Reden*, in: GA, I, ABT. Bd. 16 (2000) s. 222.

98. Karl Löwith, *My Life in Germany before and after 1933* (Champaign: University of Illinois Press, 1994), 45 (translation modified).

99. Martin Heidegger, letter to the academic rectorate, dated November 4, 1945, in Wolin, *Heidegger Controversy*, 63.

100. Jewish students were allowed to study during the first years of National Socialism. The names were taken according to the Bursar's documentation used to verify payment for the semester, UAF B 17/923.

101. Documents from the University of Marburg, Priv-Doz Dr. K. Löwith, StA MR Acc.1 1996/10.

102. Löwith was discharged from the army with a 40 percent disability payment. One of his lungs was permanently damaged; half of his chest had withered as a result of a wound he suffered on the Italian front.

103. Hermann Heidegger cites this scene in opposition to Heidegger's biographer, Ott: "Ambassador von Hassell asked my mother to wear her party badge on her English suit as so as not to be mistaken for an English woman. The British were being treated in an unfriendly manner due to the Abyssinian conflict. I have no picture of Martin Heidegger wearing the party badge (black, red, white with swastika). As Rector he sometimes wore a small silver colored pin (an eagle with a swastika). I have no memory of him wearing a party badge in Rome." See Hermann Heidegger, "Economic History and the Truth. Necessary notes to Hugo Ott's Writings on Martin Heidegger," *Heidegger Studies* 13 (1997): 184. As regards the party badge, it was the case either that Löwith mixed up Heidegger with his wife or that Heidegger was wearing "a small silver colored pin, an eagle with a swastika" at the same time that his wife was wearing a party badge and mistook it for party identification.

104. Karl Löwith, *Martin Heidegger and European Nihilism*, trans. Gary Steiner, ed. Richard Wolin (New York: Columbia University Press, 1995).

105. Heinrich Schlier, "Denken im Nachdenken," in *Erinnerung*, 221.

106. "The preparation for this Congress had been underway for one and a half years. One and a half years ago I sent a copy of the invitation I personally received from the President of the Congress to the German Ministry of Education with information in the addendum that this Descartes Anniversary would at the same time be a push on the side of the ruling liberal-democratic paradigm. The German representatives must be effective, beginning the preparation process early" (Heidegger, letter to the rector of the University of Freiburg from June 14, 1937, UAF B 24/1277).

107. All citations from Akten im UAF B 24 nr. 1277.

108. UAH, Personalakten, PA, 4369 Jaspers, Karl.

109. Martin Heidegger, Brief an den Rektor der Universität Freiburg von 16. Oktober 1942, UAF B 24 Nr. 1277.

110. Meyer's Lexikon, Bd. 8, 8. Aufl. Art. Heidegger, in völlig neuer Bearbeitung und Bebilderung, Leipzig, 1938, S. 994. Cited also by Schneeberger, *Nachlese*, 263.

111. Grunenberg, *Lukács*, chaps. 2 and 3.

112. Zimmerman, *Martin and Fritz Heidegger* (Munich: C. H. Beck, 2005), 34ff.

113. Silvio Vietta, *Heideggers Kritik* (Tubingen: Max Niemeyer, 1989), 20.

114. These are: Nietzsche, "The Will to Power (WS 1936/37); Nietzsche's Foundation in Western Thinking (SS 1937), Nietzsche's Lecture on Will to Power, (SS 1939), and Nietzsche II (II. Trimester 1942)." I follow here the list of students registered by the Bursar at the University of Freiburg in the years noted, UAF B 17/923.

115. Vietta, *Heideggers Kritik*, 36.

116. Ibid., 37.

117. Ibid., 38.

118. Ibid., 61 and 63.

119. Martin Heidegger, "Nietzsche's Word, God Is Dead," in *The Question Concerning Technology and Other Essays*, trans. and intro. William Lovitt (New York: Harper Colophon, 1977), 112.

120. Hannah Arendt, *Rahel Varnhagen: The Life of a Jewish Woman* (New York: HBJ, 1974), 214.

121. Young-Bruehl, *Hannah Arendt*, 119.

122. Adler-Rüdel, *Jüdische Selbsthilfe* (Tubingen: Mohr Siebeck, 1974), 15.

123. Ibid., 97ff.

124. See ibid., 98.

125. Adler-Rüdel, *Ost-Jüden* (1959); Adler-Rüdel, *Jüdische Selbsthilfe* (1974); see also Robert Weltsche, "Introduction," in Adler-Rüdel's *Jüdische Selbsthilfe* (1974), xiv.

126. Lotte Köhler, Notizen aus meinem Kalender Hannah Arendt betreffend, Ms. S. 4. Archive HAZ.

127. Young-Bruehl, *Hannah Arendt*, 121ff.

128. Ibid., 150–51.

129. Heinrich Blücher: Lebenslauf von 1956, masch. Ms. Archive HAZ.

130. Young-Bruehl, *Hannah Arendt*, 156ff.

131. In Lisa Fittkos's description of her work as an aid to refugees, one can find references to Hannah Arendt's escape from the Gurs camp. See Lisa Fittko, *Escape through the Pyrenees*, trans. David Koblick (Evanston: Northwestern University Press, 1985), 49 and 66.

132. See Arendt to Adler-Rüdel, letter dated April 2, 1941. The original correspondence is found in the Central Zionist Archive, Jerusalem; a copy of the correspondence is found in Archive des HAZ; it has been also presented by Katja Tenenbaum in "Hannah Arendt net."

133. Adler-Rüdel to Arendt, letter dated March 6, 1941, Archive des HAZ.

134. See Adler-Rüdel to Arendt, letter dated May 2, 1941, Archive des HAZ.

135. Adler-Rüdel to Arendt, letter dated May 20, 1943, Archive des HAZ.

"Pledge to the spirit of science," Karl Jaspers (middle), with the physiologist Fano and the art historian Carl Cornelius, August 1902. Courtesy of Hans Saner.

Abraham a Santa Clara (1644–1709), copperplate engraving, circa 1700. Photo: akg-images.

Martin Heidegger's parents: Friedrich Heidegger and his wife,
Johanna, née Kempf. Courtesy of Martin Heidegger Archiv Meßkirch.

Class photo with Martin Heidegger in Meßkirch, circa 1895. Courtesy of
Martin Heidegger Archiv Meßkirch.

Martin Heidegger in spring 1912. Courtesy of Arnulf Heidegger.

Elfride Heidegger, née Petri, in the garden, circa 1915. Courtesy of Arnulf Heidegger.

Gertrud Mayer (1879–1974), 1910. Courtesy of Hans Saner.

Gertrud and Karl Jaspers in 1911. Courtesy of Hans Saner.

Heidegger family with both sons, Jörg (born 1919) and Hermann (born 1920), Marburg, summer 1924. Courtesy of Arnulf Heidegger.

Hannah Arendt in the arms of her grandfather Max Arendt, 1907. Courtesy of the Hannah Arendt Bluecher Literary Trust.

Hannah Arendt at the age of eight with her mother, Martha Arendt. Courtesy of the Hannah Arendt Bluecher Literary Trust.

Hannah Arendt, mid-1920s.
Courtesy of the Hannah Arendt
Bluecher Literary Trust.

Martin Heidegger, 1924. Courtesy of
Martin Heidegger Archiv Meßkirch.

Heidegger's Cabin in Todtnauberg near Freiburg. Courtesy of Arnulf
Heidegger.

Hannah Arendt and Günther
Stern, who later called him-
self Günther Anders, in 1929.
Courtesy of the Hannah Arendt
Bluecher Literary Trust.

Kurt Blumenfeld (1884–1963).
Courtesy of the Hannah Arendt Bluecher
Literary Trust.

Anne Weil, née Mendelssohn, in 1967.
Courtesy of the Hannah Arendt Bluecher
Literary Trust.

Martin Heidegger, circa 1934.
Photo: akg-images.

Fritz and Martin Heidegger, in the 1960s. Courtesy of Martin Heidegger Archiv Meßkirch.

Hannah Arendt in Paris, circa 1935. Photo by Fred Stein. Courtesy of the Hannah Arendt Bluecher Literary Trust.

Hannah Arendt and Heinrich Blücher in New York, circa 1950.
Courtesy of the Hannah Arendt Bluecher Literary Trust.

A reunion 1966: (standing from left) Heinrich Blücher, Hannah Arendt,
Dwight Macdonald, with his wife, Gloria, (sitting) Nicola Chiaromonte,
Mary McCarthy, Robert Lowell. Courtesy of Vassar College Library.

Hannah Arendt and Mary McCarthy in the 1960s. Courtesy of the Hannah Arendt Bluecher Literary Trust.

Karl Jaspers giving a lecture in winter 1945–46 in the auditorium (Aula) at Heidelberg University. Courtesy of Hans Saner.

Hannah Arendt lecturing in the mid-1960s. Courtesy of the Hannah Arendt Bluecher Literary Trust.

The Heidegger family in front of the cabin with dog Fips in 1952. Courtesy of Arnulf Heidegger.

The naturalization documents of Hannah Arendt and Heinrich Blücher, 1951.

Hannah Arendt in a television interview (ZDF) with Günter Gaus, 1964.

Karl Jaspers at work, Basel 1964, photography stefan moses.

Martin Heidegger, photograph by Hannah Arendt, August 1967. Courtesy of the Hannah Arendt Bluecher Literary Trust.

Hannah Arendt 1975 in New York, shortly before her death. Courtesy of the Hannah Arendt Bluecher Literary Trust.

Martin Heidegger, manuscript page, beginning of the 1960s. Courtesy of Arnulf Heidegger.

4 Heidegger *absconditus,* or the Discovery of America

"Are saved live 317 West 95," telegraphed Hannah to her ex-husband, Günther Stern, who was living in Los Angeles, after she and Heinrich Blücher arrived in New York on May 22, 1941. Stern had worked hard to get visas for them. In Lisbon on May 10, they had boarded the SS *Guiné*; the writer Hans Sahl was on the same ship.[1] And when, weeks later, Arendt's mother, Martha, whom they had to leave behind in Marseille, arrived on the MS *Muzinho*, the relief must have been great.

Life in New York was exciting, confusing, and demanding. Everything was new and unfamiliar: the language, the skyscrapers, the speed—and the streams of pedestrians on the streets. Refugees from every European country, immigrants from all the continents of the earth, seem to have gathered there. Elegant women who shopped on Fifth Avenue, street vendors, panhandlers, and ethnicities of all kinds were among them. There were countless cars and the subway, which she certainly knew from Berlin and Paris, although this underground system branched out much farther. Like an invisible assembly line, it carried millions of people here and there underground. The whole city was like a single organism whose many arms were connected with one another under the earth and above, visibly and invisibly. Everything appeared chaotic, yet somehow held together. Nowhere was the new felt so much as here where everything was in constant motion. Every street corner provided an unfamiliar new view.

New York was also a universe of sounds: the wailing noise of police sirens, vending machines, air conditioners, the rhythmic surging and stopping of cars and buses, the calls of newspaper vendors and shoe shiners, the melodies of street musicians.

There was also the speed of life; upon her arrival she was swept along in its flow. Berlin and Paris were also cities of speed, but still no match for this lively confusion on the Hudson where the whole world seemed to have gathered and then dispersed into hundreds of thousands of activities and groups. For Hannah, the city was an unparalleled source of energy.

The exiled European intelligentsia gathered in New York. Many European greats of philosophy, sociology, music and literature, the natural sciences, architecture, and technology found themselves there. All these refugees and emigrants were looking for housing and work. They were looking for relatives and old friends and making new friends when possible. Every refugee adjusted to life in this city differently, each in accordance with his or her professional, physical, and biographical disposition; one with fortitude, another defensive and reserved, the third anxious and depressive, yet another in a carefully probing manner. The German labor lawyer Franz Neumann noted that three possibilities of existence were open for the exiled scholars: "Exiled scholars could (and sometimes did) abandon their previous intellectual position and accept without qualification the new orientation. They could (and sometimes did) retain completely their old framework of thought and either believe themselves to have the task of totally revamping American life or withdraw (with disdain and contempt) onto an island of their own. They could finally attempt an integration of their new experience with the old tradition. This, I believe, is the most difficult, but also the most rewarding solution."[2] The path some individuals chose also depended on how they handled the new world linguistically. Language meant admission into the foreign culture. The memoirs of all the immigrants were filled with complaints about the loss of language. Günther Stern spoke of the danger of falling prey to inferior speech: "The moment we were exiled, we entered the new risk, the risk of sinking into a low level of speech and becoming stammerers. And many of us did in fact become stammerers, stammerers in both languages; since while we had not yet learned our French, English, or Spanish, our German began to crumble little by little and in most cases it was so covert and gradual that we were aware of the loss as little as we are aware of becoming an adult."[3] The philosopher Ernst Bloch noticed that different types formed on the basis of dealing with language: the first type "abolished" their native culture and language and forcefully tried to adopt the new culture. The second type tried to preserve its native language and culture in the culture of the new country. The third type, described by Bloch, appeared bold in the circumstances of the day:

> In America's framework . . . we are looking for a kind of utterly human and humanly comprehensible objective distance. . . . We bring with us certain already established advantages: a formed language and an old culture to which we remain faithful both by putting it to the test on the new material and refreshing it. And we have distance: not because we want it, but because we are not comic actors. With this honest distance, we want the life around us and the problems we are dealing with to be the object of our intuitive, expressive, reality-bound language and way of thinking.[4]

When the thirty-five-year-old Hannah, who had already accumulated enough experiences for a lifetime, stepped on American soil, she undoubtedly belonged to this last type of exile. The difficulties this stance carried with it were yet to be gauged. Upon arrival in New York, the years of hectic refugee existence with the endless work of relief committees amidst all the distress of immigration were left behind. Her involvement as a Zionist, however, was not. Here Arendt's political work only assumed different dimensions. She could now plan and take advantage of the structures that were already in place. Money was also available, it simply needed to be "organized." The first source of money that she could draw upon was from the Zionist Organization of America, which gave a kind of welcome money, seventy-five dollars, to Jewish refugees. The next address was then Self-Help for Refugees.

During her exploratory trips to various authorities and relief committees, she ran into acquaintances, met new people, was drawn into debate circles, organizations, and places of employment. Each day, each month in this new home, each small success, each payment, each acquired human and professional contact confirmed the feeling that something new had begun. It was as though a new door had been opened that set free a space that had been previously closed to her. Being able to move in this space was a step into a freedom that she had never felt before. She worked relentlessly on projects, plans, and manuscripts. These included her involvement with Zionism, the beginning of her studies of the history of the Jews and the origins of European and German anti-Semitism, and—most important—constantly making friends. It was a time of enormous thirst for action.

At the same time, living conditions were anything but comfortable. Blücher, Arendt, and her mother, Martha, lived in a tiny place on the Upper West Side of Manhattan, 317 West Ninety-Fifth Street. It was a "rooming house," a hotel for permanent residents. Dozens of emigrant families and individuals lived there because the rent was cheap. The Blüchers and Martha Arendt each had a furnished room on the same floor. The bathroom was in the hallway.

Psychological frictions were added to the spatial and financial limitations. Already in Paris Heinrich Blücher and Martha Arendt had not gotten along well. In New York, the tensions increased. Martha thought that Blücher should go to work and contribute money to the household. She was of the opinion that her daughter should not have to be solely responsible for their livelihood. After a brief attempt at factory work, he, the self-made thinker, thought that he needed to find work more suitable to him and not engage in manual labor. Fortunately, in 1941 he found a position with an organization that was involved in the recruitment for the United States' entry into the war. His job was to assess the current situation in Europe. His name did not come up in the publications that emerged from this, but Blücher did not seem to mind.[5] In any event, this job was short-lived, as in the same year, 1941, the United States entered the war. Blücher then received contracts from the US Army. In the context of a training program at Camp Ritchie in Maryland, he lectured German prisoners in German history. Later he taught the structure of the French and German army to German-speaking American officers at Princeton University:[6] His calling as a military historian stemmed from this time, a time in which Arendt worked closely with him. In between these contracts, he worked in a "chemical research laboratory producing plastics."[7] In addition, he had a position as a news reporter for a German-language program for the NBC radio station.[8]

Blücher was not a man of the written word. Hannah Arendt as well as her friends repeatedly pointed out that his skills were lecture and debate. He was a genius at this and, as a result, received a good appointment in the beginning of the fifties as a philosophy professor at Bard College in upstate New York. Teaching fulfilled him, challenged him, and influenced many of his students up until today.

Unlike Blücher, who had great difficulty learning English, Arendt jumped right into the middle of the language. Barely two months after her arrival, a refugee organization sponsored a family language stay for her in Winchester, Massachusetts. The seemingly puritanically minded host family remained foreign to her; their lifestyle was contrary to her habits—including smoking, which they frowned upon. But she accepted the civic-minded self-consciousness of the people with enthusiasm, and she returned to New York with a wealth of everyday English. A year later she returned for ten days; this time she wrote about it as though it were a vacation.[9] Despite this, her American friends agreed that she had lifelong difficulties setting her thinking within the framework of the English-American language and its intellectual and cultural milieu.

The tensions between the Blüchers and Hannah's mother persisted. In 1948, after seven years of living together, Arendt's mother decided to move to her stepdaughter Eva Beerwald in England. Consequently, she took the *Queen Mary* to England in the summer of 1948. However, she suffered a severe asthma attack on the ship and died a few days after her arrival. The death of the mother was a sad caesura for the daughter, but it also brought relief to the relationship of the married couple.

At this time, Hannah and Heinrich began searching for a new apartment. They could now afford an apartment with a separate living room, an office, and an extra room that could be sublet. The new address was Morningside Drive 130. They finally had their own furniture.

It was also during this time that the first friendships grew stronger. Alfred Kazin, one of her most loyal friends, wrote: "She gave her friends—writers as various as Robert Lowell, Randall Jarrell, Mary McCarthy, the Jewish historian Salo Baron—intellectual courage before the moral terror the war had willed to us."[10] Kazin describes the inexhaustible energy that Arendt radiated. She must have attracted her guests like a magnet, and it was surely not just because of her hospitality, for which she was well known. No matter how short she was on money, there was always enough for candied fruit, cake, and port wine. Her attractiveness also lay in her glowing, sharp intellect, which so deeply impressed her friend Kazin:

> Marx-Plato-Hegel-Heidegger-Kant-Kafka-Jaspers! Montesquieu! Nietzsche! Duns Scotus! The great seminal names played a huge role in Hannah's shelter on Morningside Drive overlooking the sign of the Krakauer piano factory and the bleak unenterable enemy country that was Morningside Park.[11]
>   "The decisive break with tradition," was her constant refrain. There had been a tradition and no one was more eager and willing to bestow on you in Greek—the most essential Greek meanings of man, mind, the *polis,* the common good. But there had been a break. Definitely, there had been a break. . . . A Breaking-up—was her life and everyone's life now. . . . The longer she lived here, the more she insisted on constancy in her friends, constancy in the world of ideas—no matter how far into the past that stretched. Like her other house offering, Greek quotations, her mind instinctively sprang to some essential principle of life as tradition. And what happened to tradition? It broke.[12]

It was in this time of blossoming friendships that Arendt and her husband Heinrich Blücher formed an ever-evolving intellectual partnership. As it is not preserved in writing, it is difficult to evaluate Blücher's part in Arendt's books.[13] The marriage was based on conversation; the days began with an exchange about the morning newspapers and the nights ended in passionate debate with friends or with each other about philosophical or current questions. Conversational exchanges, which played such a large role in her thought, drew many to her. And Blücher, whom Kazin describes as "tempestuous, sometimes frighteningly intelligent" played a large role.[14] The correspondence between the married couple certainly attests to this.

Heinrich's ideas as well as those of her friends were incorporated into her first major articles and, finally, into the project *The Origins of Totalitarianism.*[15] Already at that time, the world of friends, of the *We,* a world of many perspectives, permeated the various layers of her works.

Heidegger, the magical thinker and poetic lover, withdrew into an estranged distance. Her last recorded contact with him in winter 1932–33 showed him to be in defensive posture awaiting what was coming. Her lover had joined the side of the enemy. In any event, she must have thought so.

Nowhere were there as many of the best representatives of European intelligentsia gathered together as there were at that time in New York. It must have been the best time for Jewish intellectuals, noted the poet and friend Robert Lowell jokingly, with the refugees at the time openly "unloading their European luggage."[16] A number of the German refugees saw it similarly. For example, Hans

Jonas writes that at the time America had taken over the "Leadership of the Western Spirit":

> Everything, everything happens there. There are no official academic doctrines; there is real freedom of thought, theorizing, speculation, presentation of new ideas or warming-up of the old ones. The greatest syncretism of the modern world, the confluence of intellectual ideas, points of view, and methods constantly takes place in America. . . . And, in a certain way, one could have the feeling that, at least temporarily, the most important happenings in the sciences and literature, in art and in general . . . in the realm of worldviews, are happening in America.[17]

Hans Jonas, Arendt's friend from her youth, had initially moved to England and then immigrated to Palestine after the war. In 1949 he accepted an invitation to a Canadian university. In 1955 he finally came to New York to teach at the New School for Social Research, the "University in Exile."

Hannah was a whirlwind unleashed. The city and its atmosphere were drawn into her vortex. She approached people and was a genius at making new friendships. She knocked on the doors of important Jewish organizations and magazines; she visited her old German friends, including Kurt Blumenfeld and Salman Schocken; she was further recommended and made new contacts. She began to read again and began writing. And all along, she contributed money to the household.

America, America . . .

At that time America had already emerged from the Great Depression. The economic boom which accompanied America's entry into the war in 1941 greatly improved the economic situation. The tormented years of economic crisis that had affected the entire world economy since "Black Friday" of October 24, 1929, were over. Unlike in Europe, in the United States the economic crisis did not lead to the collapse of the political order; rather, the crisis strengthened the democratic state. The New Deal and the American government's unusual role as creator of jobs and economic investor gave a considerable boost to the liberal camp.

The poverty in the country had radicalized the liberals and overnight many leftist groups sprang up. The American Left had remained true to the cause of the Russian Revolution since 1917. The distant influence of the October Revolution on the North and South American continent still seemed to persist in the 1930s. If one looks closer, however, American socialism—the Communist Party right in the center of it—was never a strong movement. Yet on occasion it produced an upheaval in the political landscape that extended well into its inner circles.

While in Europe the expansion of the radical left had been blocked by the growing number of racist movements, the socialist political groups in America in the 1930s could develop relatively peacefully. The United States seemed to be on its way to an independent socialism, at least this is what many liberal intellectuals on the East Coast believed.

In 1936 Trotsky appeared in South America. After his flight from the Soviet Union, he finally found refuge in Mexico, whose president at the time pursued a politics that was friendly to refugees from Europe. From there, Trotsky tried to organize foreign opposition to Stalin's regime. The American Left consequently split into a pro-Soviet and a pro-Trotsky camp.

Throughout the 1930s and 1940s discussions erupted as to whether the Soviet Union had shown the way that America should also follow and toward which it had already taken steps, if halfheartedly, with the New Deal; or whether (as Trotsky claimed) the Soviet Union was the fastest way to a bureaucratic military dictatorship, against which one had to fight. With this as background, the question arose: from what perspective should America, criticized from the Left as a capitalist and imperialist country, be reformed?

Conflicts like these split the New York left liberals into two large camps: the communists and their sympathizers and the Trotskyites and their followers. The huge trials that had taken place in Moscow since the mid-1930s, in which the elite leaders of the Russian communists had been exposed in their purge, deepened this rift. While Trotskyites decidedly criticized them, the followers of Stalin produced elaborate justifications.

Dwight Macdonald, journalist, essayist, and a friend of Arendt's since the mid-1940s, recalls decades later the Trotskyist scene at the time: "The Moscow Trials were undoubtedly the turning point for most intellectuals. The more reflective intellectuals were the ones that became anti-Stalinists."[18] When Hannah Arendt came to New York, these debates were in full swing. Presumably, she remained emotionally distant from the passionate feuds around the issues of socialism. To be sure, she had read Marx, but she was sober, even skeptical, in regards to the sentimental kind of leftist liberals who wrapped themselves up in a fantasy of socialism.

Another important debate, ignited in the course of the war, concerned the goals of the war and the threat to European Jews. Should America participate in the war? Admittedly, the American intervention in the First World War was decisive, but it ended abruptly. Congress refused to sign the Treaty of Versailles. Thus, there was no monetary reward for the United States' involvement in the First World War. What war goals should the United States pursue now and how should they be different from the goals of 1917? What would be its relationship to the totalitarian Soviet Union? Should the future of Germany and Europe after the end of the war be socialist or capitalist?

At the center of this debate was the leftist magazine *Partisan Review*, which Dwight Macdonald, together with Philip Rahv, Fred Dupee, William Phillips, and George Morris, founded anew in 1937, after his predecessor, who was close to the Communist Party, faded away quietly. The group was closer to Trotsky than to the communists, but it was in itself so pluralistic that the journal did not become an instrument of propaganda for the Trotskyites. Within a few years, *Partisan Review* matured to the status of *the* journal for leftist liberal intellectuals. The ingenuity of its "movers and shakers," its analytic acuity, its ability to engage in polemics skillfully, its feel for the subjects that were "in the air," and a palette rich in authors of the most disparate dispositions, were part of its success.

The magazine cultivated its own unique style: there were essays, theatre reviews, news from abroad, literary stories, and always a place for poems or unknown authors. In addition, there was gossip in everyday language.

The style was animated by a cultivated polemics and a certain joy of attack. It united that which could not be unified, as William Barrett noted in looking back on the 1930s and 1940s:

> The two M's then—Marxism in politics and Modernism in art—were the slogans that this group wrote on its banner before the world. They were enough to enlist my youthful enthusiasm in any case, for they named two regions of the spirit where my loyalties already lay. Whether the two parts of this program—a radical Marxism in politics, and a radical championship of the avant-garde in art—were really consistent with each other, did not particularly disturb us at the time.[19]

The mixture of culture, politics, and art that converged in the *Partisan Review*, in which both publishers and authors were present, was unique. Here one was always ready to confront a subject and to risk an argument. This approach defined the style for ten years, from the end of the 1930s to the end of the 1940s. *Partisan Review* seized on the important subjects of the time: politics and religion, art and modernity, Jewish identity, and so on. The journal presented key essays on the critique of capitalism and late modern society, such as, for instance, a debate on "the revolution of the manager" and the beginning of the service society. The critique, in Trotskyist colors, of the Soviet Union was also a polemic against the Stalinist milieu in some of the intellectual circles in the United States. In a series of articles called "The Future of Socialism," Trotskyites, Marxists, anti-Stalinist leftists, and liberals sharply attacked one another. Another series of articles seized on the liberal ideals in art and culture; here the Marxists criticized the liberals; the latter, in turn, opposed the Marxist curse word "liberal" with a positive liberal paradigm. There were also arguments about religion and its significance for intellectuals.

Like its contemporary rivals, the success of the journal was due to the fact that writers, poets, and essayists saw themselves as public figures and representatives of public conscience. This presupposed at least three things: first, a public that was receptive to the themes, issues, and contemporary concerns that addressed its need for insight and satisfied its intellectual curiosity. Writers of all kinds were to creatively fulfill this task, to think across genres, and to be able to be open-minded. A second fundamental presupposition was for art and literature, theater, poetry, and political essays to respond to one another in turn and to recognize those who disagreed as bearers of one and the same discourse. The 1930s and 1940s in the United States offered a fertile soil for this interweaving. The third and final presupposition was that this discourse saw itself as part of a pluralistic Western culture within which Europe and America communicated with each other. The irony of history is that in this historical moment American culture still felt itself dependent on a European culture, while at the same time European culture was radically cut off from America. After the end of the war, it was the French existentialists who first tried to rebuild this connection.

Despite their liberal openness, the publishers of *Partisan Review* did abide by some principles, although they debated vigorously about some of them. As leftists, they believed that fascism was an offspring of capitalism and therefore the struggle against it was necessarily bound up with the overcoming of capitalism. The publishing group finally became at odds with each other over their stance on the war, as the writer Mary McCarthy, founding member of *Partisan Review* and a well-known theater critic at the time, later recalled:

> At the beginning of the war we were all isolationists, the whole group. Then . . . Philip Rahv wrote an article in which he said in a measured sentence, 'In a certain sense, this is our war.' The rest of us were deeply shocked by this because we regarded it as a useless imperialist war. . . . So when Philip wrote this article, a long controversy began in *Partisan Review*. The Review was split between those who supported the war and those who didn't.[20]

Even though the journal did not have to fear either censorship or financial pressure, the Cold War provoked the formation of various camps among its members. This led to divisions. Friendships fell apart; false loyalties were declared and then betrayed.

For Dwight Macdonald, the publishers became too faint-hearted: "They didn't want to print André Gide's *Return from the USSR* because they didn't want to go that far in criticizing the Soviet Union [*sic*]—they thought it was a reactionary article."[21] In the end Macdonald prevailed. André Gide's critical travel report about the Soviet Union under Stalin was published and the political positions intensified.

In 1944 Macdonald withdrew from *Partisan Review* and founded the journal *Politics*, which was more unambiguously political and did not accept the lofty kind of cultural gossip that the *Partisan Review* had generously delivered. It placed political analyses at the center, thoroughly reported news from Europe, and undertook a huge relief program for starving European intellectuals.

Between America and Europe

For Arendt, the most important goal was to defeat Hitler. She must have found some of the leftist debates to be far removed from this reality. But, on the other hand, she liked many of these argumentative New York intellectuals; some of them became friends with whom she and Heinrich argued passionately all night long.

It therefore developed in these first years that Arendt moved in two circles of friends: the American and the European. She needed Europeans because she thought in their culture and language. She could talk about her own experiences and Europe's future with her European friends. And she needed her new American friends to get to know the country, the people, their history, and their perspective on the world. The dynamism and the frictions between the two spheres, the American and the European, yielded a tension that nourished Arendt intellectually for many years.

Waldemar Gurian was an important friend and a great support during these first years. Arendt met him in her last days in Berlin through the Zionist network and now, after her arrival in the United States, she resumed her contact with him.

It is possible that Arendt and Gurian had not lost sight of each other during their first years of exile in France (Arendt) and Switzerland (Gurian). Gurian, coming from a Saint Petersburg Jewish family, was baptized Catholic at the insistence of his mother. Yet toward the end of the Weimar Republic, he was renounced by the National Socialists because of his Jewish background. Apparently he wanted to work through this shocking experience politically. Otherwise it makes little sense that he was moving in Zionist circles at a time when National Socialism was becoming an increasingly personal threat.

Gurian's talent as an essayist and critic of the times developed in an intellectual milieu of right-wing conservative critiques of the Weimar Republic. As a student of Carl Schmitt's, he was a harsh critic of modern liberalism; as an intellectual Catholic, he shared the views of right-wing conservatives, but not their anti-Semitism. The stronger the National Socialist movement became, the more harshly he criticized it. This brought him into open opposition with Carl Schmitt and many other like-minded friends and colleagues. Since he was a Jew and a Nazi enemy, he became the center of a public attack even before Hitler's assumption of power. To avoid the threatening persecution, in 1934 he emigrated to Switzerland, where he laboriously became a publisher and a writer. Together with Otto Michael Knab, he founded one of the most important periodicals of Catholic resistance, *Deutsche Briefe*, which he copublished up until 1938. The journal, smuggled into Germany through secret channels, was a kind of information service with documents, reports, and analyses of events and developments in National Socialist Germany and abroad. The stance of two big churches (Catholic and Protestant) vis-à-vis National Socialism was the central issue. Gurian was one of the harshest critics of the collaboration of the Christian churches with the National Socialist regime.

In 1937 he got very lucky: As he tells it, he stumbled on an application for a professorship—a position at Notre Dame, the Catholic university in Indiana. Two years later, he established a journal, *Review of Politics*, that would become one of the most important journals on politics and political theory in the United States. Its unique character lay in bringing together the European debate style with American intellectual discourse. Gurian gathered a special mix of authors around him. European immigrants such as Eric Voegelin and Jacques Maritain met American thinkers (Talcott Parsons, Aron Gurwitsch, Hans Kohn, and many others, the names no longer known today), and established scientists met with young talents.

The journal located itself in the space between political theory and political commentary. It paid special attention to the changes in the West that followed from the world war. It anticipated the split of the world into two large power blocs under American and Soviet Union leadership. Always at hand were themes such as the structural relatedness of National Socialism and Bolshevism, the relationship between liberalism and democracy, understanding race ideology, imperialism, the role of education in the West, changes in morality, and the role of religion.

Like Arendt, Gurian was a passionate, eruptive person both in his likes and dislikes, as well as being a loyal and outspoken friend. Hannah and Gurian must have liked each other immediately. He must have been fascinated by the unfailing practical and intellectual vigilance of the young woman. He also recognized her ability to see matters in penetrating and surprising ways. For Arendt, Gurian was a kindred spirit; he stimulated her, he contradicted her, he lent her books, he was interested in her opinion, and he introduced his friends to her (e.g., the Frenchmen Jacques Maritain and Yves Simon). Moreover, Gurian was established in the United States; he had connections that allowed her to publish.

But how did the exiled—she who had lost her library, the books that she needed for thinking, making arguments, and writing—get by? How was she writing her articles? She visited public academic libraries. Many immigrants spent a part of their days there, as long as no other concerns were pressing. In the public library on the corner of Forty-Second Street and Fifth Avenue, to name only one among a dozen, the exiled could meet well-known and less well-known intellectuals of the New York scene. There one could borrow anything the heart desired: European, American, and world literature, one could even find one's own works again. It was warm in the winter and cool in the summer. One could work in large reading halls undisturbed by domestic constraints and make social contacts at the same time.

One can see from the friendship between Arendt and Gurian how connections in exile were made and transformed, how they were broken and renewed. Arendt took advantage of the private book exchange established both by Gurian

and the network of authors around the journal. A large part of the correspondence between them consists of reports on books that have been read, have yet
to be read, have been loaned or lost, or books to be reviewed or rejected. Books
and articles were sent back and forth nonstop. It was an ever-growing circle of
friends and acquaintances who, in this way, obtained books and essays that were
otherwise unavailable or were too expensive to buy. Last, but not least, by corresponding and exchanging books and articles, one received news and gossip about
which one fumed, discussed, and gratefully passed along.

Gurian wrote his letters by hand, with a pencil and in giant letters. Shortly
before his death he, who rejected all modern means of convenience, dictated some
of his letters on the typewriter. The tone between Arendt and Gurian is intimate,
occasionally passionate, open, and sometimes marked by an almost wounding
directness. The ups and downs of friendship resurfaced in the shifting form of
address: Dear Herr Gurian, Dear Ms. Arendt, Dear friend, Dear Waldemar, Dear
Hannah, Dear Gurian. . . .

Their first preserved letter dates back to December 1941—half a year after
their meeting in the United States—a time full of experiences with the language,
earning money, getting to know the New York libraries, contacts with Jewish
organizations and discussion circles, new friendships, worries and joys, disappointments and hopes. The letter sounds like a continuation of a conversation
just recently interrupted: "Please accept many thanks for your letter and books.
After not publishing a single line in eight years, every line I write today costs me
an old friend. You can imagine how much, under these circumstances (and of
course under any circumstances), our conversation made me happy."[22] The letter
emanates energy. The old joy in the paradoxical argument remains. With Gurian
begins a friendship that will offer her support and security in her first "American
years."

A little later Gurian suggests to Arendt that she write a book on National
Socialism. She responds:

> For days I have been carrying your suggestion in my head and turning it over.
> I am sure I do not need to say that I—above everything else—feel entirely
> senselessly and childishly flattered. But you overestimate me; I am not—or
> not yet—capable of writing such a book. Do not forget that I resumed serious
> and systematic thinking only since 1940 and this time has not by any means
> been undisturbed. There is another consideration: I, as a Jew, cannot write on
> National Socialism at all. It does not behoove me. I have no legitimacy for this.
> But what I can and would like to do is to write a chapter for *your* book, the one
> on racial anti-Semitism. This I can and may do and I could do this openly as
> a Jew: *mea res agitur.* And now write me quickly what you think about this.[23]

Evidently Gurian broached the subject again. In any event, she explains herself
for the second time:

And now on the book: since I think that there is nothing more important than to struggle with the Nazis, I would never plead another work as an excuse. So please believe me that the Jewish subject-matter is, to begin with, cogent. Not that I consider Herr Neumann to be legitimate![24] *Loin de là.* I consider your formulation of the central question to be absolutely correct; but criticizing this world does not agree with me, unless I criticize the Jewish sector, show the Jewish share of responsibility in the emergence of the plague and why the Jewish world so helplessly collapsed before it. And, secondly, please believe that I know myself well and do not suffer from false modesty; and thus know that I am not yet a match for the subject matter! If I could help in those matters that I know well, I would be very glad and believe that I could accomplish something good.[25]

Thus the plan to write a book on anti-Semitism emerged from the correspondence. In 1943 she shared this with Salomon Adler-Rüdel, a friend from the old days.[26] The topic was obvious, since Arendt had written several preparatory works. In Berlin and Paris she had worked on the history of German-Jewish assimilation; in France, she expanded the subject to the history of French anti-Semitism. Moreover, from her reflections, conversations, and heated debates with friends and Zionist comrades-in-arms in Paris, the question arose as to how European Jews could emerge from their position as a minority—and with it eternal victimhood—and organize themselves politically. Here her line of argument is presented clearly: she was walking a fine line between the minority status of the Jews, denigrated by the League of Nations, which she rejected because it was not tied in with political rights—and the demand of many Zionists for a separate state for the Jewish people.[27] Her new research project was the expansion of the one she had already worked on in Paris, while working at Youth-Alijah.

From the present perspective one sees just how much Gurian supported the writing of *The Origins of Totalitarianism*, which she published with Harcourt and Brace. One recognizes how he accompanied her intellectually as the book changed emphasis over time. The project begins with her studies on anti-Semitism, continues with her work on imperialism and race ideology, and finally concludes with a third section on the totalitarian domination and the extermination camps. Still, it all began with her claim that she, "as a Jew, cannot write on National Socialism at all."

In this initial time in America, another European was close to her, the Viennese Hermann Broch, novelist, essayist, critic of the times, and avid admirer of beautiful and intelligent women. Arendt met him in May 1946 at a party hosted by Annemarie Meier-Gräfe, Broch's partner and one of their friends, who had invited her and Blücher.[28]

At that time, she was standing at the beginning of her career as a political writer and essayist. Broch, who was twenty years older, was, as his biographer Paul Michael Lützeler notes, in the zenith of his fame, which extended to the United States. His novel *The Death of Virgil* had already been published.[29]

Despite their age difference, Arendt and Broch shared several things, including their background of assimilated Jewish bourgeois families, their rootedness in the Jewish-European culture, their burning, even tormented interest in the horrible events in Europe, and their still-unforeseeable consequences. But all of this would not have brought the two so close had there not also been an erotic connection. Broch must have been an exceptional Viennese charmer; Arendt was not indifferent to his charisma. Perhaps a sexual tension remained between them until Broch's death insofar as the much younger woman refused his persistent advances. Still it must have flattered her that this famous writer, whom she esteemed from the bottom of her heart and certainly found attractive, valued her both intellectually and erotically.

Broch, in his turn, as Lützeler points out, was drawn in by the mixture of Arendt's physical and intellectual attractiveness: he was taken by the startling freshness of her demeanor coupled with the originality of her thinking. From the outset, Heinrich Blücher was included in this affection. As Arendt's husband, he didn't seem at all bothered by Broch, neither by his letters nor by his only half-ironic pursuit of Arendt.

Arendt was so impressed by Broch's novel *The Death of Virgil* that she wrote a laudatory review for the *Nation*. She also told her friend Kurt Blumenfeld about it and advised him to read it: "When you have a lot of time and a lot of peace (prescribed by a doctor), and really want to read something good and astounding, read Hermann Broch's *Death of Virgil*. . . . We have become friends and this was the best thing that has happened since you left."[30] Broch was flattered. Since he saw her not as someone younger, but as an independent thinker, her enthusiasm must have pleased him even more. In any event, for her forty-first birthday, he sent her a typescript of the final version of *The Death of Virgil*. The following poem was attached to it:

"Oh, this is really too much"
Said the citizen of the gift
Still, that no one steal it away
He pressed it tightly in his fist:
What one receives, one takes in.

But of course it is too much—
Who has room for huge tomes!
Nonetheless I lay the Virgil

In your hands with huge congratulations,
May it remain there as symbol.

For Hannah
On the
14 October, 1947
Hermann[31]

Sending her the gift of a typescript on her forty-first birthday was a very special sign honoring their friendship. It made Arendt both self-conscious and proud.

Broch and Arendt, from similar yet quite different backgrounds, shared the conviction that as a writer one was not allowed to stand apart from the world in times that demanded thought and political analysis. Broch went so far as to put his own writer's work on hold for a time. He was convinced that he had to write political essays, not novels. He wrote several larger political texts: one of his unfinished projects was a reform of the human rights policy of the United Nations, another was a kind of mass psychology of fascism, and the third was concerned with the foundation of an international university. Broch was profoundly interested in methodology and epistemology and was—like so many of the time, including Hannah Arendt—looking for the "foundations of a plausible a-deistic metaphysics."[32] Both were convinced that that this could only be a political metaphysics.

From the correspondence with Broch, it becomes clear how thoughts and ideas were circulating in Arendt's intellectual network in New York. The intellectual challenge that Arendt received from her European friends, old and new, detecting the topics that "were in the air"—all of it makes it clear that the process of creation in the first years was also a work of community, the work of the network of friends in which topics, theses, and arguments zipped back and forth daily. They all fed on this living exchange. Those who remained outside were lonely.

With this circle of friends, always open to expansion, as a backup, America was a subject of investigation. Arendt experienced the reality of the United States both from the European and from the American perspective. She was and remained a European and became an American of a special kind. Some of her American friends criticized the resulting tension as lack of loyalty, while some of her European friends saw her as too strongly identified with America. Yet Arendt's intellectual originality and productivity was the result of this enduring exchange of perspectives.

The cultural world of the Weimar Republic, or rather what remained of it, was constantly present in New York. Those friends who had experienced it directly bonded with those in the New World who had also come from the Old World. One talked about the Old World as though it had not disappeared and kept the philosophical discourse of the years before 1933 alive.

At the same time, it was slowly becoming clear how this perspective was radically altered by the mass murder in Europe.

Martin Heidegger loomed as a great absentee in the American landscape; he was present symbolically, if not personally. But of course he was discussed. Broch condemned Heidegger's involvement with National Socialism, but without the fury with which Arendt passed it along in letters to Jaspers after 1945. On September 30, 1947, Broch writes to his friend Erich von Kahler:

> To be sure, behind all of this stands nothing other than the fundamental question: should the philosopher be a martyr if it is necessary? And it is a question that ultimately needs to be affirmed not just for the philosopher, but for everyone because it is the core of what is called decency, and the man Heidegger is thus judged in accordance with it. And his petition[33] is, in accordance with it, quite lamentable, since he of course knew what was at issue. At the same time, I am in principle rather mild in my criticism of such cases since one often does not know if a general emergency was at hand or if an individual alone precipitated his own downfall.[34]

Broch was—and here we see another link between Arendt and Broch—a critical follower of the existential philosophy of the 1920s. He studied Heidegger's *Being and Time* as well as *Kant and the Problem of Metaphysics* and other texts. His novel *The Death of Virgil* follows in the steps of Heidegger's philosophy of being. Was this also a reason that Arendt was so impressed with this book?

Broch had Heidegger's new publications sent to him after the war. He engaged with *Plato's Doctrine of Truth* and the related *Letter on Humanism* deeply and positively. However, Broch was devastating in his judgment of Heidegger's transition to "letting-be (*Gelassenheit*)," and his turn to poetic thinking which he found rambling and his "crusted" figures of speech terrible.[35] In Hermann Broch, Arendt found a kindred and reflective combatant.

In these years she persevered, attending to her network of European and Americans friends: Kurt Blumenfeld, Gershom Scholem, Martin Rosenblüth, Paul Tillich, Dwight Macdonald, Alfred Kazin, Mary McCarthy, and of course her "tribe," those who belonged to the closest circle of her friends in New York: the painter Carl Heidenreich (originally a friend of Blücher's whom Arendt met in Paris) and the artist Alfred L. Copley, who called himself Alcopley, the publicist Charlotte Beradt, the Germanist Lotte Köhler, Peter and Minka Huber, Rose Feitelson, her friend Hans Jonas from the earlier days with his wife, Eleonore, Lenchen Wieruszowski, the Wolffs, Salo and Jeanette Baron, Charlotte and Chanan Klenbort, Else and Paul Oskar Kristeller, Alice and Josef Maier, Hans Morgenthau, Robert Pick with his wife. This "tribe" was hers and Heinrich Blücher's friendly backbone throughout the years. Certainly there were lasting disagreements, such as the one connected to her book on Eichmann. Yet the tribe formed the belongingness of the "We" from which no one departed unless he or she died. This was Arendt's network. She leaned on the friends in this network through the many frustrations that lay ahead of her in these years.

Zionism in America

There are two key points in the years of her political and intellectual work: Zionism and the understanding of the events in Europe. Arendt's engagement with Zionism, which imposed itself on her under the weight of the circumstances at the end of the 1920s, took center stage in France and now assumed new forms in New York. At first there were the old friends, Kurt Blumenfeld, who actually lived in Palestine but came to New York often, and Salman Schocken, the publisher from Berlin, who was part of the Berlin Zionist circle of friends and who opened a new publishing house in New York, Schocken Books. Salo Baron was new, an important man in Jewish politics in the United States. Baron was a professor at Columbia University and the publisher of *Jewish Social Studies*. He too encouraged her to work on anti-Semitism.

Through her contact with Manfred George, the publisher of *Aufbau*, the German-language emigrant Jewish newspaper, she received an invitation to write a column on current issues in Jewish politics. This invitation came only a few months after her arrival in 1941. Evidently, her reputation as an intellectually gifted, active, and argumentative Zionist preceded Arendt not just in Europe, but on the other side of the ocean as well. Arendt saw the challenge of writing a column as an honor, as she proudly reported to Gurian.

Aufbau was *the* Jewish emigrant newspaper that presented reports of all kinds from the Old and the New Worlds, reports about the persecution of Jews in Germany and Europe, Zionist politics, and Jewish life in New York. Time and again *Aufbau* gave space to ongoing debates concerning Jewish identity and politics.

The intense debate concerning Jewish self-defense against the mass murder of the European Jews, a debate that continued for years, offered Arendt a chance to express her views. Her position on the question of how the Jews ought to defend themselves was that the creation of a "Jewish army" was the only rational solution. Coming from her own experience that "you can only defend yourself as the person you are attacked as,"[36] namely, as a Jew, Arendt passionately and against all resistance, even in her own camp, advocated this plan. In 1941 she writes that the only possible self-defense against a highly successful murderous regime that wanted to subjugate all of Europe was to form a Jewish army. The goal of the Jewish army was at the forefront of her thinking the entire year. The prospect of an independent Jewish struggle against National Socialism was, in her opinion, worth being bitten and stung in the hornet's nest of arguments, intrigues, and factional fights within the Jewish emigrant community. Moreover, the "Jewish army" was much closer to her political views than the Herzlian state project that remained suspect to her.

Her voice was quickly marginalized; on July 13, 1942, she complains in disappointment to Gurian: "In the last weeks I have barely lifted a finger, so meaningless does everything seem to me. If the question concerning the Jewish army is permanently settled, I will gladly give up the column. It would be meaningful only under the precondition of a Jewish people's politics. If it does not happen, I will withdraw from journalism, which is a plague anyway."[37] Yet, as is often the case with Arendt's firm resolution, she is angry, she is discouraged, and then she picks up the thread again. She does not spare her biting criticism of the enemies of the project: the philanthropists, Jewish notables, parvenus, and those who would rather hide behind the coattails of the Great Powers and wait there for a good opportunity to further promote the Jewish cause. Her position is clear: if it were the case, and she is firmly convinced that it is, that the Jews must defend themselves as Jews and not as Austrians, French, or Germans, then they must fight independently. In the time of war, only an army offers the opportunity to give the enemy an active response.

For Arendt, it is a *conditio sine qua non* that the Jews must stop being a powerless minority who can be arbitrarily tossed back and forth by the Great Powers. She does not tire opposing the Jewish minority status that the international community granted to the Jews as a surrogate for political status. Her years in France taught her that being in a minority makes it impossible to move beyond the historical role of the victim. However, her position also implied that she would not to go along with those who claimed Palestine as the country for the Jews stemming from biblical times.

The beginning of the 1940s was a highly emotional time when everything still seemed possible. The scattered Jewish communities, primarily those in New York and London, engaged in international politics and went back and forth on the question as to how best to win over the Great Powers in order to make Palestine a Jewish national state. The transition was not simple because the Jews were not a national movement like other minorities. Rather, they were made up of, on the one hand, many diaspora communities characterized by various religious orientations who, in part, thought in an antistate way, and, on the other hand, of Zionist factions who identified with the project of Palestine. And there was a third group: the Jewish settlers in Palestine itself.

Palestine and Israel

The debate about the Jewish army masked the question as to what should happen with Palestine. For a long time Arendt was skeptical of the majority position on the question concerning the founding of a Jewish state legitimized on the basis of the divine right of the Jewish people, which at the same time accepted the expulsion of Palestinian Arabs. Moreover, for her, the project of Palestine—despite Herzl's dreams—would not solve the problems of the Jewish minorities in Europe. In 1940 Arendt, still in France, formulated key thoughts on the Jewish perspective in Europe in a kind of memorandum for her friend and comrade-in-arms in Zionist matters, Erich Cohn-Bendit. In the face of threatening deportations and the impotent politics of the League of Nations, Arendt proposed a federated Europe be formed after the end of National Socialism within which the Jews would be acknowledged as a national minority with parliamentary representation in a European parliament.[38] In this context, the project of Palestine would then be a European settlement project in the Middle East, which would be protected both by Europe and by American Zionists.

Arendt was strongly opposed to the creation of the Palestine which crystallized at the so-called Biltmore conference in New York, according to which an Israeli state with an Arabic minority was to be created.

She was also against a two-nation state where Jews would be positioned as the minority, surrounded by an Arabic federation. The alternative she envisioned was a constitution for Palestine, in which the country would become a member of the British Commonwealth.[39]

At this time she was full of energy, active and involved. In March 1942 she and her friend and comrade-in-arms Josef (Joseph) Maier founded a discussion group of German-speaking Jews open to all, which she called "Jungjüdische Gruppe." As its addressees, they appealed to:

> Those who feel themselves not just the arbitrary victims of a catastrophic event, but also responsible for the future of the Jewish people;
> Those who, convinced of the bankruptcy of all current ideologies, are ready to rack their brains over the new foundation of Jewish politics;
> Those who know that the struggle for freedom cannot be led by either notables or world revolutionaries, but rather only by the people who want to bring it about it for their own nation.[40]

Alluding to the raging fractional fights and grudges within the Zionist movement, it meant: "we are not arrogant enough to think that our ideas could be of any consequence if they are not discussed on a democratic basis."[41] But she could not prevent the politics of the dominant groups from playing a role even in this small discussion circle.

The meetings were so conceived that either Arendt, her friend or an invited speaker began with one or two statements on the current situation. Then the discussion was opened to the group. The general subject was the political self-discovery of the Jewish diaspora and its relationship to the project of Palestine. At the end of the debate, book suggestions were given, participants were charged with being up to date on current arguments.

At one of the first sessions, on March 26, 1946, Kurt Blumenfeld made a presentation on the "History of Zionism." Following him, Arendt spoke to the critique of Zionism. In the discussion, their positions clashed fiercely: Blumenfeld reacted angrily to Arendt's radical critique of the Zionist politics. He accused her and her friends of naïveté ("politics is power"). For Blumenfeld, the only way to organize Jews politically was for them to endorse the creation of Palestine. Finally, he reproached the entire project of "Jungjüdische Gruppe": "What is desired here leads to the collapse of Palestine. There is only a struggle of life and death against it."[42]

Arendt's reaction to this threat of exclusion from Zionist solidarity is telling. Namely, she insisted on the distinction between political conflict and a war of annihilation: "For us, there is a struggle of life and death only with those who want to annihilate the Jewish people. Between Jewish patriots, there can be only differences, which are enacted politically."[43]

Yet she was nearly alone with this view on things. The closer the project of Palestine came to founding the state of Israel, the more severe the internal fight against those looking for an alternative became.

Of course, she realized that the events in Palestine pushed toward the founding of a Jewish national state, but she remained opposed to the solution advocated by the majority of Zionists. With this, she stood in open conflict both with the results of the Biltmore conference and with the majority of the currents within American Zionism.

In addition to the *Aufbau*, she published her arguments in notable Jewish or Zionist magazines, including *Commentary, Jewish Social Studies*, the *Menorah Journal, Contemporary Jewish Record, Jewish Frontier, New Currents, A Jewish Monthly*, and the *Chicago Jewish Forum*. At the beginning of the 1940s, her contributions were still accepted everywhere. Later, that changed.

In general, the *Jüdische Brigade*, founded in 1944 by the British supreme command, was all that remained of the idea of a Jewish army. At the same time, precursors to an Israeli army in Palestine emerged out of the struggle of secret Jewish paramilitary groups.

In 1947 Arendt met Judah Magnes—the legendary Zionist leader, who, like her, was on the margin and in opposition to the Zionist mainstream. Magnes must have had a charisma that overshadowed even the prominent personality of Kurt Blumenfeld. He was the first rector and chancellor of Hebrew University in Jerusalem, which had been founded under the British protectorate in 1924. Furthermore, he was the radiant embodiment of the Zionist idea of education. At the same time, he was realistic and practical, educated in the years of terror between Jews, Arabs, and the British. From these years, he had drawn certain conclusions. His experiences spoke against the seizure of Palestine by the Jews and in favor of a Jewish-Arabic federation. Magnes founded his own party in

Palestine—Ikhud (Likud)—in the hopes of being able to influence the events in such a way that the Jews would eschew founding a national state in accordance with the nineteenth century European model. From the United States in general and New York in particular, he gathered a circle of friends in support of his party. They exchanged news about Palestine, wrote memorandums, gave press releases on the events in Palestine, and, above all, collected money. Elliot Cohen, the publisher of *Commentary*; Hans Kohn, historian at Smith College in Northampton, Massachusetts; David Riesman, who later made a name in sociology (*The Lonely Crowd*); the lawyer James Marshall; Maurice Hexter from the Federation of Jewish Philanthropies; and others were part of the group.

Yet the circumstances overpowered even Judah Magnes. The position of two politicians, Golda Meir and David Ben Gurion, both of whom were present during the British protectorate of Palestine, was gradually implemented into the Zionist movement in the 1940s. Both represented the position of the Israeli Workers Party, which, supported by the British Labour Party, wanted to form an Israeli state out of the British protectorate without cooperating with the Arabs, that is to say, the Palestinians living there. For years this was the goal of various political and terrorist actions in Palestine, which the British and the League of Nations only halfheartedly fought against.

In May 1948 the state of Israel was founded in exactly the way that Magnes, Arendt, and their related circle of Zionists considered fatal: a state with a Jewish majority and an Arabic minority, surrounded by Arabic states hostile to it. Yet Magnes did not want to give up the work of persuasion. Throughout 1948, through the Jewish communities and notables, as well as through his contacts to the American government, he attempted, with his few allies, to influence the founding of the state of Israel.

Admittedly, Arendt did not agree with Magnes's grand political plans, but she shared his critique of the Zionist establishment. She worked as his mediator and confidant in the United States and created contacts with allies, mediated connections with politically influential persons, wrote press releases, and drafted speeches and petitions. She found in Magnes an ingenious debater and a fatherly friend whom she esteemed from the bottom of her heart. In October 1948 she wrote to him: "How thankful I am that the last year brought me the privilege of your acquaintanceship. Politics in our age is quite a distressful matter and I was always tempted to run from it. I can assure you that your example saved me from distress and it will remain so for many years."[44] Magnes died suddenly in October 1948. His death tore a hole in the network of friends and colleagues who endorsed a different path for Israel. In what followed, Arendt attempted to continue Magnes's initiative within the framework of a Judah L. Magnes Foundation and collected money for the Israeli educational system.

Pitfalls of Zionist Politics

Important essays that were largely the precursors of *The Origin of Totalitarianism* emerged during these years: on the cultural history of anti-Semitism ("From the Dreyfus Affair to France Today" and "Herzl and Lazare," 1942); on the question of refugees and minorities ("We Refugees," 1943; "Concerning Minorities," 1944; "The Stateless People," 1945); on the race question ("Race-Thinking before Racism," 1944); on Zionism (the *Aufbau* column and many other articles in *Aufbau* from 1941 to 1945).

In the 1945 fall issue of *Menorah Journal*, she pulled together a summary in a thirty-four-page detailed article titled "Zionism Reconsidered." The article was a summing up, condensing much of what Arendt had produced in different journals, discussion groups, and letters to friends and critics since her arrival in the middle of 1941. She did not deny Palestine's religious and mythical role or the political venture of founding a state against the backdrop of the German murder of European Jews. Nevertheless, Palestine should not be a national state. Why? Because the founding of such a state would bring about the kind of "national conflict" that had provoked the catastrophe of two world wars in Europe. In her view, the revisionist and leftist Zionists made the same mistake to which the national states of the nineteenth century had succumbed: they wanted to constitute a nation on an ethnic basis, a nation that excluded the minorities from having political status.[45] In a long review of the European, and particularly German, history of the Jews, Arendt argued that as a consequence of this decision Zionism would have to reckon with the same consequences as nationalism: race conflict and wars. For Arendt, two paths remained opened: first, the founding of an empire on the basis of a national state with all the concomitant consequences such as war and instability and, second, the creation of a Palestinian-Arabic federation.[46] Of course, she pleaded for the federation solution. Zionist politicians of every stripe and faction took her article as an affront. She received outraged reactions.

It was the years of her work in Zionist organizations and her long familiarity with the theory and praxis of Zionism that granted her the certainty in judgment hardly comprehensible by those who followed. Her experiences in Germany, her theoretical and practical knowledge of the history of Jews in Germany and Europe, her involvement in the *Jugend-Alijah* in Paris, her familiarity with Zionist literature and the programs of leading politicians, apparently granted her a pronounced self-confidence. However, in retrospect, it appears quite courageous that, lacking any powerful allies, this small, delicate woman ventured to take on the majority of the Zionist establishment. At that point, Zionist politics unfolded through powerful factions on different continents: there were the Zionist leaders in the diaspora such as Chaim Weizmann, the founders of the Jewish state (Golda

Meir and David Ben Gurion), and the paramilitary fighting groups of right-wing revisionists. In Arendt they saw not just a political enemy but a traitor. This was the power constellation that she would later become painfully aware of when she was ferociously attacked after the publication of her trial report on Adolf Eichmann.

A certainty of the heart speaks from her essays: "Here I stand, I cannot do otherwise. If you want to judge me for it, then do so." In the overheated atmosphere of the Zionist camp such a stance was an invitation to battle.

The betrayal of friends was the most painful issue with which she had to contend. It was one of her personal peculiarities that she immediately became entirely helpless in the face of a friend's betrayal and, perhaps, against her conviction, even asked for forgiveness, just to save the friendship. She had already experienced this with Kurt Blumenfeld in the Jungjüdische Gruppe. Blumenfeld's relationship to Zionism was by no means without conflict. His relationship to the founding of the state was nuanced. He recommended a moderate federalism. At the same time, he was a person of power politics and realpolitik. In case of doubt, he aligned himself with the prevailing majority line. His main point of dissent with Arendt was that he unfailingly subordinated his critique to the professed will of the Israeli people. Arendt rejected this compromise.

Blumenfeld was living in Jerusalem at the time. In the beginning of January 1946, he still asked Arendt to send him her latest articles.[47] At that time he certainly had not read "Zionism Reconsidered." Barely two weeks later he wrote to his compatriot Martin Rosenblüth in New York, also a friend of Hannah's, giving his opinion of the essay. He might have received "Zionism Reconsidered" from Gershom Scholem. He was horrified. Scholem had expressed himself even "more strongly and disdainfully."[48] Blumenfeld continues:

> I regret my letter to Hannah.[49] Not because this article was an unbearable mishmash of someone half-educated in these things, but because it revealed the character traits that led me to break off my relationship with Hannah once before. This time everything is expressed with even more clarity and ugliness. It does not matter to me that she calls us sectarians. The ignorance in things Zionist (here I am thinking not just of the remark on "general Zionists," which should not come from a real scholar) does not surprise me, since I know full well Hannah's journalistic superficiality and rashness. What is frightening is the baseness manifested in her personal judgments. A completely indifferent, heartless person, who possesses a chutzpa to which she has not even the smallest right, writes about life unfolding under the harshest conditions, about which she has formed elaborate notions through hearsay. She says about the Jewish army that it is forced upon us—who has forced it upon us? The filthy newspaper she believes in, which was concerned with these matters in America, was not founded here. . . . I never believed Hannah's Zionism. As I once told her at a gathering: "between us there is a life-and-death struggle." I was

correct, even if I was speaking in the heat of the moment. We subsequently had a very good personal friendship. Hannah gave the impression that she would miss me. In any event, I often had conversations with her in my mind. In the last years in America, we no longer had political discussions. If I began one, Hannah turned the conversation in another direction. The article in *Menorah Journal* revealed to me very clearly a psychopathic side of Hannah's being. There is a resentment which spills over into madness. The unusual controversy, pursued with such vigor, as to whether the hatred of Jews will remain or disappear is indicative of this. It is necessary for Hannah's personal, not just political, situation to predict the disappearance of anti-Semitism. I would even accept Hannah's anti-Zionism calmly if I could get over the hatefulness and the meanness of her presentation. I cannot . . . I do not know if I will have the nerve to speak against Hannah's article publicly. In a certain sense I am guilty for its development. It is possible that I once somewhat distanced her from assimilation. She has her path, the path of "revolutionary expediency," and she should walk it alone. This letter is also, certainly, meant for Hannah.[50]

It is a letter of justification to his friend Rosenblüth and a break from Hannah. Blumenfeld could not or would not distinguish between political discourse and an annihilating personal attack. This had been shown in the argument in the Jungjüdische Gruppe, and it would repeat itself tragically after Arendt's report on the Eichmann trial. Gershom Scholem wrote to her a similar letter.[51]

Both letters affected Arendt badly. She trusted these men, held their friendship in esteem, and valued their work. Certainly, the profound political differences with Blumenfeld and Scholem had been made clear time and again. Moreover, she foresaw rather clearly what her article would wreck. Earlier she had written to Gurian: "I have almost finished a big critical essay on Zionism. If *Menorah*,[52] which had requested it, accepts it, I am done with all of my Zionist friends. Frankly speaking, it was a rather heart-breaking affair. It is also the reason for the long silence. I did not feel like talking."[53] Apparently the feuds between the mainstream Zionists and minority groups had assumed an intensity that pushed Arendt to her radical critique. She, herself, was harshly criticized. Yet, unlike these two men, she insisted that these objective differences should not destroy friendships. Neither man, however, wished to separate the personal from the political.

For Scholem and Blumenfeld, all critique had to be held in check when it concerned the goal of establishing the homeland, Israel. In their view, those who did not follow this maxim placed themselves outside the Jewish people and should be scorned, at least verbally, at least for a time.

Arendt, however, could not accept that the theological foundation of Zionism should make it exempt from an earthly political discourse. For their part, Blumenfeld, Scholem, and others, did not want to understand that the conflict around *Eretz Israel* was an integral part of the process of founding the state of

Israel. Shortly thereafter, Arendt reacted to the hostilities in her own way. She reminded Blumenfeld that friendship was something that was supposed to survive argument, otherwise it was not friendship. In the middle of a letter where she complained that Rosenblüth apparently went out of his way to avoid her in New York, she exclaimed:

> Ah, children, what fools you are. Do you really believe that there is, in our inhuman world, which is becoming more inhuman every day, so much loyalty that you can afford to throw it into the corner like an old pair of shoes, which one perhaps takes out once again to re-sole, so as to wear them one last time? Friendship is rare enough and hardly available to those of us who live on the razor's edge. I really did not want to write this to you. It does not include you—or does it? What I wanted to write to you was simply that I will always care about you . . . in short, a general declaration of love, for no particular reason.[54]

Formulations like these return time and again. Arendt faithfully held on to friendship. By friendship she understood something permanent, something that survived political conflict, indeed, even stood outside it, animated by the primordial trust that was not to be shattered. However, her friends were hurt by the sharpness of her judgment. They felt personally affected by what Arendt intended as a purely political critique.

Blumenfeld, too, did not bear the split, and a couple of years later he assured Hannah again how close she was to him. She thanked him for that. And on the basis of his remark, she told him *what* she was thankful for: "I am so glad that you say that we are very close to each other. I really always wanted to write you about how much I owe you in understanding the situation of the Jews. . . . In Heidelberg you simply opened up a kind of world to me."[55] A certain style of thinking and discourse was developed in the intense conflict regarding Zionism, a style also used by Arendt. First, she rehearsed the subject matter, the event, or the context, then, switching the tone in the middle of the argument, she moved from an internal analysis to attacking the argument or the opponent directly and matter-of-factly. This struck some as cold. Her passion in the matter of the Jews was understood only by those for whom argumentative confrontation and clarity of thought was just as important as belief. For those who carried belief into politics, this woman must have had the effect of a red flag.

The Book Project on Imperialism

The engagement with Zionism and Palestine lasted until the end of the 1940s, then noticeably declined, perhaps as a result of the severe personal critique that was ever more frequent, presumably showing Arendt that the lines of demarcation drawn long ago within the Zionist movement could not be modified by her disagreement. In the meantime, the research work on imperialism came to the fore. This will become one of the precursors to *The Origins of Totalitarianism*.

She exchanged thoughts about her readings with Gurian. She recommended Joseph Conrad's *Heart of Darkness* to him, a book that stands at the center of her critique of imperialism in *Origins*: "Once again on *Heart of Darkness*: in this short [*sic*] story really and, as far as I know, for the first and the only time, a 'Nazi.' is depicted. Moreover, it is an excellent testimony to the future of the 'white man' in the 'dark continent.'"[56] In August 1943 she told Gurian that she would send him the first part of her work on imperialism.[57] Half a year later she lets him know that she was working on nationalist movements in the time between the wars, especially in the Central and Eastern European framework.[58]

In late fall of 1944, she delivered the first outline of the book project to the publisher Houghton and Mifflin. On December 17, 1946, she writes to Gurian: "Houghton Mifflin has already sent the contract for the imperialism book."[59] She asked for his permission to use both articles written for *Review of Politics*, "Race-Thinking before Racism" and "Imperialism, Nationalism, Chauvinism," in the book.

With her articles and her unusual style of argumentation, Arendt attracted attention beyond the Zionist circle. As she did not shy away from controversial topics, she was a welcome author on the liberal journal scene. It is therefore no wonder that one day Philip Rahv, one of the publishers of *Partisan Review*, contacted her, asking if she would write an article on existentialism. At that time Europe and the European intelligentsia exercised a strong fascination on the American East Coast. Sartre's plays and Camus's prose provoked great interest among New York intellectuals who saw Jean-Paul Sartre and Albert Camus as the protagonists of an exciting new direction of thought. It was clear that a leftist journal such as *Partisan Review* would address these rising stars of the intellectual world. Rahv thus invited Arendt to his editorial office for a conversation in which he could explain the direction he wanted the article to take. But Arendt did not allow him the reins. In the course of the conversation, the roles were reversed, as William Barrett, another publisher of *Partisan Review*, wrote in his memoir. Arendt took over the discussion. Rahv was the listener. It concluded with the assignment of writing an article on existentialism in accordance with Arendt's ideas.[60]

Two articles stemmed from this project. In the first issue of *Partisan Review* in 1946, she published on German existential philosophy and in the following February issue of the *Nation*, she published on French existentialism. Taken together, these articles afford a glimpse into Arendt's reflection on the German and French existential philosophy of her time.

Although she publishes the "German" article first, in it she grapples with a problem that to her mind remained unaddressed by the French existentialists. In her essay on the French, she ends her analysis of the French protagonists, Sartre and Camus, with a twofold conclusion. On the one hand, she attests to the absolute modernity of both writers, insofar as both had irrevocably departed from the tradition. However, she insisted time and again that with National Socialism and communism a new type of domination came into the world, a domination based on a complete rupture with tradition. She finds this break accomplished intellectually in Sartre and Camus. However, she did not at all agree with the conclusion that each in his own way had drawn. To the contrary, she reproached both protagonists of French philosophy and literature for moving forward only halfheartedly. The nihilism that both authors represented meant that they had not detached themselves from the tradition, but rather sought a connection with the thought of the nineteenth century (Nietzsche, Kierkegaard).[61]

The article on German existentialist philosophy served as the point of departure for the question of nihilism. The article sought to explain to the American public this enigmatic existential philosophy. At the same time, Arendt's article made clear those aspects wherein it differed fundamentally from its French counterpart.

The work on German philosophy between the wars, including the two rebels against neo-Kantianism, Karl Jaspers and Martin Heidegger, who in the meantime had become elderly, must have been strangely moving. The renewed reading of the old texts might have provoked in her contradictory feelings: familiarity, confirmation of her own insights, memories of her love of Martin Heidegger, anger, and alienation. The article takes an emphatic tone in some sections, but at times it comes across as dry and didactic.

It is the first intense confrontation with Heidegger after more than ten years. In the meanwhile, she followed what was written about him in the United States and talked about him with Hermann Broch and others.[62] She also mentioned to friends that she would use the recommendation that Heidegger wrote her for a job application in the United States.

While writing the article, she knew that Jaspers and his wife were still alive. She had been in correspondence with them since the fall of 1945. She sent packages with books, articles, canned food, and, above all, letters. For Jaspers, their resumed contact must have suddenly opened a window into the world. Even before postal service was functioning again, the young intellectual Melvin Lasky, then an officer in the American army, carried letters and packages with provisions. Lasky gave her reports on the situation in Germany and about an accidental meeting with Hans Jonas, a friend from her youth, who had become a sergeant in the "Jüdische Brigade." He also described visits with the Jaspers who were thinking about moving to Switzerland.

Through Rudolf Bultmann, another of her teachers from the Marburg days, Arendt learned that Hans Jonas had also been in Marburg and that Bultmann had big philosophical hopes for him as he had in the Weimar years. She sent Bultmann books, articles, and food, as well. However, only with Jaspers did she develop a close, constant contact. The letters between them referred back to the Old World. The teacher-student relationship became one of friendship.

The chaotic postwar conditions broke into their letters time and again. The differing experiences of the catastrophe separated the teacher and his former student. Political prospects in the zones that divided Germany were still completely unclear. The occupying powers first ordered an absolute standstill for four months: no mail, no university, no new books and articles, no newspapers, no travel. Young academics seemed dazed, oscillating between anger, frustration, and apathy.

Yet some signs of hope appeared later in 1945. In the fall, the publishing of the first newspapers was permitted. Jaspers, together with the publicist Dolf Sternberger, sociologist Alfred Weber, specialist in Roman languages Werner Krauss, and publisher Lambert Schneider, founded *Die Wandlung*, a journal that sought to follow the cultural and political changes of West Germany as it moved toward democracy. In 1946 Arendt published her text "On Imperialism," in *Die Wandlung*. Later this text was inserted into her book *The Origins of Totalitarianism*.

Postwar Era in Germany: The Question of Guilt

Immediately after the end of the war, it became clear just how deep the material and psychological damages that National Socialism had wreaked among the Germans were. Adhering to the past was simply impossible, even if many Germans could not or did not want to do otherwise. They wanted to hold on to what was reliable after the end of the trauma. At that time it was unclear how the Germans would reemerge from the disaster.

In winter semester 1945–46, after eight years of silence, Jaspers held his first lecture course, "The Intellectual Situation in Germany." The philosopher addressed his students in the plural "we" and, with this rhetorical device, implicated himself as part of the public, whose confused feelings were the topic. His audiences were young returning soldiers, invalids from the war, and many young women. According to Jaspers's description, "They are intoxicated with feelings of pride, of despair, of indignation, of defiance, of revenge, of scorn," and he asks that we "put these feelings on ice and see reality."[63]

Jaspers distinguished between four types of guilt and ways of dealing with it: criminal, political, moral, and metaphysical. By making the question of guilt multidimensional, he sought to implicate all those who wished to distance themselves from the discussion. With this categorization, Jaspers initiated, indeed, greatly influenced, the debate that would resurface regularly in the coming years in Germany. Derived from the Judeo-Christian tradition, the concept of guilt was for Jaspers, but also for both Christian churches and for part of the intelligentsia, the only remaining instrument by which to approach the crime and reflect on its effects on German culture and thinking.

Arendt adopted a different perspective. In her 1944 article "Organized Guilt and Universal Responsibility" she, too, starts out from the concept of guilt, but immediately criticizes it: "Where all are guilty, nobody in the last analysis can be judged. For exactly that guilt is mere appearance, the mere pretense of responsibility."[64]

For her there was no guilt without responsibility; only a common responsibility can be the framework in which guilt can be generally thematized. Jaspers, to whom she sent the article in January 1946, signaled agreement, but Arendt's direction of argument was entirely different from his. While Jaspers represented a view from within (how could he do otherwise after twelve years of confinement?), Arendt represented the view from outside. For her the "German problem" was to be solved only in Europe's new constitution as a confederation.[65] While Jaspers, with his recourse to a concept of guilt, remained firmly within the realm of the tradition, Arendt, time and again, unambiguously insisted that National Socialist (and communist) domination had caused a rupture in the tradition so profound that it was no longer possible to appeal to it.

The question of what was to happen with Germany and how to judge the German people and the crimes committed in their name was widely discussed internationally. There was the camp who hated Germans, represented by Lord Vansittard. Vansittard made arguments similar to those made by many in the circles of the victorious powers at the end of the First World War. In their eyes, Germany was principally responsible for the war. This meant that, even more so than after the first war, they had to pay. Some German emigrants also shared this view. Hannah Arendt strictly rejected such a position; she criticized its spokesmen as "Germans hungry for war booty."[66]

On this question, she showed solidarity with Dwight Macdonald's leftist liberal or rather post-Trotskyite stance. The latter wrote "Responsibility of Peoples" in the 1945 March issue of his journal *Politics*. Here one finds an almost word-for-word agreement with Arendt's thinking: "If everyone is guilty, no one is guilty," writes Macdonald, referring to Arendt's article "Organized Guilt and Universal Responsibility."[67] He rejected the thesis of collective guilt completely; in his view, it had to do with taking over (involuntarily) National Socialism's use of an organic concept of the people. To be sure, almost the entire American public clung to the thesis of collective guilt. "German guilt" was propagated not just by the allied veterans of the First World War, but also across the right- and left-wing party spectrum in the United States and Great Britain, by labor unions, parties, governments, and newspapers. Contrary to this, Macdonald represented the Marxist-Trotskyist maxim that wars are waged by governments, not people. However, it was already known at this time that the implication of the German people in the war crimes was much greater than supposed. It did not help that Macdonald cited Simone Weil's radical judgment, according to which modern war was a "fight of state executives and their apparatus against all arms-bearing men."[68] The mainstream had already decided on a different view.

Finally, Macdonald pleaded for a sharper differentiation—and ended at just the point where Arendt went further. For him, the real problem was that one could not find comfort in the idea that only Germans were capable of such indescribable crimes. Rather, one needed to come to terms with the thought that these atrocities were committed by completely normal people, not by beings from another planet. Arendt takes this idea further. In conversations with her husband it became clear to her that the concept of guilt could not serve as a conceptual framework for an event that in her words "should not have happened." In July 1946 Blücher wrote in a letter to Arendt, who was staying with her friend, the art historian Julie Braun-Vogelstein, in New Hampshire, after reading the Jaspers's "guilt" book:

> As I had already told you, the whole question of guilt simply serves as Christian hypocritical jabbering for the victors as a better way to get what they want, and for the vanquished as a way to continue occupying themselves exhaustively with themselves (even if for the noble purpose of self-illumination). In both cases, guilt serves the purpose of extirpating responsibility. . . . Jaspers' whole ethical purification babble leads him to solidarity with the German National Community and even with the National Socialists, instead of solidarity with those who have been degraded. . . . If Jaspers is searching for the nature of the true German, he will never find the true German conflict that has always existed in the republican-liberal will of a few against the Cossack-serf tendencies of the many.[69]

Well prior to this, Arendt had already drawn a conclusion that was diametrically opposed to Jaspers's book: She opted for a political interpretation of the event, Jaspers for a moral one. Instead of focusing on the crimes and moral responsibility, she wanted to draw attention to something that had been completely destroyed, namely, the political community for which citizens had to be held accountable. More than twenty years later she formulates the concept of "collective responsibility" as follows:

> Collective responsibility must fulfill two criteria . . . I must be held responsible for something I have not done. And the basis for my responsibility must be

my membership in a group (collective), a membership which no act on my part can sever. This means, it is a membership which is completely other than a business arrangement which I may sever at will. . . . In this sense we will all always be held responsible for the sins of our fathers in the same way that we reap the benefits of that which they have earned.[70]

However, the spokesmen in the Western world (and also in Stalin's Soviet Union) stubbornly held on to the thesis of collective guilt. The shaken elite in West Germany clung to this idea.

Heidegger from the American Perspective

The political-intellectual discourse on the future of Germany and the account-ability of the Germans preceded Arendt's reflection on existentialism and ac-companied it further. In this context, she came closer to German existential philosophy.

On the basis of the scarce information that was available to her or that others—Hermann Broch or her former classmates in Freiburg and Heidelberg—provided, she formed a view of Heidegger that was directly connected to her last correspondence with him in the winter of 1932–33. According to this view Heidegger was no longer "the secret king in the realm of thinking," but a prince of darkness. He became a National Socialist Party member. As a Nazi, he as-sumed the rectorship of Freiburg University and in this capacity forbade his old teacher, Edmund Husserl, to enter the university, which nearly cost the latter his life. After the war, he proposed to the French occupation power that he re-educate the youth. In other words, he drove the young to National Socialism in order to then present himself as their savior.

She expresses her anger in letters to Jaspers. Jaspers immediately corrects her: no, Heidegger did not personally bar Husserl from the university. Rather, it had to do with a circular given out by the Ministry regarding a ban from univer-sity grounds that every university, that is, every rector of a German university, was required to send to previously dismissed Jewish professors.[71] Arendt, how-ever, took completely different view:

Regarding the Heidegger note, your assumption about the Husserl letter is completely correct. I knew that this letter was a circular, and I know that many people have excused it for that reason. It always seemed to me that at the moment Heidegger was obliged to put his name to this document, he should have resigned. However foolish he might have been, he was capable of under-standing that. We can hold him responsible for his actions to that extent. He knew very well that that letter would have left Husserl more or less indiffer-ent if someone else had signed it. Now you might say that this happened in the rush of business. And I would probably reply that the truly irreparable things often—and deceptively—happen almost like accidents, that sometimes from an insignificant line that we step across easily, feeling certain that it is of no consequence anymore, a wall rises up that truly divides people. In other words, although I never had any professional or personal attachment to old Husserl, I mean to maintain solidarity with him in this one case. And because I know that this letter and this signature almost killed him, I can't but regard Heidegger as a potential murderer.[72]

The whole affair tormented her. In the meantime, she made inquiries about Heidegger. She spoke with Jean-Paul Sartre, whom she did not respect much, when he visited New York in 1946—and told Jaspers what she heard from him: "That four weeks (or six weeks) after Germany's defeat, Heidegger wrote to a professor at the Sorbonne (I've forgotten his name), talked about a 'misunderstanding' between Germany and France, and offered his hand in German-French 'reconciliation.' He received no reply, of course. Then, later, he wrote to Sartre. You'll be familiar with the various interviews he gave after that. Nothing but inane lies with what I think is a clearly pathological streak. But that's an old story."[73] She received a similar *On-dit* from her friend Anne Weil (née Mendelssohn) from Paris.[74]

Is Heidegger then a character with a pathological streak? Admittedly, it sounds as though she is clearly done with this man. It is as if she only needed Jaspers's confirmation. And he sees Heidegger exactly as she does.

Her article for *Partisan Review* on German existentialism informs American readers about the historical precursors of the question concerning existence and about different formulations of the question since Kant, especially in Kierkegaard and Husserl. She then addresses the further development of existential philosophy in Heidegger and Jaspers.

In its presentation of the theoretical steps of Heidegger's fundamental ontology in *Being and Time*, her essay is objective, if one-sided. However, in the beginning she deals a crushing blow to Heidegger as a person in a footnote: "Heidegger is really (let us hope) the last Romantic—an immensely talented Friedrich Schlegel or Adam Müller, as it were, whose complete lack of responsibility is attributable to a spiritual playfulness that stems in part from the delusions of genius and in part from despair."[75] The English version of the footnote made her 1946 critique even more pointed.[76] From this footnote onward the text has the character of a settling of accounts. Whoever read the footnote had in fact been already informed; one did not need to read either Arendt's article on Heidegger or even a line of Heidegger's. However, the tone of this footnote can be understood only by taking into account Arendt's profound disappointment in the readiness with which the German elite cooperated with National Socialism. One must also factor in the hopes that Arendt had placed in this man whom she loved and had not forgotten. She hoped to get, at least *post festum*, a self-critical explanation, an admission of the error. What she got instead were rumors, which, taken together with the hard facts from the 1930s, led to only one conclusion: this man had lost his mind and, with it, every shred of decency.

In the two concluding sections of the article, Arendt compares Heidegger and Jaspers. Heidegger appears as a thinker of individualistic existentialism who, following his diagnosis of Being-toward-death, must logically seek refuge in the nationalist (racial) superstition so as to somehow put back together the diagnosed collapsed world of Dasein that is directed to death:

> Later, and after the fact, as it were, Heidegger has drawn on mythologizing and muddled concepts like "folk" and "earth" in an effort to supply his isolated Selves with a shared, common ground to stand on. But it is obvious that concepts of that kind can only lead us out of philosophy and into some kind of nature-oriented superstition. If it does not belong to the concept of man that he inhabits the earth together with others of his kind, then all that remains for him is a mechanical reconciliation by which the atomized Selves are provided with a common ground that is essentially alien to their nature. All that can result from that is the organization of these Selves intent only on themselves into an Over-self in order somehow to effect a transition from resolutely accepted guilt to action.[77]

According to Arendt, this is how Heidegger came to National Socialism. In her view, this alone does not save him from nihilism; on the contrary, her judgment only clarifies how it emerged.

However, during her 1949–50 Germany trip, this view is virtually overturned. She then works intensely on giving the American intellectual public a more adequate understanding of Heidegger. In 1954 Reverend Oesterreicher, the famous Jewish-Christian priest, asked her of the depth of Heidegger's involvement in National Socialism; he wanted to see if his critical judgment of Heidegger was accurate. In her response, Arendt gave a nuanced critical judgment and took back the spontaneous judgments of 1945–46.[78] Three years later the doctoral student Calvin Schrag wrote to her. In his dissertation with Paul Tillich, he wanted to write, among other things, on Heidegger's Dasein analytic. He asked her some questions to better understand Heidegger's thought and also referred to her essay "What Is Existenz Philosophy?" She concluded her response with the sentence: "I must warn you about my essay on existentialism, especially about the part on Heidegger, which is not just entirely inadequate, but in part simply false. Please just forget about it."[79] In her article, Jaspers appears as the luminary of German philosophy, the only one who emerged authentic and decisively from the revolution against traditional metaphysics. With Jaspers, existential philosophy gave up its egoism:

> The movement of transcendence in thought [according to Jaspers—author's note], a movement basic to man's nature, and the failure of thought inherent in that movement brings us at least to a recognition that man as "master of his

thoughts" is not only more than what he thinks—and this alone would probably provide basis enough for a new definition of human dignity—but is also constitutionally a being that is more than a Self and wills more than himself. With this understanding, existential philosophy has emerged from its period of preoccupation with Self-ness.[80]

Jaspers is presented to the American public as the person who overcame the Heideggerian "solipsism." In the following years, Arendt tries to bring him closer to the American public. She frets over publishers and attends to the translation of his texts. Jaspers is thankful. Heidegger is not mentioned.

As a European in America

Probably to the broader American public, presentations of existential philosophy such as Arendt's remained foreign, just as Arendt's appearance in the American "*in-group* culture" must have seemed strange. William Barrett, who translated the article on existential philosophy for *Partisan Review*, always remembered Hannah Arendt as a foreigner from Europe: "But she could have been among us twenty years and she would still be something of a foreign presence. One part of her never quite assimilated to America. . . . She was always conscious of coming from elsewhere—of speaking for something older and deeper that she understood as European culture, something she guarded at her center. So that for us she could become a kind of incarnation of the European presence that began to be felt more and more in New York during the 1940s."[81] Some American intellectuals, schooled in pragmatism, could make little sense of Arendt's intellectual high culture. They rejected her, indeed, she infuriated them. Some thought Arendt was arrogant and haughty vis-à-vis America.[82] Delmore Schwartz, a talented poet and writer, famous for his puns, is said to have remarked sharply, according to Barrett: "That . . . that Weimar Republic flapper!"[83] Which more or less meant: this flippant woman from the times when Weimar was still dancing and young girls wore a bob, smoked cigars, had affairs with men, and had highly intellectual conversations. The background was that she did not laugh at one of his jokes, and he resented it.

However, there were people who were on the same wavelength as Arendt, in particular, Dwight Macdonald and Mary McCarthy. Coming from the Stalinist Left, Macdonald joined the Trotskyites, but in a rather American way, that is, in a nonsectarian, nearly liberal manner. Apparently, Macdonald wrote like he talked. For instance, he lifted from his friend, the writer Nicola Chiaromonte, a paradigm that the latter brought up in a conversation, used it as the title of his famous article "The Responsibility of Peoples" and then disclosed in the second half of the article that the title originated from "my friend Nicola Chiaromonte."

Macdonald liked to argue but could not defend his arguments well. Instead, he struck with a verbal sledgehammer, which often required him to apologize later. In so doing, he did not make many friends, but Arendt liked him despite his impulsiveness. He, in turn, esteemed, even venerated her a bit. Dwight was one of Arendt's most loyal friends. In any event, he remained her friend through all the ups and downs, something that cannot be said of everyone.

Mary McCarthy had a similarly temperamental disposition. With all their differences, she and Arendt had something in common: they were women with many different facets, often to the point of self-contradiction. Both met the world around them directly, not shying from judgment, leaving themselves exposed. It would be misleading to say that one, McCarthy, was a writer and the other, Arendt, a philosopher. So many of their talents were intertwined. Both had a clear, sometimes cutting, analytic mind and both called it as they saw it. Both were alert to organized lying in the public space. Both were gifted writers. Both loved literature. The only difference is that Mary wrote stories and novels and Hannah wrote political essays.

Where they were admittedly different was in the foundation of their education and thinking. While Mary McCarthy was sophisticated in her broad knowledge of culture and the arts, Arendt was historically astute due to her knowledge of antiquity. While McCarthy sought counsel in healthy common sense, with Arendt there was always a historical dimension, an ability that sometimes so discouraged her friends that they began to rebel against her.

We find ourselves in the 1940s. Mary, from a good home, lost her parents when she was six. She attended the famous Vassar College, whose culture of young women she will later turn into a bestseller, *The Group*. She married at twenty-one and divorced at twenty-four. She got to know the group around Dwight Macdonald, Philip Rahv, and William Phillips, and, together with them, founded *Partisan Review*. She wrote theater reviews and moved in with her colleague, Philip Rahv. In 1938 she married the writer and literary critic Edmund Wilson. The marriage was unhappy, but it is at this time that Mary, encouraged by Wilson, began to write short stories. In 1942 her first book, *The Company She Keeps*, came out, a book in which Mary displays her particular style of narration. Strictly oriented toward reality, she did not respect the private sphere of her contemporaries, whom she wrote about only thinly disguised. She had the reputation of being a man-devouring diva. One feared her sharp tongue. Her partner, Philip Rahv, would later file a complaint against her because he saw a caricature of himself in one of her books. However, he withdrew the complaint. When he died, Mary wrote a very loving obituary.

When the two women met, Mary McCarthy was a theater critic and a social columnist. Always elegantly dressed, she moved skillfully on the social stage.

Mary McCarthy had "class." With her clear, oval face and her hair knotted at the back of her neck in an old-fashioned style, she made a striking appearance.

She had a fine sense for the hollowness of intellectual discourse, its hidden weaknesses and its comic sides. She addressed these things in a disarming and occasionally wounding way, both in conversations and in her books. If one wanted to choose a neutral description of Mary McCarthy's character, one would describe her as "outspoken." A friend described her conversational style as based on the principle of wit. In conversations, she was the one who interrupted the banter with a sharp or witty remark. If some were piqued by Mary's bold remarks, others rejoiced at the precision of her verve. McCarthy's tone was, however, not some sign of exaggerated naïveté, something to irritate New York's intellectual society. This was not an assumed attitude; this was who she was.

When Mary McCarthy and Hannah Arendt first met in the spring 1945 in the Murray Hill bar in Manhattan, Hannah was thirty-eight years old and Mary was thirty-two. The editors of *Partisan Review* met for a social evening in the bar. Playing the *enfant terrible*, Mary suddenly announced that "she really felt sorry for Hitler, he didn't know what was happening to him, he expected the Jews to love him."[84] Arendt, who participated in the discussion, was incensed. Later she reported that she counted to 120 so as to give Philip Rahv, Mary's partner at the time, space for a riposte. When Rahv did not say anything, she exploded.[85] Loudly she said to Mary: "How can you say something like that in front of me, a victim of Hitler, who was in a concentration camp!" Mary McCarthy's attempts at justification were in vain. "I crept away," remembered McCarthy. Arendt complained further to Philip Rahv. "As a Jew how can you allow such talk in your own four walls?"[86] Reconciliation came years later, when the two women met again, this time at Dwight Macdonald's journal *Politics*. At the end of the evening, they met on an empty subway platform. Arendt plucked up her courage and said that it had struck her how often they had the same view in discussions and how they always remained in the minority. "In many respects we think quite similarly." Mary McCarthy could finally explain her much earlier remark, and Arendt admitted that she had never been in a concentration camp, only in a detainment camp.[87]

Thus began a friendship spanning more than twenty years. It was a friendship based on mutual recognition and trust, but also on surprises and reciprocal admiration. Mary McCarthy admired Arendt's capacity for thinking, her extraordinary talent to interpret events in a new way, her knowledge of ancient texts and cultures. Hannah, in turn, admired her friend's ability to write, her beauty, her erotic charisma, her spontaneous wit. McCarthy was also important for Arendt because she could decipher the American intellectual scene. Through her Arendt learned the backgrounds and the political relations and personal histories of people whom she knew. Older, Arendt felt herself to be in a protective, almost maternal role.

Arendt was active in many fields in these years: she engaged in Zionist debates, she pursued her studies of anti-Semitism, imperialism, and racism. She earned her money in various ways: a stipend, honorariums for articles, a paid university course. She was always on the lookout for "work," to make ends meet. Salman Schocken, the publisher she met in Berlin through Kurt Blumenfeld, employed her for a time as an editor. At the publishing house, she was concerned with select European writers whom she would have liked to introduce to the American public. She was especially interested in promoting Walter Benjamin, Bernard Lazare, and Franz Kafka. Under her editorship, Kafka's *Diaries* were published as well as the French poet-writer Bernard Lazare's Zionist-symbolic manifesto *Job's Dungheap*.[88] At Schocken Books she also met the poet Randall Jarrell, whose feel for the English and German languages she greatly admired. For a while, he also helped her rewrite her own texts into an English that was adequate to her thinking.[89] She also had the publishing house to thank for allowing her to meet a whole host of colleagues who became her friends or good acquaintances: Irving Howe, Nathan Glazer, Martin Greenberg, and others who were active on the New York publishing scene at the time.

It was certainly a challenge for her when she was invited to teach a course at Brooklyn College in New York. She began to teach there in mid-February 1946. This was her first time teaching in the United States.[90] Gurian wrote a recommendation for her. This course also led to the studies that would later come together in *The Origins of Totalitarianism*. She was working on them, as her biographer Elisabeth Young-Bruehl reports, almost day and night, during lunch breaks, and after dinner.[91]

In mid-May 1945 Arendt took on a kind of research assignment for the Conference on Jewish Relations. She wrote to Gurian that on behalf of this organization, which would later become part of the Commission on European Jewish Cultural Reconstruction, she would conduct "a special investigation into the condition of Jewish cultural institutions in Europe. Even though not exactly exhilarating, perhaps a little bit useful."[92] It entailed a Sisyphean project: Arendt was to trace missing Jewish cultural assets that the National Socialists had stolen from all over Europe. She was to discover who had these libraries, works of art, and cultural objects in their possession, and then ascertain the rightful owner of the stolen goods. She was to make suggestions as to which persons or Jewish institutions these cultural possessions could be returned or transferred if necessary. She remained active with this organization for six years, searching for stolen Jewish goods and destroyed Jewish history. Under the auspices of this mission, she made her first visit to Germany since the war.

Her work was a painful preparation for the reencounter with Germany from which she was driven away in 1933.

Notes

1. See Christina Heine Teixeira, Wartesaal Lissabon 1940–1941, in Spalek/Feilchenfeld, u.a. (Hg): Exilliteratur seit 1933, Bd. 3, USA, Teil 3 (2002), s. 477 und 480.

2. Coser, *Refugee Scholars* (1984), 200. Citation of Franz Neumann, "The Social Sciences," in *The Cultural Migration*, ed. Crawford (New York: Shocken, 1953), 20.

3. Günther Anders, "Lebenserlaubnis," in *Verbannung*, ed. Schwarz and Wegner (Hamburg: C. Wegner, 1964), 175–76.

4. Ernst Bloch, "Zerstörte Sprache—zerstörte Kultur," in ibid., 187.

5. See Elizabeth Young-Bruehl, *Hannah Arendt. For Love of the World* (New Haven, CT: Yale University Press,1982), 190.

6. Ibid., 184.

7. Arendt an Adler-Rüdel, letter dated February 23, 1943, HAZ Archive.

8. See Young-Bruehl, *Hannah Arendt*, 184.

9. Arendt to Gurian, letter dated September 24, 1942, Archiv des HAZ, Cont. Nr 10.7.

10. Alfred Kazin, *A New York Jew* (New York: Knopf, 1978), 197.

11. Ibid.

12. Ibid., 196–97.

13. Traces can be found in Arendt's *Denktagebuch* in which every now and again discussions of the conceptual connections unexpectedly cite or paraphrase "Heinrich." See Hannah Arendt, *Denktagebuch* (Munich: Piper, 2002), 13–14, 181, 354, 406, 416, 797, 801.

14. See Kazin, *New York Jew*, 197.

15. The influence can be seen directly here as Blücher also worked on the phenomenon of totalitarianism. See Heinrich Blücher, *Perpetual Motion. Some Texts of the Political Structure of Nazism*, Archive of the HAZ. Certainly the influence went both ways. See also Toshio Terajima, "Heinrich Blücher: A Hidden Source of Hannah Arendt's Political Thought," *Ningenkagaku Rongshu* 27 (1996): 39ff.

16. See Kazin, *New York Jew*, 191.

17. Jonas, *Erkenntnis* (Göttingen: Lamuv, 1991), 77.

18. Alan Wald, "Notes from Interviews with Dwight Macdonald, 1973," in *Interviews with Macdonald*, ed. Wreszin (Jackson: University of Mississippi Press, 2003), 107.

19. William Barrett, *The Truants* (New York: Doubleday, 1982), 11.

20. "The Art of Fiction XXVII Mary McCarthy—an Interview with Elisabeth Niebuhr 1962," in *Mary McCarthy*, ed. Gelderman (Jackson: University of Mississippi Press, 1991), 14.

21. Wreszin, *Macdonald* (2003), 129.

22. Arendt to Gurian, letter dated December 10, 1941, Archiv des HAZ, Cont. Nr.10.7.

23. Arendt to Gurian, letter dated March 21, 1942, Cont. 10.7, Archiv des HAZ.

24. She is probably referring to Franz Neumann's analyses of the power structure of National Socialism. See Franz Neumann, *Behemoth* (Oxford: Oxford University Press, 1942).

25. Arendt to Gurian, letter dated March 27, 1942, Archive des HAZ, Cont. Nr. 10.7.

26. See Arendt to Adler-Rüdel, letter dated February 23, 1943, Archiv des HAZ.

27. See Arendt to Erich Cohn-Bendit, Brief zur Minderheitenfrage, Archiv des HAZ, Cont. Nr 79.13.

28. See Lützeler, "Nachwort des Herausgebers," in *Arendt-Broch: Briefwechsel* (1996), 228.

29. Ibid.

30. *Arendt-Blumenfeld Korrespondenz* (1995), 41.

31. Herman Bloch, "Gedicht an Hannah Arendt von Oktober 1947," in *Arendt-Broch: Briefwechsel*, ed. Paul Michael Luetzeler (Frankfurt: Juedischer Verlag, 1996), 1.

32. See *Arendt-Broch: Briefwechsel* (1996), 121.

33. Because Heidegger's letter of self-justification sent to the faculty in October 1945, to which Broch is possibly referring, was first published decades later under the heading of "The Rectorship 1933/34, Facts and Thoughts," this possibly refers to a transcript or copy of this letter, mixed among information from the university faculty members in Freiburg and Heidelberg (Jaspers).

34. Hermann Broch: Brief an Erich von Kahler, in: Broch: Kommentierte Werkausgabe, Bd. 13/3 (1981), 169.

35. See Broch to Arendt, letter dated June 28, 1949, in *Arendt-Broch, Briefwechsel*, 127; see also Broch's letter to Egon Vietta from May 22, 1948, in which he gives an extremely harsh critique of Heidegger's poems and aphorisms. See Broch to Arendt, letter from October 22, 1949, in *Arendt-Broch, Briefwechsel*, 135 footnote.

36. Hannah Arendt, "The Jewish Army: The Beginning of a Jewish Politics?" in *Aufbau*, November 14, 1941, reprinted Jerome Kohn and Ron H. Feldman, eds., *The Jewish Writings: Hannah Arendt* (New York: Schocken, 2007), 137.

37. Arendt to Gurian, letter dated July 13, 1942, Archiv des HAZ, Cont. Nr. 10.7.

38. See Arendt to Erich Cohn-Bandit, letter from January, 1940, Archiv des HAZ, Cont. Nr. 79.

39. See Young-Bruehl, *Hannah Arendt*, 184.

40. Hannah Arendt and Josef Maier: Jungjüdische Gruppe lädt zu ihrem ersten Treffen (An Invitation to the first meeting of the young Jewish group) from Archiv des HAZ, Cont. Nr. 79.13.

41. Ibid.

42. Kurt Blumenfeld: Daily Discussion (*Diskussionsbeitrag*) in "Die Prokotolle der Jungjüdischen Gruppe," Nr. 3, Sitzung vom April 7, 1942, S.II., Archive des HAZ, Cont. Nr. 79:13.

43. Ibid., S.III.

44. Arendt to Judah Magnes, letter from October 3, 1948, Archiv des HAZ, Cont. Nr. 12.8.

45. See Hannah Arendt, "Zionism Reconsidered," *Menorah Journal* 33 (1945): 173. Reprinted (2007) in Kohn and Feldman, *Jewish Writings*, 343.

46 Kohn and Feldman, *Jewish Writings* (2007), 371.

47. See Blumenfeld to Arendt, letter dated January 4, 1946, in *Arendt-Blumenfeld, Korrespondenz*, 34.

48. See Blumenfeld to Martin Rosenblüth, letter from January 17, 1946, in Kurt, *Blumenfeld: Briefe* (Stuttgart: Deutsche Verlags-Anstalt, 1976), 197.

49. Perhaps this refers to a friendly letter to Arendt on January 4, 1946, in *Arendt-Blumenfeld, Correspondence* (Hamburg: Rotbuch Verlag, 1995), 33ff.

50. Blumenfeld to Martin Rosenblüth, letter from January 17, 1946, in *Blumenfeld: Briefe* (1976), 197–98.

51. See Scholem to Arendt, letter from January 28, 1946, in Gersholm Scholem, *A Life in Letters* (Cambridge, MA: Harvard University Press, 2002), 330.

52. Meant here is *Menorah Journal*, which published the article in its second volume in 1945.

53. Arendt to Gurian, letter from November 8, 1944, in Archiv des HAZ, Cont. Nr. 10.7.

54. Arendt to Blumenfeld, letter from July 17, 1946, in *Arendt-Blumenfeld: Korrespondenz* (1995), 40.

55. Arendt to Blumenfeld, letter from April 1, 1951, in ibid., 52; see also Blumenfeld to Arendt, letter from March 18, 1951, in ibid. (1995), 47ff.

56. Arendt to Gurian, letter from April 30, 1943, or May 1, 1943 (dated by Arendt), Archiv des HAZ, cont. Nr. 10.7.

57. Arendt to Gurian, letter from August 4, 1943, in Archiv des HAZ, Cont. Nr. 10.7.

58. Arendt to Gurian, letter from February 8, 1944, Archiv des HAZ, Cont. Nr. 10.7.

59. Arendt to Gurian, letter from December 17, 1946, Archiv des HAZ, Cont. Nr. 10.7.

60. See Barrett, *Truants*, 99.

61. See Hannah Arendt, "French Existentialism," *Nation*, February 23, 1946, 162. Reprinted in Hannah Arendt, *Essays in Understanding* (New York: HBJ, 1994), 193.

62. See Arendt to Gurian, letter from January 10, 1943, Archiv des HAZ, Cont. Nr. 10.7.

63. Karl Jaspers, *The Question of German Guilt* (New York: Fordham University Press, 1947), 12.

64. Hannah Arendt's "Organized Guilt" appeared in German in 1945 under the title "Organized Guilt and Universal Responsibility" in *Jewish Frontier*, January 1945; also in Kohn, *Arendt* (1994), 126.

65. See Hannah Arendt, "Approaches to the German Problem," *Partisan Review* 12, no. 1 (1945); also in Arendt, *Essays*, 26.

66. Young-Bruehl, *Hannah Arendt*, 166.

67. Dwight Macdonald, "The Responsibility of Peoples," *Politics*, March 1945, 90.

68. Simone Weil, cited by ibid., 92.

69. Blücher to Arendt, letter from July 15, 1946, in Ursula Ludz, ed., *Within Four Walls*, trans. Andrew Shields (New York: Harcourt, Brace, 1996), 84.

70. Hannah Arendt, "Collective Responsibility: Discussion of the Paper of Joel Feinberg, Rockefeller University, American Philosophical Society, December 27, 1968, Washington DC." Archiv des HAZ, Cont. Nr. 62.12, also cited in translation by Frank Stühlmeyer, MS. S. 3f, Archive des HAZ.

71. See Jaspers to Arendt, letter from June 9, 1946, in Lotte Kohler and Hans Saner, eds., *Arendt-Jaspers Correspondence*, trans Robert Kimber and Rita Kimber (New York: Harcourt, Brace, 1985), 47.

72. Arendt to Jaspers, letter from July 9, 1946, in ibid., 47–48.

73. Ibid., 48.

74. On December 30, 1945, Anne Weil wrote her that she had heard that Heidegger had written to several French university colleagues that he could not be pressured during the Nazi time and that he had, further, only supported them during the very first phase. Heidegger apparently sought to profit from the "Existentialist Fashion." He also claimed to have "rescued" German professors. See Weil to Arendt, letter from December 30, 1945, Archiv des HAZ, cont. Nr. 15.7.

75. Arendt, "What Is Existential Philosophy?," in Kohn, *Arendt*, 187.

76. "Another question worth discussing is whether Heidegger's philosophy has not generally been taken too seriously, simply because it deals with the most serious things. In any case, Heidegger has done everything to warn us that we should take him seriously. As is well known, he entered the Nazi Party in a very sensational way in 1933—an act that made him stand out pretty much by himself among colleagues of the same caliber. Further, in his capacity as rector of Freiburg University, he forbade Husserl, his teacher and friend, whose lecture chair he had inherited, to enter the faculty, because Husserl was a Jew. Finally, it has been rumored that he has placed himself at the disposal of the French occupational authorities for the reeducation of the German people.

In view of the real comedy of this development and of the no less real low level of political thought in German universities, one is naturally inclined not to bother with the whole story. On the other hand, there is the point that this whole mode of behavior has exact parallels in German Romanticism, so that one can scarcely believe the coincidence is accidental. Heidegger is, in fact, the last (we hope) Romantic—as it were, a tremendously gifted Friedrich

Schlegel or Adam Mueller, whose complete irresponsibility was attributed partly to the delusion of genius, partly to desperation." See Arendt, "What Is Existential Philosophy," 46; reprinted in Kohn, *Arendt*, 187.

77. Kohn, *Arendt*, 181–82.

78. To this, see also Arendt's exchange of letter with Father (Reverend) John Oesterreicher, Archiv des HAZ, Cont. 59.

79. Arendt to Calvin Schrag, letter from December 31, 1955, Archive des HAZ, Cont. Nr. 13.11.

80. Kohn, *Hannah Arendt: Essays in Understanding* (1994), 187.

81. Barrett, *Truants* (1982), 99.

82. Ibid., 104.

83. Ibid., 103.

84. Brock Brower, "McCarthyism. Interview with Mary McCarthy," in *Mary McCarthy*, ed. Gelderman (Jackson: University of Mississippi Press, 1991), 42ff.

85. Ibid.

86. Young-Bruehl, *Hannah Arendt*, 197.

87. Ibid.

88. See Bernard Lazare, *Job's Dungheap* (New York: Shocken, 1948).

89. Young-Breuhl, *Hannah Arendt*, 191.

90. Arendt to Gurian, letter from January 29, 1946, Archiv des HAZ, Cont, Nr. 10.7.

91. Young-Breuhl, *Hannah Arendt*, 192.

92. Arendt to Gurian, letter from April 4, 1945, Archiv des HAZ, Cont. Nr. 10.7., Bl. 2.

5 The Break in Tradition and a New Beginning, or Arendt and Heidegger in Counterpoint

IN FEBRUARY 1950, after years of flight and persecution, of disappointment, anger, and alienation, Hannah met again the great love of her youth, Martin Heidegger. She immediately writes her friend Hilde Fränkel about the encounter:

> Apart from that, yesterday I returned from Freiburg where I absolutely had to go for professional reasons. Would I have gone there otherwise? I don't know. In any case, H. almost immediately appeared in the hotel and began to perform a kind of tragedy, in which I presumably participated in the first two acts. He in no way took into account that all this happened twenty-five years ago and that he hadn't seen me for more than seventeen years. He can only be described as like a dog with his tail between its legs (that is to say, guilty). (Please don't show this letter to Paul.[1]) In addition, there was a surreal scene with his wife who, in her agitation, was always saying "your husband," when she should have said "my husband." And the things that came gushing out, things that I had neither known nor suspected—she knew what he owed me in connection with his philosophical production, etc., this, in between reproaches, toward him, about his lack of fidelity. Clearly, an often repeated scene. Despite, or rather because of this, I thank God that I came to Freiburg. I will tell you more about this veritable novel in its latest developments when I am back. In the meantime, I am overwhelmed with manuscripts and letters from him. As you know, I also have a job. In the final analysis, I am happy for the confirmation that I was right never to forget.[2]

From Arendt's point of view, Martin Heidegger was on the side of her enemies and she was angry about the betrayal of friendship that she certainly saw in Heidegger's involvement with National Socialism. However, there was something else that she had never forgotten: there was a bond between them that neither of them had ever severed.

Hannah was traveling throughout Europe and Germany. Before her departure, she had finished the rough draft of *The Origins of Totalitarianism*. At that time she was also a well-known intellectual in Germany. In 1948 Lambert Schneider—this publisher being part of the circle around the journal *Die Wandlung*—published a volume with her "six essays," which contained her contribution to the German-American debate about guilt—"Organized Guilt." Her articles in *Die Wandlung* also circulated in German intellectual circles. The newspapers reported that Arendt was traveling on behalf of *the Commission on European Jewish Cultural Reconstruction.*

In the beginning of December 1949, twelve years after her German citizenship was stripped from her, she returned to Germany to ascertain what could be saved of the huge collection of Jewish cultural treasures pillaged by the National Socialists.[3]

At this point the Germans were thinking about things other than returning stolen libraries, paintings, religious and cultural objects to the Jews. The mass murder of the European Jews under the German government had not yet penetrated public consciousness. In her report for *Commentary*,[4] which Arendt wrote during her nearly four-month-long travel across Germany, she described the collective mentality as in a stupor. Nowhere in Europe was there less mourning of the atrocities committed by Germans than in Germany. Indifference, apathy, lack of emotion, and heartlessness marked "the Germans."[5] Escape from reality, "escape from responsibility," nihilistic relativism, and self-pity characterized their everyday behavior toward the occupying powers, but also among themselves. The Germans were "in love with impotence as such."[6] They were "living ghosts, whom speech and argument, the glance of human eyes and the mourning of human hearts, no longer touch."[7] With the metaphor "living ghosts," Arendt seizes on a phrase she had already once used in a similar way, albeit in a different context. "Living corpses" was how she described refugees and the stateless in the interwar period, as well as the inmates of concentration and extermination camps. In her eyes, these people were united in that they were dispossessed of both the ability to act freely as citizens and the ability to judge—those who were victims as well as those who had committed the crimes or were complicit in them. Admittedly, in her annihilating judgment of Germany, there was a ray of light and it was Berlin. In her travels Arendt experienced only the western sector; still, Berlin, the divided city, received the best marks. In the correspondence with her husband, she gushes about how different the Berliners are: their humor, their soberness, their healthy common sense. Her positive judgment of Berlin was due in part to the Berlin taxi drivers, and partly to reconnecting with her old boyfriend, Ernst Grumach. She writes her husband: "It is almost unbelievable, but I am in Berlin again—by again I mean after seventeen years. . . . Grumach came to pick me up from the airport and we are constantly together. Delightful East-Prussian wife, enchanting child. . . . Ernst is writing poetry again."[8] She is happy to be able to speak East Prussian again. It affords her great delight. Grumach helps considerably with her job of finding and safeguarding stolen Jewish cultural treasures. Over the ensuing years, she sees him whenever she visits Berlin on business with the *Jewish Cultural Reconstruction.*

Ernst Grumach was a renowned philologist of antiquity and a Goethe scholar. He survived the National Socialist time in Berlin because he was married to a non-Jewish woman. During the war, he was forced by the Central Office of Security (Reichssicherheitshauptamt), together with many other Jewish Hellenists, Latinists, Byzantinists, Egyptologists, and Judaists, to work as an archivist for the cataloguing of stolen Jewish libraries. These had been collected at a central place in Berlin before being distributed to various institutions of the Reich as part of the so-called enemy libraries. He had accumulated an extensive knowledge of stolen Jewish cultural assets and became a sought-after expert in restitution processes after 1945.[9]

Arendt's report from Germany is directed to an American audience that had heard little about the country for years. Yet Arendt's matter of fact tone could not hide how shaken she was in the face of the devastation in the country and in the minds of its inhabitants. In the meantime, Germany had been divided. The new borders ran through the middle of Berlin, dividing the city to which she had always been loyal, the city she even now exempted from her withering judgment about Germany and its people. West Germany and the Western sector of Berlin had already endorsed a democratic constitution. In the East, the local political leaders wanted to build an "anti-Fascist democratic state" as a countermodel to Western liberal democracy. There, the local political leadership, sanctioned by the Soviet Union as occupying power, employed terrorist means to bully its political enemies.

Arendt was traveling throughout Germany, with detours to Paris, London, Zurich, and especially Basel, the new home of Karl Jaspers. She dealt with both German institutions and occupation authorities, speaking with politicians, journalists, students, professors, and random acquaintances. She reconnected with old friends. The letters to her husband Heinrich speak—in a typically sarcastic manner—of the psychic shocks that she suffered at the sight of the destroyed cities and the disoriented, embittered, spiritually impoverished, and empty people.

During this entire time she debated whether she should go to Freiburg to see Heidegger. "In Germany, everything is once again awash with Heidegger," she writes in her particular acerbic style to Heinrich Blücher:

> I will send you or bring with me *Holzwege*. Whether I'm going to see [Heidegger] or not, I don't know yet—I'll leave everything up to fate. His letters to Jaspers, the ones[10] Jaspers showed me, are just as they used to be; the same mix of genuineness and mendacity, or better still cowardice, in which both qualities are primary. With Jaspers I lost a little of my keenness for Heidegger. It always comes back to the same thing: the principle by which relationships are entered into.[11]

She writes this from London, a month prior to her trip to Freiburg—from a safe distance.

However, Arendt acted according to a different principle. Even after the supposed betrayal of friendship, their relationship was not over in her eyes. She did not want her old friendships destroyed through political polarization.

For Arendt, friends took the place of her native country and, as such, they were irreplaceable. The old love contained reminisces of an intellectual home, now destroyed.

She went to Freiburg because she had to deal with the authorities regarding the retrieval of Jewish cultural assets. The first person she met there was a friend from her university days, the Romanist Hugo Friedrich. He told her the latest news about Heidegger and gave her his address. She subsequently sent him a letter from her Freiburg hotel.

Heidegger: Fight for Honor

After the war, the Heideggers were in a precarious situation. Shortly after the French army moved into Freiburg, their house was requisitioned and they were under threat that their entire library would be taken. In 1945 their grand piano and their carpet were confiscated by the French. From summer 1945 until March 1949 a French sergeant and his family were housed there. In addition, friends and relatives had constantly been living in the house, including their friend Laslowski and his wife who were residing there at the end of the 1940s. During this time, the Heideggers were confined to Heidegger's study, used for both living and working. They also feared for their children. Both sons were in Russian captivity. One returned ill in 1947; the other returned in December 1949. Elfride Heidegger had to cope with this difficult situation; managing the house, holding the family together, and doing what was possible to relieve her husband of all practical worries.

With the French occupation in 1945, Heidegger, along with many others, was divested of his position as full professor. What followed did not catch him entirely unaware. In a postscript to a letter to Elfride in April, 1945, he already had a premonition: "Although the future is dark & forbidding, I'm confident that there are opportunities to be realized, even if teaching is denied me in future."[12] Heidegger writes this from Meßkirch, before setting foot in the city of Freiburg, much less the university. He already understood that measures would be taken against him.

Toward the end of the war, the philosophy and theology departments had been temporarily relocated to Burg Wildenstein on the Danube River. The bombings and the impending invasion of the victorious armies had made intellectual work in Freiburg impossible. Here professors could teach and their (primarily female) students could study in an improvised atmosphere; they all lived here for a couple of weeks, occasionally helping with work in the field, while Freiburg was taken over by the Allies. They did not rush back. Heidegger, in any case, went first to Meßkirch after leaving Burg Wildenstein.

The university reacted to the end of the National Socialist regime vigorously. The rectorate, members of the Senate, and several colleagues who had been opposed to National Socialism decided to launch a self-purification of the university as early as the spring 1945. Part of their decision was that the occupying powers pushed for such measures and part of it was that the university leadership wanted to do things their own way, thereby pushing back against the will of the occupiers and the local authorities. An impenetrable chaos of real and fictitious enemies of the regime emerged in which everyone sought to use the situation to their benefit. Denunciations and seeing enemies everywhere were just as common in these first few months and years after the war as during the time of National Socialism. Official state executives judged as they pleased or in eager obedience to the French occupation forces. Opportunism appeared to be the supreme rule of the day.

The leading university members of the immediate postwar time were the historian Gerhard Ritter and the economists Walter Eucken, Constantin von Dietze, and Adolf Lampe. They were all close to the Freiburg School of Economics. During the last years of National Socialism, they had been part of the Freiburg Circle (*Freiburger Kreis*), which was in contact with the German resistance.[13] In 1944 they had all been arrested. Now they became the trusted confidants of the French liaison officer in the university.[14] These men formed the core of the so-called Purification Committee internal to the university. The committee was chaired by von Dietze. The botanist Friedrich Oehlkers and a theologian also joined the committee. Franz Böhm, the acting vice-rector, a distinguished lawyer with no prior political affiliations and a friend of Walter Eucken's, joined as an adviser. The committee first met in July 1945.

The speed with which they took over Heidegger's case is surprising only at first glance. Two facts explain this: Heidegger was a famous philosopher and his involvement with National Socialism was discussed around the world. Now everyone was waiting to see what was going to happen to him. Moreover, during his short rectorate, Heidegger had made enemies who were eager to expose him to public reprobation.

In France, where the traditional attitude toward intellectuals was generally sympathetic, the attitude toward the famous German philosopher was divided. During the last years of the war and in the immediate postwar time, existentialism became the new direction in French philosophy and in French theater. Existentialism reacted to the collapse of culture and tradition in Europe with a mixture of nihilism, sorrow and revolt. Thus an "existentialist milieu" developed that ranged from philosophy to music to fashion. Still, the philosophers among the existentialists had also read their Heidegger. In 1934 Jean-Paul Sartre received a grant from the Institut Français in Berlin to study the key writings of Husserl and Heidegger. His great work, *Being and Nothingness*, was influenced by German existential philosophy. It was published in France in 1943 under the German occupation.

In July 1945 Heidegger was questioned by Adolf Lampe for the first time. It must have pained him that, of all people, the interrogator was a colleague with whom he had clashed in spring 1934, a conflict that was the decisive moment in his decision to quit as rector.[15]

During the deposition, Adolf Lampe reacted indignantly to Heidegger's remark that he had read Hitler's *Mein Kampf* only reluctantly and partially. He pointed out that Heidegger had driven entire flocks of students and young professors into the arms of National Socialism. According to Lampe's report, Heidegger argued:

> that in supporting National Socialism he saw the only and last chance to hinder an advance of Communism;
>
> that he accepted his rectorate with greatest reluctance and ultimately in the interests of the university;
>
> that he remained in this office—despite constant bad experiences—only because he wanted to prevent something worse (such as the passing of the rectorate to Herr Aly);
>
> that one had to grant him the particularly turbulent conditions under which he had to exercise his rectorate;
>
> that he averted many impending dangers that would have made the situation much worse and that he had not received credit for this;
>
> that he found no favorable resonance from his colleagues for the actual goals that he was pursuing;
>
> that later he exercised a clear critique in his lectures, especially in his Nietzsche seminars.[16]

Lampe, in turn, held the following against him: Heidegger had implemented the principle of the Führer in the university so radically that it destroyed academic autonomy. He had indoctrinated the student body in favor of National Socialism.[17] He also held complete personal responsibility for what happened after his resignation. His later critique could not be seen as compensation, as it did not risk anything at that time.[18]

The lawyer and vice-rector Franz Böhm supported, indeed took further, Lampe's arguments. Heidegger had risked his entire philosophical reputation to support Hitler. It was unthinkable for him to retain his position and remain in his office while younger professors, whom Heidegger had converted to National Socialism, were now threatened with dismissal or arrest. Heidegger had championed his views "with fanatical and terroristic intolerance." He could not give any evidence for his claim that he had been deceived by National Socialism. Böhm took as examples the looting of the Jewish fraternity house in Freiburg and posting in the university a call for the denunciation of communist students. It made him bitter:

> One of the intellectuals most responsible for the political tradition of the German universities, a man who, placed at the most decisive moment in the key position as rector of a large German university on the border, and an internationally famous philosopher, took politics in the wrong direction and preached deadly heresies in a loud voice and with intolerant fanaticism—who has to this day not retracted any of these heresies"; that this man "is only faced with suspension and obviously feels no need to answer for the consequences of the actions for which he is culpable.[19]

In October 1945 Heidegger told the philosophy department that he had received notification from the French occupying authority that he was "suspended" (*disponibel*); that is, he still formally held a position in the department. The university could do with him as it wished.[20] Böhm then announced that he would step down as vice-rector if Heidegger were allowed to remain in his position or were allowed to retire with the usual generous pension for university professors. Lampe supported his position.[21]

From the very outset of the confrontation, it is clear that his colleagues and the university leadership assessed Heidegger's responsibility to be much greater than he himself saw it. One notes that his critics argue on a different level than Heidegger. They appealed to political principles: Heidegger must take responsibility for his political conduct during his term of office. Heidegger's argument, by contrast, is confined to the private sphere. He refers to his personal errors and his individual withdrawal from academic affairs because of his change of mind.

This constellation will not change much in the coming years. Heidegger considered the accusations against him to be disproportionate. He saw the threatened punishment—forced retirement with loss of full pension and removal from the university—as grossly out of line with his offense. Some of his critics insisted on their harsh critique and demanded actual punishment; others tended toward a milder judgment, appealing to Heidegger's world fame as a philosopher.

It is evident from the documents just how deep the wounds inflicted by Heidegger's ten-month rectorate were. Many colleagues were against Heidegger's returning to the university while Rectors Metz, Mangold, and Süß, who had succeeded him, were suspended. The argument about equal treatment concealed a difficult situation. In the eyes of Heidegger's enemies, his rectorate, while short-lived, had symbolic value that extended far beyond his withdrawal and which concerned the entire time of National Socialism. That Germany's most famous philosopher had gone over to the side of National Socialism was an outrage that still hit a raw nerve in the summer of 1945 in the debates concerning self-purification.

It is clearly also the *way* in which Heidegger conducted his rectorship that threw his colleagues into a pure rage even a decade later. In their view, during his short term of office Heidegger had severely damaged the dignity of the university, its governing bodies as well as his colleagues, by introducing a style of leadership many of his colleagues considered unfit for a university. He was charged with destroying academic autonomy. Moreover, he was held partly responsible for introducing the Führer principle into the German universities, according to which the rector, among others, was nominated by the minister. By admitting students into the faculty Senate and pitting associate professors against full professors, he played various groups in the university against one another. His wife, Elfride, appears in this report as the evil spirit who planted anti-Semitism in him. Whatever the truth of this argument, such a mixture of the private and public spheres can be explained only by the tumultuous times.[22] It also indicates, however, that colleagues had clearly expected something different from him, and that there were things they simply could not fathom.

Heidegger was confronted with a responsibility that concerned not just his actual actions but also their real and symbolic effects. He must have been shaken by the force of these accusations, evidently believing that he had compensated for his involvement in National Socialism by his withdrawal from politics and his self-critical analysis of a "philosophy of action."

During the proceedings, which dragged on for years, the unified front against Heidegger gradually crumbled. Adolf Lampe, Franz Böhm, and Walter Eucken wanted to bring about his removal from the faculty via forced retirement which would have had negative effects on his pension and other rights in the university. Others such as Friedrich Oehlkers and the historian Gerhard Ritter increasingly turned away from Lampe's radical course. They considered early retirement to be a clear enough signal of the university distancing itself from its former rector. The rectors of the early postwar period (Janssen, Allgeier, and Tellenbach) also followed a moderate course, with an eye to the unclear legal situation of the time in view of which the university wanted to protect itself. At least initially, the military government and the Ministry were opposed to this milder direction: in 1946 the French authorities issued a teaching prohibition against Heidegger.[23]

From the proceedings against Heidegger, which persisted for six years, one can draw a moral portrait of the way in which the German universities handled their National Socialist past as well as their integration into the changing political circumstances of the time. The focus here, however, is on Heidegger's intellectual confrontation with National Socialism and the question of what followed from this.

On the basis of the differing views of his actions as rector, but also because he was completely surprised by the angry reaction of his former colleagues, now running the university, Heidegger felt compelled to take a stance on his past involvement in the context of the ongoing interrogations. On November 4, 1945, he wrote a long letter to the rectorate of the University of Freiburg, later included in a revised and expanded form in "The Rectorate 1933/34: Facts and Thoughts." In this letter, Heidegger describes his activities as rector and his entry into and relationship with NSDAP after 1933. He argues that he accepted the rectorate only under pressure from his colleagues and his predecessor in office. Moreover, he was convinced—and what follows is the greatest degree of openness of which he was capable with regard to his colleagues—that "an autonomous alliance of intellectuals [*der Geistigen*] could have deepened and transformed a number of essential elements of the 'National Socialist movement.'"[24]

Like many others at the time, he was deeply affected by Germany's crisis, a crisis that in his eyes was also an expression of the existential crisis of the West. Paraphrasing his inaugural speech as rector, Heidegger once again endorsed his argument regarding the intellectual turn that had become necessary and went on to discuss the difficulties of his official position, which he, however, formulated in general terms (disappointments, frictions, concessions, compromises). Nevertheless, with all of this he was convinced "especially after Hitler's May 1, 1933, speech asking for peace, that my basic intellectual position and my conception of the task of the university could be reconciled with the political will of those in power."[25] In the winter semester of 1933–34 it then became clear to him "that it was a mistake to believe that, from the basic intellectual position that was the result of my long years of philosophical work, that I could *immediately* influence the transformation of the bases—spiritual or non-spiritual—of the National Socialist Movement."[26] In January 1934 he had decided to leave the rectorate, but, unfortunately, he had to wait until April 1934. If one accepts this as true, he fully identified himself with the rectorate for only eight months.

According to him he joined the party because of the pressure of the Ministry and the leadership of the NSDAP, but it did him no good at all, as the party did not really want his counsel. In the following years, he turned away from National Socialism ever more strongly; he even criticized its nihilism in his Nietzsche lectures. Moreover, according to him, his "intellectual resistance" had been duly noticed by the National Socialist Party leaders and he was constantly punished for it by exclusion from international congresses, the refusal to publish his texts, and the surveillance of the secret police. He declined the repeated requests of the Department of Foreign Affairs to send him abroad for propaganda purposes. In conclusion: "I do not claim anything special about my intellectual resistance during the last eleven years. However, if crude claims continue to be advanced that numerous students had been 'enticed' toward 'National Socialism' by my year as rector, justice requires that one at least recognize that between 1934–1944 thousands of students were trained to reflect on the metaphysical basis of our age and that I opened their eyes to the world of spirit and its great traditions in the history of the West."[27] Heidegger develops this line of argument even further. In his later comments, he tries time and again to weaken the concrete accusations against him by referencing his intellectual critique of National Socialism. For instance, in a letter to Constantin von Dietze, he explained his politics toward the Association of German Universities (Hochschulverband) in spring 1933, as well as his particular understanding of the term *Gleichschaltung* (coordination), by which he understood a process of spiritual unification as opposed to a purely political understanding that equated coordination with the deprivation of rights and manipulation.[28] He wanted to do good, but instead had created illusions for himself, and when these illusions became clear to him, he subsequently retreated into intellectual resistance. According to him, the rupture had already taken place in 1933–34; he had simply believed for a while longer that one could change something in the system of National Socialism.

It was in this situation that Friedrich Oehlkers, who was also a member of the "Purification Committee," asked Karl Jaspers for his opinion on Heidegger's rectorate. Heidegger agreed to this. Oehlkers and Jaspers had become closer to each other during the National Socialist period because they were both married to Jewish women and suffered similarly under the discriminatory measures. Heidegger evidently hoped that his friend Jaspers would now speak in his favor, knowing that in the 1920s they both wanted what he, Heidegger, thought to implement in the 1930s. Jaspers, however, issued a sibylline judgment. On the one hand, he produced further incriminating material—Heidegger's letter with its negative judgment on the philosopher Eduard Baumgarten. On the other hand, he pointed out exonerating evidence, such as Heidegger's support of his Jewish assistant Brock, whom Heidegger assisted in finding a position in England. He agreed with Heidegger's harshest critics, such as Lampe, Böhm, and Eucken, that in no event should Heidegger get away with no punitive measures whatsoever, but pleaded—in language that was highly ambivalent—that a scholar as original as Heidegger be allowed to continue teaching: "Heidegger is a significant force, not through the content of a philosophical world-view, but in the use of speculative tools. He has a philosophical aptitude whose perceptions are interesting; although, in my opinion, he is extraordinarily uncritical and stands at a remove from true science. It sometimes appears that he combines the seriousness of nihilism with the mysticism of a magician. In the torrent of his language he is occasionally able, in a clandestine and remarkable way, to strike at the core of philosophical thought."[29] On the one hand, Jaspers argued against those who claimed that Heidegger was already a sworn anti-Semite at the beginning of the National Socialist's "seizure of power;" on the other hand, he maintained that Heidegger became an anti-Semite afterward. He agreed with the argument that Heidegger wanted to advance to the top of National Socialism and argued that the question of when he really detached himself from National Socialism must remain open. His recommendation was therefore retirement and "suspension from teaching duties for several years."[30] After a fairly long time, one would need to review what Heidegger had published in the meantime and assess the situation at the university to see whether it allowed a man of Heidegger's stature and past to be entrusted with the education of students.

The committee also returned to the discussion of the telegram that Heidegger sent to Hitler in May 1933. Walter Eucken spoke against Heidegger's claim that his actions against the Association of Universities (the telegram to Hitler was part of this action) were simply a matter of a real confrontation of the idea of *Universitas* versus the idea of a *professional* university.[31] Eucken, who was also present at the conference, pointed out that Heidegger did not even bring up this point at the meeting. Eucken also claimed that Heidegger's argument that he was deceived by Hitler was specious. The telegram was a token of his esteem for National Socialism and had a signaling effect. Two views, then, of the same event. Apparently Heidegger had raised the National Socialist leader to the stature of a revered ruler of antiquity. Did Heidegger see himself on a par with the "leader"? He the spiritual and Hitler the political leader?

Those judging in retrospect are faced with a mystery. How is it that such a significant thinker as Heidegger, like other greats from science, literature, and art, could have been attracted to the vulgar appearance of Adolf Hitler and his acolytes? How deep must their shame have been later when they—Heidegger included—became aware of the trap into which they had fallen?

Heidegger: The Difficult Years

Heidegger was fighting many defensive battles during these first postwar years. He defended himself against Jaspers's interpretation of his action against the professor Eduard Baumgarten and could prove that the transcript written from memory that Jaspers put in circulation did not agree with his actual evaluation. However, he did not contest the gist of the letter.[32]

In March 1947 the Baden Ministry of Culture and Education supported Heidegger's teaching prohibition, thereby thwarting the attempts of the university to find a quick solution to the Heidegger case.

It is interesting that at this time Catholic Church officials were also concerned with Heidegger. The archbishop of Freiburg, Conrad Gröber, influenced by the university proceeding against Heidegger, wanted to talk with him.

Evidently at the behest of the Jesuit order, Max Müller, a former student and then a colleague of Heidegger's—who was not always treated well by the latter—wrote an evaluation in which he addressed the philosophical development and the current spiritual state of his teacher. Naturally the Catholic Church was interested in where Heidegger stood with regard to it and how to interpret his hostility toward the church after 1933. They also wanted to understand Heidegger's ultimate distancing of himself from National Socialism and the specific steps that led him in that direction. Müller's text presents a balanced portrait. He counters the judgment that Heidegger is an atheist as well as the view that his philosophy aids nihilism. Concluding his report, Müller emphasizes Heidegger's inner struggle with theology and faith as central to his thinking:

> Heidegger is an extremely profound, but internally tormented and torn man who was caught by the hook of God through his baptism and his very pious upbringing. It is a hook that can never be extracted from the flesh even if it often causes insufferable pain to the point that it should be ripped out. Given this, it is perhaps understandable that he hates the Church to the same extent that he loves it. The torment of being torn apart internally makes his character often unclear, and does not allow for any final judgment. However, one thing is certain: the religious and the Christian problem are one of his central concerns and he circles incessantly around the question of the Absolute.[33]

It took until March 1949 and the end of the de-Nazification process, wherein Heidegger was classified as a "sympathizer," before things started moving again. A letter from Jaspers, this time thoroughly positive, helped. Other persons also spoke for Heidegger. The Catholic philosopher Romano Guardini, two of Heidegger's doctors, the physicist Werner Heisenberg, and District Administrator Bröse, a former student of Heidegger, all wrote letters in his favor. The effect of these efforts by Heidegger's supporters on the rector and the department was ambiguous. It became clear that Heidegger, surrounded by his friends' conjectures, rumors, and suspicions, had a somewhat limited view of things.

At the beginning of September 1949, the Ministry of Culture and Education received a letter regarding Heidegger from the High Commissioner of the French Republic. In it was written, "I have no objections to Herr Prof. HEIDEGGER's retirement."[34] However, it was now the Ministry who was creating obstacles to the retirement process. It was not until fall 1951 that the decision was finalized.

The members of the "Purification Committee" were upset that Heidegger received invitations from France during the early postwar period. For instance, in 1945 the journal *Fontaine*, the successor of *Nouvelle Revue Française*, inquired about his texts that were still unpublished. Furthermore, there was talk at that time of an invitation to Baden-Baden. Allegedly, Heidegger was to travel there to meet Jean-Paul Sartre for a discussion. Nothing came of it, first because Sartre did not come and, second, because the rectorate and the department, both those colleagues who were predisposed toward him and those who wanted to see him gone, reacted with indignation. They found it impossible to believe that Heidegger would enjoy himself at the very time that he was supposed to be justifying himself before the "Purification Committee." Even when Heidegger turned the decision regarding acceptance of the invitation over to the rector, the indignation did not subside. The mood had turned completely against him, revealing just how much emotions prevailed at this time.

It must have shaken Heidegger deeply to be questioned within the university. However, the proceeding against him was not the only reason for his physical and mental breakdown in the years 1945–46. Part of it was a romantic relationship with one of his students, Margot, Princess of Sachsen-Meiningen. Once again, he had to decide between his wife and a lover. Heidegger did not want to decide. He turned to a friend, the psychiatrist Viktor Freiherr von Gebsattel, in the sanatorium Schloß Haus Baden near Badenweiler. The doctor took him on many walks in the Schwarzwald and advised him to leave the university as soon as possible and concentrate on his work.[35]

The theme of the kind of life he would have if he no longer taught in the university runs throughout Heidegger's letters to his wife and, presumably, to his lover: "It is also clear to me that I must get away from the university atmosphere entirely, so my thinking & the evolving work retains its clear style and grounding . . . With the break with regard to the Univ. my relation to the city & everything else is also broken. Only our house & the children's home is enduring."[36] He stayed in the sanatorium from mid-February until May 1946. From there he went to the cabin in Todtnauberg, as it wasn't possible for him to concentrate on his work in the limited confines of his home in Freiburg-Zähringen.

Reflection on the Consequences

During the profoundly unsettling events of the initial postwar years, Heidegger worked on a text that sheds light on his line of thinking in this situation of existential distress. It is based on a 1946 response to Jean Beaufret.[37] This young French philosopher visited Heidegger in September 1946 in his cabin and must have been deeply impressed by their conversations. In a letter after his visit, he posed the following question: *Comment redonner un sens au mot "Humanisme"?* ("How can the word *humanism* have meaning again?")

The humanist perspective as the answer to the nihilism of the prewar and war period was passionately and critically discussed in France at the time, both in Paris and in the province, where Beaufret was teaching. The young intellectuals around Sartre, Albert Camus, and Maurice Merleau-Ponty had called into question humanism as the moral foundation of postwar society. They were looking for a new foundation, not a continuation of the old idealist understanding of humanism. This text proceeds differently than Heidegger's justificatory writings of 1945 and 1946, but is similar to the Nietzsche lectures of the 1930s. Here one can follow the development of the thought that liberated him from his involvement with National Socialism. Opposing the entire debate of "German guilt,"[38] which started at the end of National Socialism and in which both the Catholic and the Protestant Churches and the educated middle class participated, Heidegger did not join the current of those who, after the (self-)destruction of all values, claimed the beginning of a new moral age. He also did not ground his critique of the traditional moral understanding of humanism in a "break of tradition" (like Arendt), but instead in a general fallenness of Dasein.

One can see here how Heidegger integrated the now closed chapter of National Socialism into his diagnosis of the West. His response to Beaufret begins with a fundamental critique of the prevalent concept of humanism. He calls into question the paradigm of humanism as a convenient catchall phrase that could be used to conflicting ends: "When thinking comes to an end by slipping out of its element, it replaces this loss by procuring a validity for itself as *techne*, as an instrument of education and therefore as a classroom matter and later a cultural concern. By and by philosophy becomes a technique for explaining from highest causes."[39] In view of this, Heidegger argued that humanism should not be understood as a directive for moral action. For him it was not a matter of subjecting thinking to the question of its application—and here we see the old questioning from *Being and Time*—but of approaching Dasein from out of Being. Humanism, according to Heidegger's interpretation of the concept, does not manifest itself in the mobilization of moral attitudes and transporting them into "praxis," but rather in freeing the ability to think and exist from out of Being. This meant that the thinker had to withdraw into pure free thinking:

> But if man is to find his way once again into the nearness of Being, he must first learn to exist in the nameless. In the same way he must recognize the seductions of the public realm as well as the impotence of the private. Before he speaks man must first let himself be claimed again by Being, taking the risk that under this claim he will seldom have much to say. Only thus will the inestimable richness of its essence be once more bestowed upon the word, and providing man once again a home for dwelling in the truth of Being.[40]

Here Heidegger makes a link to *Being and Time*. Human beings must be brought back into their essence, "for this is humanism: meditating and caring, that man be human and not inhumane, "inhuman," that is, outside his essence. But in what does the humanity of man consist? It lies in his essence."[41]

Yet again, Heidegger distances himself from a thinking oriented toward its direct application. The text contains no "confrontation with National Socialism." The concept, or rather the historical phenomenon, is not thematized and remains in the background, under the heading of Dasein's forgetfulness of Being. At the same time, the entire history of modernity is concealed behind this. Heidegger was not able to emerge from the generality of his problematic to thematize his own actions. That was his dilemma. His critical self-reflection does not go beyond a critique of modernity's "applied" thinking. The self-critical turn remains within the framework of philosophical thinking. Addressing the conduct of Citizen Heidegger would have required going beyond this framework.

In the "Letter on Humanism," Heidegger also separated himself from the renewed reflection on the philosophy of value which began in 1945 in the European intelligentsia and was driven by Jaspers in West Germany. Heidegger also withdrew from the pull of French existentialism and its project of action. Sartre, also in 1946, published his polemical essay "Existentialism Is a Humanism" (*L'éxistentialisme est un humanisme*), which contained a radical project for individual responsibility. Heidegger saw the activist involvement of French philosophy as the reverse side of nihilism, embellished by technology that, in his view, lay at the root of the twentieth century and also, therefore, of National Socialism. Against it, his own position called for a return to freeing the relation between man and Being: the human being had to think and live from out of Being and not from that which was already given or what he had produced. If one could still infer from *Being and Time* the call to the realization of an authentic life that was appropriate to Being, here the fundamental position had become more modest. Ethics after the catastrophe means for Heidegger the freeing of a thinking that "thinks the truth of Being as the primordial element of man, as one who eksists."[42] With this, Heidegger dissolved the dichotomy between the "Is" and the "Ought" (*Sein und Sollen*). He did so, however, in a completely different way than Sartre and his friends. While the latter announced the arrival of a philosophy of perpetual contingent involvements, Heidegger stepped back, waiting, open to what could come. Thus a contradiction is hidden behind the general name of existentialism, a name that was applied to both Heidegger *and* Sartre.

Heidegger's text on humanism attracted worldwide attention; we mentioned Hermann Broch's sympathetic reading. Arendt and Blücher also read the essay carefully. It was Heidegger's first philosophical text since the end of the National Socialist disaster, and everyone was reading it against the backdrop of Heidegger's involvement with the National Socialists. Insightful commentators such as Eric Voegelin began to speculate about Heidegger's dilemma:

> An odd impression: he is much more classic-conservative (Platonist) than I realized, yet at the same time he is strangely prescient. I almost believe now that his N.S. stemmed from a place similar to that of Carl Schmitt, or similar to Laski's racism. It was an intelligent anticipation of the political on the level of the innerworldly-histories—more intelligent than the "decency" of many others whose obstinacy in the face of dangerous adventures was preserved— but of too small a spiritual stature to make its way out of the nonsense of the world-immanent processes—it never completely stretched to the "periagoge" [Turn, turning point (*Wende, Kehre*)—author's note] in the Platonic sense.[43]

In the correspondence with Jaspers, Heidegger's dilemma is shown to be a kind of intellectual captivity out of which he cannot find his way, even though there are many people standing by who wish to hand him the key in order to open the prison door.

Heidegger and Jaspers: After the End of the Friendship

The active correspondence between Jaspers and Heidegger stopped in 1936. Thirteen years later, in February 1949, Jaspers took up the thread again. He addressed his recommendation concerning Heidegger from December 1945 as well as Heidegger's recommendation concerning Baumgarten and its incriminating wording.[44] He complains that Heidegger was silent "in the long years of banishment and danger to my life." But he expresses the hope that the prevailing darkness between us will not "prevent us from exchanging a few words in philosophizing and, perhaps, also in private things."[45]

Half a year later, Heidegger sends him his thanks: he was notified about a letter, but he did not receive it. He assures Jaspers that "throughout all errancy and confusion, and an occasional souring, my relationship to you, which was established in the 1920s at the beginning of our paths, has remained untouched for me."[46] The letter contains a further allusion to the theoretical exchange in the 1920s, in which Heidegger again picks up the metaphor of the "guardian of thinking." In general, the memories of the fruitful 1920s form the continuum, the background of the resumed correspondence to which all those involved, including their wives, refer. Heidegger reflects that solitude is "the only place where those who think and poetize according to their human abilities stand by being."[47] The letter comforts and consoles. In his response of June 25, Jaspers includes a copy of his first letter. Now Heidegger must react. But how is he to respond? "Over the years, I have remained certain that the relationship between the critical points of our thinking existence is unshakable, but I found no way to a dialogue. This became even more difficult for me since the spring of 1934, when I joined the opposition and also internally severed myself from all matters at the university, for my helplessness increased."[48] He does not claim to understand and feel Jaspers's fate. He adds a reference to his own misfortune, one son still in Russian captivity, the other returned from it ill. However, he does not go into the time from 1933 until 1945: "Mere explaining will immediately go awry by becoming interminable."[49] To be sure, the confrontation with what had happened "will take the rest of our lives!"[50] Heidegger includes Jaspers in a general "we": victims and perpetrators, sympathizers and the persecuted are bound together in that they cannot get away from the event. Jaspers might have seen it as presumptuous. Heidegger's transition to a general cultural critique, the judgment of National Socialism as well as communism as an expression of the crisis of the West were also too vague for him. However, Heidegger's letters remain ambiguous. One can read them as an attempt to evade personal responsibility, but one can also have the impression that Heidegger, emerging from the disaster of 1933–34 only with great effort, had learned his lesson. Never again would he leave the site of philosophizing to enter the realm of action or political reasoning, not even to explain his turn to National Socialism.

Yet Jaspers does not give up. When Heidegger refers to the Platonic dualism between real ideas and the world of appearances from which we must twist free, Jaspers accepts the invitation to an intellectual debate, but refuses to ally himself with a shared solitude of thinking: "The *site* from which you greet me—perhaps I have never entered it, but I gladly receive such a greeting with admiration and excitement."[51] Is there an ironic undertone here?

Jaspers insists on the conversation concerning their different experiences during the Nazi time and speaks with a striking sincerity about his suffering with regard to what Germany had become: "To be a wanderer and a guest as my German fate was clear since 1934, when my eighty-four-year-old father said to me: 'My boy, we have lost our fatherland'! A sadness lies like a veil over everything. I will never come out from under it, despite the serenity of the façade."[52]

He explained why he had to leave Germany in 1948, this country where he no longer felt at ease. Too many lies, they wanted to use him as a puppet. Jaspers calls into question Heidegger's tendency to withdraw from the world, with the Platonic argument that reality is appearance. One must speak in the here and now. Also "mystical-speculative thoughts" (an allusion to Heidegger's way of questioning) "must lose their naïveté so that they do not hold us spellbound and allow us to miss what is really necessary for the age."[53] Heidegger does not take up this appeal to the thinker's responsibility as a citizen.

They are exchanging books and essays once again. Heidegger does not respond to Jaspers's invitation to speak about the difficult problem of making a transition from thinking to acting. Instead, he would rather begin a polemic concerning "technology." He complains about the slow pace of the proceeding against him at the University of Freiburg.

A small affair indicates just how tense their relationship was. Paul Hühnerfeld reviewed Jaspers's new book *Vom Ursprung und Ziel der Geschichte* in the weekly *Die Zeit*. The reviewer interpreted some passages in the book as a critique of Heidegger. Jaspers rushed to assure Heidegger that nothing he wrote was intended as an attack. Heidegger responded cryptically. Finally Jaspers wrote a letter to the newspaper in which he protested against Hühnerfeld's imputation. Heidegger seemed satisfied.

There it was again—the ambivalent tone between them that characterized the last phase before National Socialism. Both knew that they had many reservations regarding the other. Both critiqued each other in private circles and in their books but still did not dare to openly address their differences in personal letters.

Jaspers, Arendt, and Heidegger

Jaspers showed the resumed correspondence to Hannah Arendt when she visited him for the first time in December 1949 in Basel, still before her reencounter with Heidegger. She comments in a letter to Blücher: "Jaspers marvelously open in his original accusation. Heidegger accepting everything, and desperately happy that Jaspers is writing again. Quite touching, however, once again false."[54] In the same letter, she reports on how Jaspers reacted when she told him about the relationship between them. "I openly told Jaspers how things had been between Heidegger and me. He: 'Oh, how very exciting.'"

The tone in the letters between the two former friends changed temporarily under the influence of the conversations that Hannah Arendt had with each of them. Jaspers encouraged a polemic, one that could be carried out in writing, but presupposed a complete openness toward one's own thinking and the thinking of the other. If it were possible to articulate what was separating them and, in this separation, what brought them together again, the correspondence could perhaps even be published. Instead of responding to this, the letter that Jaspers must have awaited for many years finally arrives—probably as the result of conversations with Hannah. In it, Heidegger attempts to describe why he discontinued the correspondence with Jaspers in the mid-1930s. "Since 1933, I no longer came to your house, not because a Jewish woman lived there, but *because I simply felt ashamed.*"[55] For this reason he no longer visited Heidelberg, but made sure at that time that the local NSDAP leaders would undertake nothing against Jaspers and his wife.[56] He did not see how little such a promise was worth. Later, Jaspers will bitterly remark that Heidegger's shame was an "excuse."[57]

Jaspers adamantly tries to lead Heidegger to further reflection. He had sometimes thought: "You seem to behave toward the manifestations of National Socialism like a boy who dreams, who doesn't know what he is doing, who doesn't know how blindly and forgetfully he gets mixed up in an undertaking that looks to him like something completely different than what it is in reality, and then stands before a pile of rubble and allows himself to be driven further."[58] He sends him his 1946 book *The Question of German Guilt.* Heidegger does not respond to this olive branch. He seizes instead on the metaphor of the "dreaming boy." In a highly disturbing letter, he exposes himself without noticing what he has revealed. He presents the acceptance of the rectorate as if he were a sleepwalker, driven by his colleagues. He continues to be unclear about the significance of this step or of its effect on the generation of his students. He was thinking only about the university and his project of a large-scale reform: "I immediately fell into the machinery of the office; the influences, the power struggles, and the factions.

I was lost and fell, if only for a few months, into what my wife describes as an 'intoxication of power.' I only began to see more clearly at Christmas of 1933; so, in February, I resigned under protest from my office and declined to participate in the official transference of the Rectorship to my successor [Eduard Kern— author's note]."[59] Why does he date the end of the rectorate back to February and not, as the files show, to April? Did the date disappear from his memory or did he conflate the moment of decision with that of its accomplishment?

He notes that his resignation from the rectorate was public, yet it was barely noticed. In any case, he writes that it was "a step." He also notes that he was getting increasingly anxious over the course of the 1930s; in addition, he was under the surveillance of the NS secret police. Thus, he writes, the action against him in 1945 was all the more difficult to bear, although he must be clear that "at this university, *no one* dared to do what I did."[60] Even in 1945–46, he still does not comprehend the significance of his step in 1933. Although he notes that since then his questionable fame in connection with the existentialism debate has led him to some sort of an understanding. Once again, he shifts the question of guilt to the level of ontology. Once again, it becomes clear how problematic the concept of guilt as a general paradigm for coming to grips with events was for personalities such as Heidegger or Carl Schmitt. Would a debate about moral *and* political responsibility have changed that? Who would have been able to lead it at that time?

Heidegger does not see himself as responsible—he sees himself as a victim. Imagining a future in which the Russians take over Europe, a concern shared by many at the time, he feared retaliation. In Russia, his name was "once again heard." Toward the end of the letter he again conjured up the communal "we" of homelessness in which, however, a future, an "advent," was concealed.

Jaspers first returns to this letter two years later in July 1952. Meanwhile, they maintained a connection; however, they did not exchange much of substance. All sorts of negative rumors flew. Jaspers announced his unease reading Heidegger's letter from April 1950. He points out the limited nature of Heidegger's response, noting that Heidegger never engaged with his book, *The Question of German Guilt*. He attacks head-on Heidegger's tendency to engage with National Socialism and his involvement with it only ontologically. This tendency also bothers him in Heidegger's view of communism. Heidegger, on the other hand, argued that "for us, as well, there is no avoiding it, and every word and every piece of writing *is* in itself a counterattack, if all of this does not play itself out in the *political*, which itself has long been outplayed by other relations to being and leads a pseudo-existence."[61] Jaspers felt himself attacked in his role as a citizen in this remark. Should they sit face-to-face, Heidegger would experience his, Jaspers's, "flood of words, in anger and in the adjuration of reason."[62] He wondered if such a view of things did not celebrate perdition. With his "visions," Heidegger obscures the perspective on what is close, present, concrete:

> Is not a philosophy that surmises and poetizes in such sentences in your letter, that produces a vision of something monstrous, is this not, in turn, something that prepares the victory of totalitarianism by separating itself from reality? Just as, before 1933, philosophy to a great extent actually made ready the acceptance of Hitler? . . . Are you about to appear as a prophet who points to something transcendental on the basis of a secret revelation, as a philosopher who leads us away from reality? . . . With things like this, one wonders about authorization and rehabilitation.[63]

In Heidegger's remark about Stalin, Jaspers heard the stormy Heidegger of the prewar period, who declared all existing relations to be null and void. On top of everything else, Jaspers advised him again to read Arendt's "excellent book" *The Origins of Totalitarianism*.

With his attack, Jaspers thematized important fundamental positions in Heidegger's thinking, notably the juncture between thinking, acting, and responsibility. Jaspers saw Heidegger's philosophical argumentation as evasive. Between the lines, one senses disappointment, impatience, and moral superiority. Heidegger must have reacted defensively; however, nothing came of it. The tone of the letters became more conciliatory; both invoking the good old days, the years in which they were communicating openly with each other, although up until the end of the correspondence in 1963, Jaspers remained stubborn. Each of his short letters had a reference to what had not been addressed. Still, Heidegger did not react.

As we see in what follows, Jaspers is the "invisible third" in Arendt's reencounter with Heidegger. She must have faced Jaspers's judgments about Heidegger, endured the tension, and still tried to mediate between the two.

Hannah and Martin: The Reencounter

It must have been a shattering moment when Martin and Hannah approached each other in the lobby of a Freiburg hotel on February 7, 1950. She had sent him a message. In the evening he appeared with a formal letter. "I am delighted to have the chance to acknowledge our early encounter as something enduring, and to take it up now in the later part of life. . . . My wife, who knows about everything, would also like to welcome you."[64] Unfortunately, Elfriede was unable to come. He delivered the letter himself to the hotel as there was no public telephone in Zähringen where they lived. Evidently, he intended to deliver it and wait for her reaction. However, upon arrival, he asked a waiter to give her the letter and to let her know that he was waiting in the lobby. She therefore did not read the letter at all but put it in her purse. Then they walked toward one other.

That same evening they went together to Zähringen and talked for a long time, "for the first time in our lives," as she wrote to her husband.[65] What they talked about would not have been much different than what had been the topics of conversation between Heidegger and Jaspers: the transition in 1933, his rector-ate, the issue with Husserl, the how and when of his detachment from National Socialism, his estrangement from Jaspers. Surely, they also discussed her sepa-ration from him, her marriage with Stern, the breaking off of their contact in 1932–33, and her time in exile when she had sworn not to do intellectual work ever again.

What did Heidegger feel when he saw her again? Hannah, who helped him attain the height of emotion while writing *Being and Time*; Hannah, the student driven into exile; Hannah, the famous Jewish writer and thinker from America; Hannah, the reminder of his shame.

During this visit in Freiburg, Hannah met with Elfride Heidegger. In the morning of February 8, 1950, Hannah once again went to Zähringen. An emo-tional discussion between the three ensued.

Just how stirred up Arendt was can be seen in the letters that flow between the two after seventeen years. Martin tried to include his wife in the resumed relationship. He had attempted this integration time and again, in an effort to be able to keep his mistresses while not losing his wife. Heidegger asks both Hannah and Elfride that the new relationship between the three of them be one of open-ness and trust. He even wanted to include Jaspers, since he knew that Arendt was close to him:

> "Bright is beautiful." This phrase from Jaspers that you quoted last night moved me continually as the discussion between my wife and you grew from misunderstanding and scrutiny to the harmony of troubled hearts. The sole result of the exchange ought to be that the encounter between *us two*, and that which is enduring in it, can, for your sake and mine, enter the pure element of conscious trust between us three. My wife's words were aimed *only at that*; they were not meant as a demand for you to make any confession of guilt to her . . . It was because I knew that my wife would not just understand, but also affirm, the joyousness and the richness of our love as a gift of fate for which I pushed her trust aside.[66]

He attaches an ivy leaf to the letter, given by his wife, which came from Schwar-zwald and had decorated their cabin in Todtnauberg.

Elfride is a bitter woman when she meets Hannah. Her marriage and their many years of life together had been thrown off track by Martin's erotic affairs. She was the one who made it possible for him to have the life he wanted. What was lacking was her husband's recognition and intimacy. Coming from the wom-en's movement (Gertrud Bäumer), closely connected with the youth movement, Elfride's thinking had been shaped in the changing milieu between populist group culture, anti-Semitic nationalism, and a longing for authenticity. Previ-ously, she had known nothing about her husband's passionate relationship with

Hannah, at least nothing concrete. She must have felt disheartened when this woman, who was simultaneously Heidegger's lover, an intellectual, and a Jew, approached her. However, with Elfride it was difficult to determine what was concrete jealousy against the particular person Hannah, what was general jealousy against all women in Martin's vicinity, and what was anti-Semitic prejudice. Elfride was humiliated on many fronts, as a woman, as a mother, and as a wife who took care that Martin could live as he wanted: withdrawn, without any material cares or needs. During the war and after, she was the one who had to worry about their survival. Her role as an erotic partner had apparently disappeared over the years. Although it did not make the matter any easier for her, she knew that her husband needed erotic engagement in order to be able to function intellectually. A single draft of a letter of hers, written years later and never sent, is a testimony to her bitterness. She had discovered another of her husband's affairs. She writes about "lies," "most inhuman abuse of my trust," "despair," "deception," and "icy solitude."[67] She felt his affairs to be a betrayal of their love, whose previous intensity she missed. He always responded to her reproaches in the same contrite manner, a reaction that must have seemed to her ever more hollow with time.

Arendt was divided. She felt, as she wrote Martin, "a sudden feeling of solidarity" with Elfride. The following day she sent her a letter. In the first section she explains herself and even attempts a rapprochement. In the second section, she clearly distances herself. Hannah did not concede much in this encounter. She told Elfride frankly that her convictions had not changed ("You, however, never made a secret of your convictions, after all, nor do you today, not even to me."). But she also asked her to separate the personal from the political state of affairs. Politically they were enemies; yet they had a common history: "I am ready at any time, and I said as much to Martin, to talk about such issues in an objective, political way—I like to think I know a few things about them—but only on the condition that personal, intimate issues are kept out of it. The *argumentum ad hominem* is the ruin of every communication, because it includes something which stands outside of the freedom of the individual."[68] Hannah was ready to meet Elfride halfway; she had learned the hard way to distinguish between the personal and the political. In Elfride's resentment, the private and the political are mixed. How else can one explain that in their first conversation Elfride reproached Hannah for refusing to assume the role of the "German woman"? Hannah remained true to herself and expected the impossible from her shared world. However, she also could not understand Elfride because of the many things she could not possibly know about Elfride's life. She wrote to Martin the day after the meeting:

> This evening and this morning are the confirmation of an entire life. A confirmation that, when it comes down to it, was never expected. When the waiter spoke your name . . . it was as if time suddenly stood still. Then all at once I

became aware of something I would not have confessed before, neither to myself nor to you nor to anyone—how, after Friedrich had given me the address, the power of the impulse had mercifully saved me from committing the only really inexcusable act of infidelity and forfeiting my life. But one thing you should know (as we have had relatively little to do with each other, after all, and that not as openly as we might have), if I had done it, then it would only have been out of pride, that is, out of sheer crazy stupidity. Not for any good reasons.[69]

She let him know between the lines that their history is a rubble heap on which distrust and uncertainty had grown like weeds. Yet even on the rubble heap one senses the old loyalty. She makes use of the dramatic metaphors that had already come to her mind during her times of inner turmoil: "I would lose my right to live if I lost my love for you, but I would lose this love and its *reality* if I shirked the responsibility it forces on me."[70] This sentence comes from a 1928 letter and describes the existential crossroads she was at before she decided to leave Heidegger and marry, "somehow indifferent as to whom I was marrying, without being in love."[71] In 1950 the metaphor resurfaces: "committing the only really inexcusable act of infidelity and forfeiting my life," she writes to Martin. Here speaks a fidelity so radical that it was hardly bearable. Hannah was a passionate and a pragmatic woman. Radical feelings and a sober perception were equally present in her. This must have resulted in her being pulled in two directions.

During the reencounter, Hannah did not try to understand why Heidegger insisted so much on including Elfride in this revived love. However, she put a good face on the matter, all the while expressing her anger in many letters to Blücher. There Elfride appears as the evil spirit: jealous, vengeful, and resentful.

In this first conversation neither Elfride nor Martin mentioned that Martin had had many other affairs. Elfride's agitated and possibly confused demeanor, her insinuations *must* have appeared "idiotic" to Hannah because she did not know the prior history. Thus she could not have known that Elfride was confronting all Martin's other lovers in the person of Hannah.

Heidegger's histories with women were not merely physical affairs; there was always an intellectual element. His women were listeners, conversation partners who stimulated erotically. They consoled him in the solitude of thinking. They replaced the dialogue with his students, assistants, and colleagues. Apparently Elfride did not. Not anymore? Once again Heidegger was between two women and looking for harmony. At least this is how one can make sense out of his seemingly adventurous endeavor to bring together these two fundamentally different women. Having found Hannah again, he also did not want to lose Elfride, and he also wanted to keep all his other lovers. Unlike Hannah, Elfride already knew this ritual. Despite this, she sensed that Heidegger was playing both sides of the game.

Elfride again pressured Martin to justify his behavior. He once again saw himself compelled to explain his relation to marriage, to her, and to himself. He thus wrote a remarkable letter to Elfride on February 14, a week after meeting with Hannah:

> The other thing, inseparable in a different way from my love for you & from my thinking, is difficult to say. I call it Eros, the oldest of the gods according to Parmenides. By this I'm not telling you anything you don't know on your own account; nonetheless I can't quite find the terms to express it suitably. It can easily sound too free and easy & acquire a form that gives an impression of seeking to justify what is wrong and inappropriate. The beat of that god's wings moves me every time I take a substantial step in my thinking and venture into untrodden paths. It moves me perhaps more powerfully & uncannily than others when something long intuited is to be led across into the realm of the sayable & when what has been said must after all be left in solitude for a long time to come. To live up to *this* purely and yet retain what is ours, to follow the flight and yet return home safely, to accomplish both things as equally essential and pertinent, this is where I fail too easily & then either stray into pure sensuality or try to force the unenforceable through sheer work. My disposition and the manner of my early upbringing, instability and cowardice in the ability to trust & then again inconsiderateness in the abuse of trust, these are the poles between which I swing & thus only too easily & only too often misjudge & overstep the measure with regard to Hera and Eros.[72]

Elfride would not have been comforted by this self-revelation.

Hannah and Martin: Ambiguous Feelings

The symbolic value of Martin Heidegger and Hannah Arendt's meeting went far beyond their personal relationship. The disgraced philosopher, forced into the private sphere, receives a visit from the famous Jewish writer, who stands in the light of the public space. Perhaps he hopes that this could point the way to a reconciliation between the past and the present, between Jews and non-Jews. When Hannah left again, the coordinates were set. Martin's spirit was sparked. Hannah was inundated with a stream of letters and poems. This includes a poem that went back to the metaphor they had invented for young Hannah in 1925:

> *The Girl from Abroad*
> The stranger,
> even to yourself,
> she is:
> mountain of joy,
> sea of sorrow,
> desert of desire,
> dawn of arrival.

Stranger: home of the one gaze
where world begins.
Beginning is sacrifice.
Sacrifice is loyalty's hearth
still outglowing all the fires'
ashes and—
igniting:
embers of charity,
shine of silence.
Stranger from abroad, you—
may you live in beginning.[73]

This poem, a reworking of Schiller's famous poem of the same title, alludes to the *coup de foudre* of their first encounter in 1925. It situates their relationship within this internal and external tension that they both knew so well.

Hannah was relieved to have resumed the relationship, but at the same time she had concerns. This much can be gathered from her remarks about Heidegger to Blücher, Jaspers, and others. Still, distrust was lurking in the background and did not just disappear.

In any case, one may ask here: How did Hannah present her reencounter with Martin? What did she write to her husband, Heinrich Blücher, to Jaspers, and to her friends about the resumption of the relationship?

She writes from out the intensity of her anger, her relief, her love, her worry, and her profound internal conflict. Her feelings fluctuate constantly. No wonder. What else could this reencounter with the man with whom she learned to think *and* to love have generated in her?

On February 8, 1950, the day after their first meeting, she writes to Heinrich Blücher:

> On top of everything, this morning I had an argument with his wife. For twenty-five years now, or from the time she somehow wormed the truth about us out of him, she has clearly made his life a hell on earth. And he, who, always, at every opportunity, has been such a notorious liar, evidently (as was obvious from the aggravating conversation the three of us had) never, in all those twenty-five years, refuted that I had been the passion of his life. His wife, I'm afraid, for as long as I'm alive, is ready to drown any Jew in sight. Unfortunately, she is absolutely horrendous. But I'm going to try to diffuse things as much as I can.[74]

A day later she repeats once again: "the Freiburg matter was spectral: the scene with that woman, which might have hit the mark accurately twenty-five years ago, was conducted as if no time had passed."[75] She reports that she had tried to establish peace between Heidegger and Jaspers.

Blücher was more critical toward Heidegger than she. He judged from a safe distance, himself busy with an amorous liaison. Hannah, who knew nothing about it, took Heinrich with her symbolically as a constant companion on her first trip to Germany. What would she have done without him, the person to whom she could relate everything that she experienced, without embellishments, whenever she wanted to? Blücher had read Heidegger's latest texts, which made their way to America through various channels as soon as they were published. He supplied wonderfully ironic comments. In *Holzwege* Heidegger attempted "to undermine and blow up the Western concept of being. He hopes to find new territory where nothing is to be found but his Nothingness, which is leading him around by the nose."[76] Yet the irony collides with the fascination for this very different thinking. Heinrich to Hannah on March 8, 1950: "The business with Heidegger is a real tragedy, and I'm suffering on account of this metaphysical misfortune just as I'm delighted by Jaspers' stroke of luck. Both of them have shoved me deeper into my own speculation, and I'm working without interruption, to the extent that my fatigue will let me."[77] They both suffered, all the while being fascinated by the dilemmas of thinking into which Heidegger had maneuvered himself and through which he created a secret thread to the real.

Hannah also shared with Jaspers her conflicted judgment regarding Heidegger. Before meeting with Heidegger again, she characterized him to Jaspers with words such as *hypocritical, slippery, untruthful, deceitful.*[78] If one did not know any better, one would assume that she would never want to see the person in question again on the basis of these words. After their meeting, she was pulled in two directions. Karl Jaspers spoke and behaved in a similar manner. At times he tried to help revive the bond; at other times he would have preferred to see her refuse any further contact. He was equally torn at this time when he was again exchanging letters with Martin Heidegger.

Sometimes she hid her ambiguity, her anger, and her sharp critique of Heidegger behind sarcasm, for instance, in this letter to Kurt Blumenfeld: "My Europe-trip was also, as you write about yours, an entire novel. To be specific, I was in Freiburg. . . . I was there professionally and H[eidegger] showed up in the hotel. Anyway, I have thereby indirectly enriched the German language with some very beautiful poems. One does what one can."[79] In the middle of March, Hannah returned to New York. She plunged into the proofs of *The Origins of Totalitarianism*. At the end of 1950, a part of the book, "The Temporary Alliance between the Mob and the Elite," appeared in *Partisan Review*. In the years that followed, she published additional articles on specific aspects of her book.

In the meantime, she offered several leading intellectuals in West Germany a forum in *Partisan Review*. In 1949 Jaspers wrote "Science and Philosophy." In 1952 he wrote an article about Nietzsche. In 1952 Jürgen von Kempski wrote about communism; in 1953 Walter Dirks wrote about the unfinished nature of the

Enlightenment. Heidegger, too, was under consideration for *Partisan Review*, as she wrote him,[80] but it did not happen. In March 1950, Henry Regnery Company announced the publication of *Existence and Being*, a collection of Heidegger's essays. This was a clear sign for Heidegger's future presence on the American intellectual scene.

From then on, Hannah traveled regularly to Europe. She went primarily to Basel, more seldom to Freiburg. Between 1953 and 1967, she went out of her way to avoid Freiburg altogether during her stays in Germany.

Heidegger: Amid Conflicting Camps

Arendt's relationship to Jaspers was very open. However, in 1958, when he invited her to give the *Laudatio* on the occasion of his receiving the German publishers' Peace Prize—a distinction she herself had helped prepare—she had a sudden fear that Heidegger would be hurt: "Of course, this matter would only confirm what is already established, or, better, isn't established—and this, due to no fault of mine—but it would force me into unambiguously taking sides, at least to all appearances, which I do not want to do. And tied in with it is the fact that this would also be a declaration of political solidarity, or appear to be one, which needless to say I don't feel particularly comfortable with."[81] Blücher's response was inimitable. He suggested that on this occasion she should give a talk about what a good European was, "and that is just what Heidegger has coming to him anyhow, that little German shrimp."[82] The snide tone should not deceive the reader. It was not a dismissive rejection, but rather a sharp attack. However, this harsh critique of the citizen Heidegger did not alter Blücher's appreciation of his thought.

Upon her return, Hannah was occupied with the translation of Heidegger's works in the United States. Ralph Manheim, the translator of books by Jaspers and Heidegger, asked her to write an introduction to the American edition of Heidegger's *Introduction to Metaphysics*.[83] She got in touch with Edward Schouten Robinson, the translator of *Being and Time*, and corrected his translation. In 1961 she suggested to the publisher Kurt Wolff that he read Heidegger's Nietzsche book, apparently to assess the chances of a translation and subsequent publication on the American market. Both Arendt and Blücher were deeply impressed by this book.

Heidegger's letters conveyed an unreserved intimacy toward her. What was separating them simply receded into the background, but it still remained. He was fully aware that there were political worlds separating him from her, just as there was a tradition of thought and deep feelings that connected them.

In the time that followed, Arendt worked on the conflict between agreement and disagreement, trust and distrust. In an entry in her notebook from November 1952, she coined a metaphor for this difficult situation: "However one sees it, there is no question that in Freiburg I went (*without* falling) into a trap. It is also without question that Martin, whether he knows it or not, sits in this trap, is at home in it, built his house around the trap; so that one can visit him only if one visits him in the trap, goes into the trap. Thus I went into the trap to visit him. The result is that now he is again sitting alone in his trap."[84] With her skeptical rapprochement with Germany, Arendt was of course also thrown into the turbulence of the intellectual landscape in postwar Germany. In spring 1952 she once again took a European trip. In Paris, where the trip began, she stayed again with her friend Anne Weil. She met with Alexandre Koyré, Jean Wahl, and Raymond Aron. She saw the first two in New York quite often. She met Albert Camus— and had to revise her judgment made in an article for the *Nation*. In the meantime, Camus had distanced himself from Sartre's circle around the magazine *Les Temps Modernes*. Arendt was excited by this writer who was a thinker. "He is without a doubt the best man they have in France. All the other intellectuals are at most bearable," she wrote to Blücher.[85] Naturally, she visited Jaspers. During this time, she went to see Heidegger twice. She worked with him and attended his lecture "What Is Called Thinking?"[86] However, there must have been renewed tensions with Elfride, since Heidegger urged her in a letter not to visit.

Arendt was greatly affected by the fact that the intellectual atmosphere in the postwar years was deeply torn, provincial, and pervaded by personal grudges. This was not just among Heidegger and his friends, but in other parts of Germany, as well. In July 1952 she wrote to her husband about a visit to Heidelberg. There she spoke about "Terror and Ideology," a topic she had added to the German edition of *The Origins* as the concluding chapter in which she presented her thesis concerning a new form of totalitarian government for a European audience. In Heidelberg, she met few, albeit good, students, but she also noted the formation of factions within the university. With her friend Waldemar Gurian, she herself participated in a discussion in the course of which Gurian became "highly vulgar" because he felt provoked. After this, several students, professors, and the dean of the theology department left the room. There was also a formation of factions with regard to Heidegger. Under these circumstances, it was very good that Löwith was in Heidelberg.[87] From him, she expected an objective critique of Heidegger.

On the other side were people like Dolf Sternberger and Alexander Röstow, who declared metaphysics to be superfluous. This remark was directed against Arendt. They called it all a "nonsensical witches' caldron."[88]

Dolf Sternberger, copublisher of the journals *Die Wandlung* and *Die Gegenwart*, was an important personality in German public opinion. He responded to Heidegger's involvement in National Socialism with a condemnation of Heidegger's thinking. It came to a substantial clash after the appearance of his article about Heidegger in the 1952 summer issue of *Die Wandlung*. The letters between

Arendt and Sternberger reveal the intellectual situation in Germany in the 1950s as well as Hannah's inner struggle with the person and thought of Martin Heidegger. Hannah felt that she was pigeonholed by her old student friend Sternberger in a way that she wished to avoid: "Your letter . . . gives the impression . . . as though everything revolves around a war between schools of thought. If such a thing were to take place, it would certainly be without me. I would not even participate as a spectator."[89] He replied that that was never his intention.[90] She responded that the actual reason for her distrust was that his article had made a plea for common sense against metaphysics:

> You believe you can *get by* with an analysis of style, which does get many things right. I consider it impossible. Here again you criticize Heidegger and his often *desperate* stubbornness (*desperate* because of the immense objective difficulty of writing *against the tradition* with the conceptual means of the tradition; or—and this difficulty is almost greater—with new concepts that approach the tradition such that it is still understandable) with the exaggerations that we have at their clearest and worst in Nietzsche. The latter does not become a lesser philosopher because he, without a doubt, often gets on our nerves. When those who are really still rooted in the tradition discover that the thread is torn and that the great wisdom of the past answers our questions with icy silence, they are terrified and begin to talk very loudly, like children who whistle in the forest. Our situation is different. Our lot knows it either as one of the fundamental commonplaces of our communal intellectual life or is already so uprooted from the tradition, that he does not shy away from passing on the old truths as platitudes. But it is this continuation, it seems to me, and not the Heideggerian attempt, whose *immense courage* one at least ought to respect, that is a kind of counterfeit currency. That Heidegger again and again hits a wrong note is not half as bad as the counterfeit currency used professionally by Rüstow and his professional consorts without which this kind of enterprise could not go on.[91]

Sternberger, who had the same direct, sometimes gruff way as Arendt, retorted:

> Heidegger is certainly a *philosophical* problem, first, second, and third, then a political one (in addition), but, as you know, I was against his thought even when he was not yet a Nazi, at least not a declared one. However, in the 1935 "departure from metaphysics" it surprised me how contagious this radical thinking is—of course critical towards *trivial* Nazism as well as against trivial liberalism, humanism, idealism, democracy, against everyone who thinks in ordinary terms. However, at the same time this thought is contagious through the widespread popularity of the tragic-heroic. But *philosophically*—to speak roughly—I dislike it *most deeply* that he refuses to admit his original sin. And therefore death is nothing. And the human condition is nothing. *This* is what I wanted to show by means of the analysis of language. It hurt me a bit that you apparently did not see or did not *want* to see what I am getting at.

An instruction in matters of the formation of intellectual factions follows: "People like *Heidegger* are elevated, with thousands listening breathlessly (as recently in Munich). Hardly anyone dares contradict the magus, dares break the spell. Even Löwith and Krüger do so only on tiptoe without drawing the clear conclusions." According to Sternberger, it is the Restoration in Germany. In what follows, he mocks Heidegger's language and how "one" was "addicted to obscurity, hopelessness, *lovelessness*, and false poetry." Metaphysics does not matter to him, but if there is a metaphysical question, he prefers theology, which Arendt has forgotten about—an allusion to the theological studies that were left behind long ago. "In relation to Heidegger you are on the path to nowhere (*Holzwege*), and that is *very* sad."[92] With this exchange of blows, the relationship between Arendt and her student and friend Sternberger was troubled for a long time. Arendt was very angry with what she saw as a throwback to the critique of metaphysics in the 1920s and with what was common practice in many universities in the 1950s and the 1960s: colleagues from philosophy and sociology (the Frankfurt school) either mocked Heidegger or at least subjected him to a moralizing critique, themselves returning to a philosophy of value that they believed had been overcome or to a type of cultural critique that they had engaged with already in the 1920s. Many of them were also simply not willing to subject themselves to the effort of a critical engagement with Heidegger's thought.

Yet, also in the relationship to Sternberger, friendship eventually triumphed over disagreements. It becomes clear in the letters to her husband as well as to Jaspers and Sternberger how susceptible Arendt was in relation to Heidegger. She was willing to share the ins and outs of her critique of Heidegger only with her husband, at most with Jaspers, and sometimes with Kurt Blumenfeld who was so far away. She was allergic to all appeals and campaigns in the name of common sense. This was the result of her reengagement with Heidegger's thought. Her notebooks—her "journal of ideas"—eloquently reveal how she immersed herself anew in the fundamental categories of Heidegger's thought after 1951 and from this, gained clarity for her own reflection on the world after the break in tradition.

Whenever she came to Germany, she was confronted with rumors and stories about Heidegger. In a letter to Blücher, she writes:

> Löwith told me without the slightest bit of malice (Heidegger's picture hangs in his office), that Heidegger is holding seminars for professors in a farmhouse in Todtnauberg, and that, basically, he is force-feeding them his philosophy. Doubtless this is the only thing that is really alive in Germany, but I imagine in its effect it's doubtlessly disastrous. But even this has disappeared from public life. In every bookstore you find neither Jünger nor Heidegger, but Goethe and even more Goethe.[93]

She did not like the way in which the cultural elite of West Germany had taken flight into the classics or rather in classicism.

And time and again she complains about Heidegger's self-cultivation. She writes to Blumenfeld: "Just yesterday I read Heidegger's latest text on identity and difference, highly interesting but—he cites himself and interprets himself, as if it was a text from the Bible. I simply can't stand it anymore. And he is really a genius and not just highly talented. Thus: why does he need it? These unspeakably bad manners."[94] Citing oneself contradicted her intellectual ethos. This did not mean that she did not take up her own trains of thought from other contexts, but she did so only in the framework of a new narrative.

Arendt and Heidegger: The Break in Tradition and Modernity

The way of thinking pursued by Arendt was so far from Heidegger's that one can confidently speak of two worlds. However, these very different worlds contained a lively confrontation with the crisis of modernity, at the heart of which both found themselves as actors and observers, thrown and implicated in the world around them.

The greatest difference between them lay in the impulse of their thought. Hannah Arendt came to her way of thinking from the profound shock of becoming aware of a break in tradition in the actual world, represented *in extremo* by the extermination camps of totalitarianism. Heidegger grappled with the break in tradition vis-à-vis antiquity. Because of this, he had to distance himself from the living world. The way into the analysis of concrete historical situations was closed for him. Furthermore, he clearly wanted to avoid everything that could again bring him into a connection with a "philosophy of action." He had critiqued the classical acting subject of modernity already in the 1920s. The maxim "I do something in order to accomplish something else" was, in his view, one of the most fatal fallacies of all time. Presumably, he faulted himself for having acted in accordance with this fallacy personally and as a citizen. Now he was again working on the same model, like a sculptor. He deepened the perspective previously attained and cleared up its errors. Arendt, on the other hand, whose thought-sites were scattered over two continents, was compelled to approach thinking from the side of the actual historical break in the traditions of intellectual and political history.

Both, however, begin with the same question: How did the break in tradition occur in modernity? For Heidegger, the break was inaugurated by Descartes's "cogito ergo sum," which was a turn away from the thinking of being and a turn to the reflecting individual. This carried with it the illusion of being able to produce reality. The modern world and the modern subject had, in Heidegger's perspective, produced an "enframing" (*Gestell*) from which no access to a "revealed" world is any longer possible. Arendt was deeply suspicious of this kind of cultural critique since 1933. After finding her footing in the United States, she had spent years exploring the historical subterranean dimensions of totalitarianism. To do this, she had delved into the elements, motives, and mind-sets of anti-Semitism, imperialism, race ideology, National Socialism, and Soviet domination.

Both were convinced that modern liberalism was the expression of a self-induced delusion of modern human beings and of modern society. They shared these convictions with many people of their generation. As Arendt writes to Gurian: "National Socialism is the monstrous product of the hell known as liberalism in whose abyss both Christianity and the Enlightenment perished."[95] Arendt's resounding judgment from 1942 agrees not only with Heidegger's thought, but also with the positions of Georg Lukács, Theodor W. Adorno, Max Horkheimer, Herbert Marcuse, and many others. Heidegger, too, thought that modern mass democracy (as the basis of modern liberalism) distorted what was essential to human beings. Both agreed that this break was self-produced, that it was not imposed from without. Heidegger explained this break from a philosophical orientation toward life, action, and experience. Arendt, called into question the philosophical orientation itself. Her research on anti-Semitism, racism, and totalitarianism made her critical of purely contemplative philosophical thinking and its position with regard to the world of experience. Even after her reencounter with Heidegger, she did not back down from this critique.

The result of this critique was the book that she had finished before embarking on her first trip to Europe and Germany.

Elemente und Ursprünge totaler Heerschaft

Elemente und Ursprünge totaler Herrschaft (1955), the German version of *The Origins of Totalitarianism* (1951),[96] consists of three more or less independent parts.[97] The parts are devoted to anti-Semitism, imperialism, and totalitarianism. Arendt composed all three parts of the book as a single narrative. In the first part on anti-Semitism, the readers are taken to Germany, France, and England. She writes about the social structures and the political conditions of European societies that allowed for the appearance of a new kind of anti-Semitism, and about the persons who articulated it. Wilhelm von Humboldt, with his saying "I love the Jews really only *en masse, en détail* I rather avoid them,"[98] is mentioned, as well as Marcel Proust as a chronicler of fin-de-siècle society and Benjamin Disraeli as the embodiment of a Jewish parvenu. Behind the structural analysis, disguised as cultural history, is concealed a radical critique of all theories of anti-Semitism. Arendt insisted that it was the social position of the Jews in modern society and not the old Christian populist hatred that gave rise to modern anti-Semitism. It appears that she was leaning toward the Marxist critique that wanted to tie the cause of anti-Semitism to the socially "detached" role of Judaism. Yet, unlike Marx, the perspective she adopts is not the decline of the bourgeoisie and the domination of capital, but rather the lack of Jewish political organization. In other words, she saw in the lack of political self-organization one of the underlying reasons for the social and political isolation of the Jews, which then made possible their annihilation. Here we find the results of her penetrating analysis and critique of Zionism with which she had engaged throughout the 1940s.

Arendt examines the situation of the Jews in its different national variants. She thereby distances herself from, for instance, the thesis that made anti-Semitism a typically German phenomenon. Modern anti-Semitism existed in all European countries; she used the 1894 French Dreyfus affair as an example. In her view, one of the features of modernity was that it brought forth an anti-Semitism that had never before existed. Its particular characteristic is a murderous hatred of Jews aiming at annihilation. It is fueled by a nihilism in which the stealthy break in tradition comes to the fore.

In the middle part of the book, modernity is illuminated from an additional perspective, the emergence of racism. Retrospectively, it again becomes clear in this section that the racism that emerged in the second half of the nineteenth century was used against the Jews so successfully only because the latter did not politically belong to any party that could protect them. According to Arendt's thesis, the fragility of their position made it possible for racism to take over the so-called Jewish question without impediment and to assert itself without any resistance worthy of the name on the part of religion, tradition, or morals. What characterizes this modern racism? Arendt describes its emergence from out of a process of decline of the great political traditions in the main European countries. National states no longer counted in the age of imperialism, but rather, zones of influence in which the "host state" was reduced to an agent of expansion. She writes in the preface to the middle section on imperialism: "Nothing was so characteristic of power politics in the imperialist era [Arendt situates the peak of imperialism from 1884[99] until 1914—author's note] than this shift from the localized, limited and therefore predictable goals of national interest to the limitless pursuit of power after power that could roam and lay waste the whole globe with no certain nationally and territorially prescribed purpose and hence with no predictable direction."[100]

Within a few decades, through their unbridled politics of expansion, the ruling classes in Europe had undermined the political rules and regulations constructed since the seventeenth century: namely, the controlling function of the parliament as well as the separation of powers and the balance between economic and political interests. The middle classes no longer seemed interested in preserving the political traditions they themselves had created. Instead of this, the protection of property and of zones of influence emerged as the primary interest of the expansionist bourgeoisie.

In the two studies of anti-Semitism and imperialism, Arendt reveals a destructive structural phenomenon of modernity: the alliance between capital and the mob.[101] Using the conquest of the African continent as an example, she shows how the leading capitalist enterprises became tied up with an international adventurism that emerged from the uprooted victims of the European Industrial Revolution in the middle of the century. A new ideology and a praxis of exploitation came from this alliance. Here the most vulgar instincts were united with the highest social classes. She draws extensively on Joseph Conrad's report on his last trip to Africa (*Heart of Darkness*, 1902) to describe the mental transformation that took place with the agents of imperialism. She sees their mindset masterfully captured in the figure of Kurtz: "hollow to the core," "reckless without hardihood, greedy without audacity and cruel without courage."[102] In Conrad's portrait of this man, Arendt perceives the precursor to the executioners of totalitarianism: those without conscience who have lost every measure for their actions. In retrospect, the parallels with the figure of Adolf Eichmann are striking.

In Arendt's view, this new type of human being had lost every connection to civilization. She considers as a new phenomenon the fact that race ideology could gain a foothold in the highest classes because of the convergence of capitalism and the mob. It is against this backdrop that racism—the ideology of the white man's supremacy—conquered Europe. In hindsight, imperialism was, therefore, a break in modernity wherein economic expansion and racism destroyed political traditions and enabled the emergence of a new, murderous form of anti-Semitism. Thus, before the First World War in Europe, the preconditions for the downfall and self-dissolution of more or less democratically organized national states had already been created.

Arendt describes in detail how the new type of domination, *total domination*, emerged from the ruins of a shattered class society and its party structure. Instead of traditional political cultures and their institutions, it was the "movements," increasingly active all over Europe during the "period between the wars," that accelerated the collapse of parliamentary governments. The "age of the masses" was for Arendt an expression of this disintegration, inside of which the totalitarian movements of Soviet socialism and National Socialism were able to gain a foothold. In her eyes, ideology, propaganda, terror, and a permanent rotation of new governing groups formed from the mob, and brought forth a fictitious world where the contempt for the world of facts was coupled with the promise of redemption.[103] Individuals were delivered to this new domain without a single defense. The tradition that could have provided protection had been destroyed. Against this backdrop, the rise of power by National Socialism embodied for her an event in which a group on the margins of the political order seized the opportunity to take possession of a collapsing society. In her view, what was new about the National Socialist "revolution" was that ideology and terror became the foundation of a domination in which ultimately there was no resistance against the formation of concentration and extermination camps where Jews and gypsies were annihilated as races.[104]

In the last part of the book Arendt considers her own intellectual milieu and with it, her great love, Martin Heidegger. She vividly depicts the uprootedness of the German intelligentsia after the First War World. Intellectuals and artists went to war with the same guiding idea with which they returned; the destruction of the rotting structure of bourgeois society. From Arendt's perspective, the role and influence of the elite in the twentieth century was radically inverted in the imperialist age: it was not the elite that commanded the mob—the antistate and antipolitical mass movements across Europe—but rather the mob that directed them, until their Führer had no more need of them: "In all fairness to those among the elite, on the other hand, who at one time or another have let themselves be seduced by totalitarian movements, and who sometimes, because of their intellectual abilities, are even accused of having inspired totalitarianism, it must be stated that what these desperate men of the twentieth century did or did not do had no influence on totalitarianism whatsoever, although it did play some part in earlier, successful, attempts of the movements to force the outside world to take their doctrines seriously."[105] What appears at first glance as a relativization of the historical responsibility of intellectuals was instead a devastating critique of the mindset of an entire class, a critique that could not have been more severe.

Arendt wrote the last chapter—"Ideology and Terror"—for the German, or rather European, audience. Here she vividly summarizes the consequences of the destruction of civil society, which was the project of National Socialism, at the heart of which was the inescapability of terror and the destruction of the civil existence of Jews, resulting in their collective abandonment and their annihilation. Even the survivors, the witnesses to the annihilation, were robbed of their civil existence, for the civil society to which they should have been able to attach themselves had been destroyed.

The question that emerges for Arendt here is that of the implications of totalitarianism for modernity. In her view, total domination signaled the accomplishment of an irremediable break in tradition that turned the self-understanding of the West on its head. People emerged from this event desolate, facing a world that they themselves had destroyed.[106] Whether they would find a new beginning and thus take up the promise that Augustine had once formulated—"initium ut esset, creatus est homo" (that a beginning be made, man was created)—remained open.[107]

The book was not just original in its narration and its historico-evental orientation. It also went against the methodology and style in which most contemporary historians, political scientists, to say nothing of philosophers, explained historical phenomena. If one considers how Arendt's colleagues, for instance Carl J. Friedrich, Franz Neumann, Sigmund Neumann, Ernst Fraenkel, or Eric Voegelin approached the phenomenon from out of their respective juridical, historiographical, economic, philosophical, sociological, or ideology-critical perspective, Arendt's style of argumentation, in its anti-systematic character, must have been seen as almost anarchic.

It would be more accurate to speak of her systematic refusal of scientific methodology. Arendt wanted to approach the phenomenon in an entirely original way, which at first sight seemed almost stitched together. In fact, a radical critique of prevailing historical methodologies formed the basis of her approach.

Here she showed herself as a student of Heidegger. She got to the bottom of the phenomenon methodically; she could not do otherwise "according to the strengths of her understanding" (Kleist).[108] She refused to see totalitarianism as analogous with other, conventional forms of domination, such as dictatorship or tyranny.

The book, if he ever even got a hold of it, must have been an affront for Heidegger. The reader had to uncover its philosophical contents painstakingly. Heidegger was, as he said repeatedly, a slow reader. Blücher suspected that Heidegger never read the book, now with a preface by Jaspers.[109] If he did receive it—and it would have been from friends—he must have had an ambivalent reaction to it. On the one hand, he could only agree with Arendt's exposition of the abyss that modernity concealed within itself. On the other hand, he could hardly approve of the transition from the sphere of philosophy to that of political narrative. Personally, he would certainly have felt radically misjudged in her harsh critique of the "generation of the front." Indeed, it is no accident that the correspondence between them falls silent from the end of 1954 until 1959.

The methodological difficulties with which she had to struggle in her book and the critique that was waged against her persisted for a long time afterward. She reacted to various critics in many diverse ways. In 1953 she wrote her own essay on the methodological problems: "Understanding and Politics." There she presented a radical critique of historiographical and sociological methodology and discussed the methodological implications for scientific work when attempting to understand the phenomenon of total domination. The harsh critical response of her colleagues from political science that is heard even today is explained by the radicalism of her refusal to use the "proven" methodological instruments. Her thesis was that the advent of the new, total type of domination "brought to light the ruin of the categories of our thought and standards for our judgment."[110] She thereby did an about-face which the guild—even her colleagues in exile—did not find necessary. Her colleagues insisted that even the worst event could not change the fact that the process of reflective thought—as well as the person thinking—remained autonomous when faced with the event that it tries to think. She claimed the opposite: a form of domination that was rooted in the negation of human beings *as* human beings could not be analyzed with the instruments that suggested the unity of the world and the connectedness between those who judge and that which is being judged.

Her critique did not result in a cohesive new method, but she did reverse the relation between the thinker and the object of thought: the event had to be at the center and precisely as a historical occurrence (*Geschehen*) and not as an object of research. The historical event had to be examined with the most diverse methodological instruments. She did not think much of methodological rigor. However, she appealed to the validity of preunderstanding (a familiar subject from the phenomenological debates of the 1920s), the rehabilitation of the power of the imagination, of common sense, and the spontaneous power of judgment in the process of deciphering historical events—which certainly shed light on mistakes and prejudices.

Her aversion to scientific systematizing made some of her European colleagues livid. The exiled Viennese political economist Alfred Schütz, teaching at the New School for Social Research, could get truly agitated about this troubling side in Arendt's thinking:

> I listened to the author[111] socially and in our general seminar (at the New School for Social Research—author's note) several times and even though people like Gurwitsch and Jean Wahl esteem her highly, I am filled with deepest distrust. She herself was, as I hear, in a concentration camp[112] and it is only too understandable that such an experience would do immense damage to the human being and his thought. Without a doubt, she knows a lot, but she does not at all pursue theory when it concerns matters that are close to her. I believe she is something one called an "activist" in the times of the youth movement. Wanting to treat things like totalitarianism theoretically means condoning them—that is her main argument.[113]

Alfred Schütz's argument is shared by his friend Eric Voegelin *cum grano salis* and by many others wholeheartedly. Whoever reads the correspondence between Schütz and Voegelin has the impression of listening to two scholars for whom National Socialism—not to mention Soviet communism—had absolutely no effect on their approach to the scientific and extrascientific phenomena. Here reigns the continuity that Arendt, with her insistence on the break in tradition, which she took completely personally, continually called into question.

Discussions of her book on totalitarianism, especially with Gurian and Blücher, made her realize that she had not sufficiently addressed Marxism as the ideology of Soviet domination. She took this critique seriously and began to plan an additional research project "Totalitarian Elements in Marxism."[114] The study was intended to be a kind of belated component of *The Origins of Totalitarianism*.

Heidegger: The Dilemma of His Students

The book on total domination contained as its subtext Arendt's confrontation with her own history: with her background and history as a Jew, her belonging to the intelligentsia of the period between the wars, and the years of being a student of Heidegger's. She—like all Heidegger's Jewish students—was shaken by her past. In various ways every one of them had suffered a shock that each was struggling to make sense of. Almost everyone, from Arendt and Löwith to Marcuse, went to their former teacher after the war and demanded a clear statement of his distance from National Socialism. Well after the war ended, all were still reeling from having to confront Heidegger's involvement with National Socialism. All were disappointed and their disappointment could hardly disguise the fact that they were belatedly horrified by themselves as well. As Jews, how could they have followed this teacher? Reproaches to Heidegger and self-reproach went hand in hand for many of Heidegger's students. After the war, their relationship to Heidegger oscillated between esteem and aversion, between admiration and contempt, between love and hate. From among these students, we discuss three: Karl Löwith, Herbert Marcuse, and Hans Jonas.

Karl Löwith (1897–1973) came to Freiburg in 1919 where he studied under Husserl and his assistant Martin Heidegger. He finished his doctorate in Munich and then went to Marburg to write his habilitation, "The Individual in the Role of the Neighbor," with Heidegger. In 1934, as the situation was getting ever more untenable, Löwith relocated to Rome, first as a grant recipient from the Rockefeller Foundation. The University of Marburg supported him with a meager salary up until 1936.[115]

Löwith's profound personal disappointment followed in April 1936, when he met his teacher again in Rome. His relationship with Heidegger had never been without conflict. It was, however, when Heidegger appeared in Rome wearing his NSDAP badge of honor with his wife wearing her party button, and giving no indication of any distancing from National Socialism, that it became clear to Löwith, who perhaps still had hopes for Heidegger, that he could expect nothing more from him. After a stay in Japan, Löwith arrived in the United States in 1941, the same year as Arendt and her husband. They met when Löwith was invited to the New School for Social Research in 1949. In 1952 he went back to Germany to take up a professorship in philosophy in Heidelberg. Heidegger's photograph hung in Löwith's office and all of Löwith's postwar books have to do with Heidegger, the most famous entitled *Heidegger: Thinker in a Destitute Time*. In this book, Löwith attempted, on the one hand, to situate existential philosophy in the context of twentieth-century philosophy, and, on the other, he criticized Heidegger's attempt at a new foundation of metaphysics inspired by the Greeks.

As a professor in the 1950s in Germany, Löwith found himself caught between the pro- and anti-Heidegger camps at his university. Hannah Arendt told her husband on various occasions that Löwith—besides Hans-Georg Gadamer—was the only one who strove for objectivity in the polarized Heidegger hysteria. Löwith visited Heidegger after the war, yet he felt compelled to critically engage his teacher throughout his life.[116]

Heinrich Blücher aptly described the dilemma of the Jewish students when he told his wife that he agreed completely with her opinion of Löwith: if a student of a great man has nothing to propose in his own name, he has to interpret the master. "But the master has cut off this normal path for his students, particularly the Jewish ones, and so everything gets poisoned. Of course all Löwith is left with is a liberal skepticism draped in Heidegger's concepts. It would be very funny if it were not so sad."[117] Herbert Marcuse (1895–1979) also studied in Freiburg under Martin Heidegger at the beginning of the 1920s. Later in the 1920s he planned to do his habilitation with him, but he gave up this idea. In the time that followed, he went to the Frankfurt Institute for Social Research, *the* center of Marxist-oriented social research in the 1920s and early 1930s. Like other members of the institute—Theodor W. Adorno, Max Horkheimer, Leo Löwenthal, Franz Neumann, Friedrich Pollock—he emigrated to the United States in the mid-1930s. There he worked and researched for *Die Frankfurter* and, like many other exiled academics, earned money doing occasional research for the American government.

His fascination with Heidegger surfaced in the political void left in the wake of the failure of the November Revolution of 1918–19. Like many other young people at the time, Heidegger appeared to him as a savior from political and intellectual sterility.[118] Yet he made a point of claiming that he had distanced himself from Heidegger before 1932. Marcuse was deeply impressed by Karl Marx's *Economic and Philosophic Manuscripts*, which first came out in 1932. After reading them, he rethought Heidegger's philosophy of existence. In his early publications, he attempted to bring together Heidegger's way of thinking and the Marxist question of the alienation of people in modernity.

"Neither I nor my friends," Marcuse wrote in a contribution in memory of Heidegger decades later, "knew or noticed anything about Heidegger's relation to Nazism before 1933."[119] Marcuse, too, visited his former teacher after the war. The reproach that Heidegger had not distanced himself from National Socialism was at the center of two letters from Marcuse and a single reply from Heidegger from 1947–48. The disappointment of being betrayed by Heidegger was clear in both of Marcuse's letters. Even worse in his view, Heidegger had betrayed philosophy. Like the members of the "Purification Committee" in Freiburg, he continued to attribute in retrospect a highly symbolic value to Heidegger's short connection with National Socialism.[120]

The gist of Heidegger's response to Marcuse was similar to his 1945 justification letter: he expected a spiritual renewal from National Socialism and then distanced himself in 1934. During the Nazi time, he clearly set himself apart from National Socialism in his lectures and writings. However, he could not directly oppose National Socialism without putting his family in danger. After 1945 he did not want to present himself openly as an enemy of the regime because then he would be lumped with all those who at the time expressed cheap disavowals. To Marcuse's reproach that a real philosopher should have seen the character of the regime in the murder of the Jews—an argument that could be applied to Heidegger's actual situation in 1933 only by distorting the facts—and should not have kept silent about it, Heidegger responded with an analogy: he equated the Jewish victims under National Socialism with the East Germans who had been under Soviet domination since 1945. He made a similar reference in one of his letters to Jaspers, only there the analogy referred to the Soviet Union and its striving after hegemony in Europe that would turn Germany into the victim of imperial power politics. With such arguments, Heidegger echoed the fear, widespread at the time, of the Soviet Union's advance into Western Europe. The crux of his answer to Marcuse was to respond to the critique by fashioning his own (individual or collective) role of the victim (here the East Germans). Presumably, he did not see the banality of this argument.[121]

In his next letter, Marcuse described Heidegger's response as standing "outside of *Logos*"; it was not worthy of a philosopher. His letter concluded bitterly: "It looks as though the seed has fallen upon fertile ground: perhaps we are still experiencing the continuation of what began in 1933. Whether you would still consider it to be a 'renewal' I am not sure."[122] Marcuse's conclusion was stark—no wonder, two years after the end of the mass killing.

In his later publications, he still agreed with Heidegger on several issues, despite all critique; for instance, his critique of technology and his calling into question the image of the human being in mass society. However, there was no further exchange between the teacher and his former student.

Hans Jonas (1903–1993) studied philosophy, theology, and Judaism in Freiburg, Berlin, Heidelberg, and Marburg. In 1928 he earned a doctorate with Bultmann and Heidegger on "The Concept of Gnosticism." He was a convinced Zionist since the time of his study at the "University for the Study of Judaism" in Berlin in the early 1920s.[123] After 1933 he immigrated to Jerusalem via London and later served, until 1945, as a British soldier in the Jüdische Brigade. In 1955, he relocated via Canada to the United States, where he taught at various universities, including Columbia University and Princeton. He turned down a visit to his former teacher Heidegger after the war and instead sought out, still in uniform, Bultmann and Jaspers in Marburg and Heidelberg. Why did he not go to Heidegger? Jonas writes:

There are things that one cannot forgive, things that went so far that they were humanly unforgivable. There was also a philosophical bankruptcy. Philosophers are not to fall for the Nazi cause. They are not. And that the greatest philosopher of the time had failed, that he had striven for the highest level of a life devoted to truth, and yet no compassionate humanity emerged from this proximity to truth or, at the very least, this search for truth—this I saw with profound disappointment as the debacle of philosophy itself. Something was therefore not right about this claim that whoever thinks profoundly elevates their humanity and their relation to fellow human beings. And it cast a deep doubt on the power of philosophy, as we know it. It was somewhat remedied in my encounter with Jaspers where one sees a philosophical nobility that is also human.[124]

As a professor and philosopher, Jonas dedicated his life to finding a foundation for a modern ethics of responsibility in the social and political space; he attempted to do this by thinking through American Pragmatism, communitarianism, and Kantian ethics. This was his response to the existential challenge presented by a philosopher to whom he owed a great deal.

All the other students, such as Günther Anders, Arendt's ex-husband, or those whose names today are almost forgotten, such as the ancient philologist and Goethe scholar Ernst Grumach, or those who never studied under Heidegger but were fascinated with him, such as the poet Paul Celan, who loved Hölderlin as much as Heidegger, never got free from him. They harbored feelings of anger and doubt together with the awareness that this man Heidegger had penetrated spheres of thought into which almost no one could follow, thereby touching on something they felt was of profound importance.

As for Heidegger's student, Hannah Arendt, it is almost impossible to find differences between her critique of modernity and Heidegger's.

We have seen how Arendt returns to Heidegger's thought in the 1950s. In *Origins of Totalitarianism*, Arendt vividly demonstrates that political thinking requires different modes of perception, other categories, other criteria for judgment and different perspectives than philosophical thinking. She thereby highlighted her differences from Heidegger in an attempt to twist free from his thought, to use it *with* and *against* its originator, and, thereby, brought his thought into a genuinely political domain. She was the only former student who, in her critique of Heidegger, went beyond the rejection of the existential-philosophical critique of metaphysics (Löwith), ideology critique (Marcuse), and the return to the categorical imperative (Jonas).

In her eyes, it was necessary to venture a new beginning from out of the rubble of a shattered existential philosophy, without attempting to rebuild it, but also without violently eliminating the field of ruins itself.

Notes

1. Arendt is referring here to Paul Tillich, who at the time was having a stormy love affair with Hilde Fränkel.

2. Hannah Arendt to Hilde Fränkel, letter from February 2, 1950, in Archiv des HAZ Cont Nr 9.6. Nothing came of the story of the "true novel in its final sequel." Hilde Fränkel died before Hannah returned from her European trip of November 1949–March 1950.

3. In 1951 Hannah Arendt received American citizenship.

4. Hannah Arendt, "The Aftermath of Nazi-Rule: Report from Germany," *Commentary* 10, no. 4 (1950). Reprinted in Jerome Kohn, ed., *Essays in Understanding, 1930–1954* (New York: Harcourt, Brace, 1994), 249.

5. Ibid.

6. Ibid., 250ff.

7. Ibid., 254.

8. Arendt to Blücher, letter from February 14, 1950, in Lotte Köhler, ed., *Within Four Walls: The Correspondence between Hannah Arendt and Heinrich Blücher, 1936–1968*, trans. Peter Constantine (New York: Harcourt, Brace, 2000), 133.

9. See Ernst Grumanch's personal file in the Archive of Berlin-Brandenburgische Akademie der Wissenschaften.

10. Meant here are the letters from Martin Heidegger to Karl Jasper, which Jaspers shows her. See Walter Biemel and Hans Saner, eds., *The Heidegger-Jaspers Correspondence 1920–1963*, trans. Gary E. Aylesworth (New York: Humanity, 1963).

11. Arendt to Blücher, letter from January 3, 1950, in Köhler, *Within Four Walls*, 114–15.

12. Heidegger to Elfride, letter from April 17, 1945, in Martin Heidegger, *Letters to His Wife, 1915–1970*, ed. Gertrud Heidegger, trans. R. D. V. Glasgow (Cambridge: Polity Press, 2008), 189.

13. In this regard Hermann Heidegger points that Eucken and Lampe were coauthors of the "Report on the Professors—War Financing." This had been published under the title "The Source of War Financing, Inappropriate Means and War Financing." which was finished on September 12, 1939, and treated as a "secret state matter"; see Hermann Heidegger, "The Economic Historian and the Truth," *Heidegger Studies* 13 (1997): 189.

14. Hugo Ott, *Martin Heidegger: A Political Life*, trans. Allan Blunden (New York: Basic Books, 1993), 318.

15. Ibid., 209 and 248–49.

16. Adolf Lampe: Aktennotiz über die Besprechung mit Herrn Prof. Dr. Martin Heidegger am Mittwoch, den 25.7.45, UAF Akten Heidegger B 3, 522, BL.3.

17. Ibid.

18. Ibid.

19. Franz Böhm: Schreiben an den Rektor der Universität, Janssen von 6. Oktober 1945, UAF Akten Heidegger, B24, 1277, BL 3.

20. Cf. Heidegger's letter on October 10, 1945 to the philosophy faculty at the University of Freiburg, UAF Akten Heidegger, B 3, 522. In this letter, Heidegger informs them that he had, in this way, been relieved by the French occupying powers.

21. Adolf Lampe: Brief an den Rektor der Universität Freiburg vom 8 October 1945, UAF Fkten Heidegger B, 24, 1277.

22. Cf. Constantin von Dietze: Letter concerning the conclusions of the hearings of the purification committee, December 11–13, 1945, UAF B 34/31–1 and B 34/31–2, S. 14.

23. Cf. Ott, *Heidegger*, 348.

24. Martin Heidegger, "Letter to the Rector of Freiburg University," November 4, 1945, in Richard Wolin, *The Heidegger Controversy: A Critical Reader* (Cambridge: MIT Press, 1993), 61.

25. Ibid., 63.

26. Ibid. (translation modified).

27. Ibid., 66 (translation modified).

28. Martin Heidegger, "Letter to Constantin von Dietze," December 15, 1945, UAF B 34/31–1, Handakte v. Dietze, S. 2.

29. Karl Jaspers, "Letter to the Freiburg University Denazification Committee," December 22, 1945, in Wolin, *Heidegger Controversy*, 148–149 (translation modified).

30. Ibid., 150.

31. Walter Eucken: Brief an den Reinigungsausschuss der Universität Freiburg von 3. Januar 1946, UAF B 34/31–3, S. 4f.

32. Martin Heidegger, Brief [ohne Adressaten, wahrscheinlich von Dietz] von 17.1.1946, UAF B 34/31–3.

33. Max Mueller: Ein Brief an P. Alois Naber SJ zur philosophischen Entwicklung Martin Heidegger von February 2, 1947 in *Martin Heidegger: Briefe an Max Müller* (2003), S 81.

34. Der Kommissar der Republik, Delegue Superieur pour la GM de Bade vom 3.September1949 an den Herrn Badischen Minister des Kultus und Unterrichts, UAF B 3 522.

35. Cf. Heidegger's letters to his wife Elfride from Badenweiler near Freiburg, February 17, 1946, to May 8, 1946, in Heidegger, *Letters to His Wife*, 191–99.

36. Heidegger to Elfride Heidegger, letter from March 13, 1946, in ibid., 194–95.

37. Martin Heidegger, "Letter on Humanism," in *Basic Writings*, ed. David Farrell Krell (New York: Harper and Row, 1977), 213–66.

38. Antonia Grunenberg, *Die Lust an der Schuld, Von der Macht der Vergangenheit über die Gegenwart* (Berlin: Rowohlt Berlin Verlag, 2001).

39. Heidegger, "Letter on Humanism," 197.

40. Ibid., 199 (translation modified).

41. Ibid., 200.

42. Ibid., 235.

43. Voeglin to Schütz, letter from May 20, 1950, in: Schütz-Voegelin: Briefwechsel (2004), S. 375. (Trans. Note: This letter is not included in English translation of the Voeglin-Schütz correspondence.)

44. Jaspers to Heidegger, letter from February 6, 1949 in Walter Biemel and Hans Saner, eds., *Heidegger-Jaspers Correspondence 1920–1963*, trans. Gary E. Aylesworth (New York: Humanities Press, 2003), 161.

45. Jaspers to Heidegger, letter from February 6, 1949, in ibid., 162.

46. Heidegger to Jaspers, letter from June 22, 1949, in ibid., 163.

47. Ibid.

48. Heidegger to Jaspers, letter from July 5, 1949, in ibid., 164–65.

49. Ibid., 165.

50. Ibid.

51. Jaspers to Heidegger, letter from July 10, 1949, in ibid., 167.

52. Ibid.

53. Jaspers to Heidegger, letter from August 17, 1949, in ibid., 174.

54. Arendt to Blücher, letter from December 18, 1949, in Köhler, *Within Four Walls*, 107 (translation modified).

55. Heidegger to Jaspers, letter from March 7, 1950, in Biemel and Saner, *Heidegger-Jaspers Correspondence*, 185.

56. Cf. Heidegger to Jaspers, letter from March 7, 1950, in ibid.

57. Jaspers to Arendt, letter from March 9, 1966 in *Arendt-Jaspers Correspondence*, 630.

58. Jaspers to Heidegger, letter from March 19, 1950, in Biemel and Saner *Heidegger-Jaspers Correspondence*, 186.

59. Heidegger to Jaspers, letter from April 8, 1950, in ibid., 188–89.

60. Ibid., 189.

61. Ibid., 188.

62. Jaspers to Heidegger, letter from July 24, 1952, in ibid., 196.

63. Ibid., 197.

64. Heidegger to Arendt, letter from February 7, 1950, in Ursula Ludz, ed., *Hannah Arendt and Martin Heidegger Letters 1925–1975*, trans. Andrew Shields (New York: Harcourt, Brace, 2004), 57.

65. Arendt to Blücher, letter from February 8, 1950, in Köhler, *Within Four Walls*, 128.

66. Heidegger to Arendt, letter from February 8, 1950, in Ludz, *Arendt-Heidegger Letters*, 58.

67. Cf. Elfride Heidegger to Martin Heidegger (draft), letter from June 28, 1956, in Heidegger, *Letters to His Wife*, 255.

68. Arendt to Elfride Heidegger, letter from February 10, 1950, in Ludz, *Arendt-Heidegger Letters*, 62 (translation modified).

69. Arendt to Heidegger, letter from February 9, 1950, in ibid., 60.

70. Arendt to Heidegger, letter from April 22, 1928, in ibid., 50.

71. Arendt to Elfride Heidegger, letter from February 10, 1950, in ibid., 61.

72. Heidegger to Elfride Heidegger, letter from February 14, 1950, in ibid., 213.

73. Martin Heidegger, "Five Poems for Hannah Arendt," February 1950, in Ludz, *Arendt-Heidegger Letters*, 63.

74. Arendt to Blücher, letter from February 8, 1950, in Köhler, *Within Four Walls*, 128.

75. Arendt to Blücher, letter from February 9, 1950, in ibid., 129 (translation modified).

76. Blücher to Arendt, letter from February 22, 1950, in ibid., 139–40.

77. Blücher to Arendt, letter from March 8, 1950, in ibid., 144.

78. Arendt to Jaspers, letter from September 29, 1949, in *Arendt-Jaspers Correspondence*, 142.

79. Arendt to Blumenfeld, letter from April 1, 1951, in *Arendt-Blumenfeld Korrespondenz*, 22.

80. Arendt to Heidegger, letter from May 8, 1954, in Ludz, *Arendt-Heidegger Letters*, 120.

81. Arendt to Blücher, letter from May 25, 1958, in Köhler, *Within Four Walls*, 321–22.

82. Blücher to Arendt, letter from June 1, 1958, in ibid., 323.

83. Arendt to Blücher, letter from June 15, 1958, in ibid.

84. Arendt, *Denktagebuch* (2002), 1. Band, S 266.

85. Arendt to Blücher, letter from May 1, 1952, in Köhler, *Within Four Walls*, 164.

86. Elizabeth Young-Breuhl, *Hannah Arendt: For Love of the World* (New Haven, CT: Yale University Press, 1982), 304.

87. In 1952 Karl Löwith resigned from the New School for Social Research in New York and returned to Heidelberg, where he was a professor of philosophy.

88. Arendt to Blücher, letter from July 18, 1952, in Köhler, *Within Four Walls*, 205.

89. Arendt to Sternberger, Brief vom 24.10.1953, DLA, Sternberger Nachlauss, 6913 und GS 13.

90. Sternberger to Arendt, Brief vom 17.11.1953, ibid.

91. Arendt to Sternberger, Brief vom 28.11.1953, ibid.

92. Sternberger to Arendt, Brief vom 6.12.1953. Archiv des HAZ, Cont. Nr. 14.8.

93. Arendt to Blücher, letter from November 28, 1955, in Köhler, *Within Four Walls*, 294–95.

94. Arendt to Blumenfeld, Brief vom 16.12.1955, in *Arendt-Blumenfeld: Korrespondenz*, 196–97.

95. Arendt to Gurian, Brief vom 4.3.1942. Archiv des HAZ, Cont. Nr. 10.7; Arendt wrote this sentence in the context of her critique of Gurian's equating liberalism with the Enlightenment.

96. For the differences between the American, the English, and the German editions of the book, see Ursula Ludz, "Hannah Arendt and her Totalitarianism Book," in *Totalitäre Herrschaft*, ed. Grunenberg (Frankfurt: Peter Lang, 2003).

97. Arendt was not happy with the title. Initially, she wanted the book to be titled *Elements of Shame: Anti-Semitism—Imperialism—Racism*. She played with another title; however, she was even less happy with that—most likely the closest was the British edition, *The Burden of our Times*. As she later often remarked, she was not happy with the American title of the book, *The Origins of Totalitarianism*. In her opinion, the title understood totalitarianism as too determined. The German title for the 1955 West German translation—directly translated into English as *Elements and Origins of Totalitarianism*—put the stress on the incompleteness of the approach. See Young-Bruehl, *Hannah Arendt*, 236.

98. Wilhelm von Humboldt to his wife, Caroline von Humboldt, letter from April 30, 1816, in *Wilhelm und Caroline von Humboldt in ihren Briefen* (Paris: Ulan Press, 1968), 236.

99. The year 1884 was crucial for the colonization of Africa, a colonization sealed through conquest, occupation, and subsequent diplomatic conferences.

100. Hannah Arendt, *Origins of Totalitarianism* (New York: Harcourt, Brace, 1951), xviii.

101. Ibid., 147ff.

102. Joseph Conrad, *Heart of Darkness*, cited by Arendt in ibid., 189.

103. Ibid., 333.

104. Ibid., 439.

105. Ibid., 339.

106. Ibid., 478.

107. Ibid., 479.

108. "Nach Maßgabe Deiner Begreifungskraft" in Kleist an Wilhelmine von Zenge, Brief vom 16.8.1800 in Kleist: Sämtliche Briefe (1999), S 73.

109. Blücher to Arendt, letter from mid-September 1955 (dated by the German edition), in Köhler, *Within Four Walls*, 273.

110. Arendt, *Essays*, 321.

111. Here Arendt is addressed as the author of *The Origins of Totalitarianism*, which was published in 1951.

112. Schütz's information is hearsay based on the false information that Gurs was a concentration camp when it in fact was an internment camp.

113. Schütz to Eric Voegelin, letter from September 4, 1953, in Schütz, *Voegelin Briefwechsel*, ed. Ludwig Landgrebe (Paderborn: Wilhelm Fink), 482. The letter is not included in the English translation: *A Friendship That Lasted a Lifetime: The Correspondence between Alfred Schütz and Eric Voeglin* (Columbia: University of Missouri Press, 2011).

114. The project was initially supported with a Guggenheim Foundation grant, but then was abandoned owing to lack of money. See Young-Bruehl, *Hannah Arendt*, 272ff.

115. Cf. StA MR, Akte Priv-Doz. Dr. K. Löwith Acc, 1966/10.

116. Letter from Arendt to Blücher regarding Löwith, in Köhler, *Within Four Walls*, 186, 188, 194. Blücher to Arendt, letter from June 21, 1952, in ibid., 193–94.

117. Blücher to Arendt, letter from June 21, 1952, in ibid.

118. Herbert Marcuse, *Theorie und Politik, Gespräch mit Jürgen Habermas, Heinz Lubasz, Tilman Spengler,* in *Gespräche mit Herbert Marcuse,* trans. Hans-Martin Lohmann (Berlin: Suhrkamp, 1978), 10.

119. Herbert Marcuse, "Enttäuschung," in *Erinnerung,* ed. Neske (Pfullingen: Neske, 1977), 162.

120. Cf. Marcuse to Heidegger, letter from August 28, 1947, in Herbert Marcuse, *Technology, War and Fascism* (London: Routledge, 1998), 263–64.

121. Heidegger to Marcuse, letter from January 1, 1948, in ibid., 265–66.

122. Marcuse to Heidegger, letter from May 13, 1948, in ibid., 267.

123. Jonas, *Erkenntnis,* 38–39.

124. Ibid., 68.

6 *Amor Mundi*, or Thinking the World after the Catastrophe

> You will see that the book does not contain a dedication. Had things worked out properly between us—and I mean *between*, that is, neither you nor me—I would have asked you if I might dedicate it to you; it came directly out of the first Freiburg days and hence owes practically everything to you in every respect. As things are, this does not seem possible for me to do, but I wanted in some way to at least say this to you.[1]

Why did Hannah Arendt feel the need to tell Martin Heidegger about this intended dedication that she had withdrawn, rather than just remaining silent? Did she want him to be aware of the nondedication? What had happened?

In 1960 the German translation of *The Human Condition* (1958), entitled *Vita activa oder Vom tätigen Leben*, was published. Arendt made sure that Heidegger received a copy of the book. Two words in this almost brisk note draw our attention: *between us*. A dedication would have strengthened this "between us" but, apparently, something had happened that she could not resolve in the name of friendship as she had with so many others. Indeed, the relationship with Heidegger was not a friendship. More than friendship, love requires a deeper trust and openness. The trust between them had been repeatedly broken, the openness had disappeared; at the very least, she wanted to let him know that. But, in spite of everything, she did not want to become unfaithful to him. Unfaithful? In October 1950, half a year after she saw him again, she wrote in her *Denktagebuch*:

> *fidelity*, "true": true *and* faithful. As though the one who could not remain faithful had also never been true. Therefore the great crime of the unfaithful, if it is not innocent in its unfaithfulness: one murders what was true, negates that which one brought into the world, a true destruction because it is only through fidelity that we have any sway over our past. . . . All stubbornness and rigidity should be eliminated from the concept of fidelity precisely because of this connection between fidelity and truth. The perversion of fidelity is jealousy. Its opposite is not infidelity in the usual understanding—that falls under the continuation of life and vivacity—but in forgetting. This is the only true sin because it destroys truth, the truth of what has been.[2]

This text is certainly not aimed only at her relationship with Heidegger; it also expresses her efforts to come to terms with Heinrich Blücher's love affairs.

Nevertheless, one detects here that the rejected dedication to Heidegger takes on a deeper meaning: she could not dedicate a book to him because infidelity stood between them. Yet she could not really know whether he had forgotten her. Perhaps she was thinking of his letter from January 1925, which made her leave Marburg: "I forgot you—not from indifference, not because external circumstances intruded between us, but because I had to forget and will forget you whenever I withdraw into the final stages of my work."[3] In any event, she wanted this forgetting, if it had happened, not to be left as it had been before. She could not forget. She could not make her love disappear. Her book, which she could not dedicate to him, had to do with love. *Amor mundi,* love of the world, was its great theme. With her short note, she subtly indicated a special honor. She let him know that he stood at the center of her thinking. Was he able to decipher the allusions in her note?

A short text, never sent, which was found in her papers after her death, shows how strongly she was fighting with her feelings:

Re vita activa:
The dedication of this book is left blank.
How could I dedicate it to you,
One so close
To whom I remained faithful,
And not faithful, both with love.[4]

Heidegger: Life in Eros

At the time of her letter the relationship was hanging by a thin thread. She had not visited him since 1952, avoiding Freiburg on her trips to Europe and Germany. Until 1954 they had had an active correspondence. He sent her reprints and texts, and also inquired as to her work. She was pleased by his interest and let him know that since her book on totalitarianism, she had been working on three projects, (two of which subsequently became books: *The Human Condition* and *On Revolution*). At that time, Heidegger still had hoped that Arendt would mediate his relationship to Karl Jaspers. He expected that she would provide answers to Jaspers's questions, which he did not quite understand. For instance, those found in Jaspers's letter from July 1952, in which he said how angry he was with Heidegger's "ontological" remarks on the Cold War. Probably, Heidegger, once again, felt misunderstood.

In the meantime, Hannah was an active supporter of his work in the United States. She got in touch with the translators of his texts. The translator and writer, Glenn Gray, became her friend. She corrected the translations in great detail, which of course, Martin was more than happy about. He knew that with her his work was in the right hands. Then the greetings and exchanges became more infrequent, the silence returned. In 1959 he sent her two of his new texts through the publisher. One of them was *On the Way to Language*. Her note about the nonexistent dedication came eight months later. It asked a simple question: Have you forgotten me?

He had not forgotten her. But he was in the middle of another love affair, this time with the Munich artist Sophie-Dorothee, Countess of Podewils, the wife of the president of the Bavarian Academy of Fine Arts, Clemens Graf von Podewils. Again he had to explain to his wife why she did not have to feel slighted or threatened. Hannah was far away; he did not feel the need to mention anything to her. But of course his affair distanced him from her.

This time his justifications to Elfride sounded different. As usual, he assured her that this affair did not rob her of anything, but instead it added something to their relationship. He continued: "I'm not gone from you; far from it; it is simply the indestructible closeness of those who are starting to 'age.' But my character is more contradictory than yours; and I cannot prove to you by any arguments that I have to live in *eros* in order to give at least a preliminary & imperfect form to the creativity I feel within me as something unresolved and ultimate."[5] Apparently he understood his own life and thought as a way of existence that was rooted in Eros, needing love like one needs bread to live. Heidegger was sixty-five years old, Elfride four years younger.

Elfride cared for the "household" (*Lebenshaus*) in which he lived and which he regularly abandoned, but she was always there when he returned. This "household" was composed of his wife, his children, and his extended family, especially his brother Fritz in Meßkirch, who was also part of this scene, and the houses in Zähringen and Todtnauberg. All love affairs took place in the certainty that this "household" remained in place. Still, it was an old realm; its attractions were familiar. He had to leave it in order to stimulate himself, to awaken in him the eros that he needed to think and write—always with the certainty that this "home" was the backdrop.

Knowing this basic condition of his life, Elfride ought not to have felt either offended or overly affected by his love affairs, since, in his view, they took place on another level. In the best-case scenario, she was told about them. Sometimes he hid his love affairs and then had to explain himself at length when his secret was discovered. In any event, it was a practical arrangement for him. For Elfride, it was more problematic: proclaimed fidelity on the basis of perpetual promiscuity. Elfride was desexualized; hers was the role of the housewife and guardian of the children. The situation was not what she wanted. She was very aware that his affairs robbed her of the time and attention she needed.

In the meantime, everything at the university had settled down. He had become a professor emeritus and could teach when he wanted. Moreover, part of his teaching was outside the university. His network, in which professional interests and private friendships mixed, extended from his cabin in Todtnauberg to the spa hotel Bühler Höhe in Baden-Baden, passing through Konstanz, the town of his school years, Zurich, the place where his friend, the psychiatrist Medard Boss, lived, Munich and its academy for fine arts (and his new love).[6] He was connected to Heidelberg through his students and his loyal friend Hans-Georg Gadamer as well as through the Academy of the Sciences and Humanities. Throughout the years, he maintained active contact with Bremen, especially around Heinrich Wiegand Petzet and the circle "Club zu Bremen," where Heidegger sometimes gave talks. And finally he maintained his connections to Jean Beaufret and René Char in France. In the second half of the 1960s, he traveled several times to the seminars held in Le Thor.

He was now surrounded by a safety net of students and admirers with whom he had worked for quite some time. Heidegger was successful: he received invitations to give lectures and seminars at very prestigious universities. In 1957 he was nominated to the Academy of Sciences and Humanities in Heidelberg and to the Academy of Arts in Berlin. He no longer had anything to prove; he could lecture when he wanted and could choose where and with whom he did so. It was his best time. It was a time without Hannah.

Hannah Arendt: In Her Times

In the meantime, Arendt had become well known as a political theorist in the United States. The positive reception of *The Origins of Totalitarianism* secured her a place in the intellectual elite of the East Coast. Since 1953 when she was the first woman invited to be a visiting professor at the renowned Princeton University, she had frequently been invited to lecture at important American universities and conferences. In 1954 she taught at Notre Dame University where her friend Waldemar Gurian worked, and in 1955 she lectured at Berkeley. In the 1960s she taught several times at the University of Chicago at the invitation of the famous Committee on Social Thought; in 1960 she also taught at Columbia University in New York. And in 1967 she finally was offered a position at the famous "exile university," the New School for Social Research in New York. She was now an esteemed professor, part of an academic world, even though she had always passionately refused this role. However, she consciously positioned herself at the margins of the profession. She was always of two minds in her relationship to the university as an institution and to the canonization of the curriculum.

The Blüchers could afford a new apartment now that they were financially secure. In 1959 they moved from Morningside Drive to Riverside Drive, a very nice neighborhood on the Upper West Side of Manhattan. The apartment had five rooms, including a dining room and a room for guests. Each of them finally had a study. One could see the Hudson River from the windows facing the street.

In West Germany, Hannah Arendt became a speaker in high demand. Her book *Elemente und Ursprünge totaler Herrschaft* was well received by conservatives, but it was harshly criticized by left liberals and leftists. Arendt's structural comparison of German National Socialism with Stalin's Soviet Communism disturbed many widely held political viewpoints at the time. Throughout Western Europe she had to grapple with a harsh critique from the Left. Was not the Soviet Union—as the circle around Jean-Paul Sartre in France tirelessly emphasized up until the 1960s—a member of the defenders of Europe's freedom? The Soviet Union was indeed part of the democratic camp during the Second World War. And the gulag? In the eyes of many leftists, it had to do simply with a "tumor," the result of a politics that could still be set right. This is how people in several circles were thinking until 1989. Then it became known that clandestine reading groups in Central and Eastern European countries were reading Arendt's book as a guide to understanding their dictatorships and were encouraged by her in their pursuit of freedom. It was no accident that the epilogue to the 1958 English edition of the book was about the 1956 Hungarian Revolution. Arendt saw in the uprising of the Hungarian workers the resurgence of the political idea of her youth—councils. For her, the idea of councils harbored a possible answer to the aporias of national states. She was silent about the uprising of the East German workers on June 17, 1953, in the GDR.

In the German-speaking world, Arendt was seen as a controversial woman, provoking both curiosity and debate. She was a welcome guest at radio stations. She was invited to apply for a position in political science at the Free University in Berlin. In 1959 Würzburg University asked her if she was interested in a position in pedagogy and sociology.[7] A year prior, in 1958, she was nominated to the Darmstädter Academy of German Language and Poetry. The nomination made her happy insofar as she constantly emphasized that the German language and its poetry were home for her—much to the dismay of her American friends. However, publicly and with her friends, she always ironically and sarcastically downplayed such honors.

She knew what Heidegger was doing through rumors and stories from old friends. Once again, she was conflicted about him. She thought he was politically irresponsible, but regarded him as the greatest philosopher of his time. In 1953 she expressed this ambivalence in a parable:

Heidegger says, with great pride: "People say that Heidegger is a fox." This is the true story of Heidegger the fox: Once upon a time there was a fox who was so lacking in slyness that he not only kept getting caught in traps but couldn't even tell the difference between a trap and a non-trap. This fox suffered from another failing as well. There was something wrong with his fur, so that he was completely without natural protection against the hardships of a fox's life. After he had spent his entire youth prowling around the traps of people, and now that not one intact piece of fur, so to speak, was left on him, this fox decided to withdraw from the fox world altogether and to set about making himself a burrow. In his shocking ignorance of the difference between traps and non-traps, despite his incredibly extensive experience with traps, he hit on an idea completely new and unheard of among foxes: He built a trap as his burrow. He set himself inside it, passed it off as a normal burrow—not out of cunning, but because he had always thought others' traps were their burrows—and then decided to become sly in his own way and outfit for others the trap he had built himself and that suited only him. This again demonstrated great ignorance about traps: No one would go into his trap, because he was sitting inside it himself. This annoyed him. After all, everyone knows that, despite their slyness, all foxes occasionally get caught in traps. Why should a fox trap—especially one built by a fox with more experience of traps than any other—not be a match for the traps of human beings and hunters? Obviously because this trap did not reveal itself clearly enough as the trap it was! And so it occurred to our fox to decorate his trap beautifully and to hang up unequivocal signs everywhere on it that quite clearly said: "Come here, everyone; this is a trap, the most beautiful trap in the world." From this point on it was clear that no fox could stray into this trap by mistake. Nevertheless, many came. For this trap was our fox's burrow, and if you wanted to visit him where he was at home, you had to step into his trap. Everyone except our fox could, of course, step out of it again. It was cut, literally, to his own measurement. But the fox who lived in the trap said proudly: "So many are visiting me in my trap that I have become the best of all foxes." And there is some truth in that, too: Nobody knows the nature of traps better than one who sits in a trap his whole life long.[8]

The parable evokes in tone and composition an Aesopian fable, but avoids its direct moralizing. It seems rather to be inspired by Franz Kafka's story "The Burrow," a work of literature whose "lesson" is certainly complex. Her teacher is a skilled builder of traps who falls into his own trap, a fool who cannot distinguish whether he is inside or outside while everyone else can see where he is. She depicts her teacher as the naked fox who lost his fur in the troubles of the time and, deprived of its natural protection, is exposed to the attacks of the surroundings and his enemies.

However, the reader senses in her an ambivalence, that what she is describing is the dilemma of thinking itself. Did she not describe here the aporetic relation between thinking and the world, an aporia that cannot be resolved? Thus the text is not a parable of Heidegger's estrangement from the world; instead, it is a description of the dilemma of philosophical thought generally, exemplified in an important twentieth-century thinker.

Admittedly, in her personal relationship with Heidegger, she was in no position to see the situation clearly. Because she was not able to reconcile Heidegger and Jaspers, she saw herself as having failed Heidegger. On the contrary, Jaspers became more hardened over the years. For a long time he waited for Heidegger's convincing answer to the question of his National Socialist euphoria, then he tried to pry it out of him, and finally he definitively distanced himself, limiting the contact to conventional exchanges. Still Heidegger could not leave his burrow.

Moreover, her relationship to Heidegger was different than her relationships with other German friends. With Karl Jaspers, Dolf Sternberger, Hugo Friedrich, or Benno von Wiese she knew exactly where she stood. However, she never completely understood Heidegger and could not be certain that there was an indestructible ground between them.

At times she felt so unsettled that she complained to Jaspers about the role Heidegger had assigned to her: the eternally young girl, the student, the muse who has to hide her light under a bushel. They finally even argued about it. She told her husband that Jaspers had "almost given her an ultimatum," and that she had to put him in his place.[9] She also wrote to Heinrich that when it came to Heidegger, she accepted the role of the young girl, that is, she acted as though she had never written a line.[10] This paradoxical play scarcely hid her many frustrations.

She even turned to a graphologist. Following an examination of his handwriting, the wife of a publishing friend told her that Heidegger had a strong relation to language, that he was not homoerotically predisposed (apparently a recurrent fear of hers), and that his marriage meant nothing to him.[11]

Little is known of how Heidegger thought of her during these years of silence, whether he thought of her often and in which contexts. There are signs that for a time Heidegger and his circle of friends rejected her. As we have already seen, her laudatory speech on the occasion of Karl Jaspers being awarded the peace prize by the German Publishers in 1958 was not taken well. In it, she presented Jaspers as a remarkable example of a public person, an embodiment of *humanitas*, and a worthy successor of Immanuel Kant.[12] Moreover, in honoring Jaspers, she placed at the center of Jaspers's thought the element that Heidegger characterized as a deviation from the philosophical task, namely, the public space.[13] There were no congratulations from Freiburg when she received the Lessing Prize from the city of Hamburg in September 1959. Yet her speech of gratitude offers further proof of her confrontation with her former lover. She spoke of friendship, humanity, and the danger of worldlessness. One could read this homage to Lessing, the genius of friendship, as an address to Heidegger, as a plea for friendship in difficult times, an appeal for a friendship that is grounded in the world and can live with the differences between friends.

It is possible that her veiled message in the absent dedication of *The Human Condition* only deepened the distrust of Heidegger and his circle of friends. She became aware of it in July 1961, when returning from Israel, she made a stop in Freiburg at the invitation of the international law scholar Joseph H. Kaiser. She had told Heidegger about it but did not receive any response. She found out later that a colleague from the Heidegger circle had "brusquely" refused to see her, "in fact, it was clear that Heidegger had forbidden him."[14] She must have felt hurt. She was preoccupied with it for months. She complained about it to Jaspers.[15] She supposed it was her book *The Human Condition* that made him and his circle so angry, since he thought she was not capable of such an achievement.[16] Yet it was clearly her explicit nondedication that had made him angry.

Arendt: To Think a New Beginning

Whoever takes up *The Human Condition* easily recognizes that between the lines Arendt is arguing with Heidegger's thought. However, this book was not just a critical encounter with her teacher that had been on-going for many years. She *had* to write the book because at the end of her complex narrative in *The Origins of Totalitarianism*, she left her readers in the United States and Europe with a question. Having portrayed the total desolation of people in the concentration camps of both major totalitarian systems and having spoken of the "devastating sandstorms," that struck throughout the century and made the earth uninhabitable, she concluded with a quotation from Augustine: "Initium ut esset homo creatus est—that a beginning be made, man was created."[17] She thus left open whether and how at the end of the catastrophe there could be a new beginning, and with it, she distanced herself from other analyses of totalitarian domination, such as Theodor W. Adorno's and Max Horkheimer's, *Dialectic of Enlightenment*, which culminated in a radical cultural critique and a rejection of the present world. She also distanced herself from those who, after the break in tradition, were seeking to make it whole again, for instance, with a new moral philosophy, as well as from those who thought that this form of domination would disappear just as quickly as it had appeared, thereby making a return to normalcy possible. It was no accident that after 1945 many in Germany were celebrating the German classics as the indestructible purity in German culture and history.

But what were the conditions under which a new beginning was possible? The book that served as a starting point to this question was rooted in the studies on anti-Semitism, racism, and totalitarianism that Arendt undertook in the 1940s. Now the task was to reflect on the consequences of this analysis. She was very aware that the new project was inseparable from the old, as she wrote in a letter to Heidegger in 1954.[18]

Nevertheless, *The Human Condition* was a new kind of text for Arendt. If one sees *The Origins* as an intertwining of historical narratives about the European crisis, narratives whose philosophical undercurrents were accessible only to the initiated, the new text was animated instead by the debates ignited in the United States and Europe since the 1940s. Everywhere in the Western world, one witnessed political and ideological debates about the future of humankind and Western culture. They began with the question of the consequences that such an existential break, brought about by totalitarianism, would have for thinking as well as the political life of nations. In the *Partisan Review* and other journals, two currents of thought debated the question. The cultural critics understood the crisis of modernity as a cultural phenomenon within which the role of "man" and the "intellectual" had to be redefined. Those with political interests wanted to draw political conclusions from the crisis.[19] Arendt, who was certainly one of the latter, published an essay on this issue, "Tradition and the Modern Age," in *Partisan Review* in 1954.[20] Yet she had no recipe or strategy to offer. Her task was rather to trace this break in tradition that for her was rooted in the split between philosophical thinking about the world and acting in it. This split, which began with Plato and which Marx radically wanted to end, extended to the point where the two worlds were standing against each other antagonistically—the useless world of thinking and the useful world of action. For Arendt, it was *this split* that formed the basis of the erosion of political order and meaning in modernity and not some crisis of culture.

Like many intellectuals and scientists, she was thinking about the effect that the acceleration of technological transformation would have on modern society. Controversial topics of the postwar time came to the fore: the transformation of industry and working society, the automatization of work, the disappearance of certain social groups (the manual worker), the appearance of new social groups (the manager), the arrival of a "mass culture," the weakness of liberalism, the significance of religion, the agnosticism of the intellectual, and so on. It was no accident that American intellectuals had an edge in these discussions. While the European intellectual elite in the 1950s was looking back to the past, confronted with a present of destruction and depression, in the United States one was looking at the present and extrapolating the future from it. In 1952, the editors of *Partisan Review* organized a three-part discussion forum with precisely this emphasis—"Our Country and Our Culture"—in which notable liberal intellectuals of the East Coast took part. James Burnham, Leslie A. Fiedler, Norman Mailer, Reinhold Niebuhr, Philip Rahv, David Riesman, and Lionel Trilling were among them. Some maintained that there had been a paradigm shift in the relation of the United States to Europe. American culture was standing on its own and no longer had a fundamental need for Europe. Other journals—such as the Jewish intellectual journal *Commentary*—followed suit.

To be sure, the debates would not have unfolded in this way if the United States had not been so clearly an economic leader. After all, the economic boom that took place in Europe several years after the war began in the United States. The awareness that resulted from this carried over to the cultural elite.

The boom gave rise to a new type of society that required scientific and political reflection. In the post-totalitarian period, the technological development of the Western world seemed to relentlessly accelerate the expansion of a society of *job holders*. In any event, Arendt and many of her friends were convinced of this. One of the questions that emerged from this was whether work had become the sole source of the meaning of existence and, if so, what role culture would play in the face of it.

After the first atomic bomb was dropped in 1945, the United States (and later the Soviet Union) thereby demonstrating it was capable of destroying the world, the first exploration of outer space via a satellite followed in the 1950s, which was then followed with the first man landing on the surface of the moon in 1969. The dimension of complete (self-)destruction as well as the perspective of the endless expansion of the human world raised questions about the meaning of these events, which those caught up in the productive activity of work could not answer. They left such existential questions to tradition or to professional thinkers.

Arendt compared the fundamental rupture of her time to the decisive turn that Descartes carried out in his rethinking the relation of human beings to the world. Since the existence of the world was made dependent on their subjective perception, human beings began, according to Arendt's argument, to take over the space beyond the world, to transcend the earthly limits of their existence that had been accepted since antiquity.

The Human Condition is the fruit of working through these different influences. The book is written for a Western audience; it treats Europe and America as parts of a common world.

In the beginning of the 1950s, she turned, as her notebooks indicate, to the conditions under which a new political beginning in modernity was possible. For this purpose, she began to study Heidegger again and to situate him in relation to original Greek texts.

Whoever follows the Arendtian treatment of the Heideggerian categories in the 1950s and 1960s notices how these categories are transformed by her return to the original Greek texts. The reason? She concluded from her analysis of the rupture of tradition in Western history that the torn threads of the tradition could no longer be knit back together. In this she completely agreed with Heidegger. But she also considered the collapse of the *political* tradition. On the basis of this, she began a critical discussion as to how the political co-existence of human beings generally was to be rethought.

In response to Heidegger's claim that Dasein's possibilities emerge from being-toward-death, she points to birth as equally constitutive of Dasein's possibilities. The space of human action extends from birth to death. Meaning does not stop with physical death. Instead, human beings create something that continues into the future through the telling of what had happened (great actions, catastrophes) as well as through that which is most common to all, what the classics since Antiquity understood as *summum bonum* or "public happiness."

She shared Heidegger's later critique of "actionism"—which was also his self-critique—and used it positively. It is not the will to power, that is, it is not the self-sufficiency of the will that stands at the heart of our activity, nor is it a letting-be, that is, the retreat of the individual from the world, as Heidegger saw it after his steep fall. Her alternative to the violent conquering of the world is the creation of a plural world in which singular human beings are able to act with one other. This is what Arendt means when she says "world."

Arendt could not distance herself from the experiences that led her to reject pure thinking. Instead she sought to find a beginning for political thought that was open to the experience of the world. At the same time, she needed pure thought, Heidegger's thought, in order to avoid falling back into old attitudes: those of a scientist who thought and wrote "about" something. She was thus working with "Heidegger's method" when she followed the traces of the historical and linguistic uses of fundamental political categories.

She combed the texts of Antiquity and also read Heidegger against the grain, giving another meaning to certain concepts, by first calling into question, as did her teacher, their traditional significance. It was a methodological access to phenomena that Heidegger had carefully worked on from the earliest stages of his thinking and that he had followed for many years. He created a "pure realm of thought," out of which he stepped when he leaped into action—and into which he withdrew after his downfall. She used this "method" in ways that Heidegger did not. Oscillating between the pure realm of thought and experience, she, "bombarded," so to speak, this realm of thought with experiences of the twentieth century, constantly exposing it, so as to gain new insights.

Heidegger and Arendt are again in counterpoint. While Heidegger had abandoned the world of action in order to retreat into the realm of philosophy and language, Arendt came to the conclusion that one was not going to find any answers to the new questions that modernity posed in philosophical thought. Furthermore, thinking and acting were such fundamentally different spheres that one could not leap from one to the other. Bridges between the two had to be created.

In one of her notes in *Denktagebuch* from March 1952, Arendt wrote after reading Heidegger's text "The Thing":

> Heidegger: "We are—in the strict sense of the word—conditioned beings [*Be-Dingten*]. We have left behind us the presumption of all unconditionedness."[21]
> ". . . From the thinking that merely represents—that is, merely explains—to the thinking that responds and recalls."[22]
> (This is the real turning. . . .).[23]

Regardless of her appreciation of Heidegger's understanding of thinking as a thinking that remembers (as opposed to thinking-about-something), Arendt reversed his questioning. She began with the correctness of the Heideggerian supposition of having "left behind us the presumption of all unconditionedness" and then went on to examine how "various conditions," the limitations of the world, inform human action. To what degree must we detach ourselves from old representations of human beings and of life in order to allow for a new understanding of the human being as an active citizen?

Arendt was not concerned with either refuting or affirming Heidegger. She freely acknowledged that he had discovered something that eluded others. He saw that the modern connection between scientific and technological developments led to an irreversible estrangement of human beings from the world. Many thinkers of his generation arrived at a similar diagnosis. He, however, attempted a different path to find a vantage point from which to think the world. And he pursued this approach by examining the epochs of the history of thought, as well as the etymology of language. In so doing, he uncovered hidden layers of understanding that allowed for new ways of thinking. Yet he always confined his reflections to the thinking individual; he could bring worldliness into play only as a dimension of a philosophy of being. Then he stopped in his path of thought. He could not and did not want to think about plurality, conflict, and action. Thus, his ontology had limits. Heidegger did not *want*—especially after the experience with National Socialism—to overstep them. It is for this reason that he no longer entered the unknown territory of the transition to political thinking.

Arendt, on the other hand, by way of the existential shattering of the radical break in tradition revealed by National Socialism and Soviet Communism, came to the insight that Heidegger's thinking was too restrictive and that it had to be split open. In her view, one of the reasons for the modern break in tradition was that human beings were cut off from the possibility of living their life together through action. The barriers that left this realm inaccessible were created by the centralization of power in the national state, by totalitarian regimes, and by the disappearance of political spaces in modernity. It thus became clear that the task had to do not only with the remembrance (*An=denken*) of the world, as

Heidegger claimed, but with political action in it, with acting in concert with a plurality of others.

Heidegger followed Plato in understanding politics essentially as an education in truth. Truth had to be pursued by guardians and "those who knew better," that is, solitary monarchs and educators. He himself tried to pursue the Platonic *ratio* and failed. Arendt thus had to go back to the very beginnings of thinking about political life in order to understand where Heidegger had failed. Following the maxim that thinking begins with contradictions, in 1951 she began to read the ancient Greeks against the grain. She was reading Plato with the view to Heidegger's fundamental questions: What is being? What is Dasein? What is truth? How does political community emerge? Her *Denktagebuch* shows the ways in which she engages Western thought and forges new ideas in the light of Heidegger's thinking.

Over the course of this process of reading and thinking, into which she drew Heinrich Blücher who was working on similar questions, she discovered a new way of understanding the fundamental categories of thinking about the world. First of all, thinking the political—and here Heidegger would agree with her—is not thinking *about* the world, but rather thinking *in* and *of* the world. But who are the thinkers? And what is world?

In her approach to thinking in the world, one clearly sees Arendt's "turn" in opposition to Heidegger and Plato. Unlike these two philosophers, she *must* leave philosophy to enter the political realm. In her view, political thinking is related to the world and the latter is rooted in the action of the many and not in philosophical reflection. In her reading of the Old and New Testaments, she challenged the Platonic texts and those of her teacher through a different understanding of world. From the act of creation emerged not Adam alone from whose rib Eve was created. Rather, God created Adam *and* Eve. He created two different human beings, not one and not two of the same kind.[24] She expands this idea in her *Denktagebuch*: "The plurality that presents itself in its purest form in the series of numbers extending into infinity and producing themselves from out of themselves *is originally not in the multitude of things, but in the need of the human being who, born as one, has need of a second in order to ensure the progression into the third, fourth, etc.*"[25] Human beings thus need each other; they enter the world always already in a web of relationships. The world consists of what happens *between* people. Plurality emerges in the constant dynamic *between* many individuals. It has its house in language; hence the plurality of voices constitutes the world.

Plurality: here Arendt encounters one of the fundamental differences in understanding between America and Europe. The North American understanding of plurality was, among other things, the result of elaborating the traumas of the Civil War, but it was also crystallized in a historical legal case. In 1918 the anarchist Jacob Adams and other like-minded activists threw pacifist flyers from the roof of a house onto Second Avenue in Manhattan. The group was accused of posing a threat to the security of the United States and boycotting the efforts of the war. Some of them were given heavy sentences.[26] In a divergent view of the Abrams case in 1919, Oliver Wendell Holmes, an esteemed theorist of law and judge on the US Supreme Court (who could not be suspected of any sympathy for the accused), expressed an unusual understanding of plurality: "We permit free expression because we need the resources of the whole group to get us the ideas we need. *Thinking is a social activity.* I recognize your thought because it is part of my thought—even when my thought defines itself in opposition to yours."[27] In German and French history, the understanding of plurality was grounded in tolerance or rather in the commandment to tolerate differences in the name of the idea of humanity. However, if one followed the idea of Oliver Wendell Holmes, anticipated by Charles Peirce, Henry James, John Dewey, and others, society does not just tolerate divergent ideas and interests; it *requires* them. Society needs those who think differently because in these diverging activities and opinions appears part of the richness of thought of the society itself.

Such an understanding of the concept of plurality must have fascinated Arendt, even if in the actual public realm in the United States things worked differently.

Thus acting and plurality belong together. Acting is an activity by which human beings participate in a historical space created by others; this space is a framework, a web, constituted by a plurality of people who are not of the same opinion.

She agreed with her teacher only in her rejection of the will in acting—Heidegger's ultimate conclusion drawn from his downfall in 1933.

She took from Augustine that life is not simply limited by death, but also *made possible* by birth: "Initium ut esset, creatus est homo." Birth *and* death constitute the space, the only space in which we can move, which we can create—and destroy. The metaphor of birth was not foreign to Heidegger; it is indicated in concepts such as "emergence" (*Entbergen*) and also in the Greek concept of truth—*aletheia*—but it is not elaborated.

Arendt transforms the Heideggerian *thrownness* into the world (*Geworfenheit*) into *being-together* in the world.[28] Still, being-together offers no harmony. With its multiplicity of perspectives, plurality ensures that the world standing between the actors is constantly renewed. It is in the antagonism of the many perspectives, in the space *between*, that the space of action, the world, emerges.

Arendt needed to find a different relation to truth so as to turn the world into a space of historical action. She rethought Plato's concept of truth, according to which truth resided in the Ideas of things, not in things themselves. In her view, truth is not something that the (philosopher-)educator can "contemplate" and then communicate to other inhabitants of the earth. Truth is not found in ideas. But even Heidegger's idea of unconcealment, which is supposed to lead to the appearance of the truth of Dasein, does not, in her opinion, go far enough. In a daring act of thought, she relocates the concept of truth in the world of plurality. Accordingly, everyone *can* take part in truth, but only *take part*, because truth remains an object of dispute *between* many. Truth as unconcealment of what had hitherto been invisible does not then reveal what is true (*Gültige*) in an *evident* way. Instead, only in *action* does that which is true show itself. And that which is revealed, unconcealed, also includes those who are acting.

Against the Heideggerian distrust of the public world, Arendt proposes a sympathetic understanding. The world of the "they" is not simply bothersome (even if it sometimes is); it is also an existential condition for human beings.[29] The public realm emerges from the shared worldliness (*Mitweltlichkeit*) of Dasein; it is necessary for life. In the public realm, opinions collide with each other, not harmoniously, but often in a rather cacophonic way, but this is precisely what animates the public space with impulses of renewal.

To be sure, the meaning of the public space rises and falls together with the nonpublic—the private—having its recognized place. Both condition each other. To clarify this, she takes Heidegger's systematic critique of the public realm to its ultimate conclusions. If the public realm is not, as Jaspers had it, pure transparency, but rather, as Heidegger claimed, completely obscured, then distance from the public realm was the only possible way to exist for authentic Dasein. Arendt argues that the consequence of this would be everything becoming private, leaving no public space where human beings could encounter each other as actors. This would put an end to the common world.

Action requires the tribunal of the public space. The Greek polis could create this tribunal because its protagonists distinguished the political world from the realm of private needs, that is, the world of labor, work, reproduction, and family life. Participation in the public space is thus rooted in the capacity to distinguish between the public and the private. Only those who are able to make this distinction—between what belongs to the public and what must remain in the private—are capable of perceiving the public realm. It is only in this way that a political dimension can emerge—that is, a dimension that concerns everything that people have in common.[30]

With regard to the relationship between thinking and acting, in Arendt's view, Heidegger, on the one hand, posited their identity and, on the other hand, substituted the sphere of work for action. Due to her life experiences and her critique of modern history, Arendt was completely opposed to conflating thinking and acting. Her book, *The Origins of Totalitarianism*, is a refutation of this thesis.

If thinking were acting, intellectuals would be actors, pure and simple. But did she not just prove that the latter were professionally fascinated by totalitarianism? Many "thinkers by trade" created an ideological reality and passed it off as reality itself. In Arendt's view, with the arrival of totalitarianism the educational mission of philosophy was discredited. A genuine grasp of reality had to emerge from the actions of many people and from common sense. But since thinking did not come from common sense, but rather from the philosopher's retreat from the common world, thinking and acting were radically different.[31] And yet there was a faculty where they were related: speaking and judging.

On July 1955 the main idea of the new book was suddenly at hand:

> Amor Mundi: Acting in the World, it is a question of a world which is formed as a Time-Space in which human beings plural—not with and not next to each other—pure plurality is enough! (the pure between)—[the world] in which we then build our buildings, move in, want to leave behind something permanent, a world to which we belong insofar as we *are* plural, where we always remain strangers insofar as we are singular; only through this plurality can we determine our singularity. Seeing and being-seen, hearing and being-heard in the between.[32]

Amor Mundi was what she originally wanted to entitle the book before she decided on *The Human Condition*.

In this book, Arendt discusses the space—the world—that stands open to human beings when they wish to act. The subtext of the book was the question of what makes this world possible and what destroys it?

In her discussion of the underlying structures of modern society, she argues that the public realm disappears into the social. Labor stands at the center of this kind of "society." Yet, right at the beginning of her discussion, Arendt rejects the thesis that modern society is a purely "laboring society." To be sure, laborers live in it, but labor is not its only characteristic. This society also produces a world of things. Critiquing Karl Marx, she distinguishes between "labor" and "work." She defines labor as the activity necessary for maintaining the cycle of human reproduction (to be born, live, reproduce, die). This activity does not distinguish human kind from the animal species, hence the formulation *animal laborans*. In this context, the goal of human existence is to expend its labor force so as to remain alive, create progeny, and finally die. In her view, this laboring life offers no access to the common world.

On the other hand, production, which she names "work" (*Herstellen*), serves to create a sphere—the world of things—in which goods are produced that are independent of human beings. This is the world of things. This world transcends the cycle of production and consumption—which she equates with destruction—gains an enduring existence through work. In this world, things are produced that outlast an individual life. Yet it is only in speaking and acting that one has access to the common world of the *between*, the discovery of which we owe to the Greeks.

Thus, as the metaphor of birth indicates, acting goes beyond the world of labor and the world of things. Something begins with acting. She finds this idea in other thinkers, as well. Arendt, however, refines this idea. A beginning is not to be equated with the anticipation of the end. Even though I may envision the goal to be achieved, my action remains open. The consequences of my action, which involves other people, can go in unforeseen directions. Acting creates a "web of relations" in which both individuals and groups are implicated: "Action consists of weaving one's own thread into a fabric that one has not made oneself."[33] But this is possible only in the public realm.

She agrees with Heidegger that technology, work, and the world of things may distort access to the important aspects of life. She greatly appreciated his understanding of the radical consequences that the cybernatization and computerization of communication would have on the relationship between human beings and the world they created.[34]

Heidegger's difficult concept of "en-framing" (*Gestell*), a concept that crystallized his critique of modernity in the 1950s, suggested that the "true" access to being was so obscured that it was doubtful whether it was possible at all. Arendt agreed entirely with this idea.[35] Both held modern philosophical and scientific thought largely accountable for this problem. Yet Arendt saw a chance to break this spell in political acting. There she decisively disagreed with Heidegger. No fate (*Schicksal*), no destining (*Geschick*), no "en-framing" (*Gestell*) could prevent actors from breaking the spell by choosing to act and thereby begin something new.

With *The Human Condition*, Arendt introduced a new kind of thinking. She was not establishing a systematic philosophy, but rather pursuing political thought, philosophically founded, and open to other disciplines and experiences. Even further, she was reflecting on the presuppositions for the political self-organization of human beings under the complicated conditions of modernity. Essentially she was taking further what Plato and Aristotle had initiated and what Heidegger had also addressed.

At the end of *The Human Condition*, Arendt leaves her reader somewhat perplexed. She points out the victory of the society of laboring and producing, and she enumerates the obstacles to the opening of a political public realm. Then she cites once again Saint Augustine's dictum "that a beginning be made man was created." The phrase always sounds the same, but now she applies it to the political realm: What is a political beginning? How can it come about?

A "Small Book of Politics"

To Heidegger's question of what she was working on, she first mentioned the following project in 1954: "Starting with Montesquieu, an analysis of the types of states, with the goal of uncovering where the concept of authority infiltrated the political . . . and how the political sphere is constituted."[36] In her correspondence with Karl Jaspers, she described this book project as a "small book of politics." It is based on a series of lectures she gave in the 1959 spring semester at Princeton University which had to do largely with the American Revolution.

As she was preparing for citizenship in 1950–51, Arendt had begun intense work on American history and the culture of political thought. She read the writings of the American founders and their debates around the political constitution of this society of immigrants. Not only did she want to understand how the Mayflower Compact and the Declaration of Independence came about, she also wanted to understand the process by which the United States became what it was: a haven of freedom.

Prompted by her publisher Klaus Piper, she immediately planned to transform these lectures into a book about politics. Piper thought it was the right time for such a book for the German audience. But the more Arendt worked on the manuscript, the more her approach to the subject changed into a polemical writing on the ways of founding a political community, on opening up the political sphere—and on how it can be, albeit with good intentions, destroyed. The book, *On Revolution*, came out in 1963 in the United States. Two years later, the German translation, entitled *Über die Revolution*, was published.

While in *The Human Condition* Arendt discussed the conditioned nature of human existence as well as the disappearance in the modern world of the perspective of the human being as an acting being, here she spoke of how political communities were founded over the course of Western history. The book further develops the polemic concerning the loss of tradition in modernity and cites historical foundations and their dilemmas. Here, too, she also made a long detour to the question left open at the end of *The Origins of Totalitarianism*. Seeking an answer to the question of why the European mass democracy of the twentieth century could not stop the assault of totalitarian movements, she investigates the American foundation of political freedom and the difference between European and American political history.

What does the concept of "founding" (*Gründung*) mean for Arendt?

With a founding, something new begins or ends in the political realm. For Arendt, foundations in the public realm are actions of citizens that lead to the establishing of a political community. The medium of this beginning is a revolution, which does not simply break out, like a rebellion, but "was made on the foundation of reciprocal obligations and on the strength of mutual promises."[37] With the reference to "reciprocal obligations and promises," Arendt alludes to the promise before God rooted in the pietistic tradition that is simultaneously a promise among human beings, each individual before God, and all individuals among themselves *and* before God—a principle of action that is furthermore present in the Judaic tradition in the Book of Exodus. This promise stands behind the famous 1640 Mayflower Compact and the 1776 Declaration of Independence. An assembly of free human beings, similar to Greek citizens in the polis, gathered together and promised to each other and before God to found a community that should be grounded on the principle of freedom and the obligation before God. Such is the mythical story.

There is thus a *Constitutio liberartis*, a veritable constitution of freedom. In this conceptual framework, the meaning of freedom went far beyond the everyday use of the term: either being free from something or the space of freedom secured through constitutions, laws, and institutions. Freedom in the sense of the Arendtian interpretation of the American Revolution is freedom to found a political community, for instance, a republic.

In the act of founding and the narrative that accompanies it, a perspective opens that goes beyond historical facts. In the particular historical case of America, it meant that a political community was consciously founded on the Biblical tradition and a worldly promise. In Arendt's view, people in modernity, no longer living in the certitude of faith, must nonetheless carry further the question concerning the source of the meaning of origin. Without transcending itself, without a reference to something beyond itself, the political community would exhaust itself in the repetition of the reproduction cycle, in the management of social needs, in the production of useful things, and in the institution of more or less moral rules.

Here Arendt ventures into the center of Heidegger's thinking, the engagement with metaphysics, with everything that lies outside the world of things; however, she attempts to relate this realm to the realm of action and thereby avoid the trap that Heidegger had fallen into. While the latter attempted a leap from ontology into political action and remained stuck in the dualism of the leader and the follower, she ties the transcendental sphere to the plurality of many people who relate to each other and create among themselves something that reaches beyond them.

The problematic is complicated by her multifaceted concept of the *political*. It describes a domain where people can relate to each other as actors. Arendt also calls this a "political space." The exchange that takes place in this space—in acting and speaking—gives rise to the creation of the meaning of human living-together. The latter cannot be canonized for eternity, but rather must be constantly created anew.

In this context, Arendt rediscovers one of the central political concepts: power. The American founding fathers created a republic where power—based on the principle of shared power—is not divided, but rather proliferates horizontally and is thus increased. Power extends to town hall meetings in villages and towns where it becomes visible in concrete decisions. At the same time, a federation of individual states is strengthened by an admittedly strong central power: "The unique aim of the state constitutions which preceded the Constitution of the Union . . . was to create new centers of power after the Declaration of Independence had abolished the authority and power of crown and Parliament. To this task, the creation of new power, the founders and men of the Revolution brought to bear the whole arsenal of what they themselves called their 'political science,' for political science, in their own words, consisted in trying to discover 'the forms and combinations of power in republics.'"[38] Arendt thus delineates the particular path that the American Revolution followed. It did not found a centralized nation state, but rather a republican federation.

Drawing on the "American" political concept of power and consciously setting herself apart from the European theory of a centralized power, Arendt understands the concept of power positively, binding the phenomenon of power to acting in concert.[39]

Political freedom thus emerges from and consists of the acting together of the many who seek to found a political community based on the horizontal redistribution and expansion of the power of citizens acting together.

Why was this path not taken in Europe? Arendt explains this with the example of the French Revolution and one of its important thinkers, Abbot Sièyes. In his understanding, which prevailed in the French Revolution, the nation must be the supreme authority. It must be instituted as "the source of law above law."[40] Arendt criticized Sièyes for "putting the *pouvoir constituant*, that is, the nation, into a perpetual 'state of nature'"[41] from which it claimed legitimacy. This opened the flood gates to the forces that reduced the Constitution to an instrument of group interests. For the will of the nation, as Arendt argued in her interpretation of Sièyes, constantly changes. Consequently, the French constitution would always be amended. During the time of the revolution alone, four constitutions were ratified. In US history, by contrast, "the seat of power . . . was the people,"[42] not the nation. It is the people who have recourse to the state to achieve their wishes, not the state that has recourse to the people for its ends.

Only from this perspective could the principle of a federal republic, as James Madison formulated it, meaningfully appear. However, the ground for this distinctive principle lay "in the way that the American Revolution understood by power the very opposite of a prepolitical natural violence: they meant the institution and organization of promises, covenants, and mutual pledges."[43]

In contrast, the French revolutionaries, by equating the will of the people with the nation and elevating the nation to the status of a metaphysical authority, pitted the sacred will of the nation against the political deployment of power by the people themselves. Arendt's objection to the French Revolution was that "the superior right of the Revolution (Nation)," no longer anchored in the real space of action, undermined the possibility of a revolutionary process founded through the people. Whereas the French path was oriented toward the unification of the people's will, wishing to achieve this through the deification of the nation, the American path was founded, according to Arendt, on respect for the multiplicity of conflicting interests that, through representation in political institutions, could become an organized plurality able to support the system of laws (which would be called "body politic" in the language of the eighteenth century) and its institutions.

From this Arendt concluded that the centralization of power was one of the central problems for subsequent European development.

In Arendt's view, another cause of the failures of revolutions, such as the French, was turning politics into household management through social needs and interests. In *The Human Condition*, she systematically demonstrated the way in which the social realm in modernity had pushed the political sphere into the background, so that the public realm of action and the capacity of citizens to act disappeared completely. In *On Revolution*, she showed the way in which the will to found a stable political community was obscured in Europe by the problem of how to solve the "social question." The French revolutionaries saw it as their task to abolish poverty. From Arendt's perspective, this was another reason for both the success of the Americans and the failure of the French: "America did not stand under the curse of poverty. The ground of freedom could only succeed because the 'founding fathers' did not place the political under the insolvable social question; however this ground could not be a generalized matter of freedom because the residual world of the miserable masses did and would remain."[44] Compassion for the poor as well as hatred of the rich stood in diametrical opposition to the success of revolution as a political act of foundation. The constitution of freedom thus must fail in the face of the demand to produce not just the formal equality of law, but equality for all as regards living conditions. The latter could be accomplished only by force and resulted—seen in retrospect—in terror and totalitarianism.

Arendt's book on the foundation of freedom was dedicated to her friends Karl and Gertrud Jaspers. The dedication reads, "To Gertrud and Karl Jaspers: In reverence—in friendship—in love." Jaspers considered the book, as he wrote to her after a first reading, "the equal of, if not perhaps superior to, your book on totalitarianism in the profundity of its political outlook and the masterly quality of its execution."[45]

From the background of the rejected dedication, this clear and all-encompassing recognition of both the Jaspers must have felt like a slap in the face to Heidegger, if he, indeed, ever read the book.

Two Incompatible Concepts of Freedom

Does Heidegger even have a perspective of freedom?

In the 1936 summer semester, while he was still trying to dissociate himself intellectually from his traumatic rectorship and beginning to intensively delve into Nietzsche's thought, he taught a course on Schelling's treatise *On the Essence of Human Freedom*.[46]

A seminar on freedom in the middle of the success of National Socialism! Here Heidegger agreed with Schelling on the ambivalent character of freedom. Schelling interprets freedom as open for both good *and* evil. Good and evil are thus not two options available to those who act; one is always already included in the other.[47]

Second, Heidegger clearly connects the concept of freedom to the will.

In an almost Hegelian turn concerning the relation between freedom and necessity, Heidegger elevates necessity to the status of a determining presupposition of freedom: "This necessity itself is the freedom of its own deed. Freedom is necessity; necessity is freedom. These two sentences, correctly understood, do not stand in the formal mutual relation of an empty reversal. Rather, a process is contained there which goes back to itself, but in doing so never comes back to the same thing, but takes the point of departure back to a deeper understanding."[48] One can see from this passage where Heidegger's thought stopped. He could have proceeded here to the reversal of freedom into action, but he blocks the transition. After 1934 he clearly no longer intended to approach the political space. This refusal seems irritating from today's point of view. Was it not obvious that, in 1936, one had to at least mention the symbolic effect of a course on freedom? He could have systematically marked the site of transition, without touching upon its consequences politically and practically. But he did not do so.

In his texts from the 1950s, Heidegger withdrew freedom from the realm of the will entirely:

The essence of freedom is *originally* not connected with the will or even with the causality of human willing. Freedom governs the free space in the sense of the cleared, which is to say, the revealed. To the occurrence of revealing, i.e., of truth, freedom stands in the closest and most intimate kinship. All revealing belongs within a harboring and a concealing. But that which frees— the mystery—is concealed and always concealing itself. All revealing comes out of the free, goes into the free, and brings into the free. The freedom of the free consists neither in unfettered arbitrariness nor in the constraint of mere laws. Freedom is that which conceals in a way that opens to light, in whose clearing shimmers the veil that hides the essential occurrence of all truth and lets the veil appear as what veils. Freedom is the realm of the destining that at any given time starts a revealing on its way.[49]

He thus renounces many of his concepts from the 1930s: will, causality, and thus also necessity. Here he comes close to what Arendt had developed in thinking of freedom in *On Revolution*, but he did not situate freedom in the context of action.

The difference with Arendt's multilayered concept of freedom lies precisely here. It is situated ontologically, but is opened to the political space. On the one hand, drawing on antiquity where freedom and politics were one and the same, she distinguishes freedom from the act of the will, referring to the Kantian notion of spontaneity. On the other hand, she distinguishes it from the withdrawal from the world, as introduced by the Christian tradition, which equates freedom with "the freedom from politics."[50] In *On Revolution* we encounter an understanding of freedom which is identified with the collective act of *founding*.

If one compares these two approaches to the concept of freedom, it becomes clear that Arendt frees philosophical thought from the limitations of ontology. She opens up the concept of freedom to the human world by taking it out of the world of thought and exposing it to the world of action and experience.

Heidegger's understanding of history is similarly ambiguous. In *Being and Time*, he demonstrated the historicity of the philosophical world and Dasein. It was a revolutionary move at the time. Still, his discussions remained strictly within the ontological framework. When, however, in the beginning of the 1930s, the question of the event (*Ereignis*) came into play, he linked it with the *topoi* of fate (*Schicksal*), will (*Wille*), and destining (*Geschick*). Now history became something mysterious. The interpretation of historical events became in turn solemn or majestic, which, in Arendt's view, could not be attributed to them. Once again, one encountered the problem of precarious transitions. Before 1933 Heidegger associated history with the hope of fulfilling a historical task in Germany and in the West in general. He projected this hope onto National Socialism. He was even willing to overlook its violence because it was directed at a higher goal. At this time he related history to concepts like willing (*Wollen*), guiding (*Führen*), and safeguarding (*Hüten*). After his separation from National Socialism, he concerned himself more and more with the dark, ominous, and mysterious aspect of history, which he increasingly defined as destining (*Geschick*).

Confronted with the experience of totalitarianism, Arendt, in contrast, fleshed out an idea of history as the interplay of events and intervening actions. While it cannot be "produced," still history is inseparably connected with action. Without action, it cannot take place.[51] It is the actors who engender history, but it is not "made" by them, much less produced by anonymous forces. Rather, it happens in events that interrupt the course of time.[52] The actors are the "heroes" of history, but not in a traditional sense; they are heroes who have the courage to speak and to act.[53] Furthermore, history emerges from the stories that people tell to each other. In her view, Heidegger substituted the reign of history for action.[54]

In the later Heidegger, the reign of history became even more pronounced. History turned into a reigning destining (*Geschick*). In a letter dated December 15, 1952, he writes: "Meanwhile, the world keeps getting darker. Contentiousness dominates everything here. Given the disastrous situation, one would expect the opposite. 'Europe' is now only a name that can hardly be invested with a meaning at this point. The essence of history keeps getting more and more enigmatic. The rift between one's most essential efforts and its immediate ineffectuality is becoming increasingly uncanny. All this suggests that our habitual notions are limping behind the situation and will not catch up with it again."[55] At the same time he envisioned "an arrival of new mysteries—or, better said, of the ancient ones."

Karl Jaspers saw the gravity and obscurity of Heidegger's thought on history as a pure evasion. In his view, Heidegger took flight into a world of dreams. Heinrich Blücher, too, wrote biting commentaries on this. When on her 1952 trips to Europe and Germany, Arendt told him the latest *Heideggeriana*, the circulating stories and rumors, expressing her judgments on these affairs, he drew her attention to Karl Löwith's fundamental critique of Heidegger.[56] He shared Löwith's critique of Heidegger's concept of history and asked Hannah "to question his concept of historicity."[57] Hannah declined because she found Löwith's attitude toward his former teacher to be extremely questionable. But Blücher persisted: "What I meant was that Löwith had pinpointed Heidegger's sore spot, and that the master would do well to forget his pain (his disappointment with former students, the shame of so misjudging National Socialism—Author's note) and take notice. Unfortunately, his questionable and postulating concept of historicity still plays an important role with him. He is dispatching the German people into his historicity (*Geschicklichkeit*); and this one changed letter will burst the whole pustule. This is quite symbolic for such a language-oriented thinker."[58] Although Heidegger saw history as dark, speaking barely in a whisper, in retrospect many of his insights proved to be clear-sighted, notably his insights since the 1950s concerning the revolution of technology (cybernatization, computerization), which confirmed Arendt's argument in *The Human Condition* regarding the immense influence of technology on the perception of the world and on perspectives of action.[59]

The Eichmann Trial

On October 4, 1960, Arendt told Jaspers that she was going to attend the Eichmann trial in Jerusalem.[60] She had asked the publishers of the well-known magazine *The New Yorker* if they were interested in a report on the trial. She received the assignment.[61]

Eichmann, a second-rank organizer of the mass murders of European Jews, had been kidnapped in Argentina on May 1960 by the Israeli secret service and brought to Israel. This action raised a considerable international outcry, as it was an infringement on international law. The newspapers were full of commentaries about the pros and cons of this action and its consequences. Be that as it may, after the Nuremberg trial in 1947, where he was tried in absentia, Eichmann was the first high-ranking National Socialist functionary to stand trial. In Germany at this time, the persecution of those responsible for the genocide was not making any progress. In hindsight it becomes clear that the trial against Adolf Eichmann played a key function for the West German juridical landscape as it was after the trial that the German courts showed themselves to be more inclined to prosecute Nazi criminals.

The trial began in April 1961, and Arendt went to Jerusalem repeatedly to observe it. She read thousands of pages of police protocols, spoke with Israeli Prime Minister David Ben Gurion, Foreign Minister Golda Meir, Minister of Justice Rosen, and the court president Moshe Landau. She spoke with witnesses and observers, and asked for their opinions. She sat in the courtroom and formed her own view of the trial. Her reports appeared in the *New Yorker* on February 16 and 23, as well as on March 2, 9, and 16, 1963, under the title "A Reporter at Large: Eichmann in Jerusalem." The main questions were focused on what role the person of the accused played in the context of what happened as well as the situation of the Jews and the politics of their organizations (for example, the Jewish Councils) vis-à-vis the carrying out of the extermination.

Between the lines resurfaced the highly delicate question from *The Origins of Totalitarianism* of whether the murder of European Jews was not *also* the consequence of a situation in which the European Jews, having never been politically organized and thus unable to oppose deadly anti-Semitism with any resistance, had to therefore, in the end, unwillingly collaborate with their murderers.

The reports and the book that came out in the same year in New York exploded like a bomb. In one stroke, she had the entire Jewish community against her. Highly emotional and sometimes hateful indictments appeared in the press. A public campaign was launched against her. Meetings on her book were organized across the country. Rabbis preached against her in synagogues.

The parallel with 1945 almost inevitably comes to mind here. In her article "Zionism Reconsidered," she critiqued the Zionist establishment. Her enemies then attacked her personally. The abrupt disruptions of friendships over a political dispute that in her view had nothing to do with persons but with opinions and positions was for Arendt a shock that left her saddened and depressed. She struggled to save her friendships, particularly the one with Kurt Blumenfeld.

However, that dispute was nothing compared with what broke out now.

What happened? Eichmann's abduction was, for many reasons, a very particular political act. In retrospect, it seems as though the young state of Israel, fourteen years at the time, wanted to make an example out of this case. First of all, Eichmann had to be judged as a representative of the organizers of genocide. For this purpose, he had to be elevated to the status of the monster, which, in Arendt's view, did not adequately characterize him. Second, the trial had to prove to the world that the state of Israel was capable of judging the murder of the Jewish people on its own, without having to wait for post-Nazi Germany to finally decide to prosecute its criminals. Third, the trial needed to free the Jewish people from the role of victim. Finally, it needed to put an end to the profound, at times passionate, postwar conflicts that divided Israeli pioneers and Jewish communities in Europe. The division had to do with the survivors of the Holocaust and their descendants who were both openly and secretly reproached by the Zionist side for having learned nothing from being victims. The trial was meant to reconcile these divided camps. With the help of all participants—the accused, the witnesses, the prosecutor, the judge, the defendant, and the press—the trial was to establish for posterity a kind of second symbolic foundation of Israel as a state that was strong and capable of defending itself.

Hence, from the outset the trial was a mixture of politics and legal justice. In attendance were the founder of the state and prime minister, David Ben Gurion, the foreign minister, Golda Meir, and the prosecutor, Gideon Hausner. It is reported that Ben Gurion before the trial said: "There sits here not an individual, who sits in the docket of this historical process, this is also not about the Nazi regime generally, but in the docket sits anti-Semitism throughout history."[62] In addition, the assassination of Rudolf Kastner in 1957 fueled emotions. Kastner was the Hungarian Jewish functionary who had participated in the negotiations between Zionist organizations and the Nazi regime, later becoming a member of the Israeli government after the foundation of the state of Israel.

The circumstances thus could not have been more unfavorable to a critical judgment of the Eichmann case. The Israeli public demanded a positive participation in the trial and not a harsh critique of its internal contradictions and ostensible effects.

Arendt followed the history leading up to the trial in New York. She participated in discussions about the role of the Israeli state, about the problems of international law that the trial raised, as well as in discussions concerning the fundamental question about judging a murderer who had committed "crimes against humanity." She must have received background information from the intermediary Kurt Blumenfeld and her relatives, the Fürsts.[63]

With her usual analytic acuity, Arendt pointed out in her trial report the absurdities of the theatrical excess that accompanied the trial. She discussed the protagonists of the trial, above all, the accused. What was someone like who organized genocide? How did he understand his actions? How did he speak? What was his attitude toward the judges and the prosecutors? She was struck by the discrepancy between the monstrosity of the genocide, the perfection of its organization, and the shallowness of the perpetrator. She described Eichmann as an intelligent man who was, however, incapable of thinking, lacking imagination. He was a man who was not fully in command of the German language, who had fled into the apparent security of bureaucratic German during his years as an officer. This man therefore did not feel any guilt. For Arendt, he represented the mediocre type of criminal who connected his life with the Nazi regime "as destined" and for reasons of career, stood ready to murder as ordered.

She wrote to Jaspers on April 13 after the first session of the trial: "Eichmann. No eagle, rather, a ghost who has a cold on top of that, and minute by minute fades in substance, as it were, in his glass box."[64] Two days later she wrote to Blücher: "Eichmann . . . more like materialization at a séance. His only concern not to lose his composure."[65] She noticed his "pomposity" and "boasting." "In Eichmann's mouth the horrible often becomes not macabre, but decidedly comical."[66]

In the epilogue to her report on the Eichmann trial for the German edition, she noted later:

> The trouble with Eichmann was precisely that so many were like him, and that the many were neither perverted nor sadistic, that they were and still are, terribly and terrifyingly normal. From the viewpoint of our legal institutions and of our moral standards of judgment this normality was much more terrifying than all the atrocities put together, for it implied—as had been said at Nuremberg over and over again by the defendants and their counsels—that this new type of criminal, who is in actual act *hostis generis humani*, commits his crime under circumstances that make it well-nigh impossible for him to know or to feel that he is doing wrong.[67]

She saw all the weaknesses of the trial embodied in the prosecutor. In a letter to Jaspers she describes: "The prosecutor . . . very unsympathetic, is constantly making mistakes. . . . His argument artificial, overly legalistic and with gross errors, interrupted by spells of emotion. But above all immeasurably boring and full of nonexistent precedents, on which the prosecutor focuses instead of stressing the unprecedentedness of the case. He does make occasional mention of that, but the right things he says disappear under the irrelevancies."[68] The German defender: "an oily, adroit, and without a doubt thoroughly corrupt fellow, but much more clever than the public prosecutor."[69] The tribunal of the judges: "towering high, the three judges, all of them German Jews, and in the middle of them the presiding judge, Moshe Landau, who is really and truly marvelous—ironic and sarcastic in his forbearing friendliness."[70] In hindsight, one notices even more strongly than at the time, as her judgment about the role of the Jewish Councils indicates, that Arendt opposed the mixing of legal justice, politics, and history. In her view, if this trial was to be meaningful despite its flaws—the infringement on international law and the projection of the genocide into *one* single individual—it had to appear within the tradition of the Nuremberg trials. Indeed, judges started out from the dilemma of judging a crime that was committed against the human species as such and for this reason exceeded the framework of positive law. Hence the "invention" of a new category: "crimes against humanity."

A concept in her report that provoked particular anger was the "banality of evil." Her critics reproached Arendt for banalizing the crimes with this concept.[71] In fact, drawing on Kant and Schelling, Arendt defined the concept of evil in *The Origins of Totalitarianism* in an essentialist way, that is, as a radical evil that emerged from the will to do evil. She wrote in a 1951 letter to Karl Jaspers that "radical evil" "has to do with the following phenomenon: making human beings as human beings superfluous (not using them as means to an end, which leaves their essence as humans untouched and impinges only on their human dignity; rather, making them superfluous as human beings)."[72]

This characterization defined radical evil as the absolute negation of being-human and of a habitable common world. However, the Eichmann trial revealed something completely new vis-à-vis Kant's definition of evil. Arendt did not see something new in the rationality or irrationality of human annihilation or in the maliciousness of the perpetrator, but rather in the combination of absolute meaninglessness and cold calculation. From this came the systematic destruction of individuality, which in Arendt's view had never previously existed in modernity. This destruction of individuality affects the victims as well as their murderers—albeit in different ways. During her stay in Jerusalem, she confronted the phenomenon of the banality of the murderer as a person. She then coined the concept of the "banality of evil," describing a dimension that had hitherto been little considered: the complete absence of thinking and thus of conscience and self-reflection in the person of the perpetrator. Eichmann did not embody for Arendt the "bestial man" as the prosecutor Gideon Hausner presented him; he did not seem to her to be driven by personal hatred, nor did he legitimize his acts ideologically. In her view, he was a "normal" type of modern human being, a worldless human being who had lost all contact with the world inhabited by other people, a world he was part of through his birth. He was a person for whom the only foothold was submission to the orders of Nazi bureaucracy.

By formulating this concept, Arendt wanted to point out that evil could very well be part of inconspicuous normality. A mass murderer could, in normal circumstances, be a simple buffoon. His acts did not come from base instincts. He could be a good functionary and a loving father.

In the controversy around her trial report, she responded to Gershom Scholem's objection that her concept was nothing more than a "catchword": "It is indeed my opinion now that evil is never 'radical,' that it is only extreme and that it possesses neither depth nor any demonic dimension. It can overgrow and lay waste the whole world precisely because it spreads like a fungus on the surface. . . . Only the good has depth and can be radical."[73] In the subtext of her report, Arendt pursued a line of questioning that she had begun well before, a question to which she always returned: How is one to understand the disappearance of responsibility in totalitarian regimes? How can responsibility be reconstructed when its subjects are transformed into recipients of orders without any autonomous will? What is the difference between personal and political responsibility? In contrast to the juridical debates on the "state of emergency," on collective responsibility, and the diminishment of guilt in a situation of dictatorship, she held the following position: there is a type of responsibility that cannot be suspended under any circumstances, the responsibility of all for the crimes committed in their name. Behind the problem of responsibility, she saw a further problem: people give up responsibility when they are either incapable of or do not want to judge the situations in which they find themselves or the actions with which they are confronted or which they carry out themselves. In the last volume of *Life of the Mind*, Arendt intended to take up the question that emerged here, namely, how one can develop a capacity for judgment and continue to exercise this judgment under the most extreme circumstances.

If her judgment of Eichmann as an embodiment of the "banality of evil" constantly provoked critique, the way in which Arendt approached the (forced) cooperation of the Jewish councils and other Jewish organizations in the genocide was met with even harsher criticism. The style and tone in which she described the "negotiations" between National Socialist institutions and Jewish or rather Zionist relief organizations was seen as a "mockery of the victims." The tone that Arendt took up and maintained until the last page was distant, ironic, sarcastic, always walking a razor's edge that risked turning horror into comedy. It was a tone of extreme distance toward her subject, a tone that did not reveal the author's personal feelings. Her critics, such as Gershom Scholem, reproached her for this lack of empathy both toward murdered Jews as well as for the involuntary Jewish "helpers" of National Socialism.

The intense reaction to her trial report came from three different sides: from the protagonists of the *causa Eichmann* in Jerusalem, from parts of the American public, and finally from public personalities in West Germany.

In the camp of the critics, the Zionists set the tone. Ernst Simon, second-generation Zionist who emigrated to Palestine at the end of the 1920s and taught at Hebrew University in Jerusalem, criticized her for presenting the Jewish councils as enemies of Jews and for defaming the murdered Jews after their death.[74] Simon attacked her personally and suggested that her report was a continuation of her unwarranted attacks on Zionism from the 1940s. He was invited to give lectures in the United States to speak against Arendt and her book. She complained to Jaspers about this.[75] Marie Syrkin, also a second-generation Zionist, an active leftist, and coeditor of *Jewish Frontier*, who presumably knew Arendt quite well from the 1940s, published harsh critiques in *Dissent* and *Partisan Review*.[76] Michael Musmanno, an influential jurist,[77] wrote a passionate and demagogical critique against Arendt that focused on her personally.[78] Zionists from other countries were also making strong critiques.[79] Gershom Scholem, her longtime friend, who had never forgiven her for the critique of the Zionist establishment in 1945 and in whose view she was generally suspected of hating "her people," reproached her for the "heartless, even malicious tone" in her trial report. As spokesperson for the Israeli critics, he argued that she used a "cavalier style." She lacked the "tact of the heart." She did not love the Jewish people. In short, she: "had no balanced judgment, instead it's more like demagogically twisted overstatement."[80] For decades she had held Scholem in high esteem as a friend and scholar, even after his wounding 1945 judgment about her. He, too, was now in the camp of those who branded her a traitor of the Jewish people. His accusing letter and her response were published in the *Neuen Zürcher Zeitung* and in *Encounter*.

It was all the more tragic that in May 1963, in the middle of this harsh conflict, Kurt Blumenfeld died after a serious illness. Arendt visited him in the hospital and tried to explain her position to him; she must have feared that he would renounce their friendship, as he had after her article "Zionism Reconsidered." And he, in fact, seemed outraged by her report; however, as they talked with each other, he was equally outraged by two articles against Arendt that had appeared in *Aufbau*.[81]

A year later, with the controversy still in full sway, Arendt found out from a brief correspondence with a relative of Martin Rosenblüth—recently deceased—that Blumenfeld was assailed on his deathbed by people asking him to express his indignation against his friend. He was ready to do this. The reports he had heard about the book were sufficient for him.

This is precisely the constitutive feature of this scandal: Arendt's enemies did not *want* to distinguish between critical disagreement and personal attack. For them, the two belonged together. There was only an either-or: Arendt was either for the state of Israel, in which case her trial report was 100 percent false, or she was against it, in which case one had to fight her to the end and undermine her credibility in the eyes of the world.

The journals in which she had published for years turned against her. The *Aufbau*, the German-Jewish newspaper of the East Coast, for which she had written a column and a number of articles since 1941, published five articles against her.[82] In 1964 the journal *Dissent*, whose editor she considered a friend, organized a kind of tribunal focused on refuting the theses of *Eichmann in Jerusalem*. The *New York Times Book Review* published a review by Michael Musmanno that tore the book to shreds.

Prosecutor Hausner, who published a book on the Eichmann case in 1966, attacked Arendt's report during a promotional trip in the United States. Jacob Robinson, one of Hausner's assistants, wrote a book full of accusations against Arendt.[83]

The *Partisan Review* commissioned an entire series of articles on her book and published many letters from readers. The editors opened the subject with a polemical piece by Lionel Abel. Abel, a theater critic and a playwright, a former Marxist who then turned to the extreme right and for a while was part of the circle around *Partisan Review* and *Dissent*, contested all the assessments and facts in her book. His critique culminated in the scathing judgment that Arendt's book was based on aesthetic judgments—that is, judgments of taste.[84] He argued that she trivialized Eichmann. In his critique, Abel, like Simon and Musmanno, explicitly devalued her book *The Origins of Totalitarianism*. Old conflicts resurfaced.

Norman Podhoretz, another good acquaintance of Arendt's, joined Abel's critique. In his critique, he, too, extended his negative judgment to Arendt as a person and included Arendt's entire work as a political writer.

It shook her to the core that so many of her American acquaintances and friends attacked her personally. These were for the most part colleagues she met at political events, editorial conferences, and social gatherings. She talked with them, argued with them; these were the persons whom she more or less esteemed and trusted, thinking they could distinguish between intellectual critique and personal attack. It was precisely this distinction that was repeatedly undermined. It seemed that her critics began with theoretical critique only in order to follow with an attack on her personally.

Half a year after the beginning of the campaign, Mary McCarthy tried to step into the closed front of Arendt's enemies. Everyone knew that she was Arendt's close friend. She could see that Arendt was under fire from certain Jewish factions, and she tried to correct the obviously inaccurate aspects of the critiques against her; however, she failed to alter the dynamic.[85] Her old friend Dwight Macdonald also tried to help, writing a long reader's letter to *Partisan Review* in which he pointed out that the hateful attacks against Arendt stemmed from a

Jewish patriotism that viewed her book as treason against the country of Israel.[86] Apparently this came closest to the truth. What mattered to the Jewish critics was a *univocal* interpretation of the history of the horrifying experience leading to the creation of the state. Arendt, with her type of report, was in the way of this goal and she was for this reason stigmatized as an enemy of the Jewish people and of the Israeli state.

Bruno Bettelheim, Georges Lichtheim, and Daniel Bell also tried to do justice to Arendt's book, but without much success.[87] Moderating voices were not heard. Even old, very close friends were swept up in the flow of condemnations. On the one hand, when *Dissent* organized the debate around Arendt's book in 1964, her close friend Alfred Kazin declared himself opposed to the editor Irving Howe and his politics of denouncing Arendt's position;[88] on the other hand, he also thought that her thesis concerning the coresponsibility of the Jewish councils for the genocide was false and that her entire position on Eichmann and the Jews had something typically German about it—in this situation a clearly negative remark.[89]

Arendt saw the official interpretation of the Eichmann case as a manipulation of the context of a historical event that she did not want to let pass without question. Through public appearances she repeatedly tried to break the unanimity of the critiques, for instance in August 1963, in a discussion at Columbia University where she had been invited by the rabbi of the university. This worked, however, only for a short time.[90] The campaign continued.

The German side of the debate was highly illuminating. The Germans—that is, credible intellectuals of the 1960s—were in a difficult situation. On the one hand, they were deeply wrapped up in the debates concerning the punishment for mass crimes and about collective guilt; on the other hand, Israel and the German Federal Republic had established diplomatic relations. It is at this time that the history of the "special relation" between the two countries began. The German defender of Adolf Eichmann did not make a particularly good impression during the trial. How were the Germans to react when they felt themselves asked to take a position in the debate around the Eichmann book of Hannah Arendt, "the German"? The historian Golo Mann, one of Thomas Mann's sons, set the tone in West Germany by reproaching Arendt for her arrogance and for distorting the facts with regard to the Eichmann case. In particular, he harshly criticized her critique of the German resistance.[91] He could not even imagine reflecting on Arendt's rigorous critique of the lack of a democratic stance and a latent anti-Semitism among many of those in the German resistance. Heinrich Grüber, who was in the Protestant resistance, argued against Arendt in the spirit of Judeo-Christian reconciliation. Only the writer Rolf Schroers was apparently not taken in by the agitated public opinion of the time. He found the book intellectually provocative.

Her publisher, Klaus Piper, wrote her a long letter wherein he asked for changes that would make the book palatable for the West German public. He thought that Arendt's harsh critique of Nazi sympathizers, who were now part of the leading elite in West Germany in the 1950s and 1960s, went too far, specifically, for instance, in the case of Theodor Maunz.[92]

One inevitably gets the impression that many reviewers were making judgments on the basis of old conflicts. For some it was her book *The Origins of Totalitarianism*; for others it was the old feuds in the Zionist camp; at times it was her presumed Germanness, other times it was her arrogance. All sought to settle past scores by means of a critique of her book on the *causa Eichmann*.

The correspondence with Karl Jaspers and her friend, Mary McCarthy, reveals the wounds that Arendt sustained during this controversy. Certainly she was accustomed to controversy, but what she experienced these years surpassed everything she had previously known. She felt as though she had fallen into an ambush and had the impression that the campaign had taken on a life of its own—all carefully planned in advance.

A year after the publication of her book in the United States, the same year it came out in Germany, she responded to a question from the journalist Günter Gaus about her reaction to the critique from the Israeli side which called into question the tone of her presentation:

> Look, there are people who take it amiss—and I can understand that in a sense—that, for instance, I can still laugh. But I was really of the opinion that Eichmann was a buffoon. I'll tell you this: I read the transcript of his police investigation, thirty-six hundred pages, read it, and read it very carefully, and I do not know how many times I laughed—laughed out loud! People took this reaction in a bad way. I cannot do anything about that. But I know one thing: Three minutes before certain death, I probably still would laugh. And that, they say, is the tone of voice. That the tone of voice is predominantly ironic is completely true. The tone of voice in this case is really the person. When people reproach me with accusing the Jewish people, that is a malignant lie and propaganda and nothing else. The tone of voice, however, is an objection against me personally. And I cannot do anything about that.[93]

Heidegger and Arendt: A New Trust

In addition to personal wounds and the end of friendships, the controversy around the book had decisive consequences for her subsequent work. For the rest of her life Arendt concerned herself with the paradigmatic significance of Eichmann as the enemy of humanity, pure and simple. In her last book that remained incomplete, *The Life of the Mind*, she wrote that the origin of her concern with the fundamental activities of the human mind—thinking, willing, and judging—was her encounter with the *banality of evil* in the figure of Adolf Eichmann.

In her political writings, Eichmann became the archetype of the transformation of normality into terror. The themes of her essays circled around ever new variations on the fundamental topic that there were people whose capacity for thinking was lacking, who had no judging capacity, who would not assume their personal and political responsibility and who, being perfectly normal, were in spite of this or precisely for this reason, capable of the worst.

Furthermore, she used the severe attacks aimed at her personal integrity to reflect on the relation of truth and lying in the public space.[94]

Her discussion of image making came from the controversy around her Eichmann book. By image making she understood the production of a pseudo-reality for purposes of propaganda. She considered this to be a variety of totalitarianism. She took up this concept again during the Vietnam War, when it became known to what extent the Department of Defense under Presidents Lyndon B. Johnson and Richard M. Nixon had lied to the public in order to create a positive sentiment about the war in Vietnam. Image making, as opposed to political action, was for her a point of fracture wherein modern democracies began to produce totalitarian potential. Indeed, for Arendt, the production of images was equivalent to "organized public lying." Through these means, citizens were persuaded by something they ought to believe in, thereby robbing them of their judgment.[95]

All of this had little to do with Martin Heidegger. Heidegger and Eichmann belonged to opposite worlds. Yet questions that arose from her reflections on the Eichmann case found their way into her reflections on Heidegger's thought. Conversely, her reflections on Heidegger's thinking carried over into her understanding of the Eichmann case. Her discussion of responsibility brought the two figures together. Arendt argued that only a person who has actually done something, whose guilt is legally established, should be punished. For her, those who did not commit crimes, such as Heidegger, should take responsibility for the fact that the crimes were committed in the name of the political community to which they belonged. No one could simply step out of this community.[96] She was aware that Heidegger had never gotten over feelings of personal shame; however, concepts like political responsibility were not within his horizon of thought. The ruptured relationship with Jaspers made that clear.

Other concepts from Arendt's discourse, such as "guilt" and "conscience," were by no means foreign to Heidegger. He interpreted them ontologically.

Arendt did not engage with this ontological dimension. For her, conscience was hidden at the heart of thinking in the sense of the Socratic dialogue of the self with itself. But this self cannot coexist with a murderer. In the context of Arendt's thought, conscience was a guarantee against the fall of the individual into *hostis generis humani*. In any case, that is how it is meant to be. But what happens, as in the case of Eichmann, when there is no conscience because there is no thinking?

How then does one account for the case of Heidegger, for whom it would seem that the Socratic dialogue of the self with itself was there from his earliest youth and nonetheless, as a citizen, he was still susceptible to the temptation of totalitarianism? But Heidegger's understanding of thinking is such that her insight concerning the relation between thinking and moral judgments remains intact. For her, Heidegger's susceptibility lay in the nature of his own thinking, in its original inflexibility, an implacability that led him to self-indulgence (in willing) and to a false self-limitation (in responsibility) vis-à-vis the world.

Arendt's reflection on Eichmann led almost directly to the question concerning thinking itself, how thinkers of different ages understood it, and how it was linked with the everyday lived world.

As the debate around the Eichmann book began to subside, she met with Heidegger again. They had exchanged no letters, aside from formal birthday wishes, since her refused dedication of the German edition of *The Human Condition* in 1960. Now Heidegger undertook a new beginning. In October 1966 he wrote her an "autumn letter" on the occasion of her sixtieth birthday. Heidegger congratulated her, he recalled his Marburg course "The Sophist" that she had attended and where their love had begun. He told her that in the ensuing years he had gone to Greece with Elfride three times. He was clearly deeply impressed that he could feel the spirit of the Greeks so at hand after thousands of years, "the still-prevailing power of the presence of all beings and things. And no frame can disguise it."[97] He sent her Friedrich Hölderlin's poem "Autumn" and a postcard with a view overlooking the fountain and the hillside from his study in the cabin in Todtnauberg. Hannah was relieved and very happy; she, as it were, rejoiced: "Your autumn letter was the greatest joy, really the greatest possible joy. It accompanies me—with the poem and the view of the beautiful, lively fountain from the Black Forest study—and will accompany me for a long time. (Those whose hearts were brought and broken by spring will have their hearts made whole again by autumn.)"[98] She asked him about his plans and confessed that she too often thought about the course where their eyes first met.

The following summer she visited him twice in a row. On July 26, 1967, she was invited to give a talk on Walter Benjamin to the *auditorium maximum* at the University of Freiburg. Heidegger was notified about her visit and he came to listen to her talk in the packed hall. Hannah began her lecture with the following address: "Honorable Martin Heidegger, Ladies and Gentlemen!"

The address to him provoked a "bad reaction" on the part of the audience as Heidegger wrote to her later—which was surely to be expected.[99] She had also noticed this and was worried that she had embarrassed him with the direct address.[100]

By the time of the second meeting in the middle of August, they were working together. He read to her from a text he had just written and sent her his article "Kant's Thesis Concerning Being." In return, she gave him an essay drawn from Kafka's 1920 parable ("He"). They exchanged thoughts about Kafka's understanding of time.

These two meetings renewed their friendship and laid the basis for a new trust. In the years to come, they deepened their relationship of argument and thought. Their correspondence reveals clear traces of this. Parallel to this, as her *Denktagebuch* reveals, she continued her philosophical and political soliloquy with Heidegger.

After that summer she visited him every year, sometimes twice a year. They asked after each other, inquired about each other's work, and exchanged personal news. Hannah told him, as spontaneous as she was, about her impressions of America during the Vietnam War and how she wanted this war to end with America's defeat. In 1967 he congratulated her on the Sigmund Freud Prize. He himself was invited in the same year to give a lecture at the Greek academy of sciences in Athens. She became engaged with the translations of his new texts. She wrote to him about how impressed she was by his text *What Is Thinking?* At this time she was already in the middle of her work on *The Life of the Mind.* The exchange with him was now particularly valuable for her.

After the trauma of *causa Eichmann* it seemed as though a new phase had begun for Arendt, a phase of calm, friendship, and productive work.

In September 1968 she wrote in her *Denktagebuch*: "Jaspers during the farewell: 'Now you are going away and leaving me in great disarray.'"[101] During this summer she had visited him as well as Heidegger. In October Jaspers fell ill. On February 26, 1969, on his ninetieth birthday, Gertrud Jaspers sent her a telegram in which she briefly said that Karl had died. Karl Jaspers, her teacher, friend, and caring critical companion. He was her constant connection with Germany. She had done many things on his behalf in the United States; in the meantime, many of his texts had been translated. Now he was gone.

Arendt went to the funeral in Basel. On March 4, 1969, a ceremony took place at the local university; she was asked to give the main eulogy. From Basel she asked Heidegger for a meeting. Her sparse formulation—"I would very much like to see you"—gives one to understand just how urgently she needed to be reassured about herself and Heidegger now that the "invisible third" had left their company, even if his presence persisted between them. The next day she was in Freiburg. There is no written trace of their conversations.

There was no "reconciliation" between Jaspers and Heidegger. Even Arendt, who had a genius for friendship, could not bring this about. But once there had been a bond between Jaspers and Heidegger, one that neither had relinquished, even though both were unfaithful to it. Jaspers was tormented to see the passionate friendship of his youth end so banally. Still that friendship continued to challenge him intellectually. Up until the last years of his life, he was writing notes on Heidegger:

Entry 249
Heidegger
Not touching big questions.
Sexuality, friendship, marriage—the praxis of life—
profession—state, politics—education, etc.
and suddenly everything erupted in 1933—
blinded by the realities of power and himself taken
by mass hysteria—
blind, unreal, and irresponsible—
Delivering language to thieves
Suddenly the content of an empty philosophy pushed to the side.[102]

Entry 250
Heidegger
In his texts one senses the inner torment and the overcoming of the torment from which they stemmed. This is why one needs to consider them seriously in one of their sources.

What I say to Heidegger is full of contradictions.... We are all full of contradictions. In my understanding, Heidegger's contradictions are grotesque and not held together cohesively....

Fate brought us together for more than ten years. In retrospect, these years were sometimes lovely for me and sometimes confusing.

Should I praise fate? I cannot do that when I think about how I am separated from Heidegger in a silence that is different from that which I have with any other person—in a manner that seems like a betrayal on his part. I must agree with fate when I think about the experiences that would have otherwise remained inaccessible to me and about the frontiers of my human possibilities which would otherwise have remained hidden from me.[103]

The entries end with a dreamlike story dating back to 1964. Jaspers describes the meeting of two thinkers on a mountain plateau. They fight with each other over what is essential, take measure of their opponent, but remain fully in the world that lies before their eyes. Today, "one meets no one" on this plateau:

It is as though, searching in vain in eternal speculations for people who would find them important, I met one or else no one. But the latter was a polite enemy. . . . That is what happened with Heidegger. That is why I find the critiques addressed to him entirely insufficient, for they do not take place on the same high plateau. I am thus searching for a critique that would truly penetrate the substance of his thought, for a fight that would disrupt the incommunicability of the irreconcilable, for a solidarity that is still possible with what is most estranged, when it is a question of philosophy. Perhaps a critique and a fight of this kind are impossible. However, I would like to attempt to know, so to speak to, at least a shadow of this.[104]

We know very little about what Heidegger thought of Jaspers in these years. For a while he hoped that Arendt could help. Then he was silent. Perhaps he felt a kind of gratitude, insofar as his disagreement with Jaspers pushed him to further reflection.

In June of the same year, Hannah Arendt again visited Heidegger. In the meantime, the Heideggers had decided to build a bungalow on the land of their house in Zähringen, to simplify life and spare Elfride the trouble of maintaining the larger house. They needed money for this. Elfride exchanged several letters with Hannah to find out which library or private collector would give a good price for the definitive manuscript of *Being and Time*, which was also the printer's copy. Hannah advised her. At the end of May 1969, Hannah and Heinrich spent a holiday in Tegna, Switzerland. In this small village at the edge of the Maggia valley, close to Lake Maggiore, they found a hotel that suited them perfectly. They went there gladly. In Switzerland she was in the middle of Europe but could keep her distance. From there, one could also travel easily.

The Casa Barbatè was built in the style of a Japanese pavilion: one story, bright, simple, and tastefully furnished. She had a room with an exit to the garden. That is where Arendt lived when she was in Tegna. She could observe the valley from her writing desk and take short or long walks. In the beginning of June, Mary McCarthy came to visit her. In general, she had many visitors, inviting both her American and European friends.

She went to Freiburg at the end of June and then a second time on August 16, this time with Heinrich. He was warmly received and had a long conversation with Heidegger about his Nietzsche book. Heidegger held Heinrich in high esteem: "I still recall with pleasure my conversation with Heinrich about the *Nietzsche*. Such insight and perspective are rare."[105]

This same year Heidegger turned eighty. For his birthday on September 26, Arendt wrote a piece in appreciation of Heidegger's work for the jubilee. The text was written as a feature for the Bavarian radio; she recorded it in New York. The entries in her *Denktagebuch* in August and September 1969 show how hard she worked to honor Heidegger in the way that was appropriate to both of them.

She wanted to write an appraisal of his oeuvre and mark their respective positions. Agreement and difference, nearness and distance, underlined her argument.

In this text, she alluded to all the questions that she was working on in the first two volumes of *The Life of the Mind*: What is thinking? How is thinking related to the world and to acting? What happens when thinking is linked to the will?

It is a text of reconciliation between equals that at the same time does not seek harmony. She spoke of his relationship with Husserl, his friendship with Jaspers, the radical desire to renew philosophical thinking that brought the two young philosophers together in the 1920s and then later separated them. She discussed the fascination that the charismatic teacher in the small academic town of Marburg exerted on the young generation from all over Germany. Between the lines she spoke of her own fascination.

To define his position in the history of twentieth century philosophy, she found illuminating words:

> For it is not Heidegger's philosophy but, rather, Heidegger's *thinking* [author's emphasis] that has had such a decisive influence on the century's intellectual physiognomy. This thinking has a singularly probing quality that, if one wanted to grasp and trace it in words, lies in the transitive use of the verb "to think." Heidegger never thinks "about" something; he thinks something. In this entirely uncontemplative activity, he probes the depths, but not in order to discover a decisive and definitive foundation in this dimension—indeed, one might even say that this dimension simply had not been discovered in such a manner and such precision before this—not even to bring such a dimension to light, but rather, while remaining in the depths, to mark out paths and to set up "pathmarks."[106]

She acknowledged the tyrannical inclinations of most great philosophers and criticized the *déformation professionelle* that great thinkers, Heidegger included, fell prey to when they envisioned the transformation of their philosophy into an educational program. Her discussion of his National Socialist involvement did not embellish anything but gave it its proper measure. The structural fallibility of thinkers like Heidegger was always on her mind. There was no reason to underplay his involvement with National Socialism. But it did not diminish his achievement, which raised him to the status of the great thinkers in history: "For the storm that runs through Heidegger's thinking—like the one that, after millennia, still blows towards us out of Plato's work—does not come from the century. It comes from the ancient, and what it leaves behind is something consummate that, like anything consummate, reverts to the ancient."[107] To be sure, the accomplishment was not a "doctrine" and also not a "work" but a path cleared.

She took the metaphor of the "storm" from Plato's *Republic*. Heidegger closed his inaugural rector's address in 1933 with a line: "all that is great stands in the storm."[108] However, National Socialists had no need of a Plato.

In this text Arendt described herself and her teacher as two seekers in the great history of thinking. Their paths were different, but they always crossed. Seen in retrospect, this text illuminates her proximity and distance from Heidegger's thinking in a way that would have been understood by her teacher and lover. She sent him the text for his birthday and then a second one for a *tabula gratulatoria*.[109] Heidegger responded: "more than anyone, you have touched the inner movement of my thought and of my work as a teacher. These have remained the same since the *Sophist* course."[110]

She supervised the translation of *Discourse on Thinking*, which she found very good. She was pleased about his public praise for her. These later letters give the impression that the dam that had separated them had broken and allowed for a new found trust between them. A deepening of their personal and professional relationship resulted from this. At Christmas she gave him her condolences when the wife of his brother Fritz died. She noted how strangely the death of his sister-in-law and the great honors on his birthday converged: "life has such a way of putting emphasis on things."[111]

In April 1970 Martin suffered a mild stroke, from which he nevertheless recovered well. She visited him in July and August. Heinrich accompanied her to Tegna. In November Heinrich Blücher died suddenly of a heart attack. Within two years she had lost two cornerstones of her world.

It is moving how Martin tried to console her. He wrote in the way that was his own when he spoke about private relationships. He tried to lead her back to thinking and thinking back to her. With regard to Hannah's mourning, it meant breaking through the paralysis caused by the shock of the loss and creating new spaces for thinking.

In the first months she could barely write, obsessed by the feeling that part of her world had disappeared: "this tiny micro-world where you can always escape from the world, which disintegrates when the other has gone away. I go now and am quite calm and think: *away (weg)*."[112]

Heidegger interpreted her words in his reply: "when, in your last letter, I read your line 'I am quite calm and think: *away*,' I understood the last word as 'way.' That is more precise."[113] The seeming misunderstanding alters the perspective, and from the pause provoked by the experience of loss comes the vision of a new path. What in his youth seemed like pomposity and sometimes hypocrisy, his way of transferring his thinking to relations with others, here shows itself as the capacity to find peace though distance and the ability to pass on this peace. Elfride, with whom Hannah had better contact since 1967, also tried to console her.

Hannah needed many months to turn to the outside world again. On March 20, 1971, she wrote to him in anticipation of her European trip. While the letter was factual and she asked him for philosophical information, she concluded it, as it were, casually: "I have one last question, which I probably cannot manage face to face. It is at least possible that a book I am working on—a kind of second volume of *Vita Activa*—will still work out after all. On the non-active human activities: thinking, willing, judging. I have no idea whether it will turn out and, above all, when I will be finished with it. Perhaps never. But if it does work out—may I dedicate it to you?"[114] He responded on March 26, picking up on her conclusion: "Your second volume of *Vita Activa* will be as difficult as it will be important. It calls to my mind the beginning of the 'Letter on Humanism' and of the conversation in *Discourse on Thinking*. But all of that remains insufficient. We have to struggle to be at least adequate to the insufficient. You know that I will be pleased with your dedication."[115] Finally, a dedication for a book that was not yet written. Her question sounds like a request for reassurance: Are you still there? Can I count on you?

Heidegger was now the only one who remained for her.

For a while, she continued to concern herself with Jaspers's papers. In summer 1975 she again visited Europe and spent several weeks at the literary archive of Marbach to examine Jaspers's literary estate; his will named her executor. The archives also contained her own letters.

Then she left for Tessin, to work in peace in the "Casa Barbatè" on the second (Willing) and third (Judging) parts of her project *The Life of the Mind*. From Tegna she went to Freiburg in mid-August and stayed there for three days. This visit must have been traumatic for her.

The day after her return from Freiburg, on August 16, 1975, she wrote from Tegna to Glenn Gray, her friend and confidant in Heidegger matters:

> I saw Heidegger without any unpleasant incident or accidents. Still, it was a rather sad business. . . . Heidegger was tired, but that is not the word for it: he was remote, unapproachable as never before, as though extinguished (*wie erloschen*). It is true that Elfride, as you already remarked, is much kinder with him than ever before. We, Elfride and I, exchanged a few words alone and she seemed truly concerned and not at all hostile. She left Martin and me alone, but without constantly looking in from all sides. I think she was genuinely worried. He said two things of some importance: he still works at his "65 pages," I think I told you about it. These pages are supposed to give the quintessence of his philosophy, but I doubt very much that he will do more than repeat what he said before and probably ever so much better. The second utterance: in ten years—he said it very apodictically—are the Russians here; the Russian ambassador was already in Marbach to have a look at the loot.

[He is referring here to his literary archive, which he had left there—author's note.] I tried to discuss this proposition, but he sank back into his curious apathy, simply did not react at all. I did not find him very changed physically, and it seems, according to the physician, that he is quite healthy. Still, the difference against last year in everything—including movements—is enormous. Also, he is very hard of hearing; one is never quite sure whether he understood or just lets it go. Obviously, I am still very depressed.[116]

Hannah Arendt died suddenly on December 4, 1975, in New York. Martin Heidegger died peacefully in his sleep on May 26, 1976, in Freiburg-Zähringen. Elfride Heidegger died on March 21, 1992.

Notes

1. Arendt to Heidegger, letter dated October 28, 1960, in Ursula Ludz, ed., *Hannah Arendt and Martin Heidegger: Letters 1925–1975*, trans. Andrew Shields (New York: Harcourt, Brace, 2004), 124 (translation modified).

2. Arendt: *Denktagebuch*, Bd. 1 Heft II, October 1950 (2002) S 30.

3. Heidegger to Arendt, letter dated January 10, 1926, in Ludz, *Arendt-Heidegger Letters*, 40.

4. Cited by Ludz, "Commentary to Letter 89," in ibid., 261.

5. Heidegger to Elfride Heidegger, letter dated November 13, 1954, in Martin Heidegger, *Letters to His Wife: 1915–1970*, ed. Gertrud Heidegger, trans. Rupert Glasgow (Malden, MA: Polity Press, 2008), 246.

6. Dr. Gerhard Stroomann's concept of the local *spiritus rector* resembles that of Medard Boss in Switzerland. It rests on the connection between spiritual education and physical, that is, body healing. The patient or spa "Kurhaus" guest was offered lectures by famous speakers, therewith ensuring a better recovery in an atmosphere of spiritual education. The "Kurhaus" was founded in the 1920s and continued after the war. See Rüdiger Safranski, *Martin Heidegger: Between Good and Evil*, trans. Ewald Osers (Cambridge, MA: Harvard University Press, 1998), 392.

7. See correspondence with Rudolph Berlinger, especially letter dated December 7, 1959; HAZ Archive, Cont. 7.10.

8. Hannah Arendt, *Denktagebuch* (Munich: Piper, 2016), Bd. 1, Heft XVII, July 1953. Also, "Heidegger the Fox," in *Essays in Understanding 1919–1994*, ed. Kohn (New York: HBJ, 1994), 361–64.

9. Arendt to Blücher, letter dated October 31, 1956, in Lotte Kohler, ed., *Within Four Walls*, trans. Peter Constantine (New York: Harcourt, Brace, 1996), 309.

10. Ibid., 291.

11. Kurt Blumenfeld brought it up such: "Yesterday Hanna Strauss [wife of a former publisher at Schocken Books; author's note] stopped by to see me in New York. She told me she was enchanted by her talk about graphology with you. As she related that she had received two examples of writing to evaluate from you, I said, 'Heidegger and Walter Benjamin.' 'Apparently Hannah has already written you,' she replied"; see Blumenfeld to Arendt, letter dated May 21, 1958, in Ingeborg Nordmann and Iris Pilling, eds., *In keinem Besitz verwurzelt: Die Korrespondenz Hannah Arendt und Kurt Blumenfeld* (Hamburg: Rotbuch Verlag, 1995), 217.

12. Hannah Arendt, "Karl Jaspers: A Laudatio," in *Men in Dark Times* (New York: Harcourt, Brace, 1966), 71–80.

13. Ibid., 72ff.

14. Arendt to Jaspers, letter dated August 6, 1961, in *Arendt and Jaspers Correspondence*, 447.

15. Ibid., 447.

16. Arendt to Jaspers, letter dated November 1, 1961, in ibid., 457.

17. Hannah Arendt, *Origins of Totalitarianism* (New York: Shocken, 1951), 479.

18. Arendt to Heidegger, letter dated May 8, 1954, in Ludz, *Arendt-Heidegger Letters*, 120.

19. Talcott Parsons, "Max Weber and the Contemporary Political Crisis," *Review of Politics* 4 (1942): 1.

20. Hannah Arendt, "Tradition and the Modern Age," *Partisan Review* 21, no. 1 (1954). Reprinted in Hannah Arendt, *Between Past and Future* (New York: Penguin, 1968), 17–40.

21. Martin Heidegger, *Poetry, Language, Thought* (New York: Harper and Row, 1971), 181.

22. Ibid.

23. Arendt, *Denktagebuch*, Bd. 1, Heft VIII, March, 1952, Entry 28 (2002), 195.

24. See also Arendt, *Human Condition*, 8.

25. Arendt, *Denktagebuch*, Bd. 1, Heft IX, August 1952, Entry 26 (2002), S. 218.

26. Louis Menand, *Metaphysical Club: A Story of Ideas in America* (New York: Farrar, Straus, Giroux, 2001), 428.

27. Ibid., 431 (emphasis in original text). Menand goes on to say, "Holmes, James, Peirce, and Dewey wished to bring ideas and principles and beliefs down to a human level because they wished to avoid the violence they saw hidden in abstractions. This was one of the lessons the Civil War had taught them. The political system their philosophy was designed to support was democracy. And democracy, as they understood it, isn't just about letting the right people have their say; it's also about letting the wrong people have their say. It is about giving space to minority and dissenting views so that, at the end of the day, the interests of the majority may prevail. . . . Modern American thought, the thought associated with Holmes, James, Peirce and Dewey, represents the intellectual triumph of 'unionism'" (444).

28. Arendt, *Denktagebuch*, Bd. 1, Number V, August, 1951, Entry 22 (2002), 118. "Heidegger is wrong. Man is not 'thrown' 'into the world.' If we were 'thrown,' it is onto the earth—no different from the animals. Men are led into the world, not thrown, because through this a certain continuity is constituted which reveals affiliation or belonging. Woe to us, if we have been thrown into the world"; Arendt: Book XXI, August, 1955, Entry 68, in *Denktagebuch*, Bd. 1, (2002), 549f.

29. Arendt, *Denktagebuch*, Bd. I, Heft XI, October, 1953, Entry 21 (2002), S. 218–19.

30. Ibid., Bd. 1, Heft XV, October 1953, Entry 11 (2002), S. 262–63.

31. Ibid., Bd. 1, Heft XV, May 1953, Entry 21 (2002), S. 360.

32. Ibid., Bd. 1, Heft XXI, July 1955, Entry 55 (2002), S. 539.

33. Arendt, *Human Condition*, 185.

34. Arendt to Heidegger, letter dated July 28, 1970, in *Arendt-Heidegger Letters*, 170.

35. "But meanwhile even the cultivation of the field has come under the grip of another kind of setting-in-order, which *sets* upon [*stellt*] nature. It sets upon it in the sense of challenging it. Agriculture is now the mechanized food industry. Air is now set upon to yield nitrogen, the earth to yield ore, ore to yield uranium, for example; uranium is set upon to yield atomic energy which can be released either for destruction or for peaceful use"; see Martin Heidegger: "The Question Concerning Technology," in *The Question Concerning Technology and Other Essays* (New York: Harper and Row, 1969), 15. "We now name that challenging claim which gathers man thither to order the self-revealing as stand*ing*-reserve: '*Ge-Stell*'" (ibid., 19). Concerning the standing-reserve (*Ge-Stell*): "It is nothing technological, nothing on the order of a

machine. It is the way in which the real reveals itself as standing-reserve. Again we ask: Does this revealing happen somewhere beyond all human doing? No. But neither does it happen exclusively *in* man, or decisively *through* him" (ibid., 23–24). The standing-reserve can prevent an originary revealing access to being: "The rule of Enframing threatens man with the possibility that it could be denied to him to enter into a more original revealing and hence to experience the call of a more primal truth" (ibid., 28).

36. Arendt to Heidegger, letter dated May 8, 1954 in *Arendt-Heidegger Letters*, 120 (translation modified).

37. Hannah Arendt, *On Revolution* (New York: Penguin, 1963), 214–15.

38. Ibid., 149.

39. Ibid., 156.

40. Ibid.

41. Ibid., 163.

42. Ibid., 157.

43. Ibid., 181.

44. Ibid., 68–69.

45. Jaspers to Arendt, letter from May 16, 1963, in *Arendt-Jaspers Correspondence*, 504.

46. He returns to the theme of this lecture in 1941 in a second lecture and in two seminars. See Ingrid Schüßle's publisher's afterword in Martin Heidegger, *Schelling's Treatise on the Essence of Human Freedom*, trans. Joan Stambaugh (Athens: Ohio University Press, 1985).

47. Ibid., 156: "Human freedom is not the decidedness for good or evil, but the decidedness for good and evil, or the decidedness for evil and good. This freedom alone brings man to the ground of his existence in such a way that lets him emerge at the same time in the unity of the will to essence and deformation of essence aroused in him. This aroused will is spirit, as such spirit history."

48. Ibid., 155–56.

49. Heidegger, "Question Concerning Technology" (1977), 330.

50. Hannah Arendt, *The Promise of Politics*, ed. Jerome Kohn (New York: Shocken, 2005), 40.

51. Arendt, *Human Condition* (1989), 185ff.

52. Ibid., 42–43.

53. Ibid., 186ff.

54. Arendt, *Denktagebuch*, Bd. 1, Heft VIII, March 1952, Entry 28 (2002), S. 17.

55. Heidegger to Arendt, letter dated December 15, 1952, in *Arendt-Heidegger Letters*, 113.

56. Karl Löwith, "Martin Heidegger: Thinker in Destitute Times," in *Martin Heidegger and European Nihilism*, ed. Richard Wolin (New York: Columbia University Press, 1995). First appeared in German, Karl Löwith, "Martin Heidegger—Denker in Durftiger Zeit," *Die Neue Rundschau* 1 (1952).

57. Heinrich Blücher to Hannah Arendt, letter dated June 7, 1952, in Köhler, *Within Four Walls*, 186.

58. Heinrich Blücher to Hannah Arendt, letter dated June 21, 1952, in ibid., 194.

59. Heidegger, "Question Concerning Technology."

60. See Arendt to Jaspers, letter dated October 4, 1960, in *Arendt-Jaspers Correspondence*, 402.

61. See footnote 7 in the editor's introduction to "Arendt-McCarthy Briefwechsel" (1996), S. 150.

62. Cited by Daniel Bell, "The Alphabet of Justice, Reflections on 'Eichmann in Jerusalem,'" *Partisan Review* 30, no. 3 (1963): 421.

63. Blumenfeld to Arendt, letter dated February 1, 1957, in *Arendt-Blumenfeld: Korrespondenz*, (1995), 178; see also 257–59, 263, 265.

64. Arendt to Jaspers, letter dated April 13, 1961, in *Arendt-Jaspers Correspondence*, 434.

65. Arendt to Blücher, letter dated April 15, 1961, in Köhler, *Within Four Walls*, 355.

66. Hannah Arendt, *Eichmann in Jerusalem* (New York: Penguin, 2006), 129.

67. Ibid., 425.

68. Arendt to Jaspers, letter dated April 13, 1961, in *Arendt-Jaspers Correspondence*, 435.

69. Arendt to Blücher, letter dated April 15, 1961, in Köhler, *Within Four Walls*, 355.

70. Arendt to Blücher, letter dated April 15, 1961, in ibid.

71. In fact, in 2001 at a conference in Jerusalem, a passionate speech against the idea of the "banality of evil" and its creator given by Gabriel Bach, the assistant to the prosecutor and former lawyer at the highest Israeli court, went unchallenged. This made clear that Bach as well as other critics equated this idea with making evil itself banal and with a downplaying of the crime.

72. Arendt to Jaspers, letter dated March 4, 1951, in *Arendt-Jaspers Correspondence*, 166.

73. Arendt to Scholem, letter dated July 20, 1963, in Ron Feldman and Jerome Kohn, eds., *The Jewish Writings* (New York: Harcourt, Brace, 2007), 471. For a letter from Scholem to Arendt, dated June 23, 1963, see Gershom Scholem, *Gershom Scholem: A Life in Letters, 1914–1982*, trans. Anthony David Skinner (Cambridge, MA: Harvard University Press, 2002), 401–2.

74. See Ernst Simon, "Hannah Arendt—Eine Analyse," in *Die Kontroverse Hannah Arendt, Eichmann und die Juden Broschier* (Munich: Nymphenburger Verlag, 1967), 47.

75. Arendt to Jaspers, letter from October 20, 1963, in *Arendt-Jaspers Correspondence*, 522.

76. Mary McCarthy, "The Hue and the Cry," *Partisan Review* 30, no. 1 (1964): 82. See also Marie Syrkin, "Leserbrief in der Rubrik, *More on Eichmann*," *Partisan Review* 31, no. 2 (1964): 283ff.

77. Musmanno had presided over the trial against the military task forces at Nuremberg in 1947 and was therefore an expert; later he became judge of the high court of Pennsylvania.

78. See Musmanno, *Der Mann mit dem unbefleckten Gewissen in Die Kontroverse*, 85ff. See also Eine Erwiderung (an Bruno Bettelheim), in Die Kontroverse (1964), S. 114ff.

79. See also Eva Reichmann, *Eine Zionistin aus England*; see Eva G. Reichmann, *Antwort an Hannah Arendt*, in *Die Kontroverse*, 213ff.

80. Scholem to Arendt, letter dated June 23, 1963, in Scholem, *Gershom Scholem*, 396–97.

81. See "Nachwort der Herausgeberinnen," in *Arendt-Blumenfeld: Korrespondenz*, 373.

82. This relates to the articles by Hugo Hahn, Friedrich S. Brodnitz, Robert M. W. Kempner, Nehemiah Robinson, and Adolf Leschnitzer, all in *Die Kontroverse*.

83. See Elizabeth Young-Bruehl, *Arendt: For Love of the World* (New Haven, CT: Yale University Press, 1985), 355ff.

84. Lionel Abel, "The Aesthetics of Evil," *Partisan Review* 30, no. 2 (1963): 219ff.

85. McCarthy, "Hue and the Cry," 82ff.

86. Dwight Macdonald: "Arguments, More on Eichmann," *Partisan Review* 31, no. 2 (1964): 266.

87. Bell, "Alphabet of Justice" (Fall, 1963), 417ff.

88. Kazin's biographer, Solotaroff, reports, "Kazin, after listening to an endless chain of attacks on Arendt stood up, walked to the podium and said, 'That's enough, Irving. This disgraceful piling on has to stop.' Then he said a few words about the great distinction of Arendt's thought and the complexity of her book and walked out. I don't remember precisely what happened after that, except that a lot of the energy went out of the room and the meeting ended soon after." See Ted Solotaroff, *Introduction to Alfred Kazin's America: Critical and Personal Writings*, ed. and intro. Ted Solotaroff (New York: Harper, 2003), xxxvi–xxxvii.

89. Ibid., xxxviii.

90. Arendt to Jaspers, letter dated August 9, 1963, in *Arendt-Jaspers Correspondence*, 515–16.

91. Golo Mann, "Der verdrehte Eichmann," in *Die Kontroverse* (1964), 190ff.

92. See Piper to Arendt, letter dated January 11, 1963, in Archiv des HAZ.

93. Arendt, "'What Remains? The Language Remains': A Conversation with Günter Gaus," in Kohn, *Essays in Understanding* (1994), 15–16.

94. See also Arendt's entry in her *Denktagebuch*, Bd. 2, Heft XIV, 1963–1964 (2002), S. 621ff.

95. Two relevant essays were published in 1964 and 1972. See Hannah Arendt, "Wahrheit und Politik," in *Die politische Verantwortung der Nichtpolitiker*, ed. Johann Schlemmer (Munich: Piper, 1964) (the German edition was published before the American). See also "Die Lüge in der Politik: Überlegungen zu den Pentagon Papers," *Die neue Rundschau* 83 (1972): 2; the American version was published a year later. Hannah Arendt, "Lying in Politics: Thoughts on the Pentagon Papers," in *Crisis of the Republic* (New York: HBJ, 1969), 1–48.

96. Arendt had addressed the theme of responsibility in many speeches and articles, among these in a commentary on a lecture given by a colleague at the American Philosophical Society in December 1968. See Hannah Arendt: "Collective Responsibility. Discussion of the Paper of Joel Feinberg," Rockefeller University, American Philosophical Society, December 27, 1968, Washington, DC, Archiv des HAZ, Cont. 62.12.

97. Heidegger to Arendt, letter dated October 6, 1966, in *Arendt-Heidegger Correspondence*, 127.

98. Arendt to Heidegger, letter dated October 19, 1966, in ibid., 128–29.

99. Heidegger to Arendt, letter dated August 10, 1967, in ibid., 129.

100. Arendt to Heidegger, letter dated August 11, 1967, in ibid., 130.

101. Arendt, *Denktagebuch*, Bd. 2, Heft XXV, September 1968, Entry 87 (2002), S. 696.

102. Karl Jaspers, *Jaspers: Notizen zu Martin Heidegger* (Munich, Piper, 1978), 261 (question mark in the original).

103. Ibid., 262–63.

104. Ibid., 264.

105. Heidegger to Arendt, letter dated November 27, 1969, in *Arendt-Heidegger Letters*, 163.

106. Hannah Arendt, "Appraisal of Heidegger on the Occasion of His 80th Birthday," in *Arendt-Heidegger Letters*, 152.

107. Ibid., 162.

108. Heidegger, *Self-Assertion*, 39.

109. Ursula Ludz, "Commentary on Hannah Arendt's Text for Martin Heidegger's 80th Birthday," in *Arendt-Heidegger Letters*, 269.

110. Heidegger to Arendt, letter dated November 27, 1969, in ibid., 163.

111. Arendt to Heidegger, letter Christmas 1969, in ibid., 165.

112. Arendt to Heidegger, letter dated November 27, 1970, in ibid., 173.

113. Heidegger to Arendt, letter dated March 26, 1971, in ibid., 175.

114. Arendt to Heidegger, letter dated March 20, 1971, in ibid.

115. Heidegger to Arendt, letter dated March 26, 1971, in ibid., 176.

116. Arendt to Glenn Gray, letter dated August 16, 1975, Archiv des HAZ, Cont. Nr. 10.5. A few days later she wrote almost the same thing to her friend Mary McCarthy; see Hannah Arendt and McCarthy, *Between Friends 1949–1975*, ed. Carol Brightman (New York: Harcourt, Brace, 1996), 385.

Chronology

1883	February 23. Karl Jaspers born in Oldenburg. Son of civil servant and bank director Karl Jaspers and his wife, Henriette, née Tantzen.
1889	September 26. Martin Heidegger born in Meßkirch (Baden) as son of sexton and master barrel maker Friedrich Heidegger and his wife, Johanna, née Kempf.
1901	Jaspers begins to study law, then medicine.
1906	October 14. Hannah Arendt born in Hannover as only child of Engineer Paul Arendt and his wife, Martha, née Cohen.
1908–15	Jaspers works at the psychiatric clinic in Heidelberg.
1909	Jaspers becomes a medical doctor.
1909	Family Arendt moves to Königsberg.
1910	Jaspers marries Gertrud Mayer.
1911	Heidegger switches to the Faculty of Natural Sciences however continues to study under Heinrich Rickert.
1913	Arendt's grandfather Max Arendt and her father, Paul Arendt, die in the same year.
	Jaspers receives his postdoctoral degree (*Habilitation*) in psychology in Heidelberg.
1913	July 27. Heidegger receives his PhD under Arthur Schneider (coexaminer, Rickert). Theme: "The Paradigm of Judgement in Psychologismus."
	Jaspers publishes "General Psychopathology."
1914	August. War begins. Heidegger called up on October 10.
1915	July 27. Heidegger's required teaching lecture (*Probevorlesung*); he had received his postdoctoral degree with "The Categories and Paradigms of Meaning in Duns Scotus." Heidegger teaches as an adjunct professor at the University of Freiburg until winter semester 1923, as Edmund Husserl's assistant from 1919 on November 1. Heidegger transferred to Freiburg as post censor.
1916	Heidegger leaves Catholicism.
	Jaspers becomes official professor of psychology.
1917	March 21. Heidegger marries Elfriede Petri.
1918	November 16. Heidegger leaves military service.
1919	Heidegger's son Jörg born.
	Jaspers's "Psychology of World Views" published.

1920	Heidegger's son Hermann is born.
	April 8. Jaspers meets Heidegger in Freiburg at Husserl's sixty-first birthday celebration.
1922	Jaspers becomes full professor of philosophy at the University of Heidelberg.
1923	June 18. Heidegger receives an appointment as professor to the University Marburg.
1924	Winter semester, Arendt begins her studies in philosophy (main subject), Protestant theology, and Greek philology at the University of Marburg.
	November, beginning of affair between Arendt and Heidegger.
1925	Spring. Arendt writes "The Shadows" for Heidegger.
1926	In summer semester 1926, Arendt transfers to Heidelberg; in winter semester she transfers to Husserl in Freiburg and then returns to Heidelberg; meets Kurt Blumenfeld through Hans Jonas and deepens her interest in political Zionism.
1927	Heidegger's *Being and Time* is published.
1928	February. Heidegger becomes the Ordinarius for Philosophy in Freiburg, becoming Husserl's successor.
	November. Arendt receives her PhD with Jaspers. Theme of the dissertation is "The Idea of Love in Augustine."
1929	Heidegger and Ernst Cassirer at the Davos University course.
	Heidegger's *Kant and the Problem of Metaphysics* is published.
	September. Arendt and Günther Stern (Anders) marry.
1930–33	Arendt works as a freelancer; begins research on *Rahel Varnhagen*.
1931	December. Jaspers's *Philosophy* appears in three volumes.
1933	February. Stern flees to Paris.
	End of March, Heidegger's last long visit with Jaspers.
	April 21. Heidegger elected to Rector of Freiburg University.
	May 3. Heidegger becomes a member of the National Socialist Party.
	July. Arendt and her mother are arrested in Berlin; freed, they flee to Paris via the Erzgebirge, Karlsbad, Prague, and Geneva.
1933–38	Arendt works in the French section of *Jugend-Alijah*.
1934	Arendt joins the World Zionist Organization.
1934	Heidegger resigns as rector of the University of Freiburg.
1935	Arendt spends three months in Palestine.
1936	Stern emigrates to the United States.
	Spring. Arendt meets Heinrich Blücher.
1937	Arendt and Stern (Anders) divorce.
	Jaspers dismissed from the faculty at the University of Heidelberg.
	Arendt's German citizenship is revoked.

1940   January 16. Hannah Arendt and Heinrich Blücher marry.
Early summer: Arendt interned in the Gurs camp. She flees to friends in Montaubon and then with Blücher to Lisbon.
May. The Arendt-Blüchers arrive in New York.

1941–42   Arendt is a columnist for the German-Jewish newspaper *Aufbau.*

1942   End of November. The Geneva section of the Jewish World Congress report on the mass annihilation of Jews in Germany and Poland.

1945   The American Occupation Powers reinstate Jaspers as university professor; Arendt works as essayist for various publications—among them the *Partisan Review.*

1945–50   Heidegger suspended from his professorship.

1947   Jaspers publishes "On Truth."
Heidegger publishes *Plato's Concept of Truth.* He also publishes *Letter on Humanism.*
Jaspers accepts a professorial chair at the University of Basel.

1949–50   From November 1949 to March 1950 Arendt travels to Europe on behalf of the Jewish Cultural Reconstruction.
February. Arendt meets Heidegger again.
Heidegger's *Holzwege* appears.

1951   Arendt's *The Origins of Totalitarianism* is published (German edition 1955, *Elemente und Ursprünge totaler Herrschaft*).
December. Arendt and Blücher become American citizens.

1958   Jaspers receives the Peace Prize (Friedenspreis) of the German Publishers. Arendt gives the laudition.
Arendt's *The Human Condition* appears (German edition 1960, *Vita activa oder tätigen Leben*).
Arendt's *Rahel Varnhagen: The Life of a Jewess* appears (German edition 1959, *Rahel Varnhagen: Lebensgeschichte einer deutschen Jüdin aus der Romantik*).

1960   Heidegger's *Nietzsche* published.

1961   April and June. Writing for the *New Yorker,* Arendt travels to Jerusalem for the trial of Adolf Eichmann.

1963   Arendt's *Eichmann in Jerusalem. A Report on the Banality of Evil* published (German edition 1964, *Eichmann in Jerusalem: Ein Bericht von der Banalität des Bösen*).
Arendt's *On Revolution* published (German edition 1965, *Über die Revolution*).

1963–67   Arendt, professor at the University of Chicago.

1967   Arendt receives position at the New School for Social Research in New York.

1969   February 26. Karl Jaspers dies.

1970   October 31. Heinrich Blücher dies.
1975   Autumn. Arendt's last visit to Heidegger.
            December 4. Hannah Arendt dies.
1976   May 26. Martin Heidegger dies.
1992   March 31. Elfride Heidegger dies.

Index

Page numbers in italics indicate photographs. See also Chronology, pp. 293–295. HA = Hannah Arendt. MH = Martin Heidegger.

ANTONIA GRUNENBERG is Professor of Political Science and Director of the Hannah Arendt Center at Carl von Ossietzky University of Oldenburg.

PEG BIRMINGHAM is Professor of Philosophy at DePaul University. She is the author of *Hannah Arendt and Human Rights: The Predicament of Common Responsibility* (IUP, 2006), editor (with Philippe van Haute) of *Dissensus Communis: Between Ethics and Politics*, and editor (with Anna Yeatman) of *Aporia of Rights: Citizenship in an Era of Human Rights*. She is the editor of *Philosophy Today*.

ELIZABETH VON WITZKE BIRMINGHAM lives and works in Berlin. She is the translator (with Peg Birmingham) of Dominique Janicaud's *Powers of the Rational: Science, Technology, and the Future of Thought* (IUP, 1995).

KRISTINA LEBEDEVA is a doctoral student of Philosophy at DePaul University.

CPSIA information can be obtained
at www.ICGtesting.com
Printed in the USA
LVOW13s0322020917
547256LV00017B/389/P